MATHEMATICAL
METHODS
for
ARTIFICIAL INTELLIGENCE
and
AUTONOMOUS SYSTEMS

MATHEMATICAL METHODS
for
ARTIFICIAL INTELLIGENCE
and
AUTONOMOUS SYSTEMS

EDWARD R. DOUGHERTY

Fairleigh Dickinson University

CHARLES R. GIARDINA

City University of New York

PRENTICE HALL, ENGLEWOOD CLIFFS, NEW JERSEY 07632

Library of Congress Cataloging-in-Publication Data

DOUGHERTY, EDWARD R.
  Mathematical methods for artificial intelligence
and autonomous systems.

  Includes index.
  1. Artificial intelligence—Data processing.
2. Artificial intelligence—Mathematics. I. Giardina,
Charles R. (Charles Robert). II. Title.
Q336.D68 1988   006.1'01'51   87-32662
ISBN 0-13-560913-5

Editorial/production supervision
  and interior design: **Ellen B. Greenberg**
Cover designer: **Diane Saxe**
Manufacturing buyer: **Gordon Osbourne**

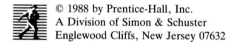 © 1988 by Prentice-Hall, Inc.
A Division of Simon & Schuster
Englewood Cliffs, New Jersey 07632

Printed in the United States of America

10 9 8 7 6 5 4 3 2

ISBN 0-13-560913-5   025

PRENTICE-HALL INTERNATIONAL (UK) LIMITED,*London*
PRENTICE-HALL OF AUSTRALIA PTY. LIMITED, *Sydney*
PRENTICE-HALL CANADA INC., *Toronto*
PRENTICE-HALL HISPANOAMERICANA, S.A., *Mexico*
PRENTICE-HALL OF INDIA PRIVATE LIMITED, *New Delhi*
PRENTICE-HALL OF JAPAN, INC., *Tokyo*
SIMON & SCHUSTER ASIA PTE. LTD., *Singapore*
EDITORA PRENTICE-HALL DO BRASIL, LTDA., *Rio de Janeiro*

To our wives' parents
Jack and Peggy Michaels
and
in memory of
Eugene and Helen Chmielewski

"A concept without a percept is empty;
a percept without a concept is blind."

Immanuel Kant

CONTENTS

PREFACE

Our purpose in writing the present text was to provide a fairly comprehensive study of the various mathematical methods that have proved valuable in the study of artificial intelligence. In doing so, we were guided by several basic considerations:

1. We wished to bridge the artificial separation between AI and the classical engineering study of autonomous systems.

2. Our goal was to concentrate on practical methodology, not on speculative theory. Consequently, we have remained close to the architectural and engineering levels.

3. In light of the previous consideration, we have provided a fairly extensive introduction to basic geometric and feature vector techniques utilized in image processing and pattern recognition.

4. Our program is conceptual, with an emphasis on modeling. Thus, we have avoided the introduction of any particular programming language.

5. In the midst of diversity, we desired unity. This is provided by the many-sorted algebra.

6. We wished to keep the mathematical level within the reach of a wide audience.

Unfortunately, a gap has developed between computer-oriented AI researchers and those whose background is engineering. For the practical implementation of real-time AI systems, this gap must be bridged. Any successful program must be grounded upon sound mathematical modeling, appropriate architecture, and satisfactory engineering implementation. In the development of fully autonomous systems, the newer algebraic models will ultimately be integrated with those employed in the classical theory of autonomous control.

Speculative theory must always exist at the leading edge of new developments. In AI, this theory takes many forms, including novel neural, reasoning, and architectural models. While we have indeed discussed the latter two notions (for instance, fuzzy logics and systolic processors), we have remained close to present-day capabilities. In today's fast-developing technologies, these capabilities are rapidly expanding and there is no doubt that a second edition of this book would contain a lengthy discussion on neural nets.

Computer vision, image processing, and pattern recognition are at the forefront of contemporary AI applications. In introducing the concept of a computer vision system, we have concentrated on basic geometric understanding and have developed methods that have already proven their worth, as evidenced by the number of software packages and parallel coprocessors that exist for the implementation of these methods. We have also connected the geometry of the image with the AI-oriented feature vector approach to image recognition.

In keeping with our modeling theme, we have refrained from the introduction of a programming language. We strongly believe that the study of an AI-oriented language such as LISP or PROLOG should not be relegated to a chapter in an AI text; rather, that study should proceed with a text on the language of interest. What should be included in a general AI text are the mathematical foundations underlying LISP and PROLOG, and these are included.

To provide unity, we have introduced the concept of a many-sorted algebra in the final chapter. Ultimately, the practical implementation of any AI algorithm will be founded upon some algebraic specification. The many-sorted algebra serves as a unifying structure in that the various algebraic models, whether they be sequential or parallel, fit into the many-sorted algebra schema. In particular, we have provided a brief sketch of the many-sorted algebra approach to image algebra. The operators in the digital image algebra yield an operational calculus for the expression of image processing (as well as other classes of) algorithms. Moreover, they do so in a manner that reveals the extensive parallelism within the algorithmic structure.

In determining an appropriate level of mathematical sophistication, we have been guided by our experience. To some extent, the book has grown out of our teaching a course entitled *Foundations of AI Theory with Applications* at Stevens Institute of Technology. As is often the case in computer science, the backgrounds of the students vary widely. Thus, the course has to be somewhat self-contained, even at the expense of occasional redundancies for various groups of students.

In writing a text such as the present one, where the scope of the methodologies is so wide, there must obviously be decisions made as to what material should be excluded. Without going into a detailed discussion of our rationale, let us simply mention two salient topics that have been excluded. We have discussed neither stochastic nor statistical methods. In this matter, our reasoning is quite straightforward. Neither topic could have been introduced in a self-contained manner without greatly expanding the text. Moreover, each of these topics should properly be studied in its own right by those interested in going beyond a general-purpose text. We have, on the other hand, given a (mainly conceptual) introduction to probabilistic reasoning, our intent being to place the analysis of data into an appropriate AI-oriented epistemology, as well as to provide certain necessary tools.

Insofar as expert systems are concerned, the logical and algebraic foundations have been included within the text and a brief discussion of the expert-system philosophy has been provided. Given that background material, a student should be prepared to take a project-based course in expert systems.

It is our hope that the present book can satisfactorily serve as (1) an introductory text for computer science and engineering students interested in pursuing the study of AI-based autonomous systems and (2) as a body of source material for those interested in finding appropriate mathematical models for their ongoing research.

Let us conclude by offering our appreciation to Professor Harry Sherman for proofreading the original manuscript.

Edward R. Dougherty

Charles R. Giardina

MATHEMATICAL
METHODS
for
ARTIFICIAL INTELLIGENCE
and
AUTONOMOUS SYSTEMS

INTRODUCTION

"What is artificial intelligence?" The question jumps out of the page and demands a straightforward answer. After all, is not *AI* the Zeitgeist, the very spirit of our age? Yet no easy answer to the question is readily available. Each discipline and subdiscipline possesses its own general answer, and refinements abound within each. Nevertheless, if our book on artificial intelligence is to have a theme, some direction to keep it from becoming, on the one hand, empty jargon, or, on the other, a kaleidoscope of disparate solutions to unconnected problems, then we must bite the bullet and commit ourselves at the outset to at least a working definition. So let us bite the bullet:

> Artificial intelligence is the structured development of theory, methodology, and physical systems that enable computers and robots to perform tasks that historically have been judged to lie within the domain of intelligence.

An immediate consequence of this definition is that, as a program, AI does not represent a radical break with the past; rather, it represents a stage in the evolution of Western thought. It draws upon, and to a certain extent brings to fruition, the dominant philosophic disciplines of our century: logic and statistics. Moreover, it is defined by and exists totally within the epistemological center of our science: specifically, the implementation of knowledge provides the power to predict, alter, and control the vicissitudes of nature, and knowledge itself is no more nor less than the mathematical description of phenomena. Now, for the first time on a massive scale, the implementation of knowledge involves the replication in machines of forms of that very knowledge.

In defining artificial intelligence, we have intentionally remained within an operational framework. It is not our intent to define intelligence; instead, we assume that there is activity that most would agree to be intelligent. At heart, the approach is phenomenological: intelligence is intentional—it points beyond itself. Rather than try to fully capture it in some logicomathematical structure, we can simply observe its accomplishments and emulate those. As an entity, we bracket it, put the bracketed entity aside, and then get on with the pragmatic replication of its activity. For some, this perspective might be too engineering oriented; nevertheless, it is an approach that is in accordance with the present state of our knowledge on the subject of intelligence and one that looks for practical solutions that fit into an overall strategy.

At the heart of any artificially intelligent system is the computer, the purpose of which is to process and store information. Many attributes that an *AI computer* should possess can be achieved through the utilization of proper architectural organization and design. Perhaps the most important attribute is speed, not only in processing algorithms, but also in CPU–memory communication and IO between incoming data from the sensors and outgoing signals to the control surfaces. To obtain functional robotic behavior in both learning and response, real-time processing is required: all processing, including IO, must be accomplished within a maximum time frame that is task dependent. To attain the necessary speed, parallel processing is essential. Substantive parallelism can be achieved in numerous ways, some of these being multiprocessing through the utilization of multiple CPUs and multiple memories, the employment of pipelining techniques in standard sequential machines, the introduction of asynchronous architectures such as data-flow, and the utilization of associative memory, where a parallel search can facilitate fast CPU–memory transferral of data and instructions.

Given an acceptable machine, where the criterion of acceptability will vary from application to application, we must algorithmically simulate whatever type of reasoning happens to be of interest. Essentially, this task requires the formulation of certain understandings concerning intelligence into formalisms that are compatible with machine implementation, while at the same time not distorting those understandings in the process of algorithm formation. There can be a great distance between an idea in the mind and a functioning program. In particular, different forms of knowledge require different representations. A suitable representation facilitates thinking in the relevant domain of application. It is also compatible with the architecture of the machine.

Of course, real intelligence exists and performs in the world, and it does so autonomously. Consequently, the paradigm of the artificially intelligent system is the autonomous system—the robot. But satisfactory robotic behavior involves far more than simply the classical chess-playing computer that crunched logic, or even the contemporary chess-playing computer, which utilizes its enormous statement-processing capabilities in conjunction with encoded knowledge elicited from experts.   The robot must interact physically with its environment.   Not only does it need to possess sophisticated electronic and mechanical control surfaces to allow it to act, but it must also be able to accumulate, process, fuse, and interpret data. It must function on the basis of valuations made on the data, with its decision procedures integrating those valuations with inference machinery that exists in either hardware or software.   But even operational decision making is not sufficient.   A truly autonomous robotic system must be adaptive: it must possess a hierarchical algorithmic system that provides for reconfiguration by higher-level algorithms, those that simulate autonomous reflection, of lower-level "behaviorial" algorithms, those that involve the direct interfacing of the robot and its environment.   Natural intelligence is adaptive, autonomously changing the way it perceives and acts as both its external and internal conditions change.   Indeed, not only must an AI system adapt to environmental variations, it must be self-rectifying in that it recognizes its own fallibility and adjusts accordingly.

We mentioned the need for data.   The autonomous system requires a sophisticated ability to organize, compress, and interpret data.   Without an extensive capability for data manipulation, it would be unable to render reasoned decisions. But what are data?   Precisely this: the readings of a needle on a meter or some other such measuring device.   The question as to what "thing" lies behind the data is not a scientific question.   That thing, be it called a particle, a wave, a particle-wave, or some other equally colloquial term, does not belong to the realm of scientific inquiry.

All scientific knowledge lies within the mathematical description of phenomena.   Yet the terms of the description do not refer to the immediate phenomena of perception; instead, it is the relationships between the terms, those relationships being logical in nature, that constitute our knowledge.   The "truth" of this essentially syntactical system depends on the degree to which the consequences of the system are compatible with the data of observation.

For robotics, such an epistemology is definitive: the mathematical apparatus that constitutes the artificial reasoning capability of the guiding machine intelligence is independent of any perceptual intuition.   Its character is syntactical rather than semantic.   Its mathematical character is limited to the fact that it possesses an organized structure that results in predefined operational decision making.   The "thinking" of the machine is purely linguistic in that there are well-defined relations between symbols, and these relations are connected to motor responses that simulate human, or perhaps superhuman, action.   And how is the worth of this action to be checked? By the acquisition of new data, of course.   The new data must be input into some auxiliary process that determines whether or not present behaviorial patterns are satisfactory.   If they are not, then self-adjustment needs to be undertaken; if they are, then the machine can continue to function as presently set.

In sum, there is the machine, the representation of knowledge, the AI algorithms (in both hardware and software), the data-based control system, and the communication between the inference machinery and both the sensors that collect the data and the control surfaces that execute the decisions.

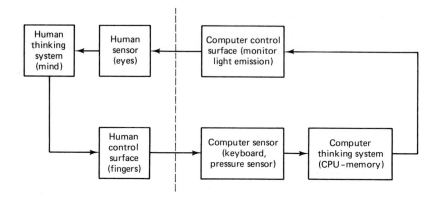

Figure I.1.   Open-loop system

Open- and Closed-loop Control

Many tasks performed by artificially intelligent systems involve direct interfacing with a human being. The computer has certain control surfaces under its command and is able to receive and interpret information from one or more sensors. Nonetheless, it is not completely autonomous. The control loop remains open unless closed by a human being, who uses his or her own sensors, brain, and control surfaces to interact actively with both the environment and the computer (see Figure I.1).

An instance of such a system is the pilot-computer coordinated control of an airplane. The computer receives information from numerous sensors, in particular, those utilized in navigation. This information is organized internally within the computer according to appropriate stochastic algorithms. Some of the processed information is passed on, in the form of signals, to control surfaces that navigate the airplane; some is passed on to instruments that can be read by the pilot (using his or her own sensors—eyes). The pilot's brain can then process this information further and, based on this processing, the pilot can send signals (using his or her own control surfaces—hands or voice) to the computer.

In a completely autonomous or fully robotic system, the control is closed-loop, in the sense that no human being is needed to close the control (decision) process. Here, the robot processes information received by way of its sensors and then sends signals to control surfaces, which then implement the control decisions made by the robot's computer brain (see Figure I.2). Unless such a closed-loop system is interrupted by either human intervention or physical failure, it continues to function according to its program.

Although autonomous (closed-loop) control is certainly a basic goal of AI, the practical employment of open-loop systems should not be overlooked. Indeed, it is the existence of automatic systems in aviation guidance that facilitates the continuous updating and implementation of navigation information. Moreover,

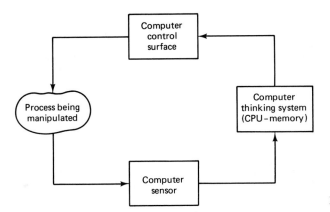

Figure I.2.   Closed-loop system

the knowledge acquired in the study of such systems and the intelligence that guides them are often directly applicable to fully autonomous systems. For instance, endowed with the appropriate image-processing and logical decision capabilities, a pilot-controlled airplane can be turned into a missile that is able to seek, find, target, and attack autonomously.

1

LOGICAL CALCULUS

1.1 THE ROLE OF LOGIC

Perhaps the foremost activity of intelligence is the construction of statements concerning facts, the manipulation of statements, and the organization of statements into hierarchical structures involving ever greater complexity. Reasoning often takes place far from the existential base upon which it is ultimately grounded. Indeed, it is the abstract manipulation of statements about facts and statements about statements, which themselves are possibly many levels removed from the facts, that tends to be associated with human thinking at its highest level.

One of the first orders of business in the construction of artificially intelligent systems is the replication of the means by which human beings carry on the act of reasoning. The ways in which statements are manipulated and understood must be reflected in machine behavior. Although it is precisely such a replication of a particular form of reasoning that has led to our conception of the modern-day digital computer, we must be careful not to attribute too much importance to any one model of reasoning. Specifically, the physical performance and the algorithmic methodology of the digital computer are both grounded in two-valued Boolean logic; nonetheless, although we must be well schooled in the basic tenets of that logic, we must not view it as the paradigm against which all modes of human thought should be judged. As our understanding of thinking, both formal and informal, increases, our ability to capture that greater understanding within the machine will depend on our ingenuity in utilizing the physical systems we have in hand. To the extent that those systems constrain our syntactical constructions and

6

the manipulations of those constructions, the formal mathematical basis of AI is also constrained.

Generally, logic is usually characterized as the science that deals with the formal principles of reasoning. Given that such principles can be articulated, an immediate goal of AI is the construction of algorithms that embody those principles. The problem, of course, is that the formal specification of rules of reasoning is a rather fuzzy notion, or at least it has turned out that way. Nevertheless, insofar as models can be created to simulate certain limited types of reason, those models can serve as the mathematical bases on which we can construct machine intelligence. Remember, the goal is to make ever smarter machines: the more sorts of thinking that can be replicated in a computer, the smarter that computer is.

In the current chapter we will briefly discuss the basic two-valued propositional calculus, which is concerned with the manipulation of atomic statements, and also present the first-order calculus, which goes deeper in that it allows analysis of the content of individual statements. These models of reasoning are referred to as calculi because they provide a calculational environment in which to formally manipulate statements according to fixed rules.

It is precisely such formal, mechanical manipulation that makes these calculi so amenable to machine implementation. Once the formal rules are encoded and appropriate computational algorithms developed, the region of human thinking that is *solely* characterized by these logics can be captured artificially. And here the word solely has been italicized for an important reason: given the machine replication of a branch of logic, it is only the logical manipulations pertinent to that branch that are automated.

To capture the hierarchical nature of reasoning within a computer, hierarchical languages need be constructed that allow the manipulation of multileveled propositions. Once again, such a system will only replicate that region of human thinking that is characterized by the syntactical and semantic constructions embodied within the formal structure of the language.

It is not our goal to present a treatise on logic; rather, we will present those fundamentals that are relevant to AI algorithm development and architectural design. It should be kept in mind that it is Boolean logic that provides the building blocks for nondeterministic logical models such as fuzzy and stochastic. Moreover, it is the inferential structure of this logic that plays the key role in current-day knowledge manipulation.

1.2 BASIC PROPOSITIONAL CONNECTIVES

The basic building blocks of the propositional calculus are sentences and the connectives that allow the interconnection of various sentences into more complex sentences, the validity of the latter depending on the lower-level input sentences and the meanings of the connectives involved.

A *sentence*, or *statement*, is a meaningful verbal or written assertion that is declarative and is either true or false, but not both true and false. Intuitively, a sentence is said to be *atomic* (or a statement *simple*) if only one fact is conveyed and the sentence is not made up of other sentences. A statement is true when it is in accordance with the facts revealed, and false otherwise.

Example 1.1

"A square is a rectangle." is a simple statement, whereas "John is tall *and* a square is a rectangle." is not a simple statement since more than one fact is conveyed. Notice that we have italicized the connective *and* when it was used within a sentence under consideration. We will continue to employ this practice so that there will be no confusion regarding the low-level usage of the word within the calculus of sentences and its higher-level use in discussions about the sentential calculus.

Given a statement comprised of simpler statements, the truth or falsity of the *compound* statement can be determined from the truth or falsity of its component statements, as long as the compound statement has been built up in strict accordance with some operational calculus. We will now describe the operations of the well-known propositional calculus.

The most elementary operation on sentences is the negation operation. For a sentence p, the *negation* (*not*) is denoted by $\sim p$. By letting 1 represent truth and 0 falsity, negation is defined by the *truth table*

p	$\sim p$
1	0
0	1

Thus, the negation of a proposition is false if the original proposition is true, and true otherwise.

Before proceeding, we should note that negation is an operation on sentences. It takes an input sentence and yields an output sentence. Moreover, the corresponding truth table defines the operation. While it is no doubt true that the truth table is in accordance with our intuitions insofar as two-valued logic is concerned, we must keep in mind that it represents an operational definition. This latter understanding leads to the mathematical formalism underlying the computational approach to propositional logic.

Whereas negation requires a single input sentence, the *conjunction* (*and*) operation requires two inputs, and thus combines sentences. The conjunction of sentences p and q (each called a *conjunct*) is denoted by $p \wedge q$ and is defined by the truth table

p	q	$p \wedge q$
1	1	1
0	1	0
1	0	0
0	0	0

It follows that the conjunction of two propositions is true when and only when each is true individually; otherwise, the conjunction is false.

Once again notice the operational role of the truth table: it gives meaning to the connective $\wedge$.

The *disjunction* (*or*) operation is also employed for combining sentences. The disjunction of p and q, $p \vee q$, has the truth table

p	q	$p \vee q$
1	1	1
0	1	1
1	0	1
0	0	0

The disjunction of two sentences is true whenever at least one of the original sentences (called *disjuncts*) is true; otherwise, the disjunction is false. The disjunction is sometimes called *inclusive or*.

There is an *exclusive or* operation, symbolized by $\oplus$, that is true if and only if exactly one of the original sentences is true. The truth table corresponding to $p \oplus q$ is provided in Figure 1.1, along with that of several other operations, some of which will be discussed subsequently.

Whenever the word *or* appears in a sentence, we will always assume that the inclusive or ($\vee$) is to be used.

An illustration will now be given showing how to find the truth value of a complex sentence from the truth values of its components when the *or* and *and* connectives are employed.

Example 1.2

All truth values associated with the sentence, "It is raining *and* the wind is blowing, *or* I am rich." will now be found. This is accomplished by associating the symbols p, q, and r, respectively, with the simple sentences, "It is raining.", "The wind is blowing.", and "I am rich." Since these are three simple sentences, each of which can be true or false, the truth value of $(p \wedge q) \vee r$ will be one of the eight values

p	q	0	$p \wedge q$	$\sim(q \to p)$	q	$\sim(p \to q)$	p	$p \oplus q$	$p \vee q$
1	1	0	1	0	1	0	1	0	1
0	1	0	0	1	1	0	0	1	1
1	0	0	0	0	0	1	1	1	1
0	0	0	0	0	0	0	0	0	0

$p \downarrow q$	$p \leftrightarrow q$	$\sim p$	$p \to q$	$\sim q$	$q \to p$	$p \mid q$	1
0	1	0	1	0	1	0	1
0	0	1	1	0	0	1	1
0	0	0	0	1	1	1	1
1	1	1	1	1	1	1	1

Figure 1.1 Binary truth functions

given in the following table. Notice that the actual truth value of the compound statement will depend on the factual conditions regarding the three atomic inputs. As the facts change, or are at least perceived to change, so too does the validity of higher-level propositions regarding an interrelationship among the facts.

p	q	r	$p \wedge q$	$(p \wedge q) \vee r$
1	1	1	1	1
0	1	1	0	1
1	0	1	0	1
0	0	1	0	1
1	1	0	1	1
0	1	0	0	0
1	0	0	0	0
0	0	0	0	0

It is important to notice that the truth values associated with the disjunction operation can be found by taking the maxima of the truth values of the component sentences. Analogously, the conjunction operation involves the minima of the truth values. Referring to Example 1.2, if, factually, it is raining, the wind is not blowing, and I am rich, then $p = 1$, $q = 0$, and $r = 1$. Hence, the truth value of $(p \wedge q) \vee r$ can be found by taking a minimum and a maximum, instead of referring to the third row of the preceding truth table. Indeed, employing the given distribution of the facts, the truth value is given by

$$\max[\min(1, 0), 1] = 1$$

We will look more closely at this maximum–minimum strategy in the following section.

Perhaps the most important operation in AI is the *conditional*, or *implication*, symbolized by $\rightarrow$. The expression $p \rightarrow q$ should be read, *if p then q*. As can be seen in Figure 1.1, $p \rightarrow q$ and $q \rightarrow p$ have different truth values; thus, implication is a noncommutative operation. For the sentence $p \rightarrow q$, p is called the *antecedent* and q is called the *consequent*. The only time $p \rightarrow q$ is false is when the antecedent is true and the consequent is false.

Very often, confusion arises from the definition of the conditional. For instance, the sentence, "*If* Julius Caesar was the discoverer of America, *then* Napolean was victorious at Waterloo," is valid (i.e., true). Indeed, since the antecedent is false, at least insofar as historical judgment is concerned, the overall conditional would be true no matter what the consequent might be. Without going into a long philosophical digression regarding the "meaning" of the definition of implication, let us simply note two points: (1) Falsehood of the conditional occurs only when the consequent is false in conjunction with the antecedent being true. (2) As a formal structure, the propositional calculus is *extensional:* there is not asserted any causal relation between the sentences connected by the conditional operator. This extensionality is in opposition to be *intensionality* that dominated philosophical logic from Aristotle through the Middle Ages. In the formal propositional calculus, sentences are operated on by the connectives, and no internal relationship between them is asserted.

The final connective to be introduced in this section is the equivalence operation $\leftrightarrow$, which is defined in Figure 1.1. Note that $p \leftrightarrow q$ is true if and only if both input sentences possess the same truth value. Thus, equivalence corresponds to the grammatical expression *if and only if*, which is often abbreviated *iff*.

Of paramount importance is the fact that, given any compound sentence formed from the fundamental operations thus far introduced, its meaning (in terms of its truth table) can be algorithmically deduced by reference to the truth tables of the connectives from which it is constructed. We need simply go step by step and apply the appropriate operational definition at each step. This is precisely the import of an operational calculus.

Example 1.3

The truth value of $[p \rightarrow (q \vee r)] \leftrightarrow p$ is given in the following table. Pay particular attention to the way in which the truth values in the fifth and sixth columns have been derived by means of the truth values in the first four columns and the first five columns, respectively.

p	q	r	$q \vee r$	$p \rightarrow (q \vee r)$	$[p \rightarrow (q \vee r)] \leftrightarrow p$
1	1	1	1	1	1
0	1	1	1	1	0
1	0	1	1	1	1
0	0	1	1	1	0
1	1	0	1	1	1
0	1	0	1	1	0
1	0	0	0	0	0
0	0	0	0	1	0

1.3 PROPOSITIONAL CONNECTIVES AND TRUTH VALUES AS MAPPINGS

Insofar as the propositional connectives thus far introduced require two input sentences, each can be viewed as a binary function f that maps a pair of sentences (p, q) into a third sentence $r = f(p, q)$. Furthermore, since each sentence can be attributed the truth value 0 or 1, it is convenient to let X denote a universal set of sentences and then define the truth function $T : X \to \{0, 1\}$, where $T(p) = 1$ if the proposition p is true and $T(p) = 0$ if the proposition is false. Consequently, as a mapping, $f : X \times X \to X$, defined by $f(p, q) = r$. For instance, the disjunctive operation, $p \vee q$, although not usually written using the prefix notation $r = \vee (p, q)$, is actually a function of two variables. In any case, the truth value of the composite statement r can be found by knowing the truth values of the sentences p and q and by knowing precisely which function f is being employed. This is the purpose of the truth table, which is actually a function, and will henceforth be denoted by F.

The following commuting diagram summarizes the foregoing discussion:

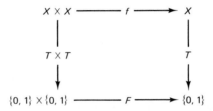

The meaning of the diagram is this: starting with a pair of sentences (p, q) in $X \times X$ possessing given truth values, the same value will be obtained by either traversing the diagram across the top and then down, or by going down first and then traversing the diagram horizontally along the bottom. In sum, the diagram states that

$$T(f(p, q)) = F(T(p), T(q))$$

Example 1.4

It was intuitively explained in Section 1.1 that the truth values of the *or* operation $f = \vee$ can be found using the maximum operation, $F = \max$, inherited from the real-number system. Thus, we have the commuting diagram

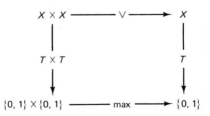

That is,

$$T(p \lor q) = \max(T(p), T(q))$$

For instance, letting p denote "a square is a circle," q denote "a triangle is a polygon," and r denote the disjunction of p and q,

$$T(p) = 0, \qquad T(q) = 1, \qquad T(r) = 1$$

and

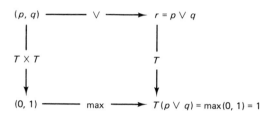

Precisely 16 binary functions appear in the table of Figure 1.1.   This corresponds to the fact that $F \in \{0, 1\}^{\{0,1\} \times \{0,1\}}$ and there are

$$\text{card}\{0, 1\}^{\text{card}(\{0,1\} \times \{0,1\})} = 2^4$$

such functions.

Example 1.5

The truth values corresponding to the conjunction operation $f = \land$ can be found using the minimum operation, $F = \min$, inherited from the real–number system. We have, for sentences p and q,

$$T(p \land q) = \min(T(p), T(q))$$

This is illustrated in the commuting diagram

$$
\begin{array}{ccc}
X \times X & \xrightarrow{\ \ \land\ \ } & X \\
\Big\downarrow T \times T & & \Big\downarrow T \\
\{0, 1\} \times \{0, 1\} & \xrightarrow{\ \ \min\ \ } & \{0, 1\}
\end{array}
$$

Example 1.6

The truth value corresponding to the negation operation $\sim$ can be found using the complement operation $'$, called *prime:*

$$': \{0, 1\} \to \{0, 1\}$$

by $0' = 1$ and $1' = 0$ or, more generally, $x' = 1 - x$.   The complement operation is traditionally given in the post-fix exponential manner just described.   We have, for

any sentence p,

$$T(\sim p) = T(p)' = 1 - T(p)$$

This is illustrated by the commuting diagram

For instance, if $T(p) = 0$, then

$$0' = 1 = T(\sim p)$$

A salient point regarding the relationship between propositional truth value and the max, min, and prime operations of the real-number system is that the problem of computing the truth value of a given expression is transformed from the "logical world" of truth-table manipulation to the "numerical world." In other words, through the use of a transform technique, the propositional calculus is embedded in the number system, in particular, that part of the number system consisting of the binary set $\{0, 1\}$, together with the three aforementioned numerical operations. Of course, we could reverse the argument, as was done by Russell, Whitehead, and Frege, and argue that a particular portion of the number system is embedded in the structure of logic. In any event, from the perspective of computational logic, the commuting diagrams provide us with an alternative methodology.

1.4 TAUTOLOGIES AND CONTRADICTIONS

In everyday grammar, there are many ways to "say the same thing." The situation is very much the same in the propositional calculus: different expressions involving sentences and connectives might in fact possess the same meaning, in that under the same distribution of the facts they are either both true or both false. Letting p and q denote the two expressions, each of which is a compound sentence, the identity between their truth values means precisely that the truth table for $p \leftrightarrow q$ is identically 1. Intuitively, the statement $p \leftrightarrow q$ is true under all circumstances.

In general, whenever the truth table for a specific sentence is identically 1, we say that the sentence is a *tautology*. No matter what the facts, a tautology is always true: we need not make any reference to the data. For instance, if we say, "Object x is a square *or* x is *not* a square," then observation of x is irrelevant, for certainly the compound statement is true.

Example 1.7

All the following sentences are tautologies:

1. $p \vee (\sim p)$.
2. $(p \wedge q) \leftrightarrow [\sim((\sim p) \vee (\sim q))]$.
3. $(p \vee q) \leftrightarrow [\sim((\sim p) \wedge (\sim q))]$.
4. $(p \leftrightarrow q) \rightarrow (p \rightarrow q)$.
5. $(p \rightarrow q) \leftrightarrow ((\sim p) \vee q)$.

For instance, sentence 4 is verified by the following truth table:

p	q	$p \leftrightarrow q$	$p \rightarrow q$	$(p \leftrightarrow q) \rightarrow (p \rightarrow q)$
1	1	1	1	1
0	1	0	1	1
1	0	0	0	1
0	0	1	1	1

Note that the last column has all 1s, assuring that a tautology exists.   Numerous other tautologies are given in Figure 1.2.

TAUTOLOGIES

1. $\sim \sim p \leftrightarrow p$
2. $p \wedge q \leftrightarrow q \wedge p$
3. $p \vee q \leftrightarrow q \vee p$
4. $(p \wedge q) \wedge r \leftrightarrow p \wedge (q \wedge r)$
5. $(p \vee q) \vee r \leftrightarrow p \vee (q \vee r)$
6. $p \wedge (q \vee r) \leftrightarrow (p \wedge q) \vee (p \wedge r)$
7. $p \vee (q \wedge r) \leftrightarrow (p \vee q) \wedge (p \vee r)$
8. $\sim(p \wedge q) \leftrightarrow \sim p \vee \sim q$
9. $\sim(p \vee q) \leftrightarrow \sim p \wedge \sim q$
10. $p \vee p \leftrightarrow p$
11. $p \wedge p \leftrightarrow p$
12. $p \wedge q \rightarrow p$
13. $p \wedge q \rightarrow q$
14. $p \rightarrow p \vee q$
15. $q \rightarrow p \vee q$

Figure 1.2   Tautologies

Returning to the problem of equivalence, two sentences p and q are said to be *logically equivalent* if $p \leftrightarrow q$ is a tautology.   Moreover, p is said to *logically imply q* if $p \rightarrow q$ is a tautology. For *p* to logically imply *q*, no distribution of the facts can ever result in *p* being true and *q* being false: the implication is independent of observation. For logical equivalence, we write $p \Leftrightarrow q$, and for logical implication, we write $p \Rightarrow q$.

Whereas implication and equivalence are operational connectives within the sentence structure of the propositional calculus, logical implication and logical equivalence are metastatements *about* sentences within the calculus. This distinction is crucial. What is interesting is that we can define higher-level notions in terms of truth values relating to the low-level equivalence operation.

To get a better understanding of logical implication, consider the statement

$$p \wedge q \rightarrow p \vee q$$

We ask whether or not the statement is a tautology. Of course, we could simply compute the truth table; however, let us proceed differently. The only time the conditional is false is when the antecedent is true at the same time the consequent is false. But for $p \wedge q$ to be true, both *p* and *q* must be true, which means that $p \vee q$ is also true. Thus, it is impossible for the conditional to be false, no matter what the distribution of the facts; that is, $p \wedge q$ logically implies $p \vee q$.

On the other hand, consider the statement

$$p \vee q \rightarrow p \wedge q$$

It is certainly possible for the antecedent to be true while the consequent is false: this condition will occur when *p* is true and *q* is false. Hence, the statement is not a tautology and $p \vee q$ does not logically imply $p \wedge q$.

According to the definition of logical equivalence, $p \leftrightarrow q$ is a tautology if and only if $p \Leftrightarrow q$. Thus, referring to tautologies 2 and 3 of Example 1.7, we have

$$p \wedge q \Leftrightarrow \sim((\sim p) \vee (\sim q))$$

and

$$p \vee q \Leftrightarrow \sim((\sim p) \wedge (\sim q))$$

respectively. These logical equivalences are known as *De Morgan's laws*.

From a computational perspective, it is useful to recognize that logical equivalence, as well as other tautologies, can be proved utilizing the truth function *T* and not by resorting to truth tables. To demonstrate logical equivalence, it must be shown that the expressions on either side of the equivalence symbol $\Leftrightarrow$ have the same truth value.

Example 1.8

Consider De Morgan's law

$$p \wedge q \Leftrightarrow \sim((\sim p) \vee (\sim q))$$

To demonstrate it, we need to show that

$$T(p \wedge q) = T(\sim((\sim p) \vee (\sim q)))$$

Applying the commuting diagrams of Section 1.3, we see that it need only be shown that

$$\min(T(p), T(q)) = [\max(T(p)', T(q)')]' = 1 - \max(1 - T(p), 1 - T(q))$$

which follows from the following well-known formulas for real numbers:

$$\min(x, y) = \frac{x + y - |x - y|}{2}$$

and

$$\max(x, y) = \frac{x + y + |x - y|}{2}$$

By identifying x with $T(p)$ and y with $T(q)$, we have

$$1 - \max(1 - x, 1 - y) = 1 - \frac{(1 - x) + (1 - y) + |(1 - x) - (1 - y)|}{2}$$

$$= \frac{2 - (1 - x) - (1 - y) - |y - x|}{2}$$

$$= \frac{x + y - |x - y|}{2} = \min(x, y)$$

Whenever the truth value of a sentence is always 0, the sentence is said to be a *contradiction*. It is immediate that p is a tautology if and only if $\sim p$ is a contradiction. Now, suppose the tautology p involves only $\sim$, $\vee$, and $\wedge$. If in p every instance of $\vee$ is replaced by $\wedge$, every instance of $\wedge$ is replaced by $\vee$, and each sentence is negated, then the resulting sentence q is a contradiction, and $p \leftrightarrow \sim q$ is a tautology. We say that the statement $\sim q$ has been obtained from p by *duality* and that the tautology $p \leftrightarrow \sim q$ results from the principle of duality. Generally, the principle of duality results from De Morgan's laws.

Example 1.9

Consider De Morgan's law

$$p \vee q \Leftrightarrow \sim((\sim p) \wedge (\sim q))$$

Note that the right side can be obtained from the left side by application of duality.

For complicated sentences, braces, brackets, and parentheses might be required to ensure that no confusion results as to what operations have which arguments. To lessen the symbology, these symbols can be removed in accordance with the following hierarchy: $\sim$ modifies the smallest sentence to the right; next, $\wedge$ is an infix operator with arguments being the two smallest sentences immediately to the left and right; $\vee$, $\rightarrow$, and finally $\leftrightarrow$ are infix operators that act in a syntactical manner similar to $\wedge$.

Example 1.10

The sentence

$$\sim p \wedge q \vee \sim r \rightarrow p \leftrightarrow q \wedge s$$

can be written as

$$\{[((\sim p) \wedge q) \vee (\sim r)] \rightarrow p\} \leftrightarrow (q \wedge s)$$

Example 1.11

The tautologies resulting in De Morgan's laws can be written as:

$$p \wedge q \leftrightarrow \sim(\sim p \vee \sim q).$$
$$p \vee q \leftrightarrow \sim(\sim p \wedge \sim q).$$

1.5 SYNTHESIS PROBLEMS

In an *analysis* problem, a sentence is given and the objective is to ascertain the truth value. This can be found by means of a truth table: given sentences p_1, p_2, ..., p_n and truth function $f(p_1, p_2, \ldots, p_n)$, find

$$T(f(p_1, p_2, \ldots, p_n))$$

Conversely, given a truth table, we might wish to find a sentence with the appropriate truth values. This is called a *synthesis* problem. In this case, for the sentences p_1, p_2, ..., p_n, $T(f(p_1, p_2, \ldots, p_n))$ is given and $f(p_1, p_2, \ldots, p_n)$ is to be found. Every synthesis problem can be solved using a sentence involving the operators $\sim$, $\vee$, and $\wedge$. An illustration of this result is given in the next example using three sentences as arguments. Generalization to n arguments is immediate.

Example 1.12

Consider the truth table involving the ternary operation f:

p	q	r	$f(p, q, r)$	
1	1	1	1	←
0	1	1	1	←
1	0	1	0	
0	0	1	0	
1	1	0	0	
0	1	0	0	
1	0	0	1	←
0	0	0	0	

The objective is to find a sentence s involving only the connectives $\sim$, $\wedge$, and $\vee$ such that s and $f(p, q, r)$ are logically equivalent; that is,

$$T(s) = T(f(p, q, r))$$

The solution is found by first noting (using an arrow) all rows for which the truth value of the final column is 1. In each of these rows, a conjunction is taken involving p, q, and r or their negations. Specifically, if $T(p) = 1$, then p is employed in the conjunction and $\sim p$ is not; conversely, if $T(p) = 0$, then $\sim p$ is employed and p is not. The sentences q and r are treated similarly. The final step is to take the disjunction of the resulting conjunctions. For the truth table under consideration,

$$s = (p \wedge q \wedge r) \vee (\sim p \wedge q \wedge r) \vee (p \wedge \sim q \wedge \sim r)$$

In general, the solution of the synthesis problem described in the preceding example is given in what is commonly called *disjunctive normal form*. Although this form is usually not minimal from the perspective of the number of operations involved, it is canonical in that the algorithm employed to obtain it always gives the desired result. Moreover, that result utilizes only negation, conjunction, and disjunction.

Example 1.13

Refer to Figure 1.1 for the truth table of $p \rightarrow q$. A disjunctive normal form possessing the same truth values, (i.e., a logically equivalent expression) can be found as in Example 1.12:

$$p \rightarrow q \Leftrightarrow (p \wedge q) \vee (\sim p \wedge q) \vee (\sim p \wedge \sim q)$$

A simpler expression can be found by noting that $T(p \rightarrow q) = 0$ only in the single instance when $T(p) = 1$ and $T(q) = 0$; so

$$\sim(p \rightarrow q) \Leftrightarrow p \wedge \sim q$$

Therefore,

$$p \rightarrow q \Leftrightarrow \sim(p \wedge \sim q)$$

Using De Morgan's law, we obtain

$$\sim(p \wedge \sim q) \Leftrightarrow \sim p \vee q$$

and so

$$p \rightarrow q \Leftrightarrow \sim p \vee q$$

which was noted in Example 1.7.

Figure 1.3 illustrates the analysis and synthesis problems. In the synthesis problem, the operation f is to be found. As noted previously, f can always be expressed (and found) in disjunctive normal form. By employing De Morgan's laws, the expression can always be reduced to a logically equivalent one involving only negation and disjunction or negation and conjunction.

But we can go even further: in fact, the synthesis operation can always be performed utilizing a single binary connective. Specifically, precisely two binary connectives can be employed alone in the construction of all truth tables: $\downarrow$ and $|$ (see Figure 1.1). The operation $\downarrow$ is sometimes called *adjoint denial* or the *Pierce arrow operation*, and it is a negation of the *or* operation. For this reason it is

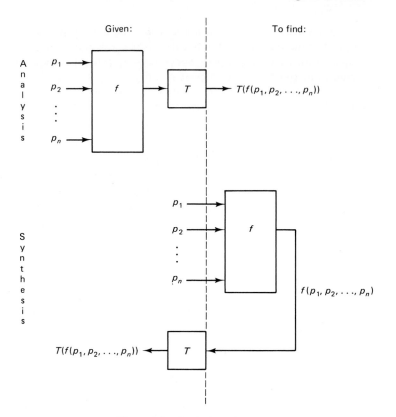

Figure 1.3   Analysis and synthesis

most often called the *NOR* operation.   Specifically,

$$p \downarrow q \Leftrightarrow \sim(p \vee q)$$

Additionally, the operation $|$ is sometimes called the *alternative denial* or the *Sheffer stroke*.   Since

$$p \mid q \Leftrightarrow \sim(p \wedge q)$$

it is most often called the *NAND* operation.   These operators will be discussed in greater detail in the next section.

1.6 COMBINATIONAL LOGIC

Leaving the electrical details aside, the logical values 0 and 1 can be seen as denoting two distinct voltages within an electrical circuit.   It is the physical manipulation of two such voltages within a system that constitutes the "thinking" done by a digital computer.   In essence, physical devices, called *gates*, serve to reconfigure voltages in accordance with the truth tables of the various propositional connectives. These gates are named according to the truth functions they simulate.   For instance, an *and* gate requires two input voltages, yields a single output voltage, and is denoted by either the block diagram

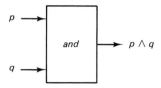

which gives the logical expression in sentential form, or by the special circuit symbol

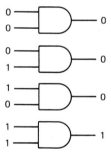

which operationally specifies the gate in terms of the input and output truth values. Using the latter symbolism, the four possible input combinations and corresponding outputs can be represented by the following four instances of the *and* gate:

The combining of logic-type connections in various physical configurations enables computers to "think and make decisions."   Such *circuit representations* constitute physical realizations of sentences within the propositional calculus.   In an actual computer, timing and storage considerations need to be taken into account; however, we will postpone discussion of the relationship between gate structure and timing until Chapter 3.   The gate structure, bereft of storage elements, is referred to as *combinational logic*.   Figure 1.4 gives the block diagrams and special symbols commonly employed in combinational logic.   The block diagrams represent propositional operations on sentences, whereas the special symbols denote operations on the truth values of sentences.   Consequently, the latter diagrams are more faithful to actual hardware.

Example 1.14

Assume that a "circuit" is to be built that will yield the truth value of the sentence, "If it is raining and it is Friday, then I will not sleep."   We will denote this sentence

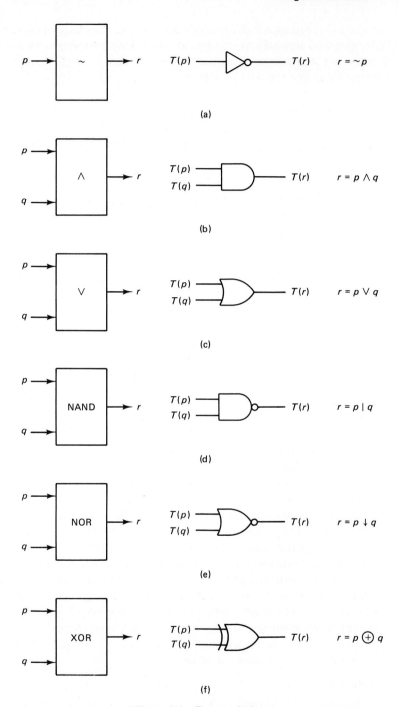

Figure 1.4 Gate symbols

by z, and let p, q, and r denote the simple sentences, "it is raining", "it is Friday", and "I will not sleep", respectively.   In the propositional calculus, z is given by the compound sentence

$$p \wedge q \to r$$

An application of the tautology

$$(x \to y) \leftrightarrow (\sim x \vee y)$$

yields the equivalent representation of z:

$$\sim(p \wedge q) \vee r$$

A block diagram representation is given by

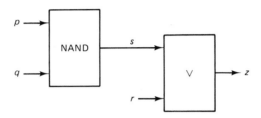

Equivalently, in special symbol form, we have

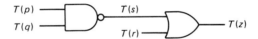

Note that, in the diagrams, s denotes the output of the NAND gate.

Physical *and* gates, *not* gates, and the like, can actually be purchased and wired according to a given block diagram.   These physical gates are usually composed of numerous transistors.   The truth values of the inputs to each gate are often given as voltage wave forms, where, for instance, the voltage may take on only one of two values, say α and β.   The actual value of α volts may represent the truth value 1, while β volts represents the truth value 0.

In practice, several simplifications for drawing circuits are employed.   Due to the commutativity of *or* and *and*, it does not matter which inputs are used on the top and bottom in their block diagrams.   Furthermore, even though the *or* and *and* operations are binary, because of their associativity, we will use them as though they are *n*-ary.   For instance, we will represent the expression $p \vee q \vee r$ in block diagram form as

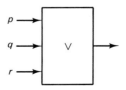

This diagram should be understood as just a simplified way of representing

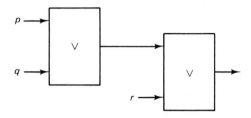

or, due to the associative law, the equivalent diagram

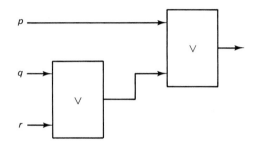

A further reduction when using block diagrams can be achieved by utilizing *fusible logic*. Unlike the circuit diagrams just presented, fusible logic cannot physically be wired as diagrammed. Rather, it is employed to simplify notation and to construct neat, orderly diagrams of logical sentences. When using fusible logic, it is customary to diagram the negation of each input sentence, even though it may not be employed in determining the output. Moreover, each *or* and *and* gate has a single wire coming in (and going out). The actual number of inputs (i.e., the arity of the operation), along with the inputs themselves, is found by observing the dots on the input wire. Each dot lies on the intersection of a horizontal and vertical line and indicates the input to be utilized.

Example 1.15

Let s denote the sentence $x \vee (\sim y) \vee z$. Then a fusible logic diagram of s is given by

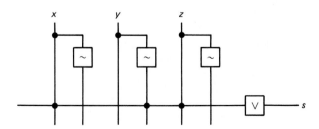

Example 1.16

A single fusible logic diagram for $r \wedge t$, where

$$r = (x \wedge y) \vee (x \wedge \sim z)$$

and

$$t = (x \wedge w) \vee (x \wedge y) \vee (z \wedge w)$$

is given by

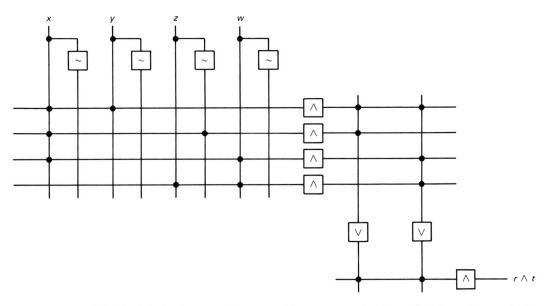

The fusible logic procedure provides an organized methodology for analysis. Indeed, numerous physical devices employ similar structures. Programmable array logic (PAL), programmable logic arrays (PLAs), and programmable read-only memories (PROMs) are three popular memory devices that employ designs similar to fusible logic.

1.7 THEOREM PROVING BY SEMANTIC TECHNIQUES

Suppose $p_1, p_2, \ldots, p_n$ and c are sentences for which

$$p_1 \wedge p_2 \wedge \cdots \wedge p_n \rightarrow c \tag{1}$$

is a tautology. Then the conjunction of the p_i logically implies c, and we say that $p_1, p_2, \ldots, p_n$ are the *premises* and c is the *conclusion* of the *syllogism* "If $p_1, p_2, \ldots, p_n$, then c." We also say the *theorem* "If $p_1, p_2, \ldots, p_n$, then c." *holds*, and we write

$$p_1, p_2, \ldots, p_n \Rightarrow c$$

If the conjunction of the p_i does not logically imply c, then we say that the theorem does not hold, and we often write

$$p_1, p_2, \ldots, p_n \nRightarrow c$$

From the definition of a syllogism, it is immediate that we need to consider the truth table of the implication in (1) to determine whether or not a theorem holds: it holds if the truth function for the implication is identically 1. Checking the verity of a syllogism by means of its truth table is known as the *semantic* method for proving a theorem.

Due to the manner in which the implication $\rightarrow$ is defined, we actually need only check the instances in which all the premises $p_1, p_2, \ldots, p_n$ are true. As long as the conclusion c is true in these instances, the overall implication will be a tautology. The technique of checking only the instances in which all the premises are true is called the method of *forward chaining*.

We can also check the verity of a syllogism by making certain that in each instance in which the conclusion is false at least one of the premises is also false. Should such be the case, then once again the implication is a tautology. This method of verifying a syllogism is called *backward chaining*. In forward chaining, we are going from the premises to the conclusion in examining the truth values, whereas in backward chaining we are beginning with the conclusion and going from there to investigate the truth values of the premises.

Example 1.17

We will prove (or disprove) the syllogism consisting of the the premises p_1 and p_2 and the conclusion c, where

$$p_1 = \text{An apple is a fruit.}$$

$$p_2 = \text{If today is Monday, then an apple is a fruit.}$$

$$c = \text{Today is Monday.}$$

The theorem to be checked is

$$p_1, p_2 \Rightarrow c$$

There are only two atomic sentences, p_1 and c, in the entire syllogism. The following truth table applies:

p_1	c	$p_2 = (c \rightarrow p_1)$
1	1	1
0	1	0
1	0	1
0	0	1

In the method of forward chaining, the theorem is true provided that in all those cases for which $T(p_1) = T(p_2) = 1$, $T(c) = 1$, also. For the first row of the truth table, this is the case; however, for the third row, this is not the case. Consequently, the theorem does not hold. Equivalently, the conclusion does not follow from the premises using backward chaining. Indeed, in the third row of the truth table, $T(c) = 0$; yet both premises are true, thereby assuring that the theorem does not hold. Thus, we write

$$p_1, p_2 \not\Rightarrow c$$

Example 1.18

Prove (or disprove) the theorem

$$p_1, p_2, p_3 \Rightarrow c$$

where

$$p_1 = x \wedge y$$

$$p_2 = x$$

$$p_3 = x \rightarrow y$$

$$c = y \vee z$$

where x, y, and z are atomic sentences. In this example, the truth table consists of eight rows and is given by

x	y	z	p_1	p_2	p_3	c
1	1	1	1	1	1	1
0	1	1	0	0	1	1
1	0	1	0	1	0	1
0	0	1	0	0	1	1
1	1	0	1	1	1	1
0	1	0	0	0	1	1
1	0	0	0	1	0	0
0	0	0	0	0	1	0

The theorem holds by backward chaining, since whenever $T(c) = 0$, $T(p_i) = 0$ for at least one i, $i = 1, 2$, or 3. Hence, we write

$$p_1, p_2, p_3 \Rightarrow c$$

Whenever $p \Rightarrow q$ and $q \Rightarrow p$ both hold, in which case p and q are logically equivalent, we write $p \Leftrightarrow q$. From the theorem point of view, $p \Leftrightarrow q$ represents two theorems, one having premise p and conclusion q and the other having premise q and conclusion p.

Figure 1.5 gives a number of well-known theorems.

Example 1.19

Theorem 2 in Figure 1.5 is often called *modus ponens:* given the truth of a sentence p and the implication $p \rightarrow q$, it always follows that the conclusion q is also true. As in all the theorems of Figure 1.5, the premises and the conclusion need not be simple. Any symbol in any of these theorems can be *instantiated* by replacing it by any sentence,

THEOREMS

1. $p, q \Rightarrow p \wedge q$
2. $p, p \rightarrow q \Rightarrow q$
3. $\sim p, p \vee q \Rightarrow q$
4. $\sim q, p \rightarrow q \Rightarrow \sim p$
5. $p \vee q, p \rightarrow r, q \rightarrow r \Rightarrow r$
6. $p \rightarrow q, q \rightarrow r \Rightarrow p \rightarrow r$
7. $p, p \rightarrow q, q \rightarrow r \Rightarrow r$
8. $p \vee (q \wedge \sim q) \Leftrightarrow p$
9. $p \wedge (q \vee \sim q) \Leftrightarrow p$
10. $p \rightarrow q \Leftrightarrow \sim p \vee q$
11. $\sim(p \rightarrow q) \Leftrightarrow p \wedge \sim q$
12. $p \leftrightarrow q \Leftrightarrow (p \rightarrow q) \wedge (q \rightarrow p)$
13. $p \leftrightarrow q \Leftrightarrow (p \wedge q) \vee (\sim p \wedge \sim q)$
14. $p \rightarrow (q \rightarrow r) \Leftrightarrow (p \wedge q) \rightarrow r$
15. $p \rightarrow q \Leftrightarrow \sim q \rightarrow \sim p$

Figure 1.5   Theorems in propositional calculus

simple or not.   For instance, by *modus ponens*, from the two premises

1. "John is big *or* Mary is short."
2. "*If* John is big *or* Mary is short, *then* it will rain today."

there follows the conclusion "It will rain today."

Example 1.20

Theorem 14 in Figure 1.5 is really two theorems; to prove it, we will show by forward chaining that, whenever the left side has truth value 1, so does the right side, and, conversely, when the right side has truth value 1, so does the left side.   We can see the verity of these two theorems by inspection of the following truth table:

p	q	r	$p \rightarrow (q \rightarrow r)$	$(p \wedge q) \rightarrow r$
1	1	1	1	1
0	1	1	1	1
1	0	1	1	1
0	0	1	1	1
1	1	0	0	0
0	1	0	1	1
1	0	0	1	1
0	0	0	1	1

In words, we have just proved that if r is *implied by p and q*, then p alone *implies* $q \rightarrow r$, and conversely.   Note the italicized terms in the hybrid English–symbolic statement of the theorem. These help to keep clear which words are connectives within the calculus and which are part of the theorem, the latter of which speaks about sentences within the calculus.

It is always possible to determine in a finite number of steps whether or not a conclusion follows from the premises by constructing a truth table. However, when a large number of atomic sentences are employed in a syllogism, the truth table is unwieldy. Fortunately, there are means other than the semantic method for proving theorems.

In the semantic technique, a transform (T) is employed: the theorem is indirectly shown to hold (or not hold) by utilizing truth values. Other methods for proving theorems are more direct and rely only on the structure of the syllogism. These are called *syntactical methods* of theorem proving and will be discussed next.

1.8 SYNTACTICAL AND AUTOMATIC THEOREM PROVING

A computer can always prove theorems using the truth table method described in the previous section; however, for a theorem comprised of n atomic sentences, 2^n rows are needed to form the table. Moreover, usually at least as many columns are needed as there are premises, and a column for the conclusion is always necessary. Due to either forward or backward chaining, it is likely that not all rows will be required; nevertheless, a large amount of computation might still be necessary. Syntactical methods often reduce this computational burden.

The syntactical method of proof utilizes a logical sequence of tautologies together with previously proved theorems to demonstrate that a conclusion follows as a logical consequence from a given set of premises. Such a demonstration is called a *derivation*. We will feel free to employ any of the tautologies in Figure 1.2 and any of the theorems given in Figure 1.5 in constructing a derivation.

Specifically, in performing a derivation to syntactically prove the theorem

$$p_1, p_2, \ldots, p_n \Rightarrow c$$

starting with the theorem as stated, we may replace any of the sentences, including the conclusion, by any stentence that is logically equivalent, we may introduce into the premises any sentence that is logically implied by any collection of sentences currently listed among the premises (at the present stage of the derivation), and we may replace the conclusion by any sentence that logically implies it. For instance, if we know beforehand that

$$p_2, p_5 \Rightarrow q$$

then we can utilize the sentence q in deriving the conclusion c by adjoining q to the collection of premises. Note that, at any step in the derivation, we can drop from the premises any number of sentences, since every collection of sentences logically implies any subcollection. In any event, the derivation is complete and the theorem is proved when (and if) both sides of the implication sign consist of exactly the same expression. Indeed, the existence of such an occurrence means that the verity of all the premises implies the verity of the conclusion, thus establishing the theorem.

In proving a logical equivalence syntactically, we utilize the fact that two logical implications are involved. Accordingly, if we only replace the premises and the conclusion by statements that are logically equivalent, then logical equivalence follows syntactically.

In essence, proving logical implication (i.e., proving a theorem) requires a sequence of expressions of the following form:

$$r_0 \Rightarrow c_0$$
$$r_1 \Rightarrow c_1$$
$$r_2 \Rightarrow c_2$$
$$\vdots$$
$$r_m \Rightarrow c_m$$

where r_0 consists of the original set of premises, c_0 is the conclusion, r_{i+1} is obtained from r_i in an acceptable manner, as described above, c_{i+1} logically implies c_i, and the final expressions r_m and c_m are identical.

It should be noted that, if at some point in the derivation process a known theorem appears as the current step, then the derivation is complete, since logical implication is thus assured. Rigorously, at such a point the premises imply the conclusion and hence they can be replaced by it, thereby resulting in the same statement being on either side of the logical implication symbol.

For those interested in a rigorous mathematical account of the methodology, we suggest a text on logic. Our sole intention is to discuss automatic theorem proving by machine, since this represents a computational simulation of an act normally associated with intelligence. The following examples should provide sufficient insight into the technique.

Example 1.21

We demonstrate the *resolution theorem*

$$p \lor r, q \lor {\sim}r \Rightarrow p \lor q$$

Since, according to Theorem 10 of Figure 1.5,

$$p \lor r \Leftrightarrow {\sim}p \to r$$

we can replace the first premise by ${\sim}p \to r$. Similarly, since

$$q \lor {\sim}r \Leftrightarrow r \to q$$

we can replace the second premise by $r \to q$. Hence, it is now sufficient to prove

$${\sim}p \to r, r \to q \Rightarrow p \lor q$$

But, by Theorem 10 of Figure 1.5,

$$p \lor q \Leftrightarrow {\sim}p \to q$$

Thus, the next step in the derivation is

$$\sim p \rightarrow r, r \rightarrow q \Rightarrow \sim p \rightarrow q$$

But this is the chain rule (Theorem 6 of Figure 1.5), and the derivation is therefore complete.

The preceding derivation can be summarized by the following sequence, which begins with the theorem to be proved and ends with an already known result:

$$p \lor r, q \lor \sim r \Rightarrow p \lor q$$

$$\sim p \rightarrow r, q \lor \sim r \Rightarrow p \lor q$$

$$\sim p \rightarrow r, r \rightarrow q \Rightarrow p \lor q$$

$$\sim p \rightarrow r, r \rightarrow q \Rightarrow \sim p \rightarrow q$$

Proofs using the resolution theorem are popular in artificial intelligence since numerous AI languages, such as PROLOG, utilize logic systems that often allow only $\land$, $\lor$, and $\sim$ operations.   However, it should be noted that resolution is nothing more than the chain rule in disguise.

Example 1.22

Another important theorem is *contraposition* (Theorem 15 of Figure 1.5):

$$p \rightarrow q \Leftrightarrow \sim q \rightarrow \sim p$$

Contraposition can be proved syntactically by using, in order, Theorem 10 of Figure 1.5, commutativity, and Theorem 10 of Figure 1.5:

$$p \rightarrow q \Leftrightarrow \sim q \rightarrow \sim p$$

$$\sim p \lor q \Leftrightarrow \sim q \rightarrow \sim p$$

$$q \lor \sim p \Leftrightarrow \sim q \rightarrow \sim p$$

$$\sim q \rightarrow \sim p \Leftrightarrow \sim q \rightarrow \sim p$$

Note that a logical equivalence was employed at each step, and hence logical equivalence results.

Example 1.23

The following derivation demonstrates that the first line is a theorem:

$$p \land q, p \land r \Rightarrow q \land r$$

$$q \land p, p \land r \Rightarrow q \land r$$

$$(q \land p) \land (p \land r) \Rightarrow q \land r$$

$$q \land [p \land (p \land r)] \Rightarrow q \land r$$

$$q \land [(p \land p) \land r] \Rightarrow q \land r$$

$$q \land (p \land r) \Rightarrow q \land r$$

$$(q \land p) \land r \Rightarrow q \land r$$

$$q \land r \Rightarrow q \land r$$

We used, in order, commutativity, the fact that the comma means conjunction, associativity, associativity, idempotence, associativity, and the trivial theorem $q \wedge p \Rightarrow q$.

Contraposition, discussed in Example 1.22, is used in proofs in a *backward chaining* manner: instead of beginning with p in $p \Rightarrow q$ and *forward chaining* (trying to show q holds), we begin with $\sim q$ and try to show $\sim p$ holds.

In *proof by contradiction*, or the method of *reductio ad absurdum*, a combination of forward and backward chaining is often employed. In this method, to show $p \Rightarrow q$, we assume that p and $\sim q$ are both true. This assumption happens to be the negation of what we are trying to show, since

$$\sim(p \rightarrow q) \Leftrightarrow \sim(\sim p \vee q) \Leftrightarrow p \wedge \sim q$$

and thus $T(p \wedge \sim q) = 1$ means that $p \not\Rightarrow q$. In the method, either forward chaining is applied starting with p and eventually showing that q is true, which is in contradiction to the assumption of $\sim q$, or backward chaining is used starting with $\sim q$ and eventually showing that $\sim p$ holds true, which is in contradiction with premise p. In either case, due to the contradiction, something must be wrong. This inconsistency can only mean that the assumption is erroneous. Therefore, it is not true that $T(p) = 1$ and $T(\sim q) = 1$; thus, $T(p \rightarrow q) = 1$ and so $p \Rightarrow q$.

Computers are easily programmed to conduct proofs by resolution, contraposition, contradiction, or a combination of other syntactical methods. However, difficulties often exist when these techniques are applied to nontheorems, that is, to unknown situations where $p \Rightarrow q$ is thought to hold but the real situation is $p \not\Rightarrow q$. For instance, if proof by contradiction is employed, the machine procedure may never terminate. Fortunately, syntactical algorithms exist for theorem proving in the propositional calculus. One such algorithm is Wang's algorithm. This algorithm always yields a solution: it always terminates after a finite number of steps, proving either that $p \Rightarrow q$ or that $p \not\Rightarrow q$.

Wang's algorithm applies to expressions of the form

$$p_1, p_2, \ldots, p_n \Rightarrow c_1, c_2 \ldots, c_m$$

where the p_i constitute the premises of the theorem and the right side represents the conclusion

$$c_1 \vee c_2 \vee \cdots \vee c_m$$

In terms of truth values, the theorem holds if

$$T(p_1 \wedge p_2 \wedge \cdots \wedge p_n \rightarrow c_1 \vee c_2 \vee \cdots \vee c_m) = 1$$

A semantic proof can be accomplished by either forward or backward chaining. In the former case, the theorem will hold if, whenever all the premises are true, so too is at least one c_j. In the latter case, the theorem is shown to be true if, whenever all the c_j are false, so also is at least one premise. In the automatic theorem-proving method of Wang, no truth assignments are utilized; however, an understanding of the semantics is necessary for a full appreciation of the algorithm.

As with most algorithms, Wang's algorithm consists of three parts: the starting conditions, the recursive procedure, and, finally, the stopping conditions. The algorithm is only intended for use in the propositional calculus and for proving theorems of the form

$$p_1, p_2 \ldots, p_n \Rightarrow c_1, c_2 \ldots, c_m$$

WANG'S ALGORITHM

I   STARTING CONDITION: Convert all sentences p_i and c_j into equivalent sentences involving only negation, conjunction, and disjunction. This can always be accomplished by employing disjunctive normal form. (This step is applied once at the beginning.)

II   RECURSIVE PROCEDURES: The objective in using the recursive procedures is to remove connectives so that the stopping conditions can be applied.

   (a) NEGATION REMOVAL: If the principal connective of any sentence is a negation, then remove it and move the sentence to the other side of the arrow. (This step is to be performed as needed.) As an illustration,

$$p, q, {\sim}r \Rightarrow {\sim}s, t$$

   becomes

$$p, q, s \Rightarrow r, t$$

   after two applications of this step.

   (b) AND/OR REMOVAL: If the principal connective of a sentence on the left side of the arrow is an *and*, then remove the *and* and put a comma in its place; if the principal connective of a sentence on the right side is an *or*, then remove it and put a comma in its place. (This step is applied as needed.) As an illustration,

$$p \wedge q, r \Rightarrow s \vee t, u$$

   becomes

$$p, q, r \Rightarrow s, t, u$$

   after two applications of this step.

   (c) THEOREM SPLITTING: If the principal connective of a sentence on the left side of the arrow is an *or*, then remove this operator and each of its arguments separately so as to split the original theorem into two "new

theorems"; if the principal connective of a sentence on the right side is
an *and*, then also split the theorem into two.   In each case, the original
expression remains the same except for the two statements resulting from
the split statement.   For instance,

$$p \vee q, r \Rightarrow s$$

becomes the two new theorems

$$p, r \Rightarrow s$$

and

$$q, r \Rightarrow s$$

each to be proved separately, whereas

$$p \Rightarrow q \wedge s$$

becomes the two theorems

$$p \Rightarrow q$$

and

$$p \Rightarrow s$$

each to be proved separately.   (This step should be applied repeatedly
as needed.)   Note the exponential growth of the number of new theorems
to be proved: In general, if there exists a total of k *or*s and *and*s as principal
connectives on the left and right sides of the arrow, respectively, then 2^k
new theorems result as a result of this step.

III   STOPPING CONDITIONS: Apply the recursive steps II(a), (b), and (c),
in any order, and as often as necessary, removing $\sim$, $\vee$, and $\wedge$ operators
until:

(a) The same sentence occurs on both sides of the arrow, in which case the
corresponding theorem holds.   For instance, the theorem

$$p, q, r, s \Rightarrow t, u, q$$

holds since q appears on both sides of the arrow.   The sentence on both
sides need not be atomic.

(b) No connectives appear in the theorem and no atomic sentences appear
on both the left and right sides of the arrow.   In this case the corresponding
theorem does not hold and, therefore, the original theorem also does not
hold.   So, for instance, if p, q, and r are distinct atomic sentences, then

$$p \Rightarrow q, r$$

is not a theorem.

(c) Either III(a) or III(b) occurs for each theorem arising by application of II(a), (b), and (c), starting with the original theorem. The original theorem is true if and only if III(a) occurs for every new theorem that eventually results from applications of II(a), (b), and (c).

Example 1.24

Suppose we wish to prove by Wang's algorithm the chain rule

$$\sim p \rightarrow r, r \rightarrow q \Rightarrow \sim p \rightarrow q$$

As has been previously shown, the chain rule is equivalent to the resolution theorem (see Example 1.21), and therefore the latter provides the starting condition:

I   STARTING CONDITION: We will prove the theorem

$$p \vee r, \sim r \vee q \Rightarrow p \vee q$$

II   RECURSIVE PROCEDURE: Use II(b) to obtain the theorem

$$p \vee r, \sim r \vee q \Rightarrow p, q \tag{1}$$

Use II(c) to obtain the two theorems

$$p, \sim r \vee q \Rightarrow p, q$$

and $\tag{2}$

$$r, \sim r \vee q \Rightarrow p, q$$

We should then apply II(c) again, this time to the second expression in (2), to obtain a total of three new theorems:

$$p, \sim r \vee q \Rightarrow p, q$$
$$r, \sim r \Rightarrow p, q \tag{3}$$
$$r, q \Rightarrow p, q$$

We apply II(a) to the middle equation, thereby obtaining the system

$$p, \sim r \vee q \Rightarrow p, q$$
$$r \Rightarrow r, p, q \tag{4}$$
$$r, q \Rightarrow p, q$$

III   STOPPING CONDITIONS: To each of the final three theorems in (4), we can apply III(a), since in each of these theorems there is a sentence in common on both sides of the arrow:

$$\widehat{p}, \sim r \vee q \Rightarrow \widehat{p}, q$$
$$\widehat{r} \Rightarrow \widehat{r}, p, q$$
$$r, \widehat{q} \Rightarrow p, \widehat{q}$$

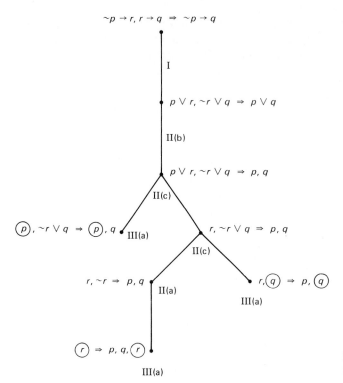

Figure 1.6 Tree diagram for Example 1.24

Hence, according to III(c), the original theorem is proved. The entire procedure is illustrated by the tree diagram in Figure 1.6.

In a diagram such as the one in Figure 1.6, when all bottom nodes satisfy III(a), the theorem holds; however, if any node satisfies III(b), then the original theorem does not hold.

Example 1.25

The tree diagram in Figure 1.7 illustrates the use of Wang's algorithm in showing that, for p and q distinct sentences,

$$q, p \to q \nRightarrow p$$

The tree need not proceed any further, since III(b) applied to the right bottom node stops the algorithm and shows that the theorem does not hold.

Although we will not go through the details, the proof that Wang's algorithm works (i.e., it terminates in a finite number of steps and produces the desired decision) follows in a straightforward manner from the definition of a theorem in terms of logical implication, together with the definitions of the negation, conjunction, and disjunction operations.

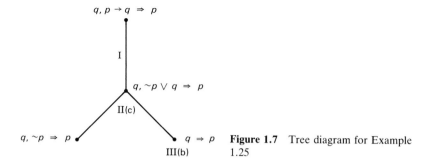

Figure 1.7 Tree diagram for Example 1.25

1.9 PREDICATE CALCULUS

The propositional calculus provides a model for a type of two-valued reasoning that involves the analysis of the connections between sentences, but it does not provide for any further breakdown of the meaning of the atomic sentences themselves.   It is concerned with a particular region of human reasoning: grammatical thinking relative to the fundamental connectives within its scope.   But there are other grammatical forms associated with reasoning.

Consider the following simple inference:

> All computers are working.
>
> The DG4 is a computer.   (1)
>
> Hence, the DG4 is working.

Although the argument certainly must be judged as "valid," the root of its validity does not lie in the structure of the propositional calculus.

Inferences in the propositional calculus result from the internal structure of sentences that are comprised of component sentences.   An atomic sentence is the smallest meaningful statement in the propositional calculus.   However, the inference in (1) requires an analysis involving a finer breakdown of structure than one stopping at atomic sentences.   Specifically, *subject–predicate* relationships need to be taken into consideration.   Moreover, the meaning of the word *all* must be specified.   The predicate calculus is an extension of the propositional calculus and is concerned with these (and other) matters that extend beyond propositional form. It often allows us to "get inside" a sentence and thereby make inferences regarding its internal substance.

The introduction of new definitions and notation is necessary to describe the predicate calculus.   To begin with, a *term* is a variable or a constant.   In English, a term is given by a noun or pronoun.   The variable x, where x stands for any object, is a term.   In (1), the constant DG4, which is an instance of x, stands for a type of computer.   Whenever a variable is set equal to or takes on a known constant value, the variable is said to be *instantiated*.

Let COMPUTER(y) indicate the fact that the object y is a computer, and let WORKING(x) indicate the property that x is working. Both COMPUTER( ) and WORKING( ) are called *predicates* and are said to be of *arity* 1, since each involves one argument. In general, predicates are relations possessing arity n, meaning there are n arguments. When all the variables, or arguments, in a predicate are instantiated, the resulting expression must be a sentence from the propositional calculus. Hence, at that point it must be true or false, When $n = 0$, we will agree that the predicate itself is a sentence. Binary, ternary, and other higher-order predicates will be introduced subsequently.

Grammatically, the instantiated predicate COMPUTER(DG4) represents the declarative statement "DG4 is a computer." and is either true or false, where, in practice, verity is based on the distribution of the facts. But what of the expression COMPUTER(x)? Factually, the expression is empty and is not a proposition. It is an example of an *open sentence*, which is defined as a declarative statement that (1) contains at least one variable, (2) is not a proposition, and (3) becomes a proposition when each of its variables is instantiated.

Condition 3 of an open sentence requires some further explanation: from where do the terms that might instantiate a predicate come? Although at first it might appear that we should not restrict the variable x, such freedom of the variable can lead to difficulties. Practically speaking, there is a field of observation that is contextually meaningful to any particular endeavor. The constant that is to replace x will be restricted by that field of observation. Terminologically, we call the set of objects that the variables in an open sentence might represent the *universe of discourse*. Although, technically, we should always articulate the universe of discourse, we often do not do so, instead allowing the context of the discussion at hand to implicitly define it.

Quantifiers are also included in the structure of the predicate calculus. We write $\forall x$[WORKING(x)] to mean that every x is working. The symbol $\forall$ is called a *universal quantifier* and stands for the grammatical expression *for all* or *for any*. Note the role of the universe of discourse: to say that every x is working without specifying the set of objects from which x might be chosen is meaningless.

Finally, we write $\exists x$[WORKING(x)] to mean that there is an x that is working. The symbol $\exists$ is called an *existential quantifier*, and it stands for *there exists*, or *there is an . . . such that*. In classical terms, the universal quantifier $\forall$ represents the word *all*, while the existential quantifier $\exists$ represents the word *some*.

Using the notions thus far introduced, the inference (1) can be symbolized by

$$\forall x[\text{COMPUTER}(x) \rightarrow \text{WORKING}(x)]$$

$$\text{COMPUTER(DG4)}$$

$$\text{Hence, WORKING(DG4)}$$

where the first line is read, "For any x such that x is a computer, x is working." Figure 1.8 illustrates the structure of (1) with the help of set theory.

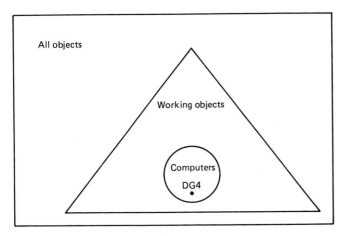

All objects

Working objects

Computers

DG4

Figure 1.8   Set-theoretic illustration of inference

In general, the expression

$$\forall x[A(x) \rightarrow S(x)]$$

indicates the fact that the set of all elements making $A(x)$ true is a subset of those elements that make $S(x)$ true. Consequently, determining its truthfulness is a matter of checking the particular instances of x for which

$$T(A(x)) = 1$$

and making certain that

$$T(S(x)) = 1$$

also holds in those cases.

Continuing in this direction, we can see that a predicate can be identified with a relation, the latter simply being a subset of some *universal set* of objects. Indeed, assuming that set $\mathcal{U}$ represents the universe of discourse for the predicate $P(\ \cdot\ )$, and $P(x)$ is to be grammatically interpreted as "x is a PRED.", then, for any x in $\mathcal{U}$, $P(x)$ is either true or false; that is, if x belongs to the class of objects for which the statement "x is a PRED." is true, then

$$T(P(x)) = 1$$

whereas if x belongs to the class of objects for which the statement "x is a PRED." is false, then

$$T(P(x)) = 0$$

Correspondingly, if we let P_0 denote the former class, then P_0 is a relation and

$$T(P(x)) = 1$$

if and only if $x \in P_0$.

Now if $Q(\ \ )$ is another predicate, with Q_0 denoting the subset of elements

x of $\mathcal{U}$ for which $Q(x)$ is true, then

$$T(\forall\, x[P(x) \to Q(x)]) = 1$$

if and only if P_0 is a subset of Q_0 $(P_0 \subset Q_0)$.

Example 1.26

Consider the universal set Y consisting of four entities:

1. A working car, denoted by JAG
2. A broken (nonworking) writing element, denoted by PEN
3. The computer DG4
4. Another computer, denoted by Z7

Thus, we have

$$Y = \{\text{JAG, PEN, DG4, Z7}\}$$

We will illustrate the manner in which the predicates COMPUTER( ) and WORK-ING( ) correspond to relations denoted COMPUTER and WORKING, respectively. To do this, we will assume that "all computers are working" is true; that is,

$$T(\forall\, x[\text{COMPUTER}(x) \to \text{WORKING}(x)]) = 1$$

Then

$$\text{COMPUTER} = \{\text{DG4, Z7}\}$$
$$\text{WORKING} = \{\text{JAG, DG4, Z7}\}.$$
$$T(\text{WORKING(JAG)}) = 1$$
$$T(\text{WORKING(DG4)}) = 1$$

and

$$T(\text{WORKING(PEN)}) = 0$$

Therefore,

$$T(\forall\, x[\text{WORKING}(x)]) = 0$$

whereas

$$T(\exists\, x[\text{WORKING}(x)]) = 1$$

Predicates need not be unary: more than a single quantifier can be employed.

Example 1.27

Consider the set

$$X = \{\text{Bill, John, Mary, Al}\}$$

and the binary predicate FATHER(x, y) defined by "y is the father of x."   Assume that

$$T(\text{FATHER(Bill, John)}) = 1$$

$$T(\text{FATHER(Mary, John)}) = 1$$

$$T(\text{FATHER(John, Al)}) = 1$$

Grammatically, John is the father of Bill, John is the father of Mary, and Al is the father of John.   Moreover, assume that there are no other father-type relationships in X.   Then we can define the relation FATHER by

$$\text{FATHER} = \{(\text{Bill, John}), (\text{Mary, John}), (\text{John, Al})\} \subset X \times X.$$

The cardinality of $X \times X$ is 16 and the truth value of each of the other 13 ordered pairs in $X \times X$ is zero.   Also,

$$T(\exists \, x[\text{FATHER}(x, \text{John})]) = 1$$

since it is true that there exists someone (Bill or Mary) in the set X who has John as a father.   However,

$$T(\forall \, x[\text{FATHER}(x, \text{John})]) = 0$$

since not everyone has John as a father; for instance,

$$T(\text{FATHER(John, John)}) = 0$$

Notice that

$$T(\exists \, x[\exists \, y[\text{FATHER}(x, y)]]) = 1$$

since there exists a father–son pair in $X \times X$.   However,

$$T(\exists \, x[\forall \, y[\text{FATHER}(x, y)]]) = 0$$

since there does not exist someone in X for whom everyone in X is his or her father.   Also,

$$T(\forall \, x[\exists \, y[\text{FATHER}(x, y)]]) = 0$$

since it is not true that everyone in X has a father in X.   Next, note that

$$T(\forall \, x[\forall \, y[\text{FATHER}(x, y)]]) = 0$$

since everyone is not everyone's father.   Finally, it should be pointed out that, in this case,

$$T((\forall \, x[\forall \, y[\text{FATHER}(x, y)]]) \rightarrow (\forall \, x[\exists \, y[\text{FATHER}(x, y)]])) = 1$$

since the antecedent has truth value 0, and therefore, as in the propositional calculus, the consequent is always logically implied.

Returning to the single-variable case, if we employ the negation operation in conjunction with the two quantifiers $\forall$ and $\exists$, then we obtain eight possible sen-

TABLE 1.1 Predicate calculus and grammatical expressions

Predicate Calculus Expression	Grammatical Expression
$\forall\, x[P(x)]$	P true for all x
$\exists\, x[P(x)]$	P true for some x
$\forall\, x[\sim P(x)]$	P false for all x
$\exists\, x[\sim P(x)]$	P false for some x
$\sim(\forall\, x[P(x)])$	P false for some x
$\sim(\exists\, x[P(x)])$	P false for all x
$\sim(\forall\, x[\sim P(x)])$	P true for some x
$\sim(\exists\, x[\sim P(x)])$	P true for all x

tences within the predicate calculus, each having an associated grammatical meaning. Table 1.1 lists the eight sentences, together with their associated meanings in the event each is true. The classical Aristotelian terms *all* and *some* are employed. Note the redundancy in that only four of the expressions are needed since each possesses an equivalent expression.

It is often convenient to represent facts in knowledge-based systems, or in AI, using flat files. This representation is commonly employed for relational databases. A *flat file* is a visual matrix-type device for displaying the n-tuples in an n-ary relation; in other words, it is a subset of the product set

$$E_1 \times E_2 \times \cdots \times E_n$$

where each E_i is a set from which the ith object is to be taken. Each row of the flat file contains an n-tuple, and there are as many rows as there are elements in the relation. For instance, the relation WORKING in Example 1.26 can be expressed as

DG4
Z7
JAG

The order of the elements in the file is irrelevant; thus, it could also be represented in five other ways, for instance, as

Z7
DG4
JAG

The relation FATHER of Example 1.27 is given by the flat file

Mary	John
John	Al
Bill	John

Of consequence is that information such as *fatherhood* can be stored within a computer in the form of flat files.   These need not be stored directly: they can be given by other flat files in conjunction with rules involving connectives from the propositional calculus and predicates and quantifiers from the predicate calculus.

Example 1.28

We will provide a set of rules that will render the flat file LIKES:

John	JAG
John	DG4
John	Z7
Al	JAG
Al	DG4
Al	Z7

The relation LIKES is a subset of the product of the universal sets X and Y from Examples 1.27 and 1.26, respectively.

Now assume that the predicate LIKES(x, y) means that "x likes y" and that the relation is satisfied whenever x is a father and y is working; that is,

$$T(\text{LIKES}(x, y)) = 1$$

if and only if

$$T(\text{WORKING}(y)) = 1$$

and

$$T(\exists z[\text{FATHER}(z, x)]) = 1$$

Hence, we will put (x, y) into the flat file LIKES for those values x that are instantiated to John or Al, these being the only fathers, and for those values y that are instantiated to working objects: JAG, DG4, or Z7.   Thus, the total of six pairs (x, y) of distinct instantiated values, called *records*, constitutes the relation LIKES.   The records can be obtained by the computer from either a directly stored file named LIKES or from the files WORKING and FATHER in conjunction with the defining rule.

Example 1.29

An example of a ternary predicate is PLAYS(x, y, z), which we take to mean "x plays y with z."   The corresponding relation PLAYS might be

John	ball	Mary
Bill	ball	Mary
Henry	golf	Susan

In this case,

$$T(\text{PLAYS}(\text{John, ball, Mary})) = 1$$

whereas

$$T(\text{PLAYS}(\text{Henry, ball, Larry})) = 0$$

since the record (Henry, ball, Larry) does not appear in the flat file PLAYS. Thus,

$$T(\sim\text{PLAYS}(\text{Henry, ball, Larry})) = 1$$

If PLAYS is a relation on

$$X = \{\text{John, Bill, Henry}\}$$

$$Y = \{\text{ball, golf}\}$$

and

$$Z = \{\text{Mary, Larry, Susan}\}$$

(i.e., PLAYS $\subset X \times Y \times Z$) then the following hold, where we have suppressed repeated use of the brackets [and] in the quantifications in order not to make the notation overly cumbersome:

$$T(\forall\ x\ \exists\ y\ \exists\ z[\text{PLAYS}(x, y, z)]) = 1$$

since every person in X has a game to play with someone in Z,

$$T(\forall\ x\ \forall\ y\ \exists\ z[\text{PLAYS}(x, y, z)]) = 0$$

since every person in X does not play every game with some person in Z,

$$T(\exists\ x\ \forall\ y\ \exists\ z[\text{PLAYS}(x, y, z)]) = 0$$

since there is no person in X who plays every game with someone from Z,

$$T(\forall\ y\ \exists\ x\ \exists\ z[\text{PLAYS}(x, y, z)]) = 1$$

since all games are played by someone in X with someone in Z,

$$T(\forall\ z\ \exists\ x\ \exists\ y[\text{PLAYS}(x, y, z)]) = 0$$

since not all persons from Z play some game with someone from X,

$$T(\exists\ x\ \exists\ y\ \exists\ z[\sim\text{PLAYS}(x, y, z)]) = 1$$

since there is someone in X and someone in Z who are not together playing a game in Y, and

$$T(\exists\ x\ \exists\ y\ \sim\forall\ z[\text{PLAYS}(x, y, z)]) = 1$$

since there is someone in X and there is a game in Y such that not everyone in Z plays the game with the given person.

Precisely how a computer determines whether or not a quantified statement is true or false in the predicate calculus will be illustrated with the help of Example 1.30. In this example, as well as in most practical situations, the universe of discourse is assumed to be finite. As a consequence, universal quantification of a given sentence corresponds to the iterated conjunction of the sentences formed by instantiating the predicate within the sentence with all values from the universe of discourse.   For instance, if $P(\ \ )$ is the predicate and the universe of discourse consists of the objects $x_1, x_2, \ldots, x_n$, then

$$T(\forall\ x[P(x)]) = 1$$

if and only if

$$T(P(x_1) \wedge P(x_2) \wedge \cdots \wedge P(x_n)) = 1$$

Similarly, existential quantification makes use of the disjunction operation:

$$T(\exists\ x[P(x)]) = 1$$

if and only if

$$T(P(x_1) \vee P(x_2) \vee \cdots \vee P(x_n)) = 1$$

Example 1.30

> Consider Figure 1.9, where a picture is given involving several large objects, a house, a tree, and a car.   Six people can be observed in this image: Joe and Russell in the house by the window, Barbara in the house by the door, Steve in the car, Mike on the roof of the house, and Johnny behind the tree.   The entire scene may be better described by introducing the binary predicates LEFT(,) and BELOW(,).   If

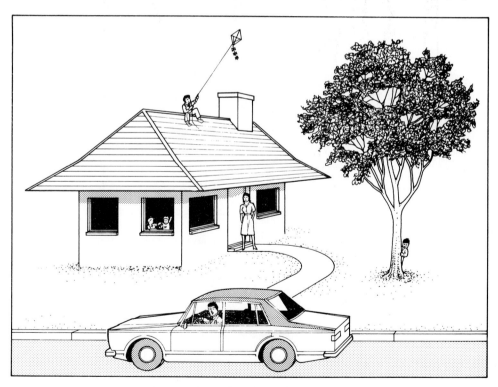

Figure 1.9   Scene for Example 1.30

object x is to the left of object y, then

$$T(\text{LEFT}(x, y)) = 1$$

On the other hand, if object w is below object u, then

$$T(\text{BELOW}(w, u)) = 1$$

Thus we have

$$T(\text{LEFT}(\text{house, car})) = 1$$
$$T(\text{LEFT}(\text{house, tree})) = 1$$
$$T(\text{LEFT}(\text{car, tree})) = 1$$
$$T(\text{BELOW}(\text{car, tree})) = 1$$
$$T(\text{BELOW}(\text{car, house})) = 1$$
$$T(\text{BELOW}(\text{tree, house})) = 1$$

The preceding information may be viewed in terms of relations or in terms of flat files stored within the memory of a computer:

LEFT

house	car
car	tree
house	tree

BELOW

car	tree
car	house
tree	house

In an analogous manner, we can also define the binary predicates ON(,), IN(,), and BEHIND(,), and corresponding relations can be obtained:

IN

Barbara	house
Steve	car
Russell	house
Joe	house

ON

BEHIND

We now demonstrate how the computer might determine whether or not the quantified sentence, " All people are in the house."

$$\forall\, x[\text{IN}(x, \text{house})]$$

is true or false. By fixing the variable $y = $ house, IN(x, house) is a unary predicate obtained from IN(x, y) and is described by the flat file

IN (x, house)

Russell
Joe
Barbara

Instantiation of the variable x by all persons in the scene yields the proposition p defined by

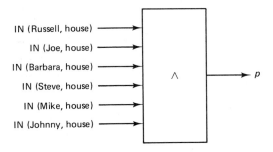

The truth value of p is 0, since all six conjuncts do not have truth value 1. For instance,

$$T(\text{IN}(\text{Mike, house})) = 0$$

since the record (Mike, house) does not appear in the flat file (relation) IN. Hence,

$$T(\forall x[\text{IN}(x, \text{house})]) = 0$$

In a similar manner, the truth value of more complex sentences involving quantifiers can be "mechanically" calculated. For instance,

$$T(\exists x \; \exists y \; \exists z \; \exists w[\text{IN}(x, y) \wedge \text{BELOW}(y, z) \wedge \text{BEHIND}(w, z)]) = 1$$

which can be automatically determined by considering the disjunction of the appropriate sentences with instantiated variables and recognizing that at least one of the sentences possesses truth value 1. Indeed,

$$T(\text{IN}(\text{Steve, car}) \wedge \text{BELOW}(\text{car, tree}) \wedge \text{BEHIND}(\text{John, tree})) = 1$$

The preceding examples illustrate how a computer can analyze subject–predicate propositions by checking the appropriate instances. If this were a course in logic, we would study formal rules of inference for proving assertions involving expressions within the predicate calculus; however, we will content ourselves with the foregoing informal presentation. What is important for the practical use of inferential and subject–predicate propositions is their structure, the type of reasoning or intelligence they model, and the manner in which their verity can be ascertained automatically in terms of the facts.

1.10 THE PREDICATE CALCULUS FOR ROBOT CONTROL: BLOCK WORLD

As an illustration of the manner in which a computer can "understand" perceptual information through manipulations involving the predicate calculus, we will consider a block world consisting of a table and three square blocks in which certain prespecified rearrangements of the blocks can be performed. The blocks are colored green (*g*), blue (*b*), and red (*r*), and a robot arm can reconfigure the blocks, subject to the constraint that all three lie on the table with common orientation, possibly on top of one another (see Figure 1.10, which illustrates several possible configurations).

We will assume that the robot has been preprogrammed as to the possible configurations of the blocks and that its knowledge of the block locations results from two imaging sensors, one on top and one on the left side of the block world. Each sensor yields the color of an observed block, along with an integer indicating the position of the block relative to the coordinate system illustrated in Figure 1.11.

Since the blocks can be piled at most three high on the table, we arbitrarily let the leftmost bottom position a block can occupy be the origin. All other possible positions are specified by utilizing the relative Cartesian coordinate system. The predicate LOC(*z*, *i*, *j*) will be interpreted to mean that the block colored *z* is at location (*i*, *j*) in the coordinate system. The integer *i* indicates the *x* location and is determined by the top sensor. The predicate TOP(*z*, *i*) will be employed to represent the output of the top sensor, *i* indicating the *x*-axis location, *i* = 0, 1, 2, of the block *x*. Analogously, the side sensor yields the output consisting of the

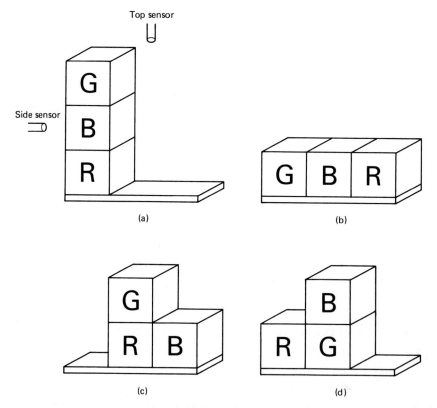

Figure 1.10   Block world configurations

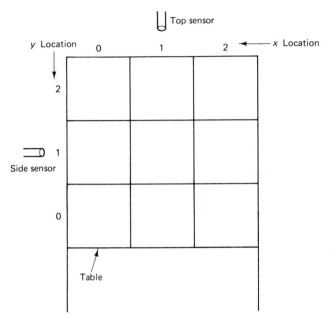

Figure 1.11   Block world coordinate system

color z of the block and the y coordinate j in the predicate $LOC(z, i, j)$.   This information is provided by the predicate $SIDE(z, j)$.

Example 1.31

Consider the block configuration portrayed in Figure 1.10(a).   Here,

$$T(LOC(g, 0, 2)) = 1$$
$$T(LOC(b, 0, 1)) = 1$$
$$T(LOC(r, 0, 0)) = 1$$

Moreover,

$$T(SIDE(g, 2)) = 1$$
$$T(SIDE(b, 1)) = 1$$
$$T(SIDE(r, 0)) = 1$$

and

$$T(TOP(g, 0)) = 1$$

(No other blocks are recorded by the top sensor.)   These truth statements are readily given as relations:

$$LOC = \{(g, 0, 2), (b, 0, 1), (r, 0, 0)\}$$
$$SIDE = \{(g, 2), (b, 1), (r, 0)\}$$
$$TOP = \{(g, 0)\}$$

Bound matrices and bound vectors provide a convenient representation for the specification of objects in a discrete coordinate system. A *bound matrix* is an m by n array-type data structure whose entries can be elements of some prespecified set X or stars (*), a star being used to indicate the absence of an element of X in a particular position. Outside the right lower side of the array, there is an integer pair (p, q) indicating the location of the first row, first column entry a_{11} in the specified coordinate system [see Figure 1.12(a)]. As a general structure for knowledge representation, bound matrices will be fully discussed in Section 4.8. Bound matrix representations for the front views of the block configurations given in Figure 1.10 are presented in Figure 1.13.

Column and row bound vectors illustrating the outputs of the side and top sensors, respectively, are also given in Figure 1.13. Note that a *column bound vector* is an m by 1 array-type structure that, like a bound matrix, has entries that are either stars or elements from a set X. On the lower-right side, outside the array, is an integer q specifying the absolute location on the y axis of the first entry

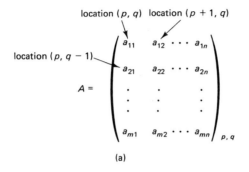

(a)

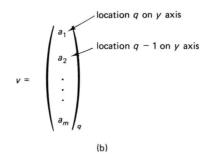

(b)

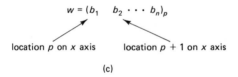

(c)

Figure 1.12 Bound matrices and bound vectors

$$P_y(A) = w = (g \quad * \quad *)_0 \qquad\qquad (g \quad b \quad r)_0$$

$$P_x(A) = v = \begin{pmatrix} g \\ b \\ r \end{pmatrix}_2 \qquad \begin{pmatrix} g & * & * \\ b & * & * \\ r & * & * \end{pmatrix}_{0,2} = A \qquad\qquad \begin{pmatrix} * \\ * \\ g \end{pmatrix}_2 \begin{pmatrix} * & * & * \\ * & * & * \\ g & b & r \end{pmatrix}_{0,2}$$

(a) (b)

$$(* \quad g \quad b)_0 \qquad\qquad (r \quad b \quad *)_0$$

$$\begin{pmatrix} * \\ g \\ r \end{pmatrix}_2 \begin{pmatrix} * & * & * \\ * & g & * \\ * & r & b \end{pmatrix}_{0,2} \qquad\qquad \begin{pmatrix} * \\ b \\ r \end{pmatrix}_2 \begin{pmatrix} * & * & * \\ * & b & * \\ r & g & * \end{pmatrix}_{0,2}$$

(c) (d)

Figure 1.13   Bound matrices for configurations of Figure 1.10

a_1 of the array.   Similarly, a *row bound vector* is a 1 by n array-type structure with entries coming from $X \cup \{*\}$.   On the lower-right side of the array is an integer p that indicates the position on the x axis of the first element b_1 of the array. Figures 1.12(b) and (c) illustrate column and row bound vectors, respectively. Figures 1.13(a) through (d) give bound matrix representations, along with bound vector representations corresponding to the top and side sensor outputs, for the block configurations given in Figures 1.10(a) through (d).   In this application, $X = \{g, b, r\}$.

If the bound matrix representation for a specific configuration is given, the corresponding sensor bound vectors can be found by projection-type operations. For instance, for the given bound matrix, call it A, of Figure 1.13(a), the x *projection* P_x yields the bound column vector v, also illustrated in Figure 1.13(a).   Intuitively, P_x gives the view of the left-side sensor.   Rigorously, and in general, P_x is given by

$$P_x(A) = v = \begin{pmatrix} a_1 \\ a_2 \\ \cdot \\ \cdot \\ \cdot \\ a_m \end{pmatrix}_q$$

where

$$a_i = \begin{cases} a_{iJ}, & J \text{ being the smallest } j \text{ such that } a_{ij} \in X \\ *, & \text{otherwise} \end{cases}$$

Similarly, the y projection P_y maps the bound matrix A into the bound row vector w illustrated in Figure 1.13(a). More generally,

$$P_y(A) = w = (b_1 \, b_2 \, \ldots \, b_n)_p$$

where

$$b_j = \begin{cases} a_{Ij}, & I \text{ being the smallest } i \text{ such that } a_{ij} \in X \\ *, & \text{otherwise} \end{cases}$$

Example 1.32

Consider the block configuration given by

$$A = \begin{pmatrix} * & * & * \\ b & * & * \\ g & * & r \end{pmatrix}_{0,\,2} = \begin{pmatrix} a_{11} & a_{12} & a_{13} \\ a_{21} & a_{22} & a_{23} \\ a_{31} & a_{32} & a_{33} \end{pmatrix}_{0,\,2}$$

There are only three array values that are not stars: $a_{21} = b$, $a_{31} = g$, and $a_{33} = r$. Consequently, the side sensor has the associated bound column vector

$$v = P_x(A) = \begin{pmatrix} * \\ b \\ g \end{pmatrix}_2$$

The top sensor has the associated bound row vector

$$w = P_y(A) = (b * r)_0$$

A more significant problem than finding projection bound vectors from a given bound matrix is the inverse problem. Given projection vectors v and w, can we find a unique bound matrix A such that $P_x(A) = v$ and $P_y(A) = w$? In general, this *back projection* problem is not solvable. However, in certain circumstances, such as the block world under consideration, a unique back projection can be found. Specifically, given the sensor input, the robot arm is precisely informed as to the identity of each block and its location. This is due only in part to the direct projection-type information provided by the sensors, since for certain block configurations, a particular block may be hidden from both sensors. This is the situation depicted in Figure 1.10(d). The first-order predicate calculus provides a convenient tool for formulating signals to control the robot arm in the event

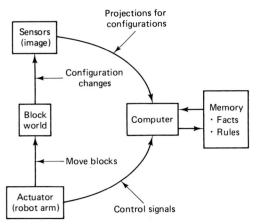

Figure 1.14   Sensor-computer-actuator interface

there is a concealed block.   Logic is employed in composing sensor outputs to keep track of hidden blocks.

Figure 1.14 illustrates the sensor–computer–actuator interface.   The robot arm reconfigures the blocks, the sensors "see" part of the reconfiguration, and the computer, using a priori information together with logic rules, provides a total picture of the new block configuration.   If it is some desired configuration, nothing more need to be done; however, if the configuration is not what is desired, control signals are sent out to instruct the robot arm to move the blocks again.   This is a standard technique for control systems.

We will now provide a more in-depth analysis of how the computer composes the projections to form the total picture of a block configuration.   Three cases will be considered.   The first, and simplest, is when all the blocks are piled vertically on top of each other.   For this configuration, the top sensor provides the common x location of the blocks, while the side sensor provides the color of each block, along with its y location.   Only one element appears on top; in fact, card(TOP) = 1 and card(SIDE) = 3 characterize this situation, where card denotes the cardinality of the relation that is its argument.   This situation is also characterized by

$$T(\exists\, z[\text{SIDE}(z, 2)]) = 1$$

Note that, in this situation, $T(\text{LOC}(z, i, 2)) = 1$, where the horizontal location i of the top block of color z is determined by $T(\text{TOP}(z, i)) = 1$.   Moreover, the other two blocks have the same horizontal location i and their heights are specified by the side sensor.   If $T(\text{SIDE}(u, 1)) = 1$, then $T(\text{LOC}(u, i, 1)) = 1$; also, if $T(\text{SIDE}(w, 0)) = 1$, then $T(\text{LOC}(w, i, 0)) = 1$.

Example 1.33

Consider the block configuration given in Figure 1.10(a).   Recall that the sensor outputs are given by

$$\text{SIDE} = \{(g, 2), (b, 1), (r, 0)\}$$

and

$$\mathrm{TOP} = \{(g, 0)\}$$

Since $T(\mathrm{SIDE}(g, 2)) = 1$, it follows that the blocks are piled three high in the first column with green on top, the latter condition being specified by

$$T(\mathrm{LOC}(g, 0, 2)) = 1$$

Furthermore, using the side sensor, we have

$$T(\mathrm{LOC}(b, 0, 1)) = 1$$

and

$$T(\mathrm{LOC}(r, 0, 0)) = 1$$

In terms of relations,

$$\mathrm{LOC} = \{(g, 0, 2), (r, 0, 0), (b, 0, 1)\}$$

The second case, also quite simple, is when there is no block on top of another (i.e., all blocks are horizontally placed on the table). Here, the top sensor specifies the block color and the x location while the side sensor provides the common y location. In terms of predicate statements, whenever

$$T(\exists z[\mathrm{SIDE}(z, 1)]) = 0$$

we must have

$$T(\forall z \; \exists i[\mathrm{LOC}(z, i, 0)]) = 1$$

Moreover, the appropriate x position i for the block of color z is obtained from the top sensor: if

$$T(\mathrm{TOP}(z, i)) = 1$$

then

$$T(\mathrm{LOC}(z, i, 0)) = 1$$

In the final case, exactly two of the three blocks are situated vertically. Card(TOP) = 2 and card(SIDE) = 2, these cardinalities characterizing the situation. Whenever exactly one block is on top of another block, one of two situations arises: either a block is hidden from both sensors or each block is seen by at least one sensor. The former situation is characterized by the existence of exactly two blocks being observed simultaneously by both sensors. The identification of these two blocks, along with position information, is found from the sensor outputs. The third block, in this case the block not sensed, is also known in that its location is beneath the higher of the two blocks registered by the side sensor. In terms of the predicate calculus,

$$T(\exists z \; \exists i[\mathrm{TOP}(z, i) \wedge \mathrm{SIDE}(z, 0)]) = 1$$

and the location of the single block of color z that fulfills the condition is immediately found from the two sensors:

$$T(\text{LOC}(z, i, 0)) = 1$$

The block of color u at height 1 is also sensed by both sensors, its location being found directly:

$$T(\text{LOC}(u, j, 1)) = 1$$

Finally, since $z \neq u$ and both are elements of $X = \{r, g, b\}$, the hidden block is the element w of $X - \{z, u\}$, and its location must be specified by

$$T(\text{LOC}(w, j, 0)) = 1$$

The last situation arises whenever both sensors detect two blocks and only one of these blocks is in common. Here, the block in common, which is on top of another block, has a location directly obtained from the sensors. The other block seen by the side sensor has a horizontal location that is exactly the same as the block above it. Finally, the third block, which must lie on the table, has a horizontal location provided by the top sensor. Using predicates, the top block of color z on level 1 has a top view, and thus

$$T(\text{TOP}(z, i)) = 1$$

Hence,

$$T(\text{LOC}(z, i, 1)) = 1$$

The block underneath this block has color u given by the side sensor. Thus,

$$T(\text{SIDE}(u, 0)) = 1$$

and hence

$$T(\text{LOC}(u, i, 0)) = 1$$

The final block has color $w \in X - \{z, u\}$ given by the top sensor, and

$$T(\text{TOP}(w, j)) = 1$$

implying that

$$T(\text{LOC}(w, j, 0)) = 1$$

Example 1.34

Suppose the output of the two sensors is given by the relations

$$\text{TOP} = \{(b, 0), (r, 2)\}$$

and

$$\text{SIDE} = \{(b, 0), (r, 1)\}$$

Since card(TOP) $= 2$, case 3 is in effect. Moreover, since the two blocks sensed by each sensor are the same, the third is hidden. It follows that

$$T(\text{LOC}(b, 0, 0)) = 1$$

$$T(\text{LOC}(r, 2, 1)) = 1$$

$$T(\text{LOC}(g, 2, 0)) = 1$$

The last truth value follows since

$$\{g\} = X - \{r, b\}$$

which means that the color of the hidden block is green. Moreover, its location is underneath the block at height 1, as determined by the side sensor. Referring to the original specification of SIDE, we see that this block is red (r). Finally, the top sensor (indirectly) gives the location of the hidden block because this block has the same location, 2, as the red block.

The purpose of this section has been to demonstrate the manner in which subject–predicate statements within the predicate calculus can be employed in the spatial description of a scene: the logic of the spatial relationships, if sufficiently simple, can be mirrored in the calculus. Should the situation be more complex, the inferential apparatus will require more information from the sensors. More specifically, the intelligence that is contained within the predicate calculus machinery can only make deductions in the presence of sufficient data: the more complicated the world, the more sensors that are required. Notice that the sufficiency of the artificial reasoning, relative to the demands on it, is a function of its ability to obtain information from the world, as well as its inferential engine.

Finally, note that the entire methodology of the present section can be implemented with the use of flat files. Consequently, properly defined searching techniques can accomplish the reasoning of the block-world robot described herein.

EXERCISES FOR CHAPTER 1

1.1. Construct truth tables for the following:
   (a) $(p \rightarrow q) \rightarrow (\sim p \wedge q)$
   (b) $[(p \rightarrow \sim q) \rightarrow (p \vee q)] \leftrightarrow (\sim p \rightarrow q)$
   (c) $(p \wedge q \wedge \sim r) \vee (\sim p \wedge q \wedge r) \vee (\sim p \wedge \sim q \wedge \sim r)$

1.2. Show that

$$\sim(p \vee q) \vee [(\sim p) \wedge q] \vee p$$

is a tautology.

1.3. Prove the tautologies of Figure 1.2 by using truth tables.

1.4. In Example 1.8, one of De Morgan's laws was demonstrated by the mapping methodology of Section 1.3. Use the same approach to verify the tautologies of Figure 1.2.

1.5. Using disjunctive normal form, synthesize a sentence having the following truth table:

p	q	r	$f(p, q, r)$
1	1	1	0
1	1	0	0
1	0	1	1
1	0	0	0
0	1	1	1
0	1	0	0
0	0	1	0
0	0	0	1

1.6. Give both block diagram and special symbol representations of the sentence in Exercise 1.2.

1.7. Employ fusible logic to express the sentence

$$[(p \wedge \sim q) \vee (\sim p \wedge \sim r)] \vee (p \wedge q \wedge r) \vee [(q \vee r) \wedge (p \wedge \sim r)]$$

1.8. By constructing appropriate truth tables, prove the theorems given in Figure 1.5 by applying both forward-chaining and backward-chaining reasoning.

1.9. Demonstrate theorems 7 through 11 of Figure 1.5 syntactically.

1.10. Apply Wang's algorithm to check the validity of the following "theorems":
(a) $(p \wedge q) \vee (p \wedge \sim q), \sim(q \vee p) \Rightarrow \sim p \vee \sim q$
(b) $\sim(p \rightarrow q) \wedge q \Rightarrow p, \sim(p \wedge q)$

1.11. Apply Wang's algorithm to verify theorems 1 through 8 of Figure 1.5.

1.12. Consider the set of people

$$X = \{\text{John, Brian, Fred, Jennifer, Sarah}\}$$

and the binary predicate FRIEND defined on $X \times X$ in accordance with FRIEND(x, y) meaning that x is a friend of y. Suppose that

$$T(\text{FRIEND}(\text{John}, \text{Fred})) = 1$$

$$T(\text{FRIEND}(\text{Brian}, \text{Jennifer})) = 1$$

$$T(\text{FRIEND}(\text{Brian}, \text{Fred})) = 1$$

and that the predicate is both reflexive and symmetric, meaning that

$$T(\text{FRIEND}(x, x)) = 1$$

and

$$T(\text{FRIEND}(x, y)) = 1 \Rightarrow T(\text{FRIEND}(y, x)) = 1$$

respectively. Determine the following truth values:
(a) $T(\exists x[\text{FRIEND}(x, \text{John})])$
(b) $T(\exists x[\text{FRIEND}(\text{Sarah}, x)])$
(c) $T(\forall x[\text{FRIEND}(x, \text{Fred})])$

(d) $T(\forall x \exists y[\text{FRIEND}(x, y)])$
(e) $T(\exists x \forall y[\text{FRIEND}(x, y)])$
(f) $T(\exists x \exists y[\text{FRIEND}(x, y)])$
(g) $T(\exists x \forall y[\sim\text{FRIEND}(x, y)])$
(h) $T(\forall x \exists y[\sim\text{FRIEND}(x, y)])$

1.13. Consider the relations LEFT and ABOVE defined by the flat files

a	b
a	c
a	d
c	d
b	d

and

a	b
d	b
c	a
c	d
c	b

respectively. For instance, a is both to the left and above b. Evaluate the following:
(a) $T(\text{LEFT}(c, b))$
(b) $T(\exists x[\text{ABOVE}(x, c)])$
(c) $T(\forall x[\text{LEFT}(x, d)])$
(d) $T(\forall x \exists y[\text{LEFT}(y, x)])$

Next, define a new relation NEW by $T(\text{NEW}(x, y)) = 1$ if and only if

$$T(\text{LEFT}(x, y) \vee \text{LEFT}(y, x)) = 0$$

Explain in words the meaning of NEW and give its flat file. Evaluate
(e) $T(\exists x[\text{NEW}(x, a)])$
(f) $T(\exists x \exists y[\text{NEW}(x, y)])$
(g) $T(\forall x \exists y[\text{NEW}(x, y)])$

1.14. Consider a block world consisting of four blocks, green (g), blue (b), red (r), and yellow (y), where once again the possible positions are confined to the locations of Figure 1.11. Because there are four blocks and only nine possible locations, no matter what the configuration,

$$T(\exists x[\text{SIDE}(x, 1)]) = 1$$

As was done in Section 1.10 for the case of three blocks, give an analysis in terms of LOC, SIDE, and TOP of the possible cases.

1.15. Repeat Exercise 1.14, except employ a fifth block, colored purple (p). Note that there are configurations where the positioning of all the blocks cannot be determined.

1.16. Repeat the block world analysis of Exercise 1.15, except this time employ three sensors, one on top and one on either side. Thus, we have the predicates LOC, LEFT, RIGHT, and TOP. Note that the problem of indeterminacy that arose in Exercise 1.15 vanishes with the addition of a sensor.

2

FUNDAMENTAL
MATHEMATICAL
STRUCTURES

2.1 SET REPRESENTATION USING MEMBERSHIP FUNCTIONS

To facilitate the subsequent introduction of fuzzy set theory, we will provide a brief discussion of regular set theory from the perspective of membership functions. For this purpose, we will assume the existence of a universal set X, of which all sets are subsets: for any set A under discussion, it is implicitly assumed that $A \subset X$; $a \in A$ implies that $a \in X$. Given the postulation of a universal set, any set A can be represented by the utilization of a *membership function* (also called a *truth function*, *valuation function*, or *characteristic function*). The membership function, $u_A(x)$, of the set A is defined on the universal set X by

$$u_A(x) = \begin{cases} 1, & \text{if } x \in A \\ 0, & \text{if } x \notin A \end{cases}$$

Consequently, any subset A of X can be represented in the form

$$A = \{x \mid u_A(x)\}$$

Specifically, each x in X is paired with its valuation (membership function value). If A is finite, it can be represented as a list of all elements of X, each followed by a slash and either a 1 or a 0, the former denoting the element belongs to A and the latter denoting it does not.

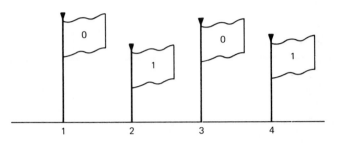

Figure 2.1 Membership function set representation

Example 2.1

Consider the universal set $X = \{1, 2, 3, 4\}$. If $A = \{2, 4\}$, then, using the membership function,

$$A = \{1/0,\ 2/1,\ 3/0,\ 4/1\}$$

The new representation is pictorially illustrated in Figure 2.1, where every subset of X consists of four points with a "flag" attached. A 0 on the flag indicates that the point does not lie in the set, whereas a 1 on the flag indicates that it does.

Of significance is that the usual set-theoretic operations possess membership-function characterizations. As a first illustration, consider the union of two sets, $A \cup B$, which is comprised of all those elements belonging to either A or B, inclusively [see Figure 2.2(d)]. Using standard "element of" representation,

$$A \cup B = \{x\colon x \in A \text{ or } x \in B\}$$

Using the membership function representation,

$$A \cup B = \{x \mid u_{A \cup B}(x), \text{ where } u_{A \cup B}(x) = \max(u_A(x),\ u_B(x))\}$$

Example 2.2

Let X and A be as in Example 2.1, and let

$$B = \{1/1,\ 2/1,\ 3/0,\ 4/0\} = \{1, 2\}$$

Then

$$A \cup B = \{1/1,\ 2/1,\ 3/0,\ 4/1\} = \{1, 2, 4\}$$

The intersection of sets A and B, $A \cap B$, is the set of all elements that belong to both A and B [see Figure 2.2(e)]. Thus,

$$A \cap B = \{x\colon x \in A \text{ and } x \in B\}$$

or, in membership function form,

$$A \cap B = \{x \mid u_{A \cap B}(x), \text{ where } u_{A \cap B}(x) = \min(u_A(x),\ u_B(x))\}$$

The set-theoretic difference of sets A and B, $A - B$, is the set of all elements that are in A but not in B [see Figure 2.2(c)]:

$$A - B = \{x\colon x \in A \text{ and } x \notin B\}$$

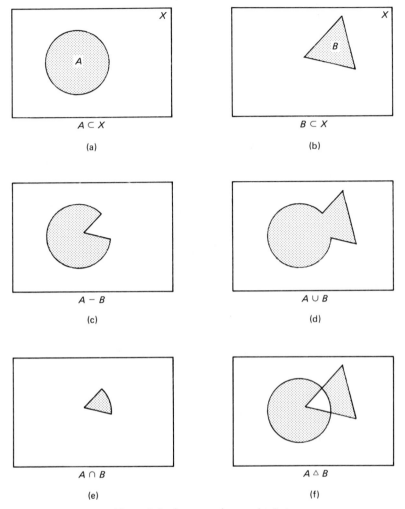

Figure 2.2 Set operations and relations

or

$$A - B = \{x \mid u_{A-B}(x), \text{ where } u_{A-B}(x) = \min(u_A(x), 1 - u_B(x))\}$$

Note that, in the case where $A = X$, we have the specification of the complement of B:

$$B^c = X - B = \{x \mid u_{B^c}(x), \text{ where } u_{B^c}(x) = 1 - u_B(x)\}$$

since

$$\min(u_X(x), 1 - u_B(x)) = \min(1, 1 - u_B(x))$$
$$= 1 - u_B(x)$$

TABLE 2.1 LAWS FOR SETS

1. Commutative laws
   $A \cup B = B \cup A$
   $A \cap B = B \cap A$

2. Associative laws
   $(A \cup B) \cup C = A \cup (B \cup C)$
   $(A \cap B) \cap C = A \cap (B \cap C)$

3. Idempotence laws
   $A \cup A = A$
   $A \cap A = A$

4. Absorption laws
   $A \cup (B \cap A) = A$
   $A \cap (B \cup A) = A$

5. Distributive laws
   $A \cup (B \cap C) = (A \cup B) \cap (A \cup C)$
   $A \cap (B \cup C) = (A \cap B) \cup (A \cap C)$

6. Smallest and largest properties
   $A \cup X = X$
   $A \cap \emptyset = \emptyset$
   $A \cap X = A$
   $A \cup \emptyset = A$

7. Involution of complement
   $(A^c)^c = A$

8. De Morgan's laws
   $(A \cup B)^c = A^c \cap B^c$
   $(A \cap B)^c = A^c \cup B^c$

9. Complementary laws (apply only to regular (nonfuzzy) subsets)
   $A \cup A^c = X$
   $A \cap A^c = \emptyset$

There are many important laws concerning set-theoretic operations. Some of the most basic are given in Table 2.1.

Example 2.3

Referring to sets A and B of Example 2.2,

$$A \cap B = \{1/0,\ 2/1,\ 3/0,\ 4/0\} = \{2\}$$

$$A - B = \{1/0,\ 2/0,\ 3/0,\ 4/1\} = \{4\}$$

$$B - A = \{1/1,\ 2/0,\ 3/0,\ 4/0\} = \{1\}$$

Using $A - B$ and $B - A$, we can find the symmetric difference of A and B, which is defined by

$$A \triangle B = (A - B) \cup (B - A)$$

and hence, in this example, is given by

$$A \triangle B = \{1/1,\ 2/0,\ 3/0,\ 4/1\} = \{1, 4\}$$

[see Figure 2.2(f)].

Because of the associative laws for union and intersection (Table 2.1), these operations can be generalized to unions and intersections of arbitrary classes of sets. If (A_i) is any family of sets indexed over the nonempty index set I, then

$$\bigcup_{i \in I} A_i = \{x : x \in A_i \text{ for some } i \in I\}$$

$$= \{x \mid u_{\cup A_i}(x), \text{ where } u_{\cup A_i}(x) = \max_{i \in I}(u_{A_i}(x))\}$$

and

$$\bigcap_{i \in I} A_i = \{x : x \in A_i \text{ for all } i \in I\}$$

$$= \{x \mid u_{\cap A_i}(x), \text{ where } u_{\cap A_i} = \min_{i \in I}(u_{A_i}(x))\}$$

If $\{A_i\}$ is empty, we define $\cup A_i = \emptyset$ and $\cap A_i = X$.

Several identities hold for arbitrary unions and intersections, in particular, De Morgan's laws:

$$\left(\bigcup_{i \in I} A_i \right)^c = \bigcap_{i \in I} A_i^c$$

and

$$\left(\bigcap_{i \in I} A_i \right)^c = \bigcup_{i \in I} A_i^c$$

2.2 FUZZY SUBSETS

In regular set theory, an element belongs to a given set or it does not. For instance, if the universal set X consists of all polygons, then the set of triangles, defined by

$$A = \{x : x \text{ has 3 sides}\}$$

is a subset of X. Moreover, given any particular $x \in X$, there are two mutually exclusive possibilities: (1) $x \in A$, in which case $u_A(x) = 1$, or (2) $x \notin A$, in which case $u_A(x) = 0$. Although such mutual exclusivity fits strictly mathematical thinking, it is, in general, not applicable to everyday reasoning. For instance, consider the universal set X of all animal species. Then one might wish to characterize the different species in terms of hostility to human beings; thus, we are led to consider the "subset" B of X defined by

$$B = \{x : x \text{ is hostile to human beings}\}$$

Clearly, there is something very different between the character of B and that of A. In fact, as it stands, B is not a set at all: given a particular species, the question of its hostility to human beings is not well defined. For instance, in a given species some may be hostile, while others are not. Moreover, the whole notion of hostility is logically fuzzy. Under what circumstances do members of a particular species demonstrate hostility; indeed, can the term "hostility" be given any deterministic meaning to begin with?

Proceeding intuitively, for A to be a properly constituted subset of a universal set X, there must be a definitive answer to the question, "Is x an element of A?" for any element x in X. Generally, if the set A is defined by some predicate formulation,

$$A = \{x : x \text{ is } \underline{\quad\quad}\}$$

then it is incumbent that the predicate be *well defined*, in the sense that it is determinative: there can be no ambiguity insofar as membership is concerned. Of course, the question arises as to whether any predicate outside the domain of mathematics can ever be determinative. Indeed, is it possible that a descriptive formulation, except one lying within some axiomatic system, can ever satisfy the criterion of determination unless it is, in fact, a listing of the elements, which would mean that the set is not defined by a predicate at all, but rather by a list? The germ of this question can be seen in Section 1.9, where we took the point of view that a predicate was equivalent to a relation (subset). In other words, we attributed no extra semantic content to the predicate beyond the strictly relational interpretation. This *nominalist* position is dominant in Western scientific circles (although it is certainly not universally accepted). Moreover, it is consistent with the principle of extensionality (see Section 1.2) in two-valued logic, since there is no attempt to impart meaning to the formulation of the subset outside the role of membership. Although we do not wish to join the philosophical battles of the twentieth century, we believe we can safely say that, insofar as the digital implementation of two-valued thinking in artificially intelligent systems is concerned, the entire matter is moot: the relevant information is stored in a finite number of memory registers, and the data are gathered and compressed according to finite algorithms; thus, no occult meaning can be attributed to predicates, since each is nothing but the name of a list.

To model indeterminate set membership, L.A. Zadeh introduced the notion of a *fuzzy* subset of a universal set X. Such a subset A is, by definition, given by

$$A = \{x \mid u_A(x)\}$$

where the membership function u_A on A takes values in the *valuation space* $[0, 1]$; that is, for any $x \in X$,

$$0 \leq u_A(x) \leq 1$$

Elements in the fuzzy subset A possess membership values between 0 and 1, whereas in classical set theory these values are either 0 or 1, precisely.

Referring to the notion of hostility discussed earlier, if we once again let X denote the set of all species, then any element x in X has a valuation $u_B(x)$ associated with it, where $u_B(x)$ is a measure of the hostility of the species x. From a modeling point of view, the species x is "more in" the "hostility set" B than is species y if and only if

$$u_B(x) > u_B(y)$$

In this instance, the membership function provides a quantitative level of the quality hostility. It is precisely such quantitative characterization of qualities that is so problematic in regular set theory. Nevertheless, quality judgments constitute a fundamental aspect of human reasoning, and the mathematical modeling of these judgments is extremely important insofar as artificial replication of that reasoning is concerned. As we will see in Section 2.6, the notion of fuzziness introduced here for sets has an immediate counterpart in logic.

Example 2.4

> Consider the set X of all robots belonging to a certain corporation. These robots, which comprise the set $X = \{a, b, c\}$, are illustrated in Figure 2.3. We wish to consider the fuzzy subset A of "intelligent" robots. If ordinary sets were to be employed, then an individual robot could either be a member of A, or not a member of A (i.e., robot a could either be considered as fully intelligent or fully unintelligent). On the other hand, the utilization of fuzzy subsets allows for gradations in intelligence to be modeled by corresponding gradations in subset membership. The more intelligent robot a is, the greater the valuation $u_A(a)$, and conversely. Intuitively, membership values near 1/2 are associated with full uncertainty regarding intelligence, although we must be careful in our use of the word *uncertainty*. In the case at hand, it simply means that a robot of middling intelligence would deserve the predicate "is intelligent" with a correspondingly middling degree of conviction.

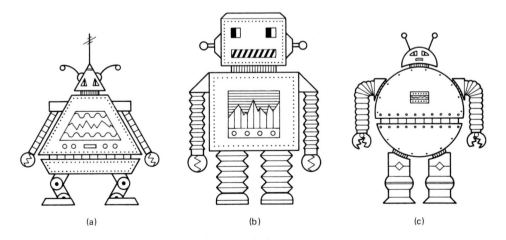

(a)   (b)   (c)

Figure 2.3   "Intelligent" robots

For the robots in Figure 2.3, it might be felt that

$$A = \{a/0.2,\ b/0.9,\ c/0.4\}$$

That is,

$$u_A(a) = 0.2$$

$$u_A(b) = 0.9$$

and

$$u_A(c) = 0.4$$

Heuristically, fuzzy membership in A corresponds to the statement "x is intelligent." Instantiating the variable x with the subject a yields neither a true nor a false statement; rather, it yields a statement whose validity has the membership value $u_A(a) = 0.2$ associated with it. In the two-valued setting, that membership value must either be 1 or 0. The utilization of a fuzzy subset has avoided the "all-or-nothing" syndrome.

Membership of elements in a fuzzy subset is indicated as follows: if $u_A(x) = 1$, then, as in ordinary set theory, we write $x \in A$; if $u_A(x) = 0$, we write $x \notin A$; and if

$$0 < u_A(x) = \lambda < 1$$

we write $x \in_\lambda A$.

Much of the basic theory of ordinary sets possesses a fuzzy variation. For instance, fuzzy subset A is said to be a subset of fuzzy subset B, written $A \subset B$, if, for every x in X,

$$u_A(x) \leq u_B(x)$$

As in conventional set theory, A is always a subset of itself, and the empty set $\emptyset$, defined by $u_\emptyset(x) = 0$ for all x, is a subset of every set. Moreover, two fuzzy subsets A and B are said to be equal, written $A = B$, if and only if $u_A = u_B$.

The operations of union, intersection, difference, and symmetric difference have fuzzy interpretations, where in each case the fuzzy operation is defined in exactly the same manner as is the membership-function version of the original. For example, $A \cup B$ is the smallest fuzzy subset of X containing both A and B, and this is characterized by the identity

$$u_{A \cup B} = \max(u_A,\ u_B)$$

Analogously, the intersection $A \cap B$ is the largest fuzzy subset of X contained in both A and B, and this is characterized by the identity

$$u_{A \cap B} = \min(u_A,\ u_B)$$

The set-theoretic difference, $A - B$, of fuzzy subsets A and B is specified by the membership function

$$u_{A-B} = \min(u_A,\ 1 - u_B)$$

As a consequence, the fuzzy complement of B, denoted B^c, possesses the membership function

$$u_{B^c} = 1 - u_B$$

Example 2.5

Consider the set X of robots given in Example 2.4, where

$$A = \{a/0.2, b/0.9, c/0.4\}$$

If

$$B = \{a/0.4, b/1, c/0.6\}$$

and

$$C = \{b/1, c/0.5\}$$

then $A \subset B$, since $u_A < u_B$. On the other hand, A is not a subset of C, since

$$u_A(a) = 0.2 \nleq u_C(a) = 0$$

Notice, however, that $C \subset B$. Next,

$$A \cup B = \{a/0.4, b/1, c/0.6\}$$

For instance, $a \in_{0.2} A$ and $a \in_{0.4} B$, and thus $a \in_{0.4} A \cup B$, membership in the union being determined by the maximum of the input membership values. Two other unions are given by

$$A \cup C = \{a/0.2, b/1, c/0.5\}$$

and

$$B \cup C = \{a/0.4, b/1, c/0.6\}$$

Employing the other fuzzy operations defined previously, we obtain

$$A \cap B = \{a/0.2, b/0.9, c/0.4\}$$
$$A \cap C = \{b/0.9, c/0.4\}$$
$$A - B = \{a/0.2, c/0.4\}$$
$$B - A = \{a/0.4, b/0.1, c/0.6\}$$
$$A^c = \{a/0.8, b/0.1, c/0.6\}$$

and

$$A \triangle B = \{a/0.4, b/0.1, c/0.6\}$$

Note that, because of the correspondence between the membership definitions of ordinary set operations and those for fuzzy sets, all the operations defined on fuzzy subsets reduce to the corresponding operations on conventional subsets when the membership value is restricted to lie in the set $\{0, 1\}$. The basic laws of fuzzy (and ordinary) set theory are provided in Table 2.1.

Example 2.6

This example shows that the complementary laws do not apply to fuzzy subsets. Let

$$X = \{u, v, w, z\}$$

and

$$A = \{u/0.5, v/0.3\}$$

Then

$$A^c = \{u/0.5, v/0.7, w/1, z/1\}$$

and hence

$$A \cup A^c = \{w/1, u/0.5, v/0.7, z/1\} \neq X$$

and

$$A \cap A^c = \{u/0.5, v/0.3\} \neq \emptyset$$

2.3 DIRECTED GRAPHS

Among the most useful structures for the representation and manipulation of knowledge is the directed graph. Special types of these graphs, as well as related structures, are employed in various AI applications. These include trees, which are useful in planning search strategies; modified directed graphs, which are employed in the representation of linked, fuzzy, and lattice-linked lists; Markov diagrams, which are a form of modified directed graph that is useful in the specification of deterministic, nondeterministic, fuzzy, stochastic, and lattice automata; many-tailed graphs, which can be employed in the transformation of abstract concepts into practical settings; and commuting diagrams, which are utilized throughout mathematics for homomorphism specification.

A *directed graph* is rigorously defined as a four-tuple

$$(P, L, f, b)$$

where

P = finite nonempty set of *points* or *nodes*

L = finite nonempty set of *directed lines* or *arrows*

f = function that indicates the node pointed to by the *front* (*head*) of the arrow,

$$f: L \rightarrow P$$

b = function that indicates the node attached to the *tail* (*back*) of the arrow,

$$b: L \rightarrow P$$

Directed graphs are drawn pictorially by using points to indicate nodes and arrows to indicate directed line segments pointing from and to appropriate nodes.

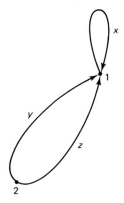

•
3

Figure 2.4 Directed graph for Example
2.7

Example 2.7

Let

$$P = \{1, 2, 3\}$$
$$L = \{x, y, z\}$$
$$f(x) = f(y) = f(z) = 1$$
$$b(x) = 1$$
$$b(y) = b(z) = 2$$

Figure 2.4 provides a graphical representation of this directed graph. Most often it is the intuition obtained from the graphical representation that helps in the solution of practical problems.

Many problems, together with their solutions, can be modeled with the help of directed graphs. The nodes are employed to represent information, states of being, or possible solutions to a problem, whereas the arrows are used to represent instructions or actions that yield other nodes. Although many directed graph applications will occur throughout the remainder of the book, we will now give a simple example to illustrate the technique.

Example 2.8

Consider the problem of finding the roots of the quadratic equation

$$ax^2 + bx + c = 0$$

where $a \neq 0$ and $c \neq 0$. The quadratic formula can be employed to find both roots:

$$x = \frac{-b \mp \sqrt{b^2 - 4ac}}{2a}$$

Multiplying this expression by

$$\frac{-b \pm \sqrt{b^2 - 4ac}}{-b \pm \sqrt{b^2 - 4ac}}$$

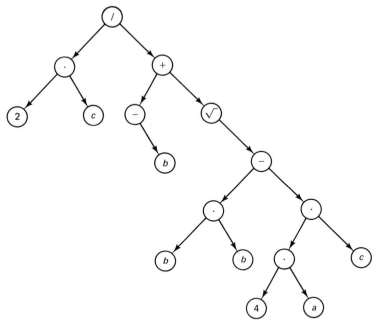

Figure 2.5   Directed graph for CITARDAUQ formula

gives, for the roots, the different expression

$$x = \frac{-2c}{b \mp \sqrt{b^2 - 4ac}}$$

known as the "*citardauq formula*" ("quadratic" spelled backward). This representation of the roots provides greater numerical accuracy in situations where the roots are far apart, the "stiff" equation situation. The directed graph diagram in Figure 2.5 provides a visual representation of the operations and data involved in finding the root

$$\frac{2c}{-b + \sqrt{b^2 - 4ac}}$$

2.4 LATTICES

A lattice is a mathematical structure that embodies the notion of order. As such, it finds extensive application in artificial intelligence. We begin with the concept of partial order.

Recall that a binary relation on a set L is a subset of $L \times L$ (see Section 1.9). If $R \subset L \times L$ is such a relation, then the elements of R are ordered pairs of the form (a, b), where both a and b are elements of L. R is said to be a *partial order relation* on L if three conditions are satisfied:

1. $(a, a) \in R$ for any $a \in$ L.
2. If $(a, b) \in R$ and $(b, a) \in R$, then $a = b$.
3. If $(a, b) \in R$ and $(b, c) \in R$, then $(a, c) \in R$.

The three conditions are known as *reflexivity*, *antisymmetry*, and *transitivity*, re-spectively. Because of the product set formulation of a binary relation, at first glance it is somewhat difficult to see the meaning of the three properties. However, if we write $a \le b$ to indicate that $(a, b) \in R$ (to mean that a and b are related), then the intent becomes transparent. Specifically, the three properties become:

   1. $a \le a$.
   2. If $a \le b$ and $b \le a$, then $a = b$.
   3. If $a \le b$ and $b \le c$, then $a \le c$.

Thus, the relation $\le$, which is reflexive, antisymmetric, and transitive, behaves similarly to the usual arithmetic order relation, and the notion of partial order is simply a generalization of that order relation. If $\le$ satisfies the property

   4. For all $a, b \in L$, either $a \le b$, or $b \le a$.

then it is called a *total order relation*.

   If $\le$ is a partial order relation on L, then the pair $(L, \le)$ is called a *partially ordered set*, or *poset*. Although it is L together with the partial order relation that is the poset, it is customary to simply say that L is a poset and assume implicitly that the partial order relation is understood from the context. Whenever $\le$ is a total order relation, L is said to be *totally ordered*. Any totally ordered subset of a poset is called a *chain*.

   An example of a totally ordered set is Z, the set of all integers, under the usual arithmetic ordering. The set of all subsets of the plane is a poset under set inclusion, $\subset$; however, it is not totally ordered.

Example 2.9

   Let

$$L = \{1, 2, 3, 4, 6, 8, 12, 16\}$$

   and let $a \le b$ mean that a divides into b with zero remainder. Then $4 \le 4$, $2 \le 4$, and $4 \le 12$, since in each case the division can be performed with remainder 0. However, $3 \nleq 4$ and $6 \nleq 16$, where the slash through the order relation means that the two elements are not related by $\le$.

Hasse diagrams are useful in representing posets. In these, each element in L is denoted by a dot (node), and whenever $a \le b$, an arrow is drawn from a to b. Very often the arrow is omitted and just a line is drawn between a and b, with a being positioned beneath b to indicate the ordering. Moreover, to simplify the diagram, two conventions are assumed: (1) since $a \le a$ for all a in L, no line is drawn running from a to a, and (2) if $a \le b$, $b \le c$, and a, b, and c are distinct, then lines are drawn from a to b and from b to c, but the line from a to c is omitted (see Figure 2.6). The Hasse diagram for the poset given in Example 2.9 is given in Figure 2.7.

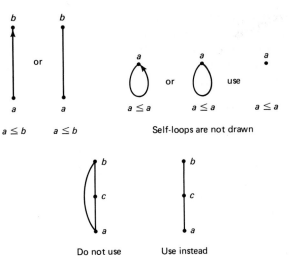

a ≤ b   *a ≤ b*   Self-loops are not drawn

Do not use   Use instead   **Figure 2.6**   Hasse diagram for poset

Example 2.10

Let

$$L = \{0, 1/2, 1\}$$

and let ≤ be the usual arithmetic ordering.   Then $(L, \leq)$ is a totally ordered set, and it is illustrated in Figure 2.8.

Example 2.11

Let L be the set of all subsets of the set $\{x, y, z\}$, and let $A \leq B$ mean that $A \subset B$. Then $(L, \subset)$ is a poset and is illustrated in Figure 2.9.

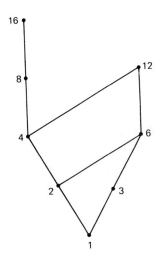

Figure 2.7   Hasse diagram for Example 2.9

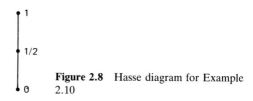

Figure 2.8   Hasse diagram for Example 2.10

If R is a subset of L and u is an element of L such that $r \leq u$ for any r in R, then u is said to be an *upper bound* for R.   Moreover, u in L is called the *least upper bound* or *supremum* of R if u is the "smallest" among all upper bounds for R.   Rigorously, u is the supremum if u is an upper bound for R, and if u' is any other upper bound for R, then $u \leq u'$.

Proceeding analogously, l is a lower bound for a subset of R of the poset L if $l \leq r$ for any r in R.   It is called the *greatest lower bound* or *infimum* if, for any other lower bound l', $l \geq l'$.   The least upper bound and greatest lower bound are abbreviated as LUB and GLB, or as sup and inf, respectively.

Example 2.12

Consider the poset of Example 2.9, which is illustrated in Figure 2.7.   Let

$$R = \{4, 6, 8\}$$

Then there is no upper bound for R, since there does not exist an element u in L for which $4 \leq u$, $6 \leq u$, and $8 \leq u$.   Consequently, there is no supremum for R.   On the other hand, $l = 1$ and $l = 2$ are both lower bounds, whereas $l = 3$ is not a lower bound.   The greatest lower bound is $l = 2$.

Example 2.13

If $L = [0, 1]$ and we consider the usual arithmetic ordering, then $(L, \leq)$ is a totally ordered set, and every subset possesses both an LUB and a GLB.

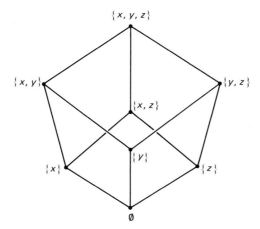

Figure 2.9   Hasse diagram for Example 2.11

TABLE 2.2   LAWS FOR LATTICE OPERATIONS

1. Commutative laws
$$x \vee y = y \vee x$$
$$x \wedge y = y \wedge x$$
2. Associative laws
$$x \vee (y \vee z) = (x \vee y) \vee z$$
$$x \wedge (y \wedge z) = (x \wedge y) \wedge z$$
3. Idempotence laws
$$x \vee x = x$$
$$x \wedge x = x$$
4. Absorption laws
$$x \vee (y \wedge x) = x$$
$$x \wedge (y \vee x) = x$$

A poset L is called a *lattice* if every subset R consisting of two points possesses both an LUB and a GLB.   We denote the LUB of $\{x, y\}$ by $x \vee y$, and the GLB by $x \wedge y$.   The poset given in Example 2.9 is not a lattice, since the subset $\{12, 16\}$ does not possess an LUB in L.   The posets given in Examples 2.10, 2.11, and 2.13 are lattices.   In general, every totally ordered set must be a lattice, since $x \vee y$ must equal x or y, and similarly so for $x \wedge y$.   Table 2.2 gives the fundamental properties satisfied by the sup and inf.

Not only are the four properties given in Table 2.2 characteristic of lattices, they, in fact, characterize the concept of a lattice.   Specifically, if L is any set with binary operations $\vee$ and $\wedge$ satisfying the four properties, then L is a lattice under the order relation $\leq$ defined by $a \leq b$ if and only if $b = a \vee b$.

For instance, in the propositional calculus, if L consists of all well-formed sentences, if we identify logically equivalent sentences, and if $\vee$ denotes *or* and $\wedge$ denotes *and*, then L, together with the operations $\vee$ and $\wedge$, is a lattice.   If p and q are two statements, then $p \leq q$ means $q = p \vee q$.

An important type of lattice is the *distributive lattice*.   Not only do its sup and inf operations satisfy the four properties of Table 2.2, but they also satisfy

5. Distributive laws
$$x \wedge (y \vee z) = (x \wedge y) \vee (x \wedge z)$$
$$x \vee (y \wedge z) = (x \vee y) \wedge (x \vee z)$$

Both the propositional calculus and the collection of subsets of the plane (under union and intersection) are distributive lattices.   So, too, are the lattices illustrated in Figure 2.10.   In general, any totally ordered set is a distributive lattice.

Example 2.14

The two lattices, M_5 and N_5, illustrated in Figure 2.11 are not distributive.   Moreover, these two lattices characterize all nondistributive lattices, in that a lattice L is non-

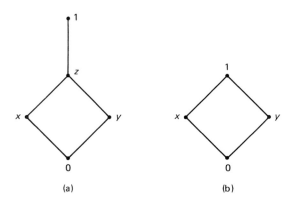

(a)   (b)   **Figure 2.10** Two distributive lattices

distributive if and only if it possesses a sublattice that is isomorphic to either M_5 or N_5. For N_5, note that

$$y \vee (x \wedge z) = y \vee 0 = y$$

whereas

$$(y \vee x) \wedge (y \vee z) = 1 \wedge z = z$$

and so it is not distributive.

A *bounded* lattice, or a lattice with *units*, possesses two elements, denoted 0 and 1, which are the smallest and largest elements, respectively, in the lattice. Whereas a general lattice is, from an algebraic point of view, a triple $(L, \vee, \wedge)$, a bounded lattice is a quintuple

$$(L, \vee, \wedge, 0, 1)$$

for which the four properties of Table 2.2 hold, as well as the following property:

6. $x \wedge 0 = 0$
$\quad x \vee 1 = 1$

The lattices given in Figures 2.9, 2.10 and 2.11 are bounded.

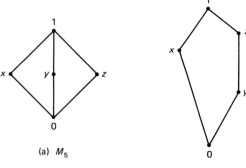

(a) M_5

(b) N_5

Figure 2.11 Two nondistributive lattices

A lattice L is said to be *complemented* if, for any element x in L, there exists an element x', called a *complement* of x, such that

$$x \vee x' = 1$$

and

$$x \wedge x' = 0$$

The closed interval $[0, 1]$, endowed with the usual arithmetic order relation, is a distributive, bounded lattice; however, it is not complemented.

Example 2.15

The lattice M_5, which is illustrated in Figure 2.11, is complemented. Note that the element x in M_5 possesses two complements, y and z. This shows that the complement need not be unique.

A distributive, bounded, and complemented lattice is called a *Boolean algebra*. Whereas in Example 2.15 the complement was not unique, it can be shown that it is always unique in a Boolean algebra. Because it possesses two binary operations, $\vee$ and $\wedge$, a unary operation called complementation, and two units, 0 and 1, a Boolean algebra is algebraically a sextuple

$$(L, \vee, \wedge, ', 0, 1)$$

with binary operations $\vee$ and $\wedge$ and unary operator $' : L \to L$.

Example 2.16

The lattice in Figure 2.10(b) is a four-point Boolean algebra in which $x' = y$. The two-point Boolean algebra $\{0, 1\}$, with $0 \leq 1$, is probably the most important Boolean algebra, since it is used to support the language by which digital computers "think" and process information.

A *Heyting algebra* is a sextuple,

$$(L, \vee, \wedge, \to, 0, 1)$$

where $(L, \vee, \wedge, \to, 0, 1)$ is a bounded, distributive lattice, and $\to$ is a binary operation, called *implication*, on L satisfying the following conditions:

H1. $x \to x = 1$
H2. $(x \to y) \wedge y = y$
H3. $x \wedge (x \to y) = x \wedge y$
H4. $x \to (y \wedge z) = (x \to y) \wedge (x \to z)$
H5. $(x \vee y) \to z = (x \to z) \wedge (y \to z)$

If

$$(L, \vee, \wedge, ', 0, 1)$$

is a Boolean algebra, and if $a \to b$ is defined as $a' \vee b$, then

$$(L, \vee, \wedge, \to, 0, 1)$$

is a Heyting algebra. Note that, in making a Boolean algebra into a Heyting algebra, we define the operation $\to$ in a manner analogous to the logical equivalence between the implication

if a, then b

and the sentence

(not a) or b

in the propositional calculus.

Finally, a lattice L is said to be *complete* if every subset R possesses a supremum or, equivalently, every subset R possesses an infimum.

2.5 SWITCHING ALGEBRA

In the present section we present a standard mathematical model for switching mechanisms. The significance of the model can be recognized by realizing that a digital computer consists of devices that switch states. Throughout the section, we will be considering the two-state Boolean algebra $\{0, 1\}$, and we will be using $+$ to denote the supremum, and $\cdot$, or simple concatenation, to denote the infimum. Keep in mind that our main concern is with expressions in the propositional calculus, and, therefore, it is worthwhile to think of $+$, $\cdot$, and $'$ as *or*, *and*, and *not*, respectively. It should be noted that the presentation can easily be extended to more general Boolean algebras.

A *switching expression* over the n variables $x_1, x_2, \ldots, x_n$ is defined recursively as follows:

1. 0 and 1 are switching expressions.
2. x_j is a switching expression for $j = 1, 2, \ldots, n$.
3. If A and B are switching expressions, then so are $A + B$, AB, and A'.

If $f(x_1, x_2, \ldots, x_n)$ represents a switching expression, then, by allowing the variables x_j to take on the values 0 and 1, a function on the n-fold product space

$$\{0, 1\} \times \{0, 1\} \times \cdots \times \{0, 1\}$$

results. Such a function is known as a *switching function* or *switching polynomial*. The collection of all such functions constitutes the *switching algebra*. Note that we will freely employ metasymbols such as parentheses in order to avoid ambiguity in the representation of switching expressions.

As in the propositional calculus, where certain statements are logically equivalent, certain switching expressions yield the same switching function.

Example 2.17

Consider the switching expressions

$$f(x_1, x_2) = (x_1 x_2) + x_1$$

and

$$g(x_1, x_2) = x_1$$

By the absorption law, f and g represent the same switching function.

Just as truth tables can be employed to check the logical equivalence of statements within the propositional calculus, truth tables can also be employed to check the equivalence of switching expressions. If there are n variables in the expression, then there are 2^n rows in the table.

Given a particular switching expression f, we would like to find an equivalent minimal expression g, where we will define minimality in terms of the number of terms in a *sum-of-products* expression. Specifically, if

$$f(x_1, x_2, \ldots, x_n) = A_1 + A_2 + \cdots + A_m$$

where each A_j, called a *minterm*, is a product of symbols of the form x_i and x_i', then we wish to minimize the number of symbols in the "summation." The required minimization can be implemented through the use of *Karnaugh maps*.

To illustrate the method, we consider the case of three symbols x, y, and z. Referring to Figure 2.12, we see that there are eight squares making up the Karnaugh map for three symbols. Each square is labeled by a binary-encoded integer between 000 and 111, the labeling scheme being written along the left and top sides. For instance, the second square in the second row, is labeled 101. We let the first bit in the encoding represent the the first variable, 1 for x and 0 for x'; the second bit represent the second variable, 1 for y and 0 for y'; and the third bit represent the third variable, 1 for z and 0 for z'. Note that each possible three-variable multiplication corresponds to exactly one square. For instance, the switching expression $xy'z$ is represented by the 101 square.

To use the Karnaugh map to reduce a sum-of-products expression, we place a 1 in each square to which the minterm corresponds. If the minterm utilizes all three variables, then it corresponds to exactly one square; if it consists of two variables, then it corresponds to two squares; and if it consists of a single variable,

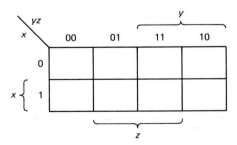

Figure 2.12 Schema for Karnaugh map with three variables

it corresponds to four squares.   For instance, the minterm yz' corresponds to the squares labeled 010 and 110.   This is because these squares both correspond to the case $y = 1$ and $z = 0$, which is precisely the conditions under which the minterm yz' assumes the value 1.   Note that the value of x is irrelevant to the value of yz', and hence plays no role in the choice of 1-valued squares.

Once the appropriate squares are filled with 1s, adjacent marked squares are grouped together, where the groups must occur in rectangular blocks whose numbers of squares are powers of 2.   In the three-variable case, blocks must contain 1, 2, 4, or 8 squares.   Of fundamental importance is that adjacency can result from "wrapping" the map.   As a result, square 000 is adjacent to square 010, and square 100 is adjacent to square 110.   Once a collection of grouped squares has been obtained, the original minterm-to-squares mapping can be inverted, and this inversion process will reduce the redundancy in the original sum-of-squares expression.   As an example, if two separate three-variable terms yield two adjacent squares, then, upon inversion, the pair of adjacent squares yields a single minterm consisting of only two variables.   Although the explanation of the methodology is rather wordy, in practice the technique is completely straightforward.

Example 2.18

Let

$$f(x, y, z) = x'y'z' + xy'z' + x'y'z + xyz$$

The appropriate Karnaugh map is given in Figure 2.13.   Note that squares 000 and 100 have been blocked, as well as squares 000 and 001, and that no other blocking is possible.   Hence, the reduced expression for f is

$$f = y'z' + x'y' + xyz$$

where $y'z'$ represents the inversion of the block pair {000, 100}, and $x'y'$ represents the inversion of the pair {000, 001}.   Indeed, if $y = 0$ and $z = 0$, then the sum of minterms

$$x'y'z' + xy'z'$$

in the original expression has value 1, and conversely.   Similarly, $x = 0$ and $y = 0$ if and only if

$$x'y'z' + x'y'z$$

has value 1.

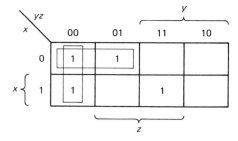

Figure 2.13   Karnaugh map for Example 2.18

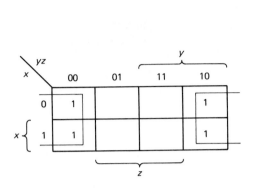

Figure 2.14 Karnaugh map for
Example 2.19

Figure 2.15 Schema for Karnaugh map
with four variables

Example 2.19

The Karnaugh map for

$$f = x'y'z' + xy'z' + yz'$$

is given in Figure 2.14. Note that the minterm yz' has resulted in the filling of two
squares, 010 and 110. Since the end squares are adjacent, there is a rectangular block
of four labeled squares, and, consequently, inversion yields $f = z'$.

The map methodology for the minimization of switching functions over more
than three variables is analogous to the three-variable case. For example, in the
four-variable case, we look for rectangular blocks of size 1, 2, 4, 8, or 16, the
original Karnaugh map diagram being 4 by 4. Once again, each bit in a 4-bit word
corresponds to an appropriate variable, and once again minterms in the original
expression result in the labeling of corresponding squares. For instance, referring
to Figure 2.15, the minterm $xy'w$ results in the labeling of squares 1001 and 1011,
since it is equivalent to the sum

$$xy'z'w + xy'zw$$

which has value 1 if x, y, z, and w take on the values corresponding to either of
the labeled squares. Keep in mind that, in the four-variable situation, the wrapping
of the diagram results in the four corner squares being adjacent. It is as if the
map were folded into a torus (see Figure 2.16 for three-variable torus).

Example 2.20

The Kanaugh map for

$$f = x'y'z'w' + xy'z'w' + x'z + xz$$

is given in Figure 2.17. There is a four-square blocking consisting of the corner
squares, and there is an eight-square blocking consisting of the two right-hand columns.

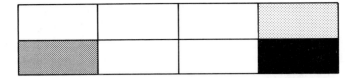

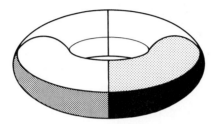

Figure 2.16   Karnaugh map converted into a torus

Therefore, f can be reduced to

$$f = y'w' + z$$

Note the transformation:

$$y'w' \leftrightarrow \{0000, 0010, 1000, 1010\}$$

$$z \leftrightarrow \{0011, 0010, 0111, 0110, 1111, 1110, 1011, 1010\}$$

Although the consideration of more than four variables is possible, we will not go further, the technique being completely analogous.

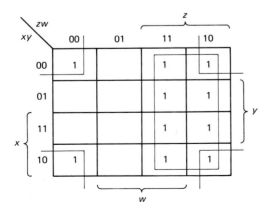

Figure 2.17   Karnaugh map for Example 2.20

The relationship between the synthesis methodology of Section 1.5 and Karnaugh map reduction should be recognized. Specifically, given a logical function in terms of its truth values, a propositional expression can always be constructed in disjunctive normal form that possesses those values. Since each minterm in a disjunctive normal form expression contains the maximum number of variables, either complemented or uncomplemented, each corresponds to exactly one square in a Karnaugh map. As a consequence, if the values, 0 or 1, of the input variables are listed in the truth table so that the resulting rows represent a binary counting from 0 to $2^n - 1$, then not only is there a one-to-one correspondence between the appropriate rows, minterms, and squares of the Karnaugh map, it is also true that the rows and squares that are in correspondence possess the same binary codes. For example, should there be three variables, and the truth function values of the eight possibilities correspond to a desired combinational gate system, a minimal *and-or-not* gate system can be obtained by the use of a Karnaugh map.

Example 2.21

Suppose we wish to design a combinational logic circuit that will receive an encoded message and, based on the message, take one of two actions, which we will denote by 0 and 1. The message will be a binary-encoded integer between 0 and 15, and the action 1 will be taken if and only if, in base 10 notation, the received integer ends in a 4, 5, 6, or 7. Letting x, y, z, and w denote the 4 bits, from left to right, forming the received binary integer, and assuming a truth table labeled in accordance with a binary count from 0 to 15, the truth table has, in order, and from top to bottom, the values

$$0, 0, 0, 0, 1, 1, 1, 1, 0, 0, 0, 0, 0, 0, 1, 1$$

The corresponding Karnaugh map is given in Figure 2.18, and the appropriate switching function is

$$f = x'y + yz$$

Note that the value of the units bit is irrelevant since neither w nor w' appear in the reduced switching expression. Thus, the units bit can be ignored by the system. The required combinational circuit is given in Figure 2.19.

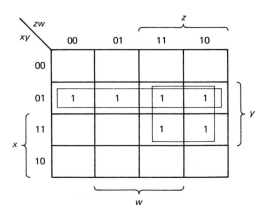

Figure 2.18 Karnaugh map for Example 2.21

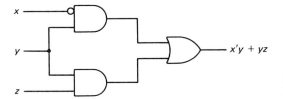

Figure 2.19 Combinational circuit for Example 2.21

2.6 FUZZY LOGICS AND LATTICE VALUATIONS

Regular and fuzzy subsets of a universal set X involve membership functions that take values in the totally ordered valuation spaces $\{0, 1\}$ and $[0, 1]$, respectively. These valuation spaces are both lattices under the usual arithmetic ordering: $\{0, 1\}$ is a Boolean algebra and $[0, 1]$ is a distributive lattice with units.

Numerous structures employ membership-type functions, for instance, the truth function T discussed in Section 1.3. Recall that T mapped statements in the propositional calculus into the values 0 or 1, where 0 and 1 meant false and true, respectively.

Valuation spaces are not limited to $\{0, 1\}$ and $[0, 1]$; valuations can be taken in partially ordered sets, totally ordered sets, and lattices. An example of a lattice valuation function occurs in the lattice-valued automata discussed in Section 5.6.

For the present, we shall concern ourselves with a more rudimentary example, *Kleene's three-valued logic system*. In this system, as in the propositional calculus, a statement is mapped by a truth function into a totally ordered set; however, in the Kleene system, the valuation space is the three-point set

$$\{0, 1/2, 1\}$$

under the usual arithmetic ordering. Intuitively, $T(a) = 1$, $T(a) = 0$, and $T(a) = 1/2$ mean that a is true, false, and undecided, respectively. As in the propositional calculus, the connectives $\sim$ (*not*), $\wedge$ (*and*), $\vee$ (*or*), $\rightarrow$ (*implies*), and $\leftrightarrow$ (*if and only if*) are defined, their definitions being given in Table 2.3. Since each statement can have one of three values, a proposition employing n distinct statements is analyzed using a truth table consisting of 3^n rows. However, rather than employ truth tables, we can employ a commuting diagram methodology similar to that demonstrated in Section 1.3. In the Kleene system, valuations of T, subsequent to the operations of negation, conjunction, disjunction, and implication, are given by

$$T\,(\sim a) = 1 - T(a)$$

$$T(a \vee b) = \max(T(a),\ T(b))$$

$$T(a \wedge b) = \min(T(a),\ T(b))$$

and

$$T(\,a \rightarrow b) = \max(1 - T(a),\ T(b))$$

respectively.

TABLE 2.3   KLEENES THREE-VALUED LOGIC SYSTEM

A	~A
1	0
0	1
1/2	1/2

A	B	$A \wedge B$	$A \vee B$	$A \rightarrow B$	$A \leftrightarrow B$
1	1	1	1	1	1
1	0	0	1	0	0
1	1/2	1/2	1	1/2	1/2
0	1	0	1	1	0
0	0	0	0	1	1
0	1/2	0	1/2	1	1/2
1/2	1	1/2	1	1	1/2
1/2	0	0	1/2	1/2	1/2
1/2	1/2	1/2	1/2	1/2	1/2

Example 2.22

Consider the statements a, b, and c given by

"ROBY can see the block."

"ROBY contains an X2 computer control system."

and

"ROBY will pick up the block."

(see Figure 2.20). The truth table corresponding to the proposition

$$(a \wedge b) \rightarrow c$$

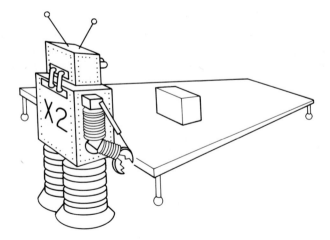

Figure 2.20   ROBY and block

is given in Table 2.4.   For instance, if $T(a) = 1$, $T(b) = 1/2$, and $T(c) = 0$, then, reading from the sixth row of the table,

$$T((a \wedge b) \rightarrow c) = 1/2$$

which means that the proposition is undecided given the input conditions.   The same result can be obtained by using the truth function methodology.   Proceeding thusly,

$$T(a \wedge b) = \min(T(a), T(b)) = \min(1, 1/2) = 1/2$$

and hence

$$T((a \wedge b) \rightarrow c) = \max(1 - T(a \wedge b), T(c))$$
$$= \max(1/2, 0) = 1/2$$

Kleene's three-valued logic system is an extension of the conventional propositional calculus: if undecided values are never used, then the usual two-valued system results.

TABLE 2.4   TRUTH TABLE FOR EXAMPLE 2.22

a	b	c	$a \wedge b$	$(a \wedge b) \rightarrow c$
1	1	1	1	1
1	1	1/2	1	1/2
1	1	0	1	0
1	1/2	1	1/2	1
1	1/2	1/2	1/2	1/2
1	1/2	0	1/2	1/2
1	0	1	0	1
1	0	1/2	0	1
1	0	0	0	1
1/2	1	1	1/2	1
1/2	1	1/2	1/2	1/2
1/2	1	0	1/2	1/2
1/2	1/2	1	1/2	1
1/2	1/2	1/2	1/2	1/2
1/2	1/2	0	1/2	1/2
1/2	0	1	0	1
1/2	0	1/2	0	1
1/2	0	0	0	1
0	1	1	0	1
0	1	1/2	0	1
0	1	0	0	1
0	1/2	1	0	1
0	1/2	1/2	0	1
0	1/2	0	0	1
0	0	1	0	1
0	0	1/2	0	1
0	1	0	0	1

We next discuss the fuzzy logic system, which is to the two-valued propositional calculus as fuzzy set theory is to the usual two-valued set theory. Because of the similarity of both motivation and interpretation, we will not go through a detailed discussion of the meaning of the predicates in fuzzy logic as we did in Section 2.2 for fuzzy set theory; indeed, the semantic interpretation is the same.

The fuzzy logic system employs statements as in the propositional calculus and the Kleene three-valued logic system. Connectives $\sim$, $\wedge$, and $\vee$, similar to those utilized in the other systems, are also employed. However, in the fuzzy system, the truth function T maps statements into real values in the lattice valuation space $[0, 1]$. When $T(a) = 0$, a is said to be *false*; when $T(a) = 1$, a is said to be *true*; otherwise, a is said to be *neither true nor false*, with values of $T(a)$ close to 1 corresponding to a being close to being true and values of $T(a)$ close to 0 corresponding to a being close to being false.

As in the Kleene system, the statements $\sim a$, $a \wedge b$, and $a \vee b$ possess truth values that are defined in accordance with the negation, minimum, and maximum rules discussed in Section 1.3 for the propositional calculus. In other words, the commuting diagrams of that section are used once again; however, in the fuzzy setting, the operations apply to truth values that are in the valuation space $[0, 1]$. Specifically, for the negation $\sim a$ (*not a*),

$$T(\sim a) = 1 - T(a)$$

for the conjunction $a \wedge b$ (*a and b*).

$$T(a \wedge b) = \min(T(a), T(b))$$

and for the disjunction $a \vee b$ (*a or b*),

$$T(a \vee b) = \max(T(a), T(b))$$

At first glance, we might think that truth tables utilizing an uncountable number of situations are required to analyze propositions involving n distinct statements; however, such is not the case. In fact, we require truth tables with only $2^n n!$ rows. Although this can be shown using an induction argument, we will content ourselves with an intuitive explanation.

When $n = 1$, a single statement a is involved, and either

$$T(a) \leq T(\sim a)$$

or

$$T(\sim a) \leq T(a)$$

There is no other possibility. Thus, with a single statement, there exist $2^1 1! = 2$ possibilities.

For the case of two statements, say a and b, there are $2^2 2! = 8$ possibilities. If

$$T(a) \leq T(b)$$

then

$$-T(b) \leq -T(a)$$

which implies that

$$1 - T(b) \leq 1 - T(a)$$

and so

$$T(\sim b) \leq T(\sim a)$$

Thus, assuming $T(a) \leq T(b)$, four possibilities exist:

$$T(a) \leq T(b) \leq T(\sim b) \leq T(\sim a)$$

$$T(a) \leq T(\sim b) \leq T(b) \leq T(\sim a)$$

$$T(\sim b) \leq T(a) \leq T(\sim a) \leq T(b)$$

and

$$T(\sim b) \leq T(\sim a) \leq T(a) \leq T(b)$$

These four cases can be rewritten using the suggestive notation

$$a \mid b \mid \sim b \mid \sim a$$

$$a \mid \sim b \mid b \mid \sim a$$

$$\sim b \mid a \mid \sim a \mid b$$

and

$$\sim b \mid \sim a \mid a \mid b$$

respectively.   In this notation, the ordering from left to right represents increasing truth values.   Continuing the case of two input statements, four other possibilities arise:

$$\sim a \mid b \mid \sim b \mid a$$

$$b \mid \sim a \mid a \mid \sim b$$

$$\sim a \mid \sim b \mid b \mid a$$

$$b \mid a \mid \sim a \mid \sim b$$

Thus, there are eight rows in the truth table, one for each of the preceding possibilities, and in each row there appears each of the four quantities a, $\sim a$, b, and $\sim b$.   As a result, there are 4^8 distinct propositions involving two variables.

As an illustration of the use of truth tables for the fuzzy logic system, consider the (fuzzy) De Morgan laws, which say that

$$T(a \wedge b) = T(\sim(\sim a \vee \sim b))$$

TABLE 2.5   TRUTH TABLE FOR FUZZY LOGIC

	1	2	3
	$a \vee b$	$\sim a \wedge \sim b$	$\sim (\sim a \wedge \sim b)$
$ab \sim b \sim a$	b	$\sim b$	b
$\sim b \sim aab$	b	$\sim b$	b
→ $\sim ab \sim ba$	a	$\sim a$	a
$\sim ba \sim ab$	b	$\sim b$	b
$a \sim bb \sim a$	b	$\sim b$	b
$b \sim aa \sim b$	a	$\sim a$	a
$\sim a \sim bba$	a	$\sim a$	a
$ba \sim a \sim b$	a	$\sim a$	a

and

$$T(a \vee b) = T(\sim(\sim a \wedge \sim b))$$

The validity of the second law is established by the truth table in Table 2.5, since columns 1 and 3 are identical. As an illustration of how the table is derived, consider the third row. According to column 1 of that row,

$$T(a \vee b) = T(a)$$

which follows from the third row condition

$$T(\sim a) \le T(b) \le T(\sim b) \le T(a)$$

since, under this condition,

$$T(a \vee b) = \max(T(a), T(b)) = T(a)$$

Similarly, under the third row condition, the $\sim a$ entry in column 2 follows from

$$T(\sim a \wedge \sim b) = \min(T(\sim a), T(\sim b)) = T(\sim a)$$

Finally, the column 3 entry a follows from

$$T(\sim(\sim a \wedge \sim b)) = 1 - T(\sim a \wedge \sim b)$$
$$= 1 - T(\sim a)$$
$$= 1 - (1 - T(a))$$
$$= T(a)$$

In sum,

$$T(a \vee b) = T(\sim(\sim a \wedge \sim b))$$

The other De Morgan law can be validated in like manner; however, rather than employ a truth table, the definitions can be directly applied as in Example 1.8. In fact, that example proves the theorem in the fuzzy case, since the method that was used for the valuation space {0, 1} applies directly to the valuation space [0, 1].

As a further illustration of the use of direct definitions, rather than the truth-table approach, for proving identities, consider the absorption laws

$$T(a \lor (b \land a)) = T(a)$$

and

$$T(a \land (b \lor a)) = T(a)$$

Letting $x = T(a)$ and $y = T(b)$, the first law follows from

$$T(a \lor (b \land a)) = \max[T(a), \min(T(b), T(a))]$$

$$= \max\left[x, \frac{(x + y) - |x - y|}{2}\right]$$

$$= \frac{x + \dfrac{x + y - |x - y|}{2} + \left|x - \dfrac{x + y - |x - y|}{2}\right|}{2}$$

$$= \frac{3x + y - |x - y| + |x - y + |x - y||}{4} = x$$

In the above, the outer absolute value signs in

$$|x - y + |x - y||$$

are not needed since the inside expression is nonnegative.

The foregoing methodology is often easier to apply than the truth-table approach. Indeed, when three distinct statements are employed, 48 rows in a truth table are required, and 6^{48} distinct propositions can arise. In general, the number of distinct propositions using n distinct statements is $(2n)^{(n!2^n)}$.

For the incorporation of the implication connective into fuzzy logic, several varying approaches have been taken, each leading to a different extended fuzzy logic system.

Perhaps the most straightforward method for defining the truth value of $a \to b$ is to imitate both the propositional calculus and the Kleene three-valued system by letting

$$T(a \to b) = \max(1 - T(a), T(b))$$

When $T(a)$ and $T(b)$ lie in {0, 1}, the usual implication truth table results, and thus the new definition is consistent.

From a modeling point of view, it might be felt that when

$$T(a) > T(b) = 0$$

$T(a \to b)$ should equal 0. To satisfy this modeling constraint, the truth value of the implication is sometimes defined by

$$T(a \rightarrow b) = \begin{cases} T(b), & \text{if } T(a) > T(b) \\ 1, & \text{otherwise} \end{cases}$$

This definition, too, is consistent with the propositional calculus. However, the operation is not continuous: a small change in the truth value of a or b can cause a great change in $T(a \rightarrow b)$. For instance, if $T(a) = 0.1$ and $T(b) = 0$, then $T(a \rightarrow b) = 0$; however, if $T(a) = 0$ and $T(b) = 0$, then $T(a \rightarrow b) = 1$.

To conclude the section, we will briefly consider the situation where the valuation space is not necessarily a totally ordered lattice. Proceeding in exactly the same manner as before, if X is a universal set and L is a lattice with units, a *lattice subset A of X* (also called an L *subset*) is a collection of pairs

$$A = \{x \mid u_A(x)\}$$

where $u_A(x) \in L$ for any $x \in X$.

Example 2.23

     Let

$$X = \{u, v, w, x, y, z\}$$

and let L be the lattice given by the following diagram:

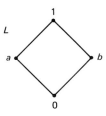

An example of an L subset is

$$A = \{u/a, v/b, x/1, y/1\}$$

Both x and y belong to A with full certainty; however, u and v belong to A with certainties a and b, respectively. Note that the lattice values a and b are not comparable; nevertheless, both u and v belong to A "more" than z and "less" than x.

2.7 STRINGS

A string is a finite sequence of symbols used to convey information between processing systems, either human or machine. For instance, in Figure 2.21, strings are transmitted, encoded, manipulated, decoded, transformed, interpreted, and processed by various entities. Generally, a computer program is nothing more than a string of characters that is converted (encoded) into a new string representing

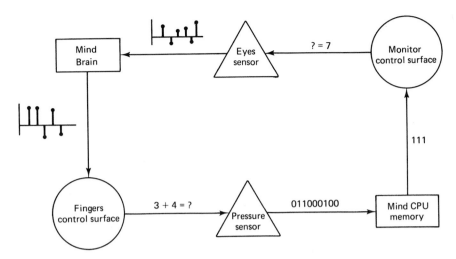

Figure 2.21   Manipulations involving strings

a desired result, which is itself then decoded into a string of characters recognizable by a human, whose brain might then issue signals that result in the production of another string to initiate a repetition of the entire process.

There exists a number of standard methods for encoding, including ASCII (American Standard Code for Information Interchange), BCD (Binary Coded Decimal), EBCDIC (Extended Binary Coded Decimal Interchange Code), and Hollerith.   Each of these codes employs strings of fixed length.   Others, such as the Shannan–Fano and Huffman encoding schemes, produce optimal codes in the maximum entropy sense (see Sections 6.5 and 7.6).   In these, characters that are used with greatest frequency are encoded with fewest bits.

Proceeding formally to the definition of a string, we consider a finite set A, called an *alphabet*, with elements called *letters*.   A *word*, or *string*, of symbols over the alphabet A is a finite sequence of letters, usually written as a concatenation. Thus, if $a_1, a_2, \ldots, a_n$ are elements of A, a word w of length n will be written

$$w = a_1 a_2 \cdots a_n$$

instead of

$$w = (a_1, a_2, \ldots, a_n)$$

Letting A^* denote the set of all strings, a binary *concatenation* operation is defined on A^* as follows: for two strings

$$w = a_1 a_2 \cdots a_n$$

and

$$s = b_1 b_2 \cdots b_m$$

a new string t is formed as

$$t = ws = a_1 a_2 \cdots a_n b_1 b_2 \cdots b_m$$

A possibly different string in A^* is

$$r = sw = b_1 b_2 \cdots b_m a_1 a_2 \cdots a_n$$

Since t need not equal r, the commutative law need not hold. Nevertheless, the associative law does hold:

$$r(st) = (rs)t = rst$$

The empty word, denoted ε, is the neutral element for concatenation: for any word w,

$$\varepsilon w = w \varepsilon = w$$

Example 2.24

If $A = \{y, a, c, t\}$, then A^* is the set of all strings formed from letters of A. For instance, *acat* is a string of length 4, and *aayyata* is a string of length 7.

Sometimes strings that are nonintelligible to humans (or computers) can be made intelligible with only slight modification.

Example 2.25

Consider the string of symbols in the citardauq formula used in finding the roots of a quadratic equation (see Example 2.8). If written as

$$x = 2 \cdot c / -b + \sqrt{\ } b \cdot b - 4 \cdot a \cdot c$$

the string is completely meaningless because it is ambiguous; however, modified by a judicious placement of parentheses, it becomes intelligible:

$$x' = (2 \cdot c)/(-b + \sqrt{\ } (b \cdot b - 4 \cdot a \cdot c))$$

EXERCISES FOR CHAPTER 2

2.1. Let $X = \{a, b, c, d\}$ and consider the subsets A, B, and C of X, where $A = \{a, b, c\}$, $B = \{b, c, d\}$, and $C = \{a, c\}$. Using conventional set operations, find:
   a) $A \cup B - (A \triangle B)$
   b) $(A \triangle B) \triangle (A \cap B)$
   c) $A \triangle (A \cap B)$
   d) $A \cap (B \triangle C)$

2.2. Show, using conventional set operations, that if A, B, and C are arbitrary subsets of any set X, then
   a) $(A \cup B) - (A \triangle B) = A \cap B$
   b) $(A \triangle B) \cup (A \cap B) = A \cup B$
   c) $A \triangle (A \cap B) = A - B$

d) $A \cap (B \triangle C) = (A \cap B) \triangle (A \cap C)$

Note that to show the conventional set-theoretic equality, $A = B$, one must show that $x \in A$ if and only if $x \in B$.

2.3. Using conventional set operations, show the following properties hold in the class 2^X of all subsets of a given nonempty set X ($A, B, C \in 2^X$):

a) $A \triangle B \in 2^X$

b) $A \triangle (B \triangle C) = (A \triangle B) \triangle C$

c) $\emptyset \triangle A = A \triangle \emptyset = A$, and $\emptyset$ is the only set in 2^X having this property for arbitrary A.

d) $A \triangle A^c = A^c \triangle A = \emptyset$, and for given A, A^c is the only set in X having this property.

e) $A \triangle B = B \triangle A$

f) $A \cap B \in 2^X$.

g) $(A \cap B) \cap C = A \cap (B \cap C)$

h) $A \cap (B \triangle C) = (A \cap B) \triangle (A \cap C)$ and $(B \triangle C) \cap A = (B \cap A) \triangle (C \cap A)$

i) $X \cap A = A \cap X = A$, and X is the only set in 2^X having this property for arbitrary A.

j) $A \cap B = B \cap A$

The fact that a through j hold shows that the set of all subsets of the given set X forms a commutative ring with identity; that is, the structure $(2^X, \triangle, {}^c, \emptyset, \cap, X)$ is a commutative ring of sets with identity.

2.4. In Exercise 2.3 above, which identities do not hold when fuzzy set operations are employed?

2.5. Illustrate the directed graph specified by

$$P = \{1, 2, 3\}$$
$$L = \{x, y, u\}$$
$$f(x) = f(y) = 3$$
$$f(u) = 2$$
$$b(x) = b(y) = 1$$
$$b(u) = 2$$

2.6. Consider the poset L illustrated in Figure 2.7. If $S = \{2, 6, 4\}$, then find
    a)   all upper bounds for S in L
    b)   all lower bounds for S in L
    c)   the LUB for S in L
    d)   the GLB for S in L

2.7. Give an example of a totally ordered set that is also a complemented lattice.

2.8. Give an example of a totally ordered set that is bounded and is not a complemented lattice.

2.9. Show that in a Boolean algebra $(L, \vee, \wedge, ', 0, 1)$, if the term $a \to b$ is defined as $a' \vee b$, then the structure $(L, \vee, \wedge, \to, 0, 1)$ is a Heyting algebra.

2.10. Employ Karnaugh maps to reduce the expressions

$$R = r'suv + rsuv' + rs'u'v' + rs'u'v + rs'uv + rs'uv'$$

$$S = r's'u'v + r'su'v + r'suv + rsu'v$$

$$U = rsuv' + rs'u'v' + rs'u'v + rs'uv + rs'uv'$$

to

$$R = r'suv + rsuv' + rs'$$

$$S = r'u'v + r'sv + su'v$$

$$U = rsuv' + rs'$$

respectively.

2.11. Using fuzzy truth tables, show that $\sim(a \wedge b)$ is equivalent to $(\sim a) \vee (\sim b)$.

2.12. Strings over a nonempty set A are more rigorously defined as a set of functions f mapping finite sets of nonnegative integers of the form $Z_n = \{0, 1, 2, \ldots, n - 1\}$ into A. Here, $n = 1, 2, \ldots$, with $n = 0$ reserved for the function that maps the empty set into A, which corresponds to the empty string ε. An operation $\odot$, corresponding to string concatenation, is defined for $f: Z_n \to A$ and $g: Z_m \to A$ by

$$f \odot g: Z_{n+m} \to A$$

where

$$(f \odot g)(k) = \begin{cases} f(k), & \text{for } k = 0, 1, 2, \ldots, n - 1 \\ g(k - n), & \text{for } k = n, n + 1, \ldots, m - 1 \end{cases}$$

Show that $(f \odot g) \odot h = f \odot (g \odot h)$ in this system.

3

PARALLEL
ARCHITECTURES

3.1 CONVENTIONAL COMPUTER SYSTEMS

Most present-day computer systems are classified as *single-instruction, single-data* systems (SISD). These computers have central processor units (CPUs) that process a single instruction at a time and manipulate only a single piece of data at a time. This is in contrast to the machines to be discussed in the ensuing sections, which can process multiple instructions and manipulate several pieces of data concurrently.

An ordinary CPU contains *combinational logic* circuits of the type discussed in Section 1.6. It also possesses some form of memory, often in the form of *sequential circuits*. In contrast to combinational circuits, these are capable of storing, or "remembering," information. Moreover, their present outputs depend on past inputs.

A simple memory element is the *delay*, which is denoted by a block diagram with $1/z$ in the block

The delay circuit has output $g(t) = f(t - 1)$. Information entering the circuit remains stored there for one unit of time, after which it exits and is replaced by a new input, which will itself be stored for a unit of time. This process is repeated sequentially as the program is executed.

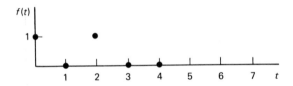

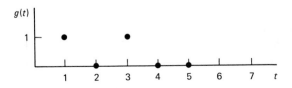

Figure 3.1   Binary input and delayed signal

Example 3.1

Consider the binary input signal $f(t)$ illustrated in Fig. 3.1. The signal is a function of clock pulses and hence possesses a domain that is a subset of Z, the set of integers. In the figure, f has a domain consisting of the five clock pulses in the set $\{0, 1, 2, 3, 4\}$. Moreover, it can be represented as the bound vector (see Section 1.10)

$$f = (1 \quad 0 \quad 1 \quad 0 \quad 0 \quad *)_0$$

where the subscript 0 denotes the absolute location of the first tuple. Recall that the star $(*)$ is used to indicate that f is not defined at $t = 5$, and that it is understood that stars appear at each point where f is undefined. If f is input into the delay element $1/z$, then the output is the function

$$g = (* \quad 1 \quad 0 \quad 1 \quad 0 \quad 0)_0$$

$$= (1 \quad 0 \quad 1 \quad 0 \quad 0)_1$$

illustrated in Figure 3.1.

Most machines are binary: the input and output strings consist of two-valued elements, which, as is customary, we will denote by 0's and 1's. For the computer to process commands given by a human, as in the open-loop control system discussed in the Introduction, it must encode these commands into strings of zeros and ones. The input strings of zeros and ones are processed by being converted to new strings of zeros and ones. The conversion is performed utilizing *not*, *and*, and *or* gates in conjunction with delay elements and can be accomplished in either software or hardware. The circuits are configured so as to render a faithful implementation of the desired behavior.

To illustrate the manner in which desired algorithmic manipulation can be carried out in hardware, we will design a simple computer to solve a specific word-recognition problem. The design will be highly idealized and ignore such things as circuitry to control the clock pulses. Nevertheless, the essence of the interplay between combinational and sequential elements will be revealed.

Consider a simple word-recognition system, similar to a spelling checker, where, for convenience, there are only four letters: a, c, t, and y. Strings consisting of these letters are input to the computer by a human working at a keyboard, and if the word *cat* appears anywhere in the string, the computer will recognize it. The recognition procedure works in the following manner. For each input letter, there will appear an output letter on the monitor, either a y or a t. The output will be a y, no matter what the input, until an input t concludes the first spelling of the word *cat*. For this letter t and all subsequent input letters, the output will be a t. Insofar as the human observer is concerned, the monitor will output a string of successive y's, which possibly will change to a string of t's (should the word *cat* eventually appear). The place where a t first occurs on the monitor denotes the t in the first spelling of the word *cat*. For instance, if the input string is

cyattaccataytt

then the output string will be

yyyyyyyyyyttttt

the tenth symbol appearing on the monitor denoting the first spelling (and in this case, the only spelling) of *cat*.

The essential details of a computer that performs the foregoing recognition task are illustrated in Fig. 3.2. No timing, power, or input–output devices are included. The following chart gives the input coding (i.e., the 0–1 string) corresponding to each letter the human inputs from the keyboard.

Input	Encoded input (*uv* Boolean expressions)
y	0 0
c	0 1
a	1 1
t	1 0

The next chart gives the output encoding, the 0 or 1 that results from the computer processing being output to the monitor as either a y or a t.

Encoded output (*U* Boolean variable)	Output
0	y
1	t

Note that, in the schema of Figure 3.2, we will initialize the variable string *rs* to 00.

The recognition process is much like opening a safe: if the proper sequence of numbers is input, then the safe pops open and remains open. Pursuant to the

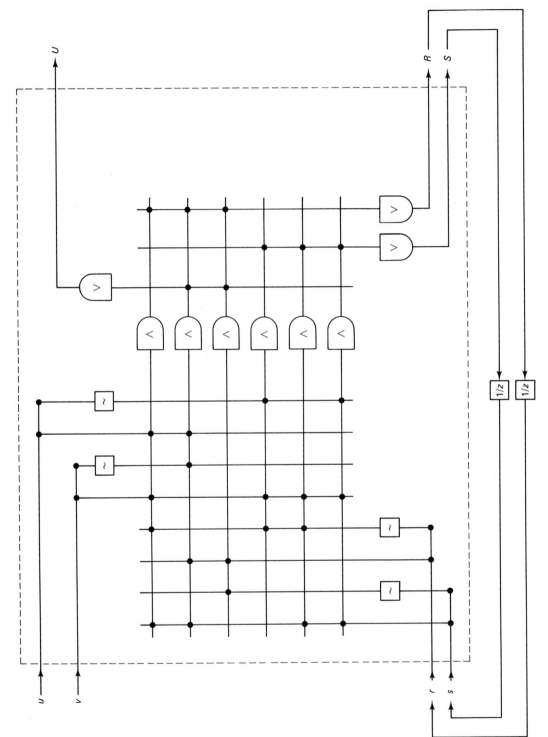

Figure 3.2 Sequential circuit for recognition system

TABLE 3.1   TRACE OF STATE VARIABLES

Clock pulse	1	2	3	4	5
Input	y	c	a	t	t
Encoded input uv	0 0	0 1	1 1	1 0	1 0
Encoded old state rs	0 0	0 0	0 1	1 1	1 0
Encoded new state RS	0 0	0 1	1 1	1 0	1 0
Encoded output U	0	0	0	1	1
Output	y	y	y	t	t

analogy, a *y* appearing on the monitor indicates that the safe is closed, whereas a *t* indicates it is open.

Now, imagine a human involved in an open-loop control structure sitting at a keyboard with only four keys: *y*, *c*, *a*, and *t*. The human starts the computer or presses a reset button, thus making the internal mechanism within the machine go to the initial state, which, in the present application, corresponds to *rs* = 00.   The human enters a string of letters by touching the appropriate keys one at a time. For instance, the string might be

$$ycatt$$

Unknown to the human, and perhaps of no concern, is that the string is encoded. Eventually, a 0–1 output string will be decoded, the encode–decode pair enabling the computer and the human to communicate.

The action of the computer upon entry of the string *ycatt* is summarized in Table 3.1.   In the table, note that *r* and *s* are delayed versions of *R* and *S*, respectively:

$$r(t) = R(t - 1)$$

and

$$s(t) = S(t - 1)$$

As a result, *r* and *s* are called the *encoded old state variables*, and *R* and *S* are called the *encoded new state variables*.   Encoded values for *R*, *S*, and *U* in Table 3.1 are found by utilizing the *and*, *or*, and *not* gates in Figure 3.2.   The encoded output string is finally decoded to provide the desired output appearing on the monitor:

$$yyytt$$

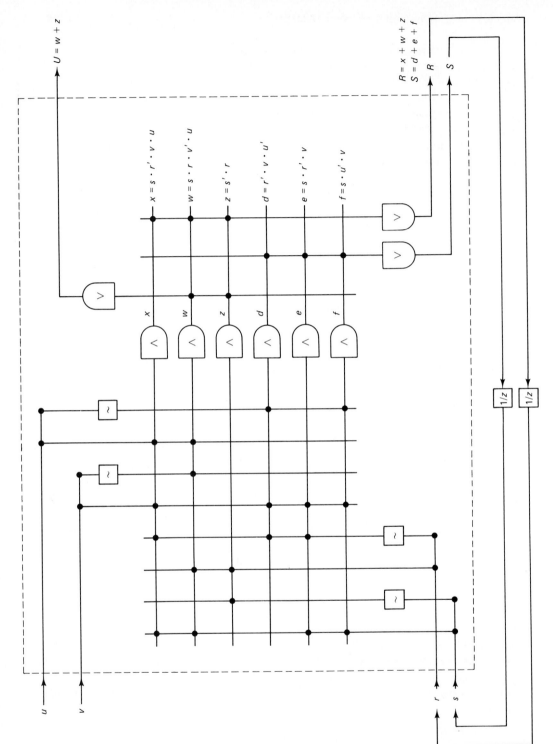

Figure 3.3 Sequential circuit with intermediate variables

We will now give a detailed walk-through to illustrate how the computer performs the recognition task given the input *ycatt*. We will refer to Fig. 3.3, in which the intermediate variables x, w, z, d, e, and f supplement the circuitry of Figure 3.2, and in which the symbols $+$, $\cdot$, and $'$ are used to denote *or*, *and*, and *not*, respectively. Recall that initially the Boolean expressions r and s are both set to 0 and that the human input y is encoded to be $u = 0$ and $v = 0$.

On the first clock pulse, the initial values are input to give the intermediate variables the following values:

$$x = 0 \cdot 1 \cdot 0 \cdot 0 = 0$$

$$w = 0 \cdot 0 \cdot 1 \cdot 0 = 0$$

$$z = 1 \cdot 0 = 0$$

$$d = 1 \cdot 0 \cdot 1 = 0$$

$$e = 0 \cdot 1 \cdot 0 = 0$$

$$f = 0 \cdot 1 \cdot 0 = 0$$

Therefore, since $U = w + z$, $R = x + w + z$, and $S = d + e + f$,

$$U = 0 + 0 = 0$$

$$R = 0 + 0 + 0 = 0$$

$$S = 0 + 0 + 0 = 0$$

The output variable $U = 0$ is decoded and the human sees a y as the output. The values R and S go into memories and remain there until the second clock pulse, at which time they will come out and become the values of r and s, respectively. The action at the first clock pulse is summarized in the first column of Table 3.1.

The second clock pulse utilizes the values r and s (both 0) in the delay elements and the encoded value of c, which is $u = 0$ and $v = 1$. Voltages corresponding to the values $r = 0$, $s = 0$, $u = 0$, and $v = 1$ travel through the *not*, *and*, and *or* gates and thereby provide values for the intermediate variables, which are given by

$$x = 0 \cdot 1 \cdot 1 \cdot 0 = 0$$

$$w = 0 \cdot 0 \cdot 0 \cdot 0 = 0$$

$$z = 1 \cdot 0 = 0$$

$$d = 1 \cdot 1 \cdot 1 = 1$$

$$e = 0 \cdot 1 \cdot 1 = 0$$

$$f = 0 \cdot 1 \cdot 1 = 0$$

The resulting outputs are

$$U = 0 + 0 = 0$$

$$R = 0 + 0 + 0 = 0$$

$$S = 1 + 0 + 0 = 1$$

As before, the computer decodes the output U and again y appears on the monitor. Moreover, the values $R = 0$ and $S = 1$ enter their respective memories; they will pop out on the next clock pulse. The second column of Table 3.1 describes the condition of the variables following the second clock pulse.

The third clock pulse involves the values $s = 1$, $r = 0$, $v = 1$, and $u = 1$, which, according to Figure 3.3, yield the intermediate values $x = 1$, $w = 0$, $z = 0$, $d = 0$, $e = 1$, and $f = 0$ and the output values $U = 0$, $R = 1$, and $S = 1$. The output $U = 0$ is decoded and y appears on the screen. The third column of Table 3.1 summarizes these results.

At the completion of the fourth clock pulse, $U = 1$, and a t appears on the monitor. The human observer then knows that the word *cat* has been completed and that the letters c, a, and t are the second, third, and fourth entries, respectively, in the original input string. Although we will not go through the details of the intermediate variable values in this stage, or in the fifth and last, a complete synopsis is provided in Table 3.1.

While the preceding illustration was based on a very simple architecture, in fact, SISD computers have CPUs consisting of elements no more advanced than those illustrated in Figure 3.2. However, these compuuters usually possess storage units, called *memories*, that consist of a large number of addressable cells, each containing a piece of data or an instruction. It is the conventional use of memory elements that we now wish to address.

Generally, the CPU of an SISD computer interfaces with memory by reading information from and writing information to it. *Coordinate address* storage is frequently employed for this purpose. Here, the CPU reads information from a specific cell in memory by specifying the address (i.e., location or name) of the cell, along with the instruction READ. Conversely, the CPU can change the contents of a cell, or write into a specific cell, by specifying the address of the cell, together with the instruction WRITE and the information to be written in. This information is encoded using a string of zeros and ones, as, too, is the address and the commands READ and WRITE.

The basic building block of most memory cells is the delay element; however, to be able to store information indefinitely, some sort of feedback is required. A straightforward device for accomplishing indefinite storage is the *flip-flop*, of which a popular type is the *set–reset*, or *RS*, flip-flop (the letters R and S having no relation to the Boolean variables employed in Figure 3.3). The R stands for *reset* (storing 0 in memory) and the S for *set* (storing 1 in memory). Figure 3.4 shows the block diagram of an *RS* flip-flop, where, even though a clock is required, no timing circuitry is explicitly depicted. Two inputs, labeled R and S, appear in the

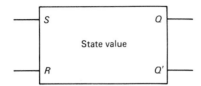

Figure 3.4   RS flip-flop

RS flip-flop.   Moreover, it is assumed that 0 or 1 is already stored in the flip-flop, that value being called the *old state value*.   During the pulse of the clock, 0 or 1 appears on each of the R and S input lines, with the combination of $R = 1$ and $S = 1$ being forbidden.   At that time, the old state value appears on the output line Q, and the complement of this value simultaneously appears on the output line Q'.   The new value stored in the flip-flop, called the *new state value*, will be 1 if $R = 0$ and $S = 1$; it will be 0 if $R = 1$ and $S = 0$; it will equal the old state value if both $R = 0$ and $S = 0$.   This is summarized in Table 3.2.

The *RS* flip-flop is utilized in forming coordinate memory, a single cell of which is illustrated in Figure 3.5.   The old value of memory, the old state value, is held in the flip-flop.   The cell functions whenever the address is *enabled*, or called, and the value in memory can only change under the WRITE mode.   Each cell of memory represents 1 bit and forms the fundamental building block for the storage of larger-sized strings: for a word of memory consisting of n bits, n such cells, having a common address and select line, and individual input and output lines, are employed (see Figure 3.6).   Consequently, the whole word of memory can be addressed as an entry and read into the CPU, or the CPU can write to the address a whole word of memory.   Each word of memory has a unique address, and only by knowing and utilizing this address can information be transferred to and from memory by the CPU.   Table 3.3 summarizes the workings of the 1-bit memory cell.   It is assumed that the address is enabled, for otherwise the device does not operate.   Most importantly, in the READ mode, the output equals the old state value; in the WRITE mode, the new state value equals the input value.   Moreover, in the READ mode, the new state value equals the old state value, a characteristic of more modern *read-out protect* integrated-circuit memories.

TABLE 3.2   STATE VALUES FOR RS FLIP-FLOP

Inputs		Old	Outputs		New
S	R	State	Q	Q'	State
0	0	0	0	1	0
0	0	1	1	0	1
0	1	0	0	1	0
0	1	1	1	0	0
1	0	0	0	1	1
1	0	1	1	0	1

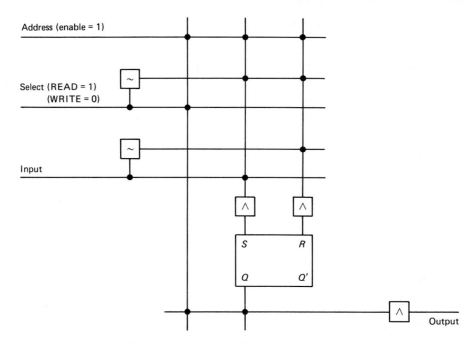

Figure 3.5 Circuitry for a bit of coordinate memory

In most SISD machines, there is synchronized communication between the CPU and memory. Instructions to be executed by the computer are stored in memory. The CPU specifies addresses of memory that contain instructions needed in the execution of data. The process of obtaining the instruction from memory is often called *fetching the instruction*, or just *fetching*. For a sequence of instructions $i_1, i_2, \ldots, i_n$ to be carried out in the proper order, the computer must first fetch the corresponding instructions and then execute each in turn. This action can be symbolized by the sequence.

$$f_1, e_1, f_2, e_2, \ldots, f_n, e_n$$

where f_j denotes the fetching of instruction i_j and e_j denotes the execution of

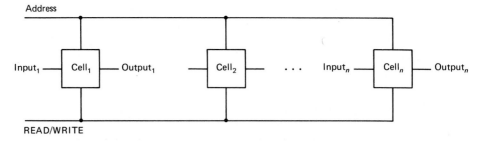

Figure 3.6 Word of coordinate memory

TABLE 3.3 WORKINGS OF ONE-BIT MEMORY CELL

	Select	Input	Old state	Output	New state
READ	1	1	1	1	1
	1	1	0	0	0
	1	0	1	1	1
	1	0	0	0	0
WRITE	0	1	1	0	1
	0	1	0	0	1
	0	0	1	0	0
	0	0	0	0	0

instruction i_j. This fetch–execute sequence demonstrates the sequential behavior of most SISD machines: fetch j occurs after the execution of instruction i_{j-1}.

In some computers, the fetch circuitry and the execution circuitry are disjoint from one another, thereby allowing the fetching of the jth instruction to occur during the same time that the $(j - 1)$th instruction is being executed. This is a type of concurrency called *pipelining*. Intuitively, assuming that each fetch and each execution take a single clock pulse, then, with pipelining, instead of taking $2n$ clock pulses to perform the sequence of n instructions, it takes only $n + 1$ clock pulses. Figure 3.7 illustrates the concurrency of pipelining. Other types of parallel machines will be discussed in the ensuing sections.

Clock pulse	1	2	3	4		n	$n + 1$
Execution circuitry		e_1	e_2	e_3	. . .	e_{n-1}	e_n
Fetch mechanism	f_1	f_2	f_3	f_4	. . .	f_n	

Figure 3.7 Pipelining concurrency

3.2 MULTIPLE-INSTRUCTION, SINGLE-DATA MACHINES

An important ingredient in building intelligent machines is the incorporation of as much concurrency as is practically feasible, for concurrency enhances processing speed in both the learning and response modes. Generally, any machine that can process two or more instructions simultaneously is called a *multiple-instruction, single-data machine* (*MISD machine*). The pipelining methodology introduced at the end of the preceding section results in a rudimentary MISD machine, since two instructions are processed concurrently.

More sophisticated pipeline computers exist that allow several instructions to be processed simultaneously, not just a concurrent fetch and execution. Architecturally, these require disjoint hardware to permit the performance of concurrent operations (see Figure 3.8). Each disjoint processing circuit is called a *pipe*, a *stage*, or a *segment*. Each segment is like a stage in an assembly line, where partial

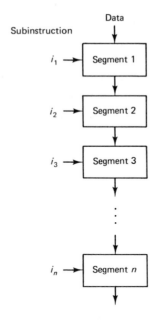

Figure 3.8 Pipelining stages

assembly is being performed concurrently with assembly at other stages. At each stage, different resources are made available and distinctive operations are carried out, the final result being obtained after the item has visited all necessary stages.

Pipelining necessitates the decomposition of *macro* operations into a sequence of more primitive operations. These primitive operations are ultimately employed in a concurrent manner by overlapping steps in the instruction cycle. Complicated instructions may often require the same resource several times (i.e., a stage in the pipeline may need to be visited more than once). As a consequence, pipeline scheduling difficulties may exist, and collisions may occur if inadequate scheduling is performed. Scheduling difficulties, and possible solutions to these difficulties, will be illustrated for a pipeline computer that performs the same fixed operation repeatedly. Such computers are not uncommon; for instance, fast Fourier transform (FFT) processors perform a butterfly-type operation consisting of repeated multiplications and additions.

Suppose an instruction p consists of subinstructions p_i, and the segment s_i is employed in processing this subinstruction. Moreover, assume that a unit of time is needed to process each subinstruction. A pipeline scheduling routine can be found in this case by making a *reservation table*. The top of the table is labeled with the names of the segments that are required to process the instruction. On the left side of the table appear times, in clock pulses, at which segments are required. An X is used in the jth row, s_ith column to denote that the segment s_i is required at time j (see Figure 3.9 for an example of a reservation table). If any segment s_i is needed at time j and also at time $j + 1$, then instructions cannot be initiated or staggered one unit apart in the pipeline process without having collisions occur. More generally, if a segment is required simultaneously at times j and k, $k > j$, then instructions cannot be staggered $k - j$ units apart.

	Segments			
	s_1	s_2	s_3	s_4
Time 1	×			
2		×		
3	×			
4			×	
5				×
6		×		
7		×		

Figure 3.9 Reservation table

The *forbidden list* provides an indication of where collisions can occur. It is useful in determining the *minimum constant latency* (i.e., the smallest positive time that must elapse between initiation of distinct subinstruction sequences), and it consists of a set of nonnegative integers derived from the reservation table. Specifically, if segment s_i is needed at time j and also at time k, $k > j$, then $k - j$ is entered into the forbidden list. The minimum constant latency m is found from the forbidden list: it is the smallest positive integer such that no positive integral multiple of it occurs in the list. Thus, $m \geq 1$ and, for any integer $k \geq 1$, mk is not an element of the forbidden list.

	s_1	s_2	s_3	s_4
1	a			
2		a		
3	a			
4	b		a	
5		b		a
6	b	a		
7	c	_a_	b	
8		c		b
9	c	b		
10	d	_b_	c	
11		d		c
12	d	c		
13	e	_c_	d	
14		e		d
15	e	d		
16	f	_d_	e	
17		f		e
18	f	e		
19	g	_e_	f	
20		g		f
		.		
		.		
		.		

Figure 3.10 Execution trace for pipeline processor

Example 3.2

Consider a pipeline processor that is to execute instruction p repeatedly, and assume that it takes 7 clock pulses to execute p. Moreover, assume that instruction p consists of subinstructions requiring segments s_1, s_2, s_3, and s_4, as specified in the reservation table of Figure 3.9. The forbidden list for this processor is

$$F = \{1, 2, 4, 5\}$$

and the corresponding minimum constant latency is $m = 3$. Therefore, instead of initiating instruction processing 7 clock pulses apart (as in an SISD computer), instructions can be repeated only 3 clock pulses apart, thereby giving a savings of over 50%. A time trace for the first 20 clock cycles is given in Figure 3.10, where consecutive use of instruction p is denoted by the letters a, b, c, d, and so on, and underlined letters indicate an end to the execution of the instruction. By time 19, five instructions have already been completely executed. Note that at some times three subinstructions are being processed simultaneously.

3.3 CONTENT-ADDRESSABLE MACHINES AND OTHER SIMD PROCESSORS

Another method for incorporating concurrency into computers is to enable numerous pieces of data to be manipulated by a single instruction. *Single-instruction, multiple-data (SIMD)* types of computers possess this capability. A specific type of such a machine is a *vector* or *array* processor. Such a machine is useful in tasks where the same sequence of instructions is applied repeatedly to varying data, as is the case in image recognition and computer vision.

Images are often represented by partial functions from $Z \times Z$ into R, the set of real numbers, with the real values indicative of the gray levels (see Section 4.8). When domains of these functions are large, it becomes prohibitive to utilize SISD-type machines for processing; instead, array processors are often employed.

Example 3.3

Consider the images f and g, both with domains

$$A = \{(0, 0), (0, 1), (1, 0), (1, 1)\}$$

and with gray values determined by the respective formulas

$$f(p, q) = p^2 + q^2$$

and

$$g(p, q) = 2pq + 1$$

If the addition of f and g, denoted by $\text{ADD}(f, g)$, is defined pointwise by

$$[\text{ADD}(f, g)](p, q) = f(p, q) + g(p, q)$$

then the output is defined on A and is given by

$$[\text{ADD}(f, g)](p, q) = (p + q)^2 + 1$$

In an array processor the four pointwise additions, one for each (p, q) in A, are done in parallel. The process is illustrated in Figure 3.11, where a circle has been drawn around the gray level at the origin. The single instruction, in this case ADD, causes four regular arithmetic additions to occur in parallel:

$$\begin{array}{cccc} 0 & 1 & 1 & 2 \\ \underline{+1} & \underline{+1} & \underline{+1} & \underline{+3} \\ 1 & 2 & 2 & 5 \end{array}$$

To accomplish such parallelism, array processors are built with replicated arithmetic-logic units (ALUs).

Another computer design of SIMD type is the *content-addressable processor*. Such a machine contains intelligent memory, known as *associative* or *content-addressable memory*, that is quite different from the coordinate addressable memory discussed in Section 3.1. Content-addressable memory is a storage device with built-in search capability. When presented with data, it can automatically compare that data with data stored in memory and indicate those locations in memory where there is agreement. No addresses are required: information is found by *what* it is and not *where* it is. Moreover, content-addressable processors can write in parallel into all those memory locations where agreement has been determined, and part or all of the agreeing words can be modified. Often, array-processing-type operations can be emulated using content-addressable processors. Not only are content-addressable machines fast, but they are also relatively easy to program.

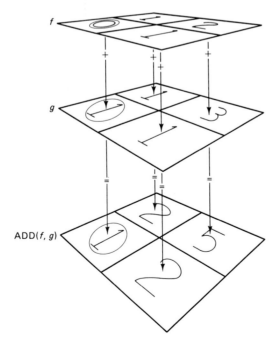

Figure 3.11   Array processing of an image

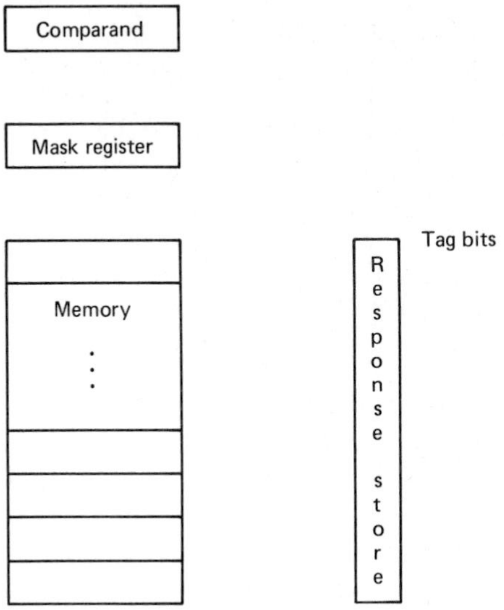

Figure 3.12 Structure of content addressable memory

Finally, the amount of hardware associated with them is only slightly greater than that associated with coordinate addressable memory.

A content-addressable memory can be thought of as a flat file (see Section 1.9); indeed, this type of memory is conducive to carrying out relational database-type operations. Besides the location where actual information is stored, there are basically three other parts to the memory structure. There is the *comparand*, in which information to be retrieved is placed, and a *mask register*, which is used in blocking out certain bits in the comparand that are not to be checked in the retrieval process. When a COMPARE instruction is issued, certain cells in memory are marked, these being the cells containing a word that matches the unmasked bits in the comparand. Memory cells are marked using a tag memory, also known as a *response store*. Those places where a match exists are set equal to 1 in the response store. Figure 3.12 illustrates the structure of content-addressable memory.

Example 3.4

Consider a flat file R consisting of people's names, ages, and grades in two courses:

R

JOE	20	A	B
JOHN	21	C	B
ABE	22	A	C
STEVE	20	A	A
BARB	20	A	B
MARY	22	B	B
MIKE	20	C	A

Suppose the comparand is set to

JOE   20   A   B

and the mask register contains the 4-bit word

1   1   1   1

which means that all fields in each record are compared to the comparand. Then the first record in R is tagged in the response store. If the mask register is changed to

0   1   1   1

then all records in the database consisting of people who are 20 years old and who received grades of A and B are tagged. There are two such records. If records are desired for all persons who received a grade of A in the first course, then the mask register should be set to

0   0   1   0

Other information can be extracted from the database by utilizing different comparands and masks.

A single cell of content-addressable memory is depicted in Figure 3.13. Each cell consists of a single *RS* flip-flop together with some *and* and *or* gates. A word consisting of n bits is comprised of n such cells. Moreover, for each word there is a 1-bit response store. The ith bit cell in every word is connected to the ith bit in the mask register and the ith bit of the comparand. The tag bits are all preset to 1 prior to any search involving memory. If any bit in word j for which the mask bit is 1 does not match the corresponding bit, then the jth bit in the response store is reset (to 0); otherwise, it will remain set at 1, indicating a match for that word (see Table 3.2). Referring to Figure 3.13, there will be a 1 coming out of the *or* gate belonging to the memory cell of the ith bit of the jth word when search enable is 1, mask bit i is 1, and the content of the memory cell differs from the content of the comparand (at bit i).

Compared to a usual coordinate address memory, reading information out of a content-addressable memory and writing into such a memory requires only three additional *and* and/or *or* gates per cell. Information can be read from, or written into, the words for which the response store contains a 1.

As demonstrated in Example 3.4, programming a content-addressable processor often entails judicious, yet simple manipulation of the comparand and mask registers. We will further illustrate this point by describing an algorithm to determine the minimum number in memory, where each word of memory consists of n bits, is binary, and is interpreted as a nonnegative integer. The algorithm involves n concurrent searches of the database, irrespective of the number of entries (records).

Recall that, when using the content-addressable memory illustrated in Figure 3.12, all tag bits should be preset (to 1) prior to the search. Initially, the comparand should be set to all 0s and the mask register should have a 1 in the most significant bit and 0s elsewhere. A search should then be conducted using the content-

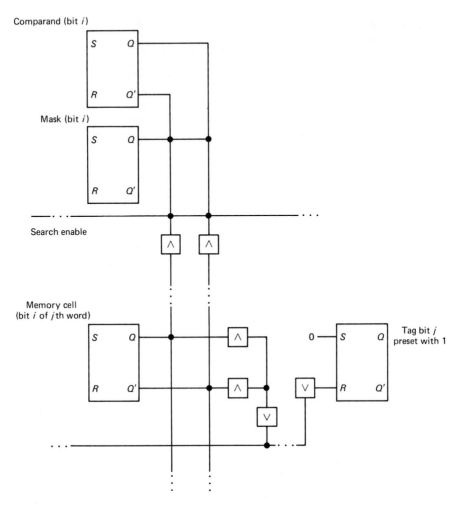

Figure 3.13   Single cell of content addressable memory

addressable processor. If any tag bits remain set, then there is a match and it is therefore known that the most significant bit of the smallest number in the data base is 0. If no match is obtained, then it is known that the most significant bit is 1, and the comparand is changed to reflect this conclusion. In either case, the highest address bit of the smallest number has been found. The next highest address bit is found next: the mask is altered so as to have two 1s in the two highest-ordered bits and a second search is performed. The second-highest bit in the comparand is then adjusted to generate a match. Continuing, the mask is then modified to include three 1s in the three highest-ordered bits, and the process is repeated. In total, the entire process is repeated n times, the desired answer being contained in the comparand at the conclusion of the nth step. We now summarize the algorithm.

START CONDITIONS: Comparand 0 0 0 ... 0
                           Mask   1 0 0 ... 0

RECURSIVE CONDITIONS: Do n times.
If a match is found, then change the leftmost 0 in the mask to 1. Otherwise, change the 0 in the comparand above the rightmost 1 in the mask to a 1, and change the leftmost 0 in the mask to a 1.

STOPPING CONDITIONS: Read out the least integer in the database, it being the contents of the comparand at the conclusion of the nth step in the recursion.

Example 3.5

Assume that words in memory are 4 bits long and are given by

$$1 \quad 1 \quad 1 \quad 1$$
$$0 \quad 0 \quad 1 \quad 0$$
$$1 \quad 1 \quad 0 \quad 0$$
$$1 \quad 0 \quad 0 \quad 0$$
$$0 \quad 1 \quad 0 \quad 1$$

Since $n = 4$, at most four manipulations of the comparand and mask register will be required, these resulting in four searches of the database. The initial search, using

Comparand: 0 0 0 0

Mask: 1 0 0 0

results in a match. Therefore, the mask (only) is modified by changing the leftmost 0 to a 1. The second search uses

Comparand: 0 0 0 0

Mask: 1 1 0 0

which also results in a match. Therefore, the mask is modified by changing the leftmost 0 to a 1. The third search uses

Comparand: 0 0 0 0

Mask: 1 1 1 0

which does not result in a match. Therefore, the comparand is modified by changing the 0 above the rightmost 1 in the mask to a 1, and the leftmost 0 of the mask is changed to a 1. The fourth search uses

Comparand: 0 0 1 0

Mask: 1 1 1 1

which results in a match, and since there are no more 0s in the mask, the algorithm concludes. The answer is given by the contents of the comparand.

Determining a maximum with a content-addressable processor is just as straightforward as determining a minimum. The median, as well as other *order statistics*, can also be found using binary search-type algorithms. Moreover, arithmetic and other more involved operations can also be performed solely with a content-addressable processor. However, such machines attain their maximum benefit when used in conjunction with conventional memories so as to allow the programmer to employ whichever memory scheme best suits his or her purposes.

3.4 DATA-FLOW SYSTEMS

Thus far we have considered parallelism from the perspective of either multiple instruction execution or multiple data computation. In both, control flow is sequentially determined by the original program and, in that sense, such parallel architectures remain within the scope of standard sequential design. In data-flow architecture, however, control flow is determined by the availability of data (operands), rather than by any specific control apparatus within the program. Whereas traditional architectures are sequential, control being maintained by a program counter that causes processing to follow a user-determined path (or flow chart), data-flow design does away with sequentiality and allows the stream of computation to proceed along a program graph without regard to any prerequisite control.

The principle is quite straightforward: if the operands for a specific operation are available and the destination of the result is prepared to receive it, then there is no need to await the processing of other operands elsewhere within the program. Data-flow processors execute their instructions as soon as all required operands have arrived. After the execution (or *firing*) of an instruction, the result is transmitted to all other instructions that require it as an input. Counters are employed for each instruction in order to keep count of the number of operands that have arrived, as well as how many more are needed for instruction execution. There being no overall program counter to synchronize instruction execution, instructions are executed in an *asynchronous* manner. One consequence of the flow-oriented design is that data-flow machines utilize graphical languages that are similar to directed graphs.

In representing the dynamics of a data-flow system, logical entities called *tokens* are employed. Besides carrying an operand, each token specifies the operation to be performed (i.e., its destination). During actual (physical) processing, tokens are often held in queues.

A data-flow operator of arity n, which is represented as a node on the program graph, can be in one of several states. These are illustrated in Figure 3.14, where a dot is used to denote the presence of a token. Part (a) of the figure illustrates the *waiting state*. Here, the function cannot be executed since not all input lines

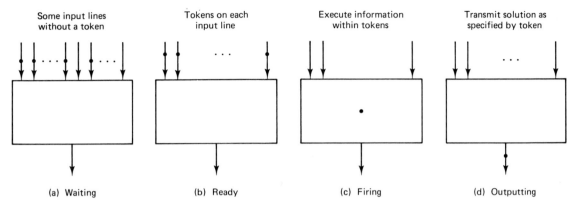

Figure 3.14   States in a data-flow machine

contain a token.   Part (b) depicts the *ready*, or *enabled*, state, where all necessary tokens have arrived and the input lines are full.   Part (c) illustrates an activated data-flow function firing, and part (d) shows a data-flow operator outputting the result generated.

It is possible that several tokens might be present on an input line to a data-flow operation.   This situation is illustrated in Figure 3.15, where no feedback mechanism is employed: execution proceeds on a first-come, first-served basis.

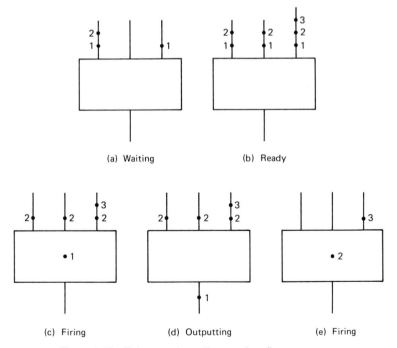

Figure 3.15   Tokens on input lines to data-flow processors

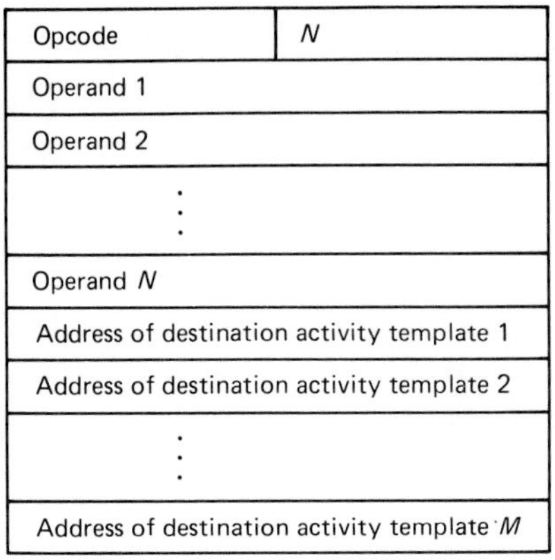

Opcode	N
Operand 1	
Operand 2	
$\vdots$	
Operand N	
Address of destination activity template 1	
Address of destination activity template 2	
$\vdots$	
Address of destination activity template M	

Figure 3.16   Activity packet

Information in a data-flow system is often organized utilizing *activity packets* (or *activity templates*).   At the top of an activity template (see Figure 3.16), the opcode of the operation to be performed is specified.   The number of operands required for execution of the instruction is also specified in the template.   As operands arrive, this number is decremented in a special counter until it reaches zero, at which point execution of the instruction occurs.   There is room in the template to store each of the operands as it arrives, as well as the addresses of all other activity templates that need the result of the operation.   As soon as an operation fires, the result is transmitted to all specified addresses and stored as an operand in each destination activity template.   The following example illustrates the use of activity packets in the specification of a data-flow algorithm.

Example 3.6

Consider the citardauq formula discussed in Example 2.8 for finding roots of the quadratic equation.   The formula

$$ x = \frac{-2c}{b \pm \sqrt{b^2 - 4ac}} $$

will be described using activity packets in data-flow language (see Figure 3.17).   To start, three multiplications can be performed in parallel, or as desired.   The minus operation on top can only be performed after the multiplication of 2 and c, while the subtraction operation whose activity packet appears near the center of the figure can be applied only after the multiplications of $2a$ by $2c$ and b by itself are performed. Once the subtraction is executed, the square root, and then, subsequently, the addition of the root with b can be implemented.   Utilizing the outputs of MINUS and ADD, the division can be performed to provide the root x_1.   Using SUB instead of ADD, the second root x_2 can be obtained in parallel.   Note that in the SUB activity template, the subtrahend is above the minuend.

Although the introduction of asynchronous design might at first appear some-

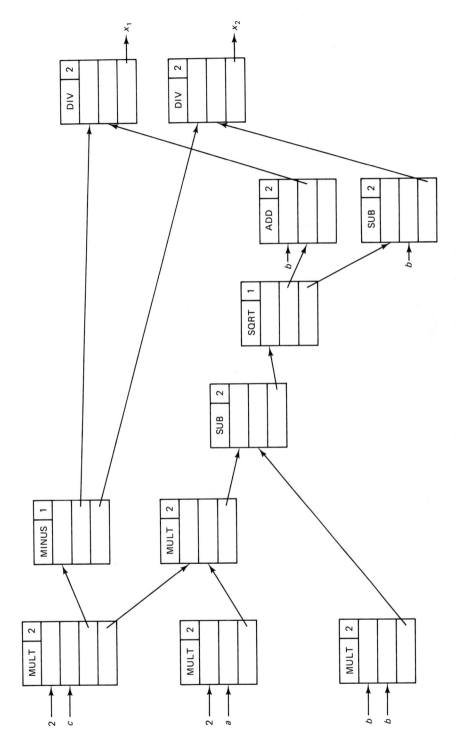

Figure 3.17   Data-flow program for citardauq formula

what odd to those familiar with classical synchronous architecture, it is fairly easy to see the motivation behind asynchronicity. To date, the parallelism necessary for increased operating speeds has, for the most part, been achieved by multiprocessing. The principle has not been to depart from sequentiality, but instead to allow several processors to work simultaneously. Augmenting the increased number of processors has been the utilization of multiple memory modules. However, since the program must continue to run according to the predetermined control sequence, a complex switching network is necessary to route instructions and data between distinct processors and memory modules. As the number of processors increases, so does the complexity of both the switching network and the data paths. As a consequence, memory latency occurs: processors remain idle while they await responses to requests for data.

Cache memories, high-speed buffer memories that act as stores between the CPU and the main memory, do not provide a fully satisfactory solution, since, unless there is a complicated see-through design, changes made by one processor in a location present in its cache may cause side effects unknown to another processor. While it is true that cache memories are useful wherever there exists a high degree of spatial locality in data references, it is nevertheless necessary to provide some mechanism to maintain cache coherency.

Generally, it is the inevitability of complex control devices that gives an upper bound to the pragmatic achievement of ever greater parallelism as long as traditional synchronous architecture is maintained. Data-flow systems are one response to this problem. Other potential solutions will be explored in the next two sections.

3.5 SYSTOLIC PROCESSORS

A systolic system consists of a set of interconnected cells, each capable of performing a simple operation. Information in such a system flows in a pipelined fashion, and communication with the outside world only occurs at *boundary cells*. Systolic architectures were designed to handle *compute-bound* types of applications. Here, the number of operations in a computation is large compared to the amount of input–output instructions. Ordinary matrix multiplication represents a compute-bound task.

An array of systolic cells will be implemented in this section to illustrate the ordinary matrix multiplication application. In this, as well as in any other application using systolic architectures, data are used effectively at each cell while being *pumped* from cell to cell along the structure. The synchronous pulsing of data is ensured at the algorithmic level by using an external clock.

A systolic array usually has a simple (geometric) structure involving local connections. Each cell performs simple identical tasks.

Each systolic cell in the following discussion operates in identical fashion. There are two inputs to each cell: an upper input x_i and a left input y_i:

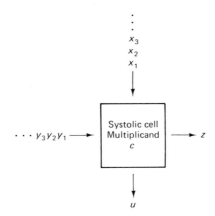

Outputs for each cell appear to the right (z) and below (u). The lower output equals the upper input unchanged, but delayed by one unit of time. The right output equals the sum of the left input with the product of c and the upper input. An execution trace follows.

After clock pulse 1 occurs, we have

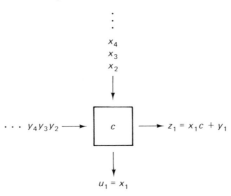

Upon the conclusion of the second clock pulse,

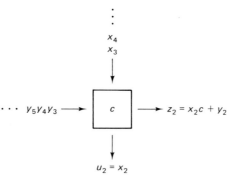

and so on.

These cells are connected to perform various specialized operations. If this is done, each cell operates independently from one another in a synchronous fashion. An external clock is employed to ensure rhythmic operation of the systolic array with all processor operations in unison.

A cell can be connected in various ways, but usually the right (bottom) output of a cell is connected to the left (upper) input of another cell. To illustrate this horizontal connection, consider the following diagram:

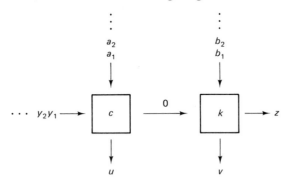

After the first clock pulse, we obtain

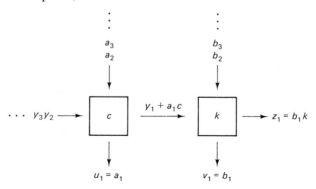

After the second clock pulse,

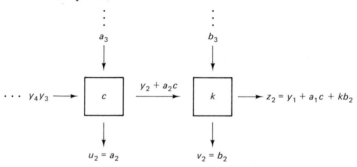

In general, after the nth clock pulse, $u_n = a_n$, $v_n = b_n$, and $z_n = y_{n-1} + a_{n-1}c + kb_n$. To reinforce these ideas, consider Example 3.7.

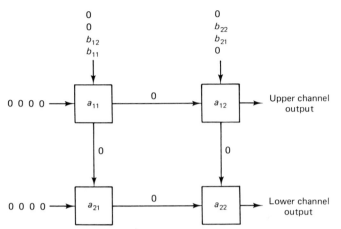

Figure 3.18 Initial Systolic Configuration

Example 3.7

We wish to form the product of two 2 by 2 matrices,

$$\begin{pmatrix} a_{11} & a_{12} \\ a_{21} & a_{22} \end{pmatrix} \begin{pmatrix} b_{11} & b_{12} \\ b_{21} & b_{22} \end{pmatrix} = \begin{pmatrix} c_{11} & c_{12} \\ c_{21} & c_{22} \end{pmatrix}$$

using a systolic array. Generalization to n by n matrices is immediate. First, we describe the way the input should be set up. This is followed by how the desired output is obtained. Finally, an execution trace is provided giving a step-by-step account of the input, the output, and each processor's status after every clock pulse.

The initial configuration is depicted in Figure 3.18. Only four inputs are illustrated in this diagram since four clock pulses would be needed to obtain the desired result. The output of the array will be as follows:

After clock pulse	4	3	2	1
Upper channel output	0	c_{12}	c_{11}	0
Lower channel output	c_{22}	c_{21}	0	0

This is seen in detail in Figures 3.19 through 3.22.

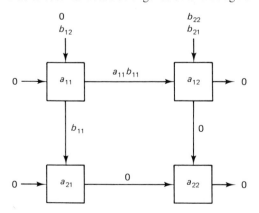

Figure 3.19 Systolic Configuration after 1st Clock Pulse

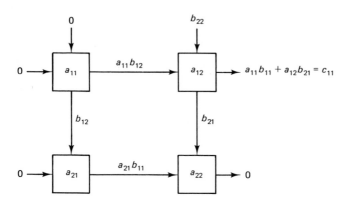

Figure 3.20 Systolic Configuration after 2nd Clock Pulse

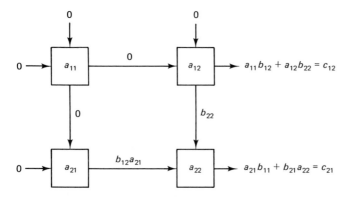

Figure 3.21 Systolic Configuration after 3rd Clock Pulse

During the first clock pulse, b_{11} is utilized from the top in the upper-left systolic processor, and there is a zero input into all the other processors, thus giving the configuration of Figure 3.19 at the completion of the pulse. After the second clock pulse, the array is as given in Figure 3.20. We notice that the first desired output c_{11} appears from the upper channel. It has resulted from summing $a_{11}b_{11}$ (the left input) with the product of the multiplication of the upper input and a_{12}. After the third clock pulse, two more desired outputs are provided (Figure 3.21). When the fourth clock pulse is completed, we are left with the result in Figure 3.22.

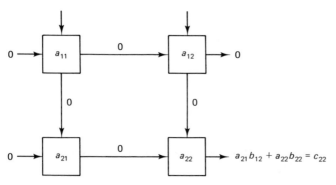

Figure 3.22 Systolic Configuration after 4th Clock Pulse

3.6 WAVEFRONT ARRAY PROCESSORS

Wavefront array processors fit right into the VLSI revolution. Once again, emphasis is placed on massive parallelism, simple connections, modular design, and regularity. Similar to the systolic array, a repetitive modular structure is employed with localized communications. However, unlike systolic processors, there is no external clock, and, in fact, wavefront array processors perform their task in an asynchronous manner. Information is transmitted whenever it has been computed, and computing begins once all the operands are present. Thus, a wavefront array processor is also a data-flow processor. Wavefront array processors are a cross between systolic processors and data-flow processors; they make use of the best points of each.

The main objective of this section is to show how a wavefront processor processes information and to illustrate this on matrix multiplication, as was done using the systolic processors. It will be assumed that each cell is programmed to perform the same repetitive simple operation described next.

A wavefront array cell has two input channels, a left and a top. When both inputs are present, the procesor multiplies the inputs together and adds the result onto the contents of an internal memory within the cell. The top input is shipped out to the bottom output, and the left input is transmitted out to the right output:

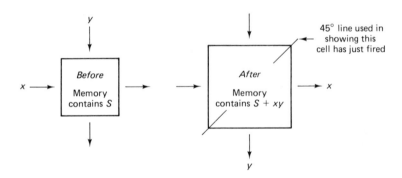

A powerful special-purpose data-flow computer results by connecting numerous cells together. A cell can fire only when both inputs are present. A 2 by 2 matrix multiplication is performed in Example 3.8; generalization to n by n matrices is immediate.

Example 3.8

If we want to use a wavefront array to perform the matrix multiplication

$$\begin{pmatrix} a_{11} & a_{12} \\ a_{21} & a_{22} \end{pmatrix} \begin{pmatrix} b_{11} & b_{12} \\ b_{21} & b_{22} \end{pmatrix}$$

and obtain the matrix

$$\begin{pmatrix} c_{11} & c_{12} \\ c_{21} & c_{22} \end{pmatrix}$$

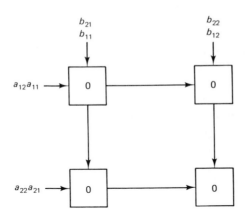

Figure 3.23 Initial Wave Front Array
Process Conditions

Figure 3.24 Upper-Left Cell Fired

the appropriate input scheme is illustrated in Figure 3.23. Note that the initial content of each cell's internal memory is set equal to zero.

The desired output for this processor appears inside each cell after all the inputs are used up, that is, after each cell has executed twice. Cells execute at different times from one another; there is no external clock. At the outset, only the leftmost, uppermost cell executes, since only it has both operands available (see Figure 3.24). Then all cells except the right-bottommost cell execute, as illustrated in Figure 3.25, which shows two waves of information. Then all but the leftmost, uppermost cell executes, as depicted in Figure 3.26, and the waves move forward and down. Finally, the bottom-right cell executes for the second time. Now all the cells can be read and the results obtained (see Figure 3.27).

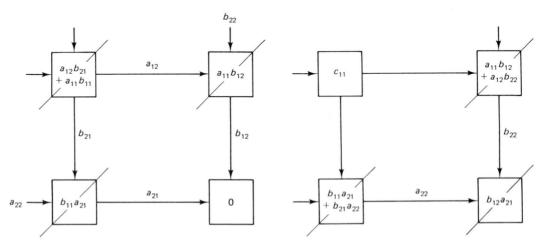

Figure 3.25 Left and Upper Cells
Fired

Figure 3.26 Bottom and Right Cells
Fired

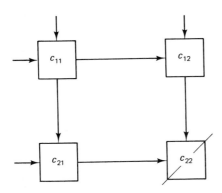

Figure 3.27   Bottom-Right Cell Fired

3.7 AND/OR GRAPHS

Having described several parallel architectures in the preceding sections, we will conclude the chapter with two mathematical models describing parallelism.   The first of these models is the and/or graph, to be discussed in the current section, and the second is the Petri net, to be discussed in the subsequent section.

And/or graphs, otherwise known as *biological graphs*, are similar to directed graphs and are used for representing parallelism in programming computations, processing, and general systems.   They can also be employed to represent search strategies.   In an and/or graph, the nodes, drawn as circles (see Figure 3.28), represent statements within a parallel program.   Arrows denote control or data links between nodes, which possess both input and output control.   *Source nodes* with two or more arrows leaving (as outputs) must be labeled with a disjunctive $\vee$ or *or* operation or with a conjunctive $\wedge$ or *and* operation.   The same holds for *destination nodes* with two or more arrows coming in.

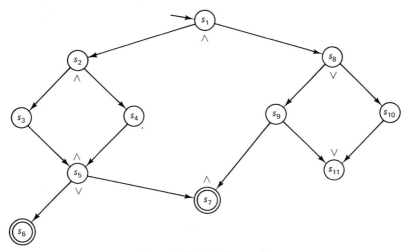

Figure 3.28   And/or graph

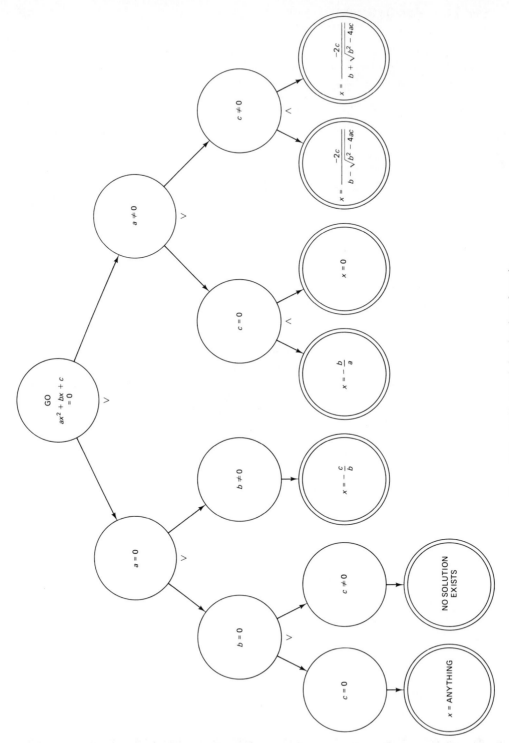

Figure 3.29 And/or graph for citardauq formula

Whenever an instruction within a node is executed, the node is said to *fire* or to be *activated*. For disjunctive input control, a statement node fires whenever one (and, in this discussion, exactly one) arrow entering the node has been activated. For conjunctive input control, a statement node fires whenever all arrows entering the node are activated. Disjunctive output from a firing node activates one (and, in this discussion, exactly one) arrow leaving the node. Conjunctive output from a firing node activates all arrows leaving the node. A pointer is used for showing at which node the process starts, and double circles are used to represent *concluding nodes*, which are employed to represent the solution to the problem. Concluding nodes usually do not have any arrows emanating from them.

Example 3.9

Consider the problem of finding all solutions to the quadratic equation

$$ax^2 + bx + c = 0$$

where a, b, and c are any real numbers. We will employ an and/or graph to represent an algorithm for finding the solutions (see Figure 3.29). The starting node contains the equation together with instruction GO. With the execution of GO, the starting node fires, causing exactly one arrow leaving the node to be activated. The head of the activated arrow points to the appropriate node to be activated, and so exactly one of the two instructions, $a = 0$, or $a \neq 0$, is executed. Referring to Figure 3.29, we can see that, if GO, $a = 0$, $b = 0$, and $c = 0$ have all been activated, then the concluding node

$$x = \text{ANYTHING}$$

is activated, thus yielding the desired solution. If GO, $a = 0$, $b = 0$, and $c \neq 0$ have fired, then

NO SOLUTION EXISTS

also fires. In the case where GO, $a \neq 0$, and $c \neq 0$ have all fired, since the node $c \neq 0$ possesses conjunctive output, two output arrows are activated and two concluding nodes fire, one for each root given by the citardauq formula.

And/or graphs have been used for aiding search strategies, as well as for the modeling of various issues in both parallel programming and parallel processing. By and large, as a tool for the handling of parallelism in both systems analysis and processing, these graphs have been supplanted by Petri nets, a topic to be discussed in the following section.

3.8 PETRI NETS

Like an and/or graph, a Petri net is an abstract model used in representing parallel systems and processes. Petri nets are most often depicted through the use of directed graphs, and they are among the most popular formalisms for the description of the interaction within a parallel dynamic system.

Rigorously, a *Petri net* is a seven-tuple

$$(P, T, V, f, g, N, m_0)$$

where

P = nonempty finite set of *places*

T = nonempty finite set of *transitions* that is disjoint from P

V = valuation space $\{0, 1\}$

f = binary function used in determining the connections from places to transitions; thus,

$$f: P \times T \rightarrow V$$

and if $f(p, t) = 1$, then place p connects to transition t; otherwise, it does not

g = binary function used in determining which transitions connect to which places; thus,

$$g: T \times P \rightarrow V$$

and a connection exists from transition t to place p if and only if $g(t, p) = 1$

N = set of *markings:* $\{0, 1, 2, \ldots\}$

m_0 = *initial marking* function

$$m_0: P \rightarrow N$$

Petri nets are usually illustrated by means of directed-type graphs, such as the one in Figure 3.30, where there exists a node for each element in $P \cup T$.

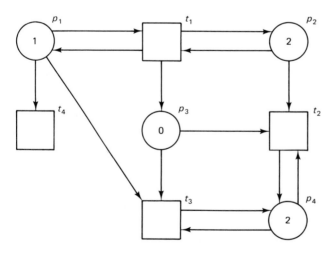

Figure 3.30 Petri net graph

Nodes for places are denoted by circles, while those for transitions are drawn as squares. Each node is labeled by writing the appropriate place or transition symbol next to it. An arrow goes from a place p to a transition t whenever there is a connection from p to t ($f(p, t) = 1$) and from the transition t to the place p whenever there is a connection from t to p ($g(t, p) = 1$). The arrows are not labeled.

Each place p has a *marking*, denoted $m(p)$, associated with it. The marking is integer valued, is written within the circle for place p, and denotes the number of tokens stored in the place p. Recall (Section 3.4) that a token is a logical entity that, in the data-flow scheme, is used to carry a piece of data. Structurally, a Petri net represents a dynamic parametric process: the graph structure does not change; only the markings change. The beginning net is labeled with the initial marking given by m_0, and different markings occur due to the firings of specific single transitions. Once a firing has occurred, a *new* Petri net, with new markings, results. Moreover, transition t fires for a given marking m provided each input place for t possesses at least one token: t fires if, for any p such that $f(p, t) = 1$, $m(p) \geq 1$.

Example 3.10

Consider the Petri net illustrated in Figure 3.31, where there are three distinct transitions t_1, t_2, and t_3, and the places have markings given by

m	p_1	p_2	p_3	p_4
	1	2	0	2

Only one transition can fire, that being t_1; indeed, all places connected to (inputting into) t_1, p_1 and p_2, have nonzero markings. Transition t_2 cannot fire since $f(p_3, t_2) = 1$, but $m(p_3) = 0$.

If a given transition t fires for a given marking m, a new marking m' results;

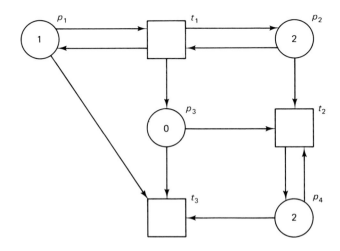

Figure 3.31 Petri net before firing

this new marking is found by reducing the marking in each input place of transition t by 1, and adding an additional token onto each output place to which the transition is connected.   Thus, if transition t fires, then, for all places p,

$$m'(p) = m(p) - f(p, t) + g(t, p)$$

Example 3.11

Again refer to the Petri net given in Figure 3.31.   If transition t_1 fires, the Petri net illustrated in Figure 3.32 results.   Notice that the (graphical) structure of the two distinct Petri nets in Figures 3.31 and 3.32 is the same; they differ only in the markings, which, for the new Petri net, are given by the function m_1:

m_1	p_1	p_2	p_3	p_4
	1	2	1	2

Notice that in the new Petri net any of the three transitions can fire.   In general, transitions fire in an asynchronous manner, one at a time, with each firing resulting in a new Petri net.   If no transition can fire, then the process ends.

Example 3.12

Referring to the Petri net in Figure 3.32, suppose transition t_2 fires.   Then the marking m_2, given by

m_2	p_1	p_2	p_3	p_4
	1	1	0	2

is obtained.   Then, if t_1 fires, marking m_3, given by

m_3	p_1	p_2	p_3	p_4
	1	1	1	2

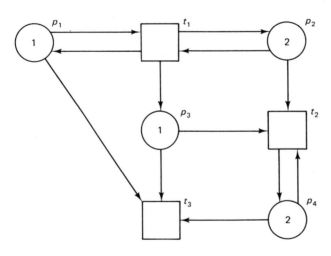

Figure 3.32   Petri net after firing

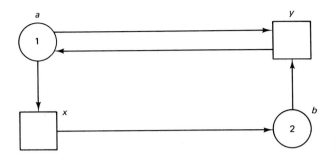

Figure 3.33 Petri net for Example 3.12

results. Finally, if t_3 fires, marking m_4 is obtained:

m_4	p_1	p_2	p_3	p_4
	0	1	0	1

At this point, since no transition can fire, the process ends.

Notice that, if the Petri net illustrated in Figure 3.31 is employed and t_1 fires repeatedly, the process never terminates.

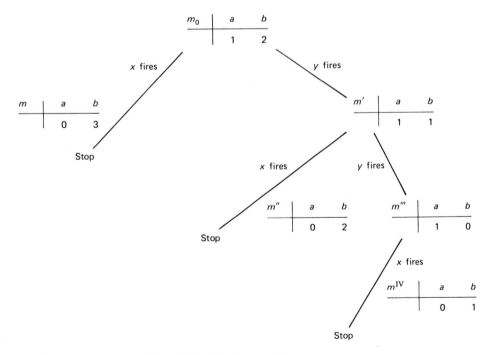

Figure 3.34 Petri net transition sequences

Example 3.13

Consider the Petri net given by

$$P = \{a, b\}$$

$$T = \{x, y\}$$

f	x	y
a	1	1
b	0	1

g	a	b
x	0	1
y	1	0

m_0	a	b
	1	2

and illustrated in Figure 3.33. The diagram in Figure 3.34 illustrates the possible sequences of transition firings.

EXERCISES FOR CHAPTER 3

3.1. Referring to Figure 3.2, show how the outputs of Table 3.1 are obtained.

3.2. If $sruv = 1101$ in the fusible logic diagram of Figure 3.3, what corresponding values are attained by S, R, and U? Is the output a y or a t in this case?

3.3. How much does the pipeline schema (illustrated in Figure 3.7) increase the throughput of a computer?

3.4. Using the pipeline processor of Example 3.2, show that, at time 19, four instructions have been completely executed. What is the increase in throughput for this computer over an SISD computer?

3.5. Consider the flat file R of Example 3.4 with the comparand as given there. If a mask 0001 is employed, what is the resulting flat file?

3.6. Write a content-addressable machine program that finds the maximum of the numbers given in Example 3.5.

3.7. Draw a data-flow diagram to find the roots of a second-order equation using the quadratic formula.

3.8. A digital signal is a partial function from the class Z of integers into the class R of real numbers. For instance, the function f with domain $\{1, 2, 3, 4\}$ that is defined by $f(1) = 4, f(2) = 1/2, f(3) = 7$, and $f(4) = 5$ is a digital signal. A finite digital signal is one possessing a finite domain, such as f. Given two finite digital signals g and h, we define the digital signal $g*h$ by

$$(g*h)(k) = \sum g(n)h(k - n)$$

where the summation is taken over all n in the domain g for which $k - n$ is in the domain of h. The function $g*h$ is called the *convolution* of g and h. Draw a data-flow diagram illustrating the convolution operation.

3.9. Let $g(4) = 2$, $g(5) = 1$, $g(6) = 3$, $h(2) = 2$, $h(3) = 0$, and $h(4) = -1$. Find the convolution of g and h using the data-flow methodology developed in Exercise 3.8.

3.10. Show how to perform a 3×3 matrix multiplication using systolic processing and illustrate with an example.

3.11. Develop a systolic processor for the convolution of two digital signals, where each possesses a domain of three consecutive integers. Compute the convolution of the signals in Exercise 3.9 using the processor. (This problem is difficult.)

3.12. Repeat Exercise 3.10, except employ a wavefront array processor.

3.13. Repeat Exercise 3.11, except employ a wavefront array processor. (This problem is also difficult.)

3.14. Write an and/or graph much like the one illustrated in Figure 3.28 to solve the quadratic equation.

3.15. For the Petri net of Figure 3.30, what are the markings corresponding to the firing sequence t_1, t_1, t_1, t_2, t_3?

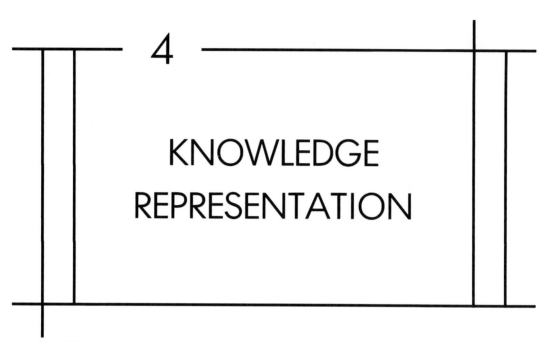

4
KNOWLEDGE REPRESENTATION

4.1 GAMES AND PUZZLES

This section is dedicated to providing several simple games and puzzles that are subsequently used to illustrate the advantages of various representations that arise through the utilization of different data structures.

The game of *fifteenzy*, or *number scrabble*, can be played by two humans, two computers, or one of each (see Figure 4.1). In the game, there are nine chips, marked 1 through 9, spread out on a playing board, and each of the two players alternately picks up one chip of his, her, or its choice at a time. The first player to pick is chosen by lot. The first player to possess, among the chips held, exactly three chips whose numbers sum to 15 is the winner. If all 9 chips have been selected and neither player has a sum of 15 among the ones held, then the game commences again with the player who first went second now going first.

Rather than begin the game with the number placement presented in Figure 4.1, suppose we utilize the placement of Figure 4.2, where numbers along any row, column, or main diagonal sum to 15. Now the game of fifteenzy is seen to be equivalent to the game of *tic-tac-toe*. Perhaps from the point of view of a human, the latter representation appears more natural, but from the perspective of a computer, the opposite might very well be true. The better representation lies in the eye of the beholder—computer or human.

The next game we consider is the *magic nine square puzzle*, which consists of eight numbered, movable tiles organized in a three by three frame. Each tile is labeled with a unique integer between 1 and 8, and an empty space allows the

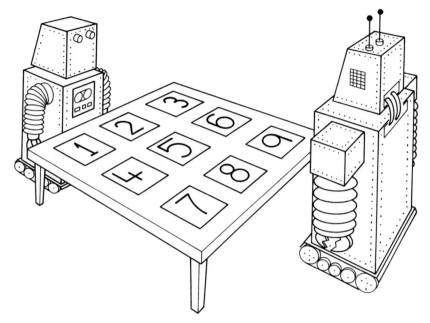

Figure 4.1.   Game of fifteenzy

2	7	6
9	5	1
4	3	8

Figure 4.2.   Alternate representation of fifteenzy

tiles adjacent to it to be moved into it, thereby vacating the square previously occupied by the translated tile.   A game begins with the puzzle being in some initial configuration, say

1	6	7
2	5	8
4	3	*

where the star (*) denotes the blank.   The object is to move the tiles so that a final configuration, say

1	2	3
4	5	6
7	8	*

is obtained.

Representations for solving the magic nine square puzzle problem will be discussed in subsequent sections; however, even at this point, it is useful to represent the actual physical action of the tiles in terms of the movement of the blank cell. For instance, if a tile moves to the right and thereby occupies the empty cell, this process can be represented as the blank cell moving to the left. Thus, at any point, there are several possible moves involving the blank cell and several impossible moves. Valid moves depend on the configuration (or state) of the game. A total of 9! = 362,880 distinct configurations are possible, and therefore, to simplify matters, we will consider the magic four square puzzle.

In the four-square case, there are three tiles, labeled 1, 2, and 3, organized in a two by two manner, again with a blank cell. For each configuration, there exist two possible and two impossible moves of the blank. There will be a starting configuration, say

2	3
1	*

and a final or desired configuration, say

1	2
3	*

For future consideration, note that graphical methods can be employed to keep track of previous and future moves, search trees can be used to transform the initial configuration into the desired configuration, and automata can be programmed to play the game (see Example 5.6).

The *Tower of Hanoi* puzzle utilizes three pegs, labeled 1, 2, and 3, together with 64 rings of different exterior diameters that fit onto the pegs. Initially, all 64 rings are on peg 1 and form a pyramid-type structure, no larger ring being atop

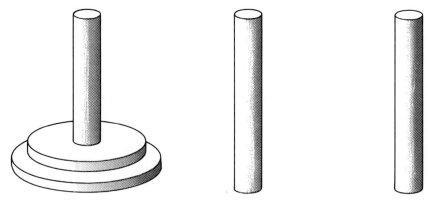

Figure 4.3. Tower of Honoi game

a smaller ring. The object of the game is to transfer all the rings to peg 3 so that the same tower structure results. The rules are (1) a single ring is to be moved at a time, (2) peg 2 is employed as an intermediate (memory-type) structure, and (3) no larger ring can be placed atop a smaller ring. Due to the vast number of possible configurations, we will restrict our attention to the game consisting of only two rings, a large one denoted by b (big) and a small one denoted by s (small) (see Figure 4.3). In this simplified version, only 12 configurations are physically possible, and only 9 of these are legal. An automaton designed to play the Tower of Hanoi game is constructed in Example 5.5.

4.2 TREE REPRESENTATIONS AND SEARCHING STRATEGIES

A tree is a type of directed graph that is useful for representing knowledge and operations performed on knowledge. Trees are also useful in providing visual insight into searching strategies. Among the important search methodologies are the breadth-first and depth-first procedures, each to be discussed in the present section.

Fundamental to the subsequent discussion is the notion of a cycle within a graph. Intuitively, a cycle is a closed sequence of arrows, and the traversal of the sequence from any point in the cycle will lead back to the starting point. Rigorously, if (P, L, f, b) is a directed graph, with front function f and back function b, the distinct arrows $x_1, x_2, \ldots, x_n$ form a *cycle* of length n if

$$f(x_1) = b(x_2)$$

$$f(x_2) = b(x_3)$$

$$\vdots$$

$$f(x_n) = b(x_1)$$

A cycle of length 1 is called a *self-loop*, or just a *loop*. Figure 4.4 provides an illustration of a directed graph containing a cycle of length 3.

A directed graph is said to be a *tree* if the following two conditions are satisfied:

1. There are no cycles.
2. There exists a point p, called the *root*, such that

$$f: L \xrightarrow[\text{onto}]{1-1} P - \{p\}$$

Trees in AI applications will be drawn with the root on top and arrows going down. Moreover, the heads of the arrows will usually be omitted since it is understood that they point downward. Figure 4.5 provides two illustrations of the same tree, whose root is 9.

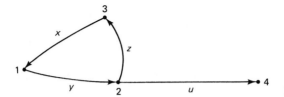

Figure 4.4. Cycle of length 3

The *leaves* of a tree are those points q in P that are not in the range of b; that is, leaves are points in the graph that have no arrow emanating from them. Intuitively, leaves are points on the bottom of the graph.

A useful characterization of the *depth* of a point in a tree is its *level*. Proceeding inductively, the root p of a tree is, by definition, on level 0. The subset P_1 of points $f(x_i)$ in P for which

$$b(x_1) = b(x_2) = \cdots = b(x_n) = p$$

constitutes level 1. Thus,

$$P_1 = \{f(x_1), f(x_2), \ldots, f(x_n)\}$$

The set P_k of points in level k is defined recursively in terms of those in level $k - 1$ as follows: if

$$b(x_i) \in P_{k-1}$$

for $i = 1, 2, \ldots, j$, then

$$P_k = \{f(x_i): i = 1, 2, \ldots, j\}$$

It is important to realize that a computer "sees" a directed graph differently than humans, who tend to pay attention to the graphical representation. A ma-

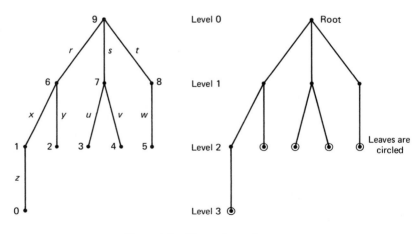

Figure 4.5. Illustrations of a tree

chine is only "aware" of the quadruple (P, L, f, b).   Thus, all manipulations of directed graphs must be accomplished utilizing only the quadruple.

The next example illustrates the manner in which a computer might perform a *breadth-first* search, one in which all nodes of level i are visited before any node of level $i + 1$ is visited.

Example 4.1

Consider the tree illustrated in Figure 4.5.   Insofar as the computer is concerned, it sees only a mathematical description of the tree; that is,

$$P = \{0, 1, 2, 3, 4, 5, 6, 7, 8, 9\}$$

$$L = \{r, s, t, x, y, u, v, w, z\}$$

and the two functions f and b are given by

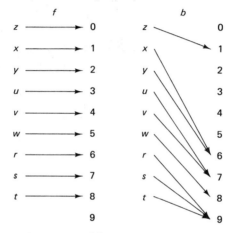

Note that f is 1–1 and onto $P - \{9\}$; thus, by definition, 9 is the root of the tree and the set of level 0 nodes is given by

$$P_0 = \{9\}$$

The points of level 1 are those that are pointed to by arrows emanating from the root. Since

$$b(r) = b(s) = b(t) = 9$$

the relevant arrows are r, s, and t.   Thus,

$$P_1 = \{f(r), f(s), f(t)\}$$

$$= \{6, 7, 8\}$$

In a breadth-first search, if the desired point lies in level 1, then the search ends; otherwise, the next level is found.   Proceeding, level 2 is found by first determining the set of all arrows whose backs touch a point in level 1.   Since

$$b(x) = b(y) = 6$$

$$b(u) = b(v) = 7$$

and

$$b(w) = 8$$

it follows that

$$P_2 = \{f(x), f(y), f(u), f(v), f(w)\}$$
$$= \{1, 2, 3, 4, 5\}$$

If the desired quantity is in this level, the search ends; if not, we proceed to the next level, which is found by determining all arrows whose backs touch elements of level 2. Since $b(z) = 1$ and since no other values of b occur in P_2,

$$P_3 = \{f(z)\} = \{0\}$$

Depth-first searching can also be implemented on a computer through the utilization of the functions f and b. This type of search is characterized by starting at the root and then traveling "nonstop to the leaves by following contiguous arrows." More precisely, a sequence of distinct branches $x_1, x_2, \ldots, x_n$ is employed, where

$$b(x_1) = p \quad \text{(the root)}$$
$$b(x_2) = f(x_1)$$
$$.$$
$$.$$
$$.$$
$$b(x_n) = f(x_{n-1})$$

and there does not exist an x_{n+1} in L such that

$$b(x_{n+1}) = f(x_n)$$

which means that $f(x_n)$ is a leaf. Such a sequence is said to be *maximal*. In practice, leaves should be marked. (In Figure 4.5 circles are used.) If the desired node is not found, then a different maximal sequence of branches is employed to find another leaf. The process is continued until the desired node is located or until all leaves have been reached by maximal sequences.

Example 4.2

We will employ a depth-first search on the tree in Figure 4.5. Beginning with the root, $p = 9$, maximal sequences of contiguous arrows must be determined. For instance, r, x, and z form such a sequence, since

$$b(r) = 9$$
$$b(x) = f(r)$$
$$b(z) = f(x)$$

and $f(z) = 0$ is a leaf. If $f(r)$, $f(x)$, or $f(z)$ is the desired node, then the process terminates; otherwise, a distinct maximal sequence is found, one possibility being r

and y, since

$$b(r) = 9$$
$$b(y) = f(r)$$

and $f(y) = 2$ is a leaf.   Other distinct maximal sequences are s and u, s and v, and t and w.   These sequences terminate at the leaves 3, 4, and 5, respectively.

Actual computer searching need not perform backtracking; that is, there is no need to begin at the root each time a leaf is found in a depth-first search.   For instance, in the previous example, since $b(r) = 9$, begin with arrow r, and then, since

$$b(x) = b(y) = f(r)$$

choose either x or y and save the other for later use.   Supposing that x is selected, since $b(z) = f(x)$, the leaf $f(z)$ is found.   Now, instead of going back to the root, go back to y and continue from there, thus arriving at the leaf $f(y)$.

Compared to a parallel-search methodology, such as the utilization of content-addressable memory, the preceding tree search techniques are very time consuming. To reduce the number of steps, and, concomitantly, the time required for searching, a priori knowledge must be employed.   Often this knowledge involves rules of thumb, heuristics, and the like.   This additional information is utilized in the form of a *cost function*, which must be minimized while the search is being conducted.

From a practical standpoint, information, states of being, or various stages of a problem can be represented as the nodes of a tree, with the root denoting the original problem to be solved.   Each arrow often represents an instruction that, when executed, results in a transition to the state to which the arrow points.

Example 4.3

Consider the magic four square puzzle introduced in Section 4.1, with initial configuration

2	3
1	*

and goal (desired result)

1	2
*	3

Letting the root be the initial configuration, a tree can be drawn whose nodes represent the configurations resulting from movements of the blank, a single movement yielding the level 1 nodes, two movements yielding the level 2 nodes, and so on.   Figure 4.6 illustrates the first three levels of this tree representation, where each arrow is labeled according to whether the blank moves up, down, left, or right, the four possible movements being denoted by bu, bd, bl, and br, respectively.   Note that some con-

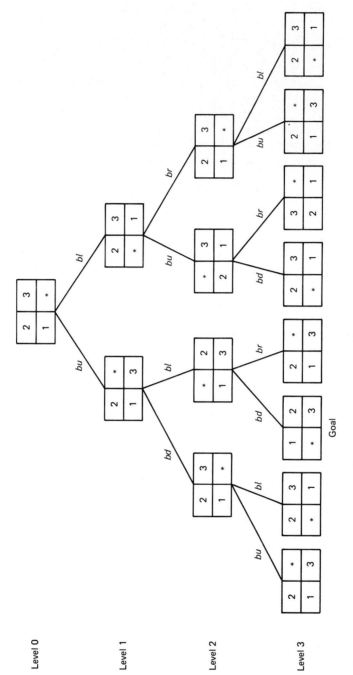

Figure 4.6. Tree representation of magic four puzzle

Level 0

Level 1

Level 2

Level 3

Goal

figurations repeat, and thus it would appear that a directed graph that is not a tree might yield a more appropriate representation.

A plausible cost function c can be defined as the sum of the level and the number of cells that do not match the goal configuration, the latter being known as the *distance* from the goal. The maximum distance is 4; however, at a particular node it might be less. For instance, the distance between the original configuration and the goal configuration is 4, but the distance between

2	3
*	1

and the goal configuration is only 3. The cost at each node illustrated in Figure 4.6 is given in Figure 4.7. In utilizing the cost function, the decision at each node would be to choose as the next node the one having the smallest cost. In case of a tie, a node is chosen arbitrarily from among the ones having minimal cost. When the cost equals the level, the puzzle has been solved.

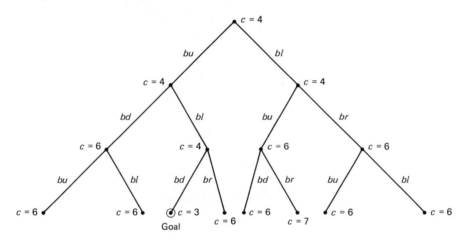

Figure 4.7.   Search cost for magic four puzzle

4.3 BINARY TREES

A *binary tree* is a tree (P, L, f, b) such that (1) for any p in P there are at most two arrows x in L such that $b(x) = p$, and (2) each arrow has a value l for left or r for right, this value being given by a function h, where

$$h: L \rightarrow \{l, r\}$$

By convention, nodes are drawn as circles, and each arrow emanating from a node is drawn leaving from either the left or the right, to indicate that it is labeled l or r, respectively (see Figure 4.8).

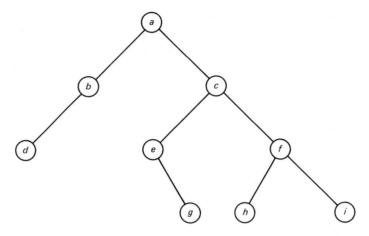

Figure 4.8. Binary tree

Note that the two binary trees illustrated in Figure 4.9 are distinct. As trees, both are characterized by the quadruple (P, L, f, b), where

$$L = \{x\}$$
$$P = \{a, b\}$$
$$f(x) = b$$

and

$$b(x) = a$$

However, for the binary tree in Figure 4.9(a), $h(x) = l$, whereas for the binary tree in Figure 4.9(b), $h(x) = r$.

Ignoring names of arrows and nodes, there are

$$\frac{(2n)!}{(n + 1)!n!}$$

distinct binary trees involving n nodes, $n \geq 2$. For instance, as was seen in Figure 4.9, there are two distinct binary trees having two nodes. There are five distinct binary trees having $n = 3$ nodes, and these are illustrated in Figure 4.10.

Several binary tree traversal procedures can be rigorously specified using the

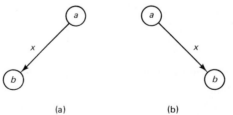

(a)   (b)

Figure 4.9. Distinct two-node binary trees

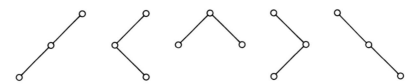

Figure 4.10.   Distinct three-node binary trees

functions f, b, and h; however, it is more expedient to employ the concept of a subtree.   Given a node $p \in P$, we consider the binary tree consisting of the arrows leaving p, the nodes to which these arrows point, the arrows leaving these nodes, the nodes to which these arrows point, and so on.   The resulting structure can take one of two forms: (1) if p is a leaf, the new structure is an isolated node; (2) otherwise, it is a tree with root p.   In either event, the new structure is called a *subtree with root p*.   In sum, each node of a binary tree, if it is not a leaf, will possess a left subtree (the one emanating from the left node beneath it), a right subtree (the one emanating from the right node beneath it), or possibly both a left and right subtree.

In traversing a binary tree, we will say that a node is *visited* whenever it is reached in the traversal.   Moreover, any traversal can be represented by the string of nodes in which the order within the string reflects the order of visitation.   We assume that each node is visited exactly once.

The *preorder traversal* of a binary tree is defined recursively by

1. Visit the root.
2. Traverse the left subtree in preorder.
3. Traverse the right subtree in preorder.

Example 4.4

Consider the binary tree in Figure 4.8. Preorder traversal yields the string

$$a\ b\ d\ c\ e\ g\ f\ h\ i$$

Figure 4.11(a) illustrates the procedure whereby the node values are converted into the above string. Note that the result is a total order relation on the nodes of the tree, the relation being induced by the traversal methodology. Moreover, note how the recursive definition of preorder traversal leads to the actual traversal obtained.

Inorder traversal of a binary tree proceeds in accordance with the following recursive definition:

1. Traverse the left subtree in inorder.
2. Visit the root.
3. Traverse the right subtree in inorder.

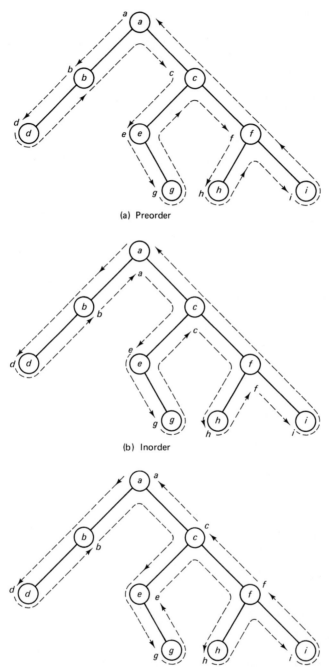

(a) Preorder

(b) Inorder

(c) Postorder

Figure 4.11. Traversals of a binary tree

Example 4.5

For the tree illustrated in Figure 4.8, inorder traversal yields the string

$$d\ b\ a\ e\ g\ c\ h\ f\ i$$

In this representation, the traversal proceeds by continuing to the left until it cannot go any further, whereupon a visit is made and the output letter is recorded. The traversal then proceeds to the right, recording letters as it goes; but once it can go left again, it proceeds as far left as possible before recording a visit. This procedure is continued until all nodes have been visited [see Figure 4.11(b)].

The final traversal method to be introduced is *postorder traversal*; it is defined recursively by:

1. Traverse the left subtree in postorder.
2. Traverse the right subtree in postorder.
3. Visit the root.

Example 4.6

For the tree illustrated in Figure 4.8, postorder traversal yields the string

$$d\ b\ g\ e\ h\ i\ f\ c\ a$$

[see Figure 4.11(c)].

Binary trees are useful in the representation of knowledge. Consider a string consisting of data, together with binary and unary operations involving the data. The string can be represented using a binary tree in which each node corresponds to precisely one letter in the string and where the structure of the tree has been obtained in accordance with the hierarchy of operations to be performed. If the tree is traversed in conformity with some traversal procedure, a new string results from the enumeration of the visited nodes, the new string being a permutation of the original.

To enunciate the type of procedure we have in mind, we will consider the string

$$x = (3 \cdot a) + (- \ 4 \ / \ b)$$

In representing such a string in a binary tree, we will place the final operation, which in the present case is $+$, at the root, and we will ignore parentheses. Since $+$ is binary, two arrows (left and right) emanate from the root. We now proceed inductively, repeating the process for the final operations in each of the subexpressions and placing these at the roots of the left and right subtrees. If only data exist in a subexpression, then this information is placed in the leaves of the appropriate subtree. Should a unary prefix operation, such as minus $(-)$, be encountered, the subtrahend is placed in the subsequent right-hand node; on the

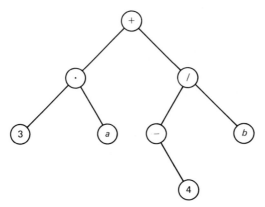

Figure 4.12. Binary tree for arithmetic operations

other hand, should a unary postfix operation, such as a factorial, be encountered, the operand preceding it is placed in the left-hand node subsequent to the node holding the operation itself. If, when the tree is completed, an inorder traversal is made, the original string (without parentheses) is obtained. This string is called an *infix* string. Applying the methodology to the string under consideration, the appropriate tree is given in Figure 4.12, and inorder traversal yields

$$3 \cdot a + - 4 / b$$

This string, absent the tree from which it is derived, is meaningless due the ambiguity that has resulted from the loss of all hierarchical information (which was contained in the placement of the original parentheses).

Of interest is that both preorder and postorder traversal of a binary tree resulting from the immediately preceding methodology provide meaningful strings in terms of the desired operations, even though parentheses are not utilized. These representations are called *prefix* and *postfix*, respectively, and, using a stack, a computer can interpret the representations correctly. This is significant in programming language interpretation when stacks are employed for string evaluation. Stack memories are somewhat similar to coordinate memories, in that information is loaded into a stack in a sequential manner using a PUSH operation and retrieved from the stack by employing a POP operation.

Example 4.7

Employing the graphic representation

to portray an empty stack, the sequence of instructions

$$\text{PUSH}(x), \text{PUSH}(x), \text{PUSH}(y), \text{POP}(y), \text{POP}(x), \text{PUSH}(z)$$

results in the following sequence of stack conditions:

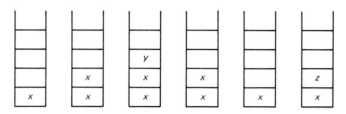

Given a prefix string of data and operation symbols, a stack can be utilized to yield a correct interpretation of the string. Working from the right side of the string, data variables and constants are pushed onto the stack one by one. Operation symbols do not enter the stack. When a unary operation is encountered, the stack is popped, the operation is applied to the popped datum, and the result is pushed back onto the stack. When a binary operation is encountered, the stack is popped twice, the operation is applied to the popped data, and the result is again pushed back onto the stack. In the binary case, since the operation need not be commutative, the first operand popped, called *top*, is employed as the left operand, and the second operand popped, called *next top*, is employed as the right operand.

The prefix string associated with the tree in Figure 4.12 is

$$+ \cdot 3\, a\, /\, -\, 4\, b$$

Figure 4.13 contains a stack evaluation of the preorder expression. The diagram should be read from right to left.

Example 4.8

In Example 2.25, the citardauq formula is given as

$$x = 2 \cdot c/(-b + \sqrt{(b \cdot b - 4 \cdot a \cdot c)})$$

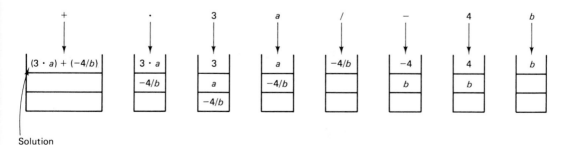

Figure 4.13.   Stack machine processing of arithmetic operations

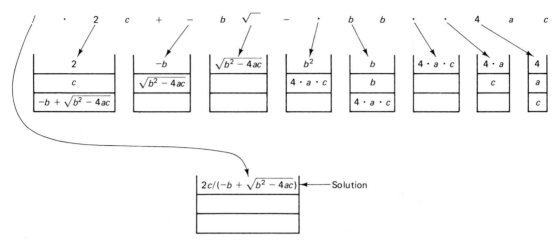

Figure 4.14.   Stack machine processing of citardauq formula

Moreover, Figure 2.5 gives the binary tree.   A stack evaluation of the prefix string is depicted in Figure 4.14.

Postfix expressions can be evaluated using stack machines in a manner similar to that employed for prefix strings.   Furthermore, strings involving ternary operations, as well as operations of higher arity, can be handled using nonbinary trees; however, such operations, when utilized in the context of finite sets, can always be expressed as compositions of binary operations.

4.4 SEMANTIC NETWORKS

Knowledge engineering involves the manipulation of facts in accordance with a calculus of rules.   As was seen in Section 1.9, logic, in the form of flat files and relational database representations, can provide an operational calculus.   Other methods are possible, some of which will be discussed in the present section.
Consider the functional or predicate-type notation

$$A(O) = V$$

interpreted to mean that for *object O*, the *value* of *attribute A* is *V*.   For instance, we might write

$$\text{Color(Door)} = \text{Brown}$$

to indicate that the given door has color brown.   This form of representation is known as *object–attribute–value* $(O–A–V)$ representation.   The same information can be conveyed graphically as in Figure 4.15, where a structure similar to a directed

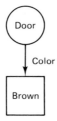

Figure 4.15.   O-A-V diagram

graph is employed.   There, the source node is labeled with the object, the arrow is labeled with the attribute, and the destination node is labeled with the value. The relational-type $O-A-V$ structure can be utilized to store information in a compact manner.   Moreover, through the use of flat files, $O-A-V$ representation can be employed to answer questions regarding unknowns among attributes, values, and objects.

Example 4.9

Consider the flat file R whose first, second, and third fields respectively contain the names of objects (in this case machines), the values of sound levels observed from the various machines, and the conditions of the machines that are related to the sound levels:

	R	
Object	Attribute (sound level)	Attribute (condition)
a	loud	broken
b	low	good
c	loud	good
d	low	good
e	medium	broken

Using the $O-A-V$ functional notation, questions can be written and answers given relative to the flat file:

Question: What is the condition of object a?

$$\text{Condition}(a) \ = \ ?$$

  Answer: $? \ = $ broken

Question: What is the sound level of object b?

$$\text{Sound level } (b) \ = \ ?$$

  Answer: $? \ = $ low

Question: Which objects are in a broken condition?

$$\text{Condition}(?) = \text{broken}$$

Answer: ? =

Object
a
e

Question: What attribute of object a is loud?

$$?(a) = \text{loud}$$

Answer: ? = sound level

Question: What are the conditions of all objects?

$$\text{Condition}(?) = ?$$

Answer:

Object	Condition
a	broken
b	good
c	good
d	good
e	broken

Question: What are the values of all attributes of object a?

$$?(a) = ?$$

Answer:

Object	Sound	Condition
a	loud	broken

Question: What are the attributes and corresponding objects that have value good?

$$?(?) = \text{good}$$

Answer:

Object	Condition
b	good
c	good
d	good

Question: ? (?) = ?
Answer: R

Semantic networks are directed-graph-type representation schemes that generalize the graphical $O-A-V$ triple (see Figure 4.16). Nodes are used to represent

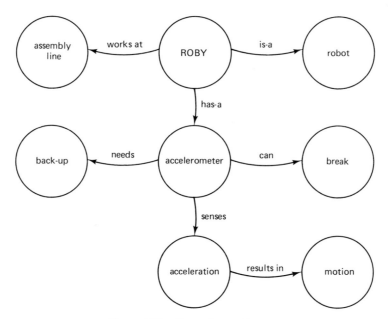

Figure 4.16.   Semantic net diagram

both objects, which might be physical or conceptual, and descriptors of objects. The arrows in the graph relate objects and their descriptors and therefore represent relations.   Several types of attributes are often employed, for instance, the class instance relation *is-a* and the possession relation *has-a*.   Examples of these relations are given by

"A dog *is-a*(*n*) animal."

and

"A chair *has-a* leg."

respectively.   In $O-A-V$ functional notation, these relations take the forms

is-a(dog) = animal

and

has-a(chair) = leg

Causality relations are also commonly employed in semantic networks.

Frames provide another representation for storing knowledge.   In these, slots are used to hold the knowledge associated with some object.   For instance, values of attributes may be entered in a slot in a fashion analogous to storage in a semantic network.   Moreover, other forms of knowledge, such as procedural information, can be used in slots.   In the case of procedures, a sequence of instructions that yields a desired result is entered into a slot.   Exception conditions, as well as

ROBY	
Slot	
Is-a	Robot – See _____ Frame Robot
Has-a	Accelerometer that measures acceleration $a(t)$
Moves at	Velocities $v(t)$ between -10 and $+10$ ft/sec, where $$v(t) = \int_0^t a(s)\,ds$$
Is located at	Distance $x(t)$ found from $$x(t) = \int_0^t v(s)\,ds$$
Has IQ	180

Figure 4.17. Frame diagram

pointers to other slots, can also be utilized. Figure 4.17 illustrates a frame-type structure.

Common to all the aforementioned representations is a convenient and illustrative structure that provides a skeleton for the symbolic portrayal of fact manipulation. In each instance, as well as in the flat-file representation of the predicate calculus, commonly employed reasoning procedures are delineated in a manner that is compatible with their customary semantic interpretations. The intent is to provide the knowledge engineer with the requisite scaffolding for whatever reasoning model he or she wishes to capture in machine form.

4.5 SET-THEORETIC DATA STRUCTURES

Set-theoretic data structures (STDS) enable the use of conventional set-theoretic operations on *n*-tuples of information, as well as on normal sets. This is achieved, in the case of finite sets, by the use of a common representation.

Without going into a too mathematically rigorous discussion, we will explain how the common representation is accomplished. First, if A is a finite set of elements, it is rewritten as the same set, except that each element is given the superscript 1. For instance,

$$A = \{a, b, c, d\}$$

is given the representation

$$A = \{a^1, b^1, c^1, d^1\}$$

Next, an *n*–tuple of elements is replaced by a set consisting of elements representative of the components. Specifically, the first component is given the superscript 1, the second component is given the superscript 2, and so on.   The final component is given the superscript n.   Thus, if

$$B = (a, b, c, 3, d)$$

the new representation is

$$B = \{a^1, b^2, c^3, 3^4, d^5\}$$

As mentioned previously, the benefit of the STDS representation is that set-theoretic operations can now be defined on ordered component structures, whereas normally they cannot.   We simply transform the n-tuples into their STDS forms and apply the set-theoretic operations to the resulting sets.   For instance,

$$\{a, b, c, d\} \cap (a, b, c, 3, d)$$

and

$$\{a, b, c, d\} \Delta (a, b, c, 3, d)$$

can be evaluated using STDS representation.   Indeed,

$$A \cap B = \{a^1\}$$

and

$$A \Delta B = (A - B) \cup (B - A)$$
$$= \{b^1, c^1, d^1, b^2, c^3, 3^4, d^5\}$$

The following examples should provide some insight into the manner in which STDS representations can be employed in the presentation and manipulation of descriptive information.

Example 4.10

Suppose two different records of information are given by n-tuples.   Let the first record be the triple

$$C = (\text{Henry, green, 22})$$

where the first component gives a name, the second an eye color, and the third an age.   Let the second record be the quadruple

$$D = (\text{Joe, green, 22, A})$$

where the first three components give the same types of information as the corresponding components of C, and the fourth gives a grade in a particular course.   Suppose the question is raised as to what component values are in common for the two records.   Putting both C and D into STDS form, the answer is given by

$$D \cap C = \{\text{green}^2, 22^3\}$$

The second components are the same: both Joe and Henry have green eyes.   Also, the third components are the same: both are 22 years old.

Example 4.11

Consider the database consisting of records of information whose first two fields give parents names, mother and father, and whose third field gives the names of children (one or more).   An example would be the flat file

Mother	Father	Child
Jane	Joe	Sam
Ann	Bill	Sally
Sue	Ike	Ira, Ed

Use of STDS notation provides a consistent mathematical description for each record:

$$\{Jane^1, Joe^2, Sam^3\}$$

$$\{Ann^1, Bill^2, Sally^3\}$$

$$\{Sue^1, Ike^2, Ira^3, Ed^3\}$$

The superscripts 1, 2, and 3 indicate mother, father, and child names, respectively.

Example 4.12

Consider the image of the triangle with legs given in Figure 4.18.   We wish to provide an STDS description that will capture three important relations within the image structure: (1) the connectivity between vertices, (2) the relative horizontal locations of the vertices, and (3) the relative vertical locations of the vertices.   An appropriate encoding of this information is given by the STDS structure

$$\{\{\{d^1, a^2\}, \{a^1, b^2\}, \{a^1, c^2\}, \{e^1, b^2\}, \{b^1, c^2\}\}^1, \{\{d^1, e^2\}, \{a^1, b^2\}\}^2, \{\{d^1, a^2\}, \{e^1, b^2\}, \{b^1, c^2\}\}^3\}$$

where the superscripts 1, 2, and 3 on the next-to-the-outermost braces denote connectivity, horizontal relative location, and vertical relative location, respectively.   Inside the next-to-the-outermost braces with a 1 there is $\{d^1, a^2\}$, which is an encoding

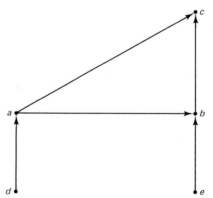

Figure 4.18.   Triangle with legs

of the fact that node d has an arrow leaving it that points to node a. Similarly, $\{a^1, b^2\}$ means there is an arrow pointing from a to b. In general, connectivity information is contained within these braces. Inside the next-to-the-outermost braces with a 2 is $\{d^1, e^2\}$, which represents the fact that node d is to the left of node e. Similarly, $\{a^1, b^2\}$ denotes that node a is to the left of node b. Finally, the next-to-the-outermost braces with a 3 contain information regarding which node is beneath another node; for instance, entry $\{d^1, a^2\}$ means that node d is underneath node a.

4.6 FORMAL LIST STRUCTURES

Most computers utilize coordinate address memories: data are stored and retrieved by where they are, not by what they are (as is the case with content-addressable memory). Searching in a coordinate address memory is performed by the software and is often very time consuming. To facilitate searching, list structures are used to organize data into modules that are hierarchically related and can therefore be accessed independently. In this section we will explain how data are changed, created, and destroyed using list structures.

Before proceeding rigorously, it would be profitable to intuitively discuss sequential memory and linked memory allocation. In sequential memory, information, in the form of data or instructions, is stored sequentially by address. For instance, consider the set of information

$$I = \{\text{dog, cat, rat, bat}\}$$

that is to be stored alphabetically and for which four adjacent (contiguous) memory locations are available. Suppose these addresses are given by

$$N = \{2, 3, 4, 5\}$$

Then each available address will be assigned a unique piece of data from I. Intuitively, we might imagine a function performing the assignment; indeed, such a function will be defined in the subsequent formal presentation of list structures. In any case, the information in I might be stored in a manner described by the *memory map* given in Figure 4.19, where an arrow points to the location (2) in memory where the string of alphabetical names begins.

Such memory organization is not always conducive to speedy CPU–memory transfer. For one thing, a contiguous chunk of memory might be required to store a large amount of information. Second, due to the necessity of interrogating all previous entries, an inordinate amount of searching is required to access the last entry

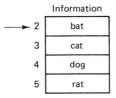

Figure 4.19. Memory map

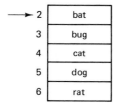

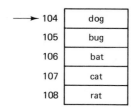

Figure 4.20.
Reconfigured
memory map

Figure 4.21.
Additional memory for
reverse alphabetical
representation

in the string. Next, deletion and creation of new packets of information in a sequentially organized memory can entail the movement of large blocks of memory. For instance, suppose that, in the situation depicted in Figure 4.19, the additional piece of information "bug" is to be stored alphabetically together with the data already in memory. Either an additional word in memory at location 1 or 6 is required, or a new block of memory consisting of five contiguous locations must be found. In any event, to write the new datum into the sequential memory organization, other data must be moved. Thus, if location 1 is not free, but location 6 is free, then the block of memory consisting of the information "cat," "dog," and "rat" would, of necessity, be moved down one address, and the datum "bug" would be entered into location 3, the result being the memory map given in Figure 4.20.

Another troublesome feature of sequential memory is the inability to order the data in a way other than by address alone. Should it be desired that the information in Figure 4.20 be ordered alphabetically relative to reverse spellings, then a whole separate block of memory would be necessitated (see Figure 4.21).

Linked memory allocation overcomes the difficulties associated with sequential memory, except perhaps the excessive time required for searching. Briefly, linked memory allocation utilizes list structures in which links are used to point to the next address. To accomplish the linking, each word of memory has several fields. Information is stored in the first field, and the other fields are used to point to the addresses of other information. A transition function is utilized in the linking process (see Figures 4.23 and 4.24). A formal presentation of linked memory allocation will be given next.

A *list* is a nine–tuple

$$(N, I, \varepsilon, Z, V, f, g, M, \delta)$$

where

N = finite nonempty set of addresses

I = finite nonempty set of information

ε = unique element of I denoting empty, or blank, information

Z = finite nonempty set of *linking labels*

$V = \{0, 1\}$ is a *valuation space*, 1 and 0 being used to indicate that an action does or does not occur

f = *entry address function*,

$$f: N \to V$$

If $f(n) = 1$, then n is an *entry point*, or *entry address*, to the list; otherwise, it is not. Normally, access to a list can only take place by starting at an entry address.

g = *information locating function*,

$$g: N \times I \to V$$

For each $n \in N$, there exists one and only one $a \in I$ such that $g(n, a) = 1$; thus, at each address there is exactly one piece of information. The ordered pair consisting of the address and the associated information is called a *record*.

M = set of records; that is,

$$M = g^{-1}(1)$$

and so $M \subset N \times I$, with the first component being the address and the second component being the unique piece of information located at that address.

δ = the *delta* or *linking* function,

$$\delta: M \times Z \times N \to V$$

where for each $(m, z) \in M \times Z$, there exists at most one $n \in N$ such that $\delta(m, z, n) = 1$.

If $\delta(m, z, n) = 1$, it is said that the record m *points* to the address n under (or using) the linking label z, or, more briefly, the linking label z points from the record m to address n. If $\delta(m, z, n) = 0$, then there is no z link from record m to address n.

Although the formal definition of a list at first appears abstract, those familiar with a programming language, such as PASCAL, that employs pointers should recognize the essence of the structure.

Example 4.13

Suppose five memory locations are available, and these are the elements of the set

$$N = \{1, 2, 4, 7, 8\}$$

The four words "dog," "cat," "rat," and "bat" are to be placed into memory. Two linking labels, x and y, are available, the former for linking alphabetically and the latter for alphabetically linking two words according to reverse spellings. Then, utilizing the notation in the list definition,

$$I = \{\text{dog, cat, rat, bat, } \varepsilon\}$$

and

$$Z = \{x, y\}$$

Assuming that the information is entered in the order given,

$$g(1, \text{dog}) = 1$$

$$g(2, \text{cat}) = 1$$

$$g(4, \text{rat}) = 1$$

$$g(7, \text{bat}) = 1$$

$$g(8, \varepsilon) = 1$$

and all other values of g are zero.   Therefore, the set of all records is

$$M = \{(1, \text{dog}), (2, \text{cat}), (4, \text{rat}), (7, \text{bat}), (8, \varepsilon)\}$$

The delta function is employed in connecting together the records in accordance with the desired lexicographical ordering:

$$\delta((1, \text{dog}), x, 4) = 1$$

$$\delta((2, \text{cat}), x, 1) = 1$$

$$\delta((4, \text{rat}), x, 8) = 1$$

$$\delta((7, \text{bat}), x, 2) = 1$$

$$\delta((1, \text{dog}), y, 7) = 1$$

$$\delta((7, \text{bat}), y, 2) = 1$$

$$\delta((2, \text{cat}), y, 4) = 1$$

and all other values of δ are defined to be zero.

Note that the first entry above says that "rat" follows "dog" alphabetically, and therefore there was no choice as to the valuation.   On the other hand, the fact that (4, rat) points to 8 under x is not necessitated by the alphabetical lexicography.

Theoretically, any number of nodes, including none, can be entry nodes for the list; however, from a practical point of view, since "bat" is the first word under the linking variable x and "dog" is the first word under the linking variable y, it is convenient to let

$$f(7) = f(1) = 1$$

It might also be convenient to point to empty "pieces of memory," and so we let $f(8) = 1$.

A record, as defined previously, is an ordered pair consisting of an address, together with information.   An *extended record*, or *record with links*, is an n-tuple, $n \leq \text{card}(Z) + 2$, consisting of the address of the record, a single piece of information, and up to n addresses that are pointed to by n linking labels, the particular labels being agreed upon a priori.   For instance, in Example 4.13, ex-

	Information	x	y
1	dog	4	7
2	cat	1	4
3			
4	rat	8	
5			
6			
7	bat	2	2
8	ε		

Figure 4.22.   Memory map of list

tended records can be utilized that have four entries: the record address, the information at the address, the value of the x linking label, and the value of the y linking label.

Figure 4.22 gives a memory map for the list of Example 4.13 that employs extended records. In the diagram, note that the arrows point to the entry points and that addresses 3, 5, and 6 are not part of the list structure. In practice, entry point addresses are stored in other memory locations such as designated registers. Note also in Figure 4.22 that some extended records, such as the one with address 4, do not have a link associated with each linking variable—in the case of the nonextended record (4, rat),

$$\delta((4, \text{rat}), y, n) = 0$$

for every $n \in N$.

For human understanding, a graphical representation like the one in Figure 4.23 is often employed to depict a list structure. In such a representation, instead of putting the actual link values in the link variable fields, arrows are drawn from the fields to the appropriate locations (addresses). For instance, since in Example 4.13

$$\delta((7, \text{bat}), x, 2) = 1$$

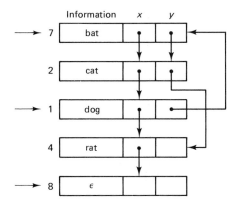

Figure 4.23.   Linked list structure

in Figure 4.23 there is an arrow from the x field of the extended record at address 7 pointing to address 2. As in the case of an ordinary memory map, arrows are used to point to entry addresses.

Data are accessed in a list by first entering the list utilizing an entry address and then traveling the appropriate links in order to find the desired information. For instance, in Example 4.13, to find the second alphabetically ordered entry, which is "cat," the list would be entered at address 7, the entry point for (forward) alphabetically ordered entries. Then the x link is followed because it is the linking label determining the next (forward) alphabetically ordered entry. Thus, since

$$\delta((7, \text{bat}), x, 2) = 1$$

address 2 is checked. Since

$$g(2, \text{cat}) = 1$$

the desired information is obtained.

Compared to content-addressable memory methods, searching by following links can be very time consuming. So, too, is the changing of list structures, as well as are the creation and destruction of records. Generally, the modification of a list structure must be preceded by a search to find the record that is to be changed or removed or to find the place where new records are to be inserted. Mathematically, any change in a given list results in a new and different list.

Example 4.14

Consider the list, herein to be called OLD, given in Example 4.13. Suppose we wish to modify it by the insertion of a new record, say (3, bug). A new list, called NEW, with this record in its appropriate spot, is given in Figure 4.24. Searches, as well as link modifications, had to be performed on OLD to transform it into NEW. As an illustration, letting δ be the delta function for OLD,

$$\delta((7, \text{bat}), x, 2) = 1$$

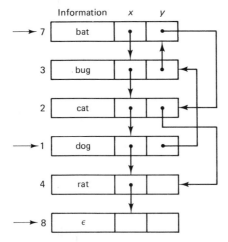

Figure 4.24. Insertion into linked structure

After searching, the delta function, δ', for NEW is found by first letting

$$\delta'((3, \text{bug}), x, 2) = 1$$

and then by letting

$$\delta'((7, \text{bat}), x, 3) = 1$$

A similar procedure can be given for the y link.

4.7 FUZZY AND LATTICE LINK STRUCTURES

The linked list provides a precise method for the organization of data; indeed, the following are specified exactly:

1. Information at a given address
2. Entry addresses
3. Address to which each link points

To introduce uncertainty into the model, we can employ a fuzzy linked list, where, instead of the two-point Boolean algebra {0, 1}, the valuation space is the interval [0, 1]. As in the customary interpretation of fuzzy values, valuations close to 1 are used to indicate a high degree of certitude, while those close to 0 indicate negligible certitude. For instance, with regard to 1 through 3 above, fuzzy valuation allows for lack of certainty regarding information location, entry addresses, and addresses specified by pointers, respectively.

Like a list, a *fuzzy linked list* is a nine–tuple

$$(N, I, \varepsilon, Z, V, f, g, M, \delta)$$

Due to the similarity of the definitions, we will only point out the differences. As mentioned previously, in the fuzzy case $V = [0, 1]$. Thus, the entry address function f, the information location function g, and the delta function δ take values in [0, 1]. The following restrictions apply:

1. For each $n \in N$, there exists one and only one $a \in I$ such that $g(n, a) \neq 0$. Any ordered pair (n, a) for which g is not 0 is called a record.
2. For any $(m, z) \in M \times Z$, there exists at most one $n \in N$ such that

$$\delta(m, z, n) \neq 0$$

In such a case, we say that the record m using the z link points to address n with certainty $\delta(m, z, n)$.

Example 4.15

Consider the address space

$$N = \{1, 2, 3, 5, 6\}$$

and the information set

$$I = \{a, b, c, d, \varepsilon\}$$

Let there be a single linking variable z, a certain entry point at 1 $[f(1) = 1]$, an uncertain entry point at 2 [say, $f(2) = 0.7$], and no other entry points. Moreover, let

$$g(1, a) = 1$$

$$g(2, b) = 0.6$$

$$g(3, a) = 0.8$$

$$g(5, \varepsilon) = 1$$

$$g(6, c) = 1$$

and let all other values of g be 0. Note that at locations 1, 5, and 6 there is certainty that the data a, ε, and c are respectively stored. To a lesser degree of certainty, datum a is stored at location 3, and to a still lesser degree of certainty, datum b is stored at location 2. Finally, define the linking function by

$$\delta((1, a), z, 3) = 1$$

$$\delta((3, a), z, 6) = 0.9$$

$$\delta((2, b), z, 5) = 0.8$$

with all other values of δ being 0. Note that the label z points from the record $(3, a)$ to the address 6 with less than certainty.

A memory map depiction of the fuzzy list defined in Example 4.15 is given in Figure 4.25. Note that the relevant valuations are included in the map: data in the information and linking fields have the appropriate valuations written adjacently (separated by a slash), and entry address arrows are labeled with the appropriate degrees of certainty defined by the function f.

A graph structure can also be employed to depict a fuzzy linked list. Figure 4.26 gives the graphical representation for the fuzzy list of Example 4.15. Note that the linking arrows are labeled with the proper valuations.

General lattice linked lists are defined analogously to fuzzy linked lists, with the exception that the valuation space V is a lattice with units 0 and 1. Restrictions

	Information	Link
1 ⟶ 1	a/1	3/1
0.7 ⟶ 2	b/0.6	5/0.8
3	a/0.8	6/0.9
4		
5	ε/1	
6	c/1	

Figure 4.25. Memory map of fuzzy linked list

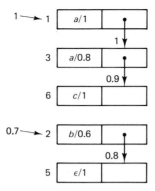

Figure 4.26.   Fuzzy linked list structure

(1) and (2) above apply.   Memory maps and graphical representations are constructed in exactly the same manner as for fuzzy linked lists.

Example 4.16

Let

$$N = \{1, 2, 3, 4\}$$

$$I = \{a, b, c, d, e, \varepsilon\}$$

$$Z = \{z\}$$

and V be given by the diagram

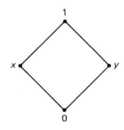

Let

$$f(1) = 1$$

$$g(1, a) = x$$

$$g(2, b) = x$$

$$g(3, c) = y$$

$$g(4, e) = 1$$

$$\delta((1, a), z, 2) = 1$$

$$\delta((2, b), z, 3) = x$$

$$\delta((3, c), z, 4) = y$$

$$\delta((4, e), z, 1) = x$$

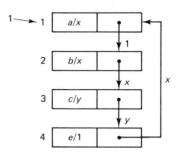

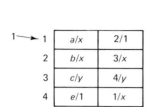

Figure 4.27. Memory map
of lattice linked list

Figure 4.28. Lattice linked list
structure

and let all other values of f, g, and δ be 0. Note that the valuations x and y are not comparable. Figures 4.27 and 4.28 give the memory map and the graphical representation, respectively, of the lattice list.

4.8 BOUND MATRICES AND DIGITAL IMAGES

In Section 1.10, bound matrices were briefly introduced in order to provide a convenient framework for the description of a block world. It was explained there that the entries in a bound matrix can be taken from any abstract set. In the present section, we will reintroduce the bound matrix data structure from the perspective of digital images; indeed, it is in such a setting that the structure was originally utilized. From a practical standpoint, nothing essential is lost in this approach. The form of a bound matrix is the same no matter what the nature of its entries, and the operations defined on and between bound matrices can always be reinterpreted for more general settings whenever, of course, a particular operation is meaningful in a given setting. For instance, if the entries come from a lattice, then sup and inf operations are relevant, whereas add and multiply operations might not be. In any event, the most important applications occur when the entries are real-valued.

Insofar as knowledge representation is concerned, it is important to recognize at the outset that the theory of bound matrices subsumes that of ordinary matrices. Consequently, all forms of knowledge that have been historically represented by matrices are ipso facto representable by bound matrices. In particular, all ordinary matrix operations can be implemented in terms of operations on bound matrices. The advantage of bound matrix algebra is that it includes many operations that are fundamental to AI and that have no counterparts in ordinary matrix algebra. More generally, bound matrices form the most practically significant category within the general image algebra (see Section 9.2).

From a classical mathematical perspective, a *digital image* is a real-valued function defined on some subset of the integral lattice $Z \times Z$. To understand the reason for such a model, imagine the *xy* plane being partitioned into square regions, much like graph paper, with each square centered at a lattice point (i, j) in $Z \times Z$. Each square is called a *pixel*, short for *picture element*, with the square centered

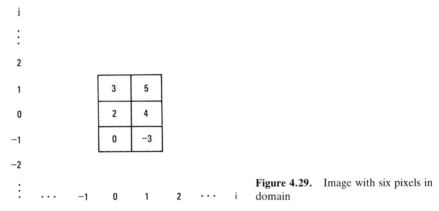

Figure 4.29.   Image with six pixels in domain

at (i, j) being called the (i, j)th pixel.   A digital image is obtained by assigning to each pixel a value, called a *gray value*, which, before processing, is indicative of the level of gray (white to black) at the given pixel.   Once processing has begun, the gray level can take on both noninteger and negative real values.   As a result, gray levels are assumed to be values in the set of real numbers.   Since each pixel square is addressed by the lattice point at its center, we do not mathematically differentiate between the center and the square itself.   To wit, we also call the lattice point a pixel, and the definition of an image takes a subset of $Z \times Z$ as the domain of the image.

By practical necessity, every digital image has gray values on only a finite set of pixels.   Consequently, there are always an infinite number of lattice points on which no gray value is defined; thus, each digital image is considered to be of the form $f: D \rightarrow R$, where D is a *finite* subset of $Z \times Z$, and R is the set of real numbers.

Example 4.17

Consider the digital image f illustrated in Figure 4.29.   The domain consists of the six pixels darkly outlined.   Rigorously, the image $f:D \rightarrow R$, where $D = \{(i, j): i = 0,$ 1 and $j = -1, 0, 1\}$. The gray value at $(i, j) \in D$ is $f((i, j))$ or, more conveniently, $f(i, j)$.   Thus $f(0, 0) = 2$, $f(0, -1) = 0$, $f(1, -1) = -3, f(1, 0) = 4, f(0, 1) = 3$, and $f(1, 1) = 5$.

A bound matrix representation can be constructed for any finite digital image with rectangular domain D.   If the image f has an $m \times n$ rectangular domain given by $D = \{(i, j): r \leq i \leq r + n - 1 \text{ and } s \leq j \leq s + m - 1 = t\}$, then f can be represented as

$$\begin{pmatrix} a_{11} & a_{12} & \cdots & a_{1n} \\ a_{21} & a_{22} & \cdots & a_{2n} \\ \vdots & \vdots & & \vdots \\ a_{m1} & a_{m2} & \cdots & a_{mn} \end{pmatrix}_{r, t}$$

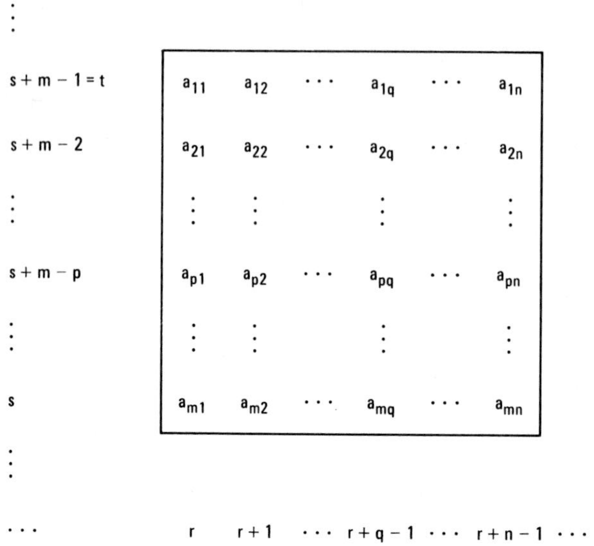

Figure 4.30. Overlay of matrix and grid structures

The values of gray for the image are given as a_{pq} in the bound matrix $(a_{pq})_{rt}$. Here p denotes the matrix row and q the matrix column for the location of the value a_{pq}. The integers r and t specify the leftmost and uppermost pixel (r, t) in D, the domain of the image f. The gray value at this pixel is a_{11}; that is, $f(r, t) = a_{11}$. For any other pixel (i, j) in D, it can be seen that

$$f(i, j) = a_{m+s-j,\ i+1-r} = a_{t+1-j,\ i+1-r}$$

or, equivalently,

$$a_{pq} = f(q + r - 1, m + s - p) = f(q + r - 1, t + 1 - p)$$

The preceding relationships can best be seen by overlaying the matrix representation on the pixel grid structure ("hanging" the matrix), as in Figure 4.30.

Example 4.18

Let f be the image given in Example 4.17. Then employing the notation of bound matrices, we obtain

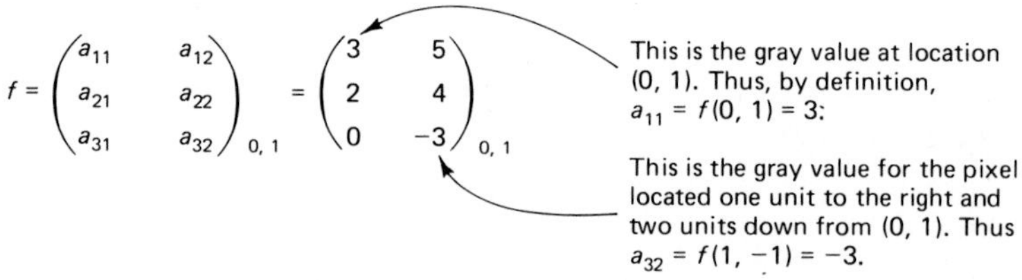

$$f = \begin{pmatrix} a_{11} & a_{12} \\ a_{21} & a_{22} \\ a_{31} & a_{32} \end{pmatrix}_{0,\ 1} = \begin{pmatrix} 3 & 5 \\ 2 & 4 \\ 0 & -3 \end{pmatrix}_{0,\ 1}$$

This is the gray value at location (0, 1). Thus, by definition, $a_{11} = f(0, 1) = 3$:

This is the gray value for the pixel located one unit to the right and two units down from (0, 1). Thus $a_{32} = f(1, -1) = -3$.

While it can be seen from the positioning that $a_{32} = f(1, -1)$, this relationship can be directly computed from $f(i, j) = a_{t+1-j, i+1-r}$. The algorithm for obtaining the values of f from the values in the bound matrix, and vice versa, is important for computer implementation and for mechanization purposes. However, in this text it will generally suffice to have a good understanding of the geometric explanation for identifying the appropriate pixel locations.

A rigorous definition of a bound matrix will now be given. Consider the array-type structure consisting of m by n entities:

$$
\begin{pmatrix}
a_{11} & a_{12} & \cdots & a_{1n} \\
a_{21} & a_{22} & \cdots & a_{2n} \\
\vdots & \vdots & & \vdots \\
a_{m1} & a_{m2} & \cdots & a_{mn}
\end{pmatrix}_{r,\,t}
$$

where

1. each a_{pq} is a real number or a $*$ (star)
2. $1 \le p \le m,\ 1 \le q \le n$
3. r and t are integers

Such a data structure is called a *bound matrix*, or an $m \times n$ bound matrix, and the stars denote values that are not known. The location in $Z \times Z$ of the a_{11} entry, which may be a $*$, is (r, t). The location of the entry a_{pq} in $Z \times Z$ is $(q + r - 1, t + 1 - p)$. The star will be utilized to allow nonrectangular images to be represented by bound matrices. It is helpful to visualize all values *outside* a bound matrix to be stars.

Because the value at the origin plays a key role in many applications, we often omit the subscript (r, t) and simply circle the bound matrix entry corresponding to the origin. Given the origin position, it is possible to find (r, t), and vice versa. When using this convention, one must keep in mind that it is the subscript that is stored in the computer.

Example 4.19

Consider the image $f : D \to R$, where $D = \{(1, 1), (1, 2), (2, 2)\}$ and $f(1, 1) = 8$, $f(1, 2) = 4$, and $f(2, 2) = 6$. Then a bound matrix representing f is given by

$$
\begin{pmatrix}
4 & 6 \\
8 & *
\end{pmatrix}_{1,2}
$$

Another bound matrix representing the image f is

$$
\begin{pmatrix}
* & 4 & 6 \\
* & 8 & * \\
* & * & *
\end{pmatrix}_{0,2}
=
\begin{pmatrix}
* & 4 & 6 \\
* & 8 & * \\
\circledast & * & *
\end{pmatrix}
$$

Note that in the origin specification the circle is always around the gray value for the (0, 0) pixel. In this example that pixel happens not to be part of the image; nevertheless, the notation must be used in a consistent fashion.

When we say that an $m \times n$ bound matrix $(a_{pq})_{rt}$ *represents* a (necessarily finite) image $f:D \to R$, we mean that the gray values of f lie in $(a_{pq})_{rt}$ in the proper position and that all other values (if any) of a_{pq} are $*$. Rigorously, $(a_{pq})_{rt}$ represents the finite image $f:D \to R$ if for every (i, j) in D there corresponds the element $a_{t+1-j,\ i+1-r}$ in $(a_{pq})_{rt}$, where $a_{t+1-j,\ i+1-r} = f(i, j)$. Furthermore, all other a_{pq} in $(a_{pq})_{rt}$ must have the entry $*$.

It is important to know how to go from a picture representation of an image to a bound matrix representation, and vice versa. This is most simply done geometrically by overlaying one structure on the other. There is no need to memorize the formula for relating gray values using matrix notation a_{pq} with the function notation $f(i, j)$. The complexity of the relation arises from the somewhat backwardly rotated notation used in representing tuples in matrices relative to the xy coordinate labeling.

For any digital image f with finite, nonempty domain, a *minimal bound matrix* can be found to represent f. The minimal bound matrix for f is simply that representation for which m and n are as small as possible. In Example 4.19, the first bound matrix given is the minimal one. It is simply the representation that contains no extraneous rows or columns of stars.

4.9 BOUND MATRIX ALGEBRA

There exists an operational algebra defined on bound matrices. It is many-sorted (see Section 9.1) in that different sorts or entities are involved—for instance, arrays, real numbers, and the bound matrices themselves. There are unary operations having a single bound matrix input, and binary operations such as the addition of bound matrices and the scalar multiplication of a bound matrix by a real number. As mentioned in Section 4.8, ordinary matrix algebra is a subalgebra of bound matrix algebra. So, too, is the set-theoretic algebra of finite subsets of $Z \times Z$. From an operational perspective, bound matrix algebra is a powerful tool for the representation and manipulation of information. In particular, it provides a relatively simple framework within which to embed digital image-processing algorithms (see Chapter 8).

Due to the identification of images and bound matrices, we will often not distinguish between the two concepts. It should be kept in mind that the image model that we employ is mathematically quite general and, as a consequence, possesses applications outside the area of computer vision. Indeed, the more general image algebra of Section 9.2 should not be viewed as a study within image processing; rather, it is the processing of images that forms one use, albeit an important one, of the general image algebra.

The *addition* of images is performed *pointwise* (or, more appropriately, *pixelwise*). The gray values of corresponding pixels are added numerically. To be precise, ADD is a binary (two input) operation defined by

$$[\text{ADD}(f, g)](i, j) = \begin{cases} f(i, j) + g(i, j), & \text{if } f \text{ and } g \text{ are both defined at } (i, j) \\ *, & \text{if either } f \text{ or } g \text{ is undefined at } (i, j) \end{cases}$$

where f and g are the input images. Saying that the sum is $*$ simply means ADD (f, g) is undefined whenever either f or g is undefined. Hence the domain of ADD(f, g) is the intersection of the domains of f and g. The block diagram for ADD is

$$f \longrightarrow \boxed{\text{ADD}} \longrightarrow \text{ADD}(f, g)$$
$$g \longrightarrow$$

Example 4.20

Consider the images f and g in Figure 4.31. The image f has the domain D_f $=\{(0, 0), (0, 1), (1, 1), (2, 1)\}$ and g has the domain $D_g = \{(0, 0), (0, 1), (0, 2), (1, 1)\}$. Furthermore, $f(0, 0) = 3, f(0, 1) = 2, f(1, 1) = 1$, and $f(2, 1) = 4$. Also, $g(0, 0) = 3, g(0, 1) = -7, g(0, 2) = 8$, and $g(1, 1) = 4$. Operating by ADD yields

$$\text{ADD}(f, g) = \begin{pmatrix} -5 & 5 \\ 6 & * \end{pmatrix}_{0,1} = \begin{pmatrix} -5 & 5 \\ \boxed{6} & * \end{pmatrix}$$

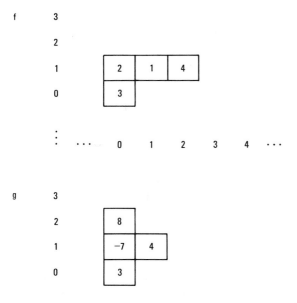

Figure 4.31. Images with different domains

That is,

$$[ADD(f, g)](0, 0) = 3 + 3 = 6$$

$$[ADD(f, g)](0, 1) = -5$$

$$[ADD(f, g)](1, 1) = 5$$

Moreover, $[ADD(f, g)](1, 0) = *$, since both f and g are undefined at $(1, 0)$. Equivalently, $f(1, 0) = g(1, 0) = *$. It should be recognized that, if just one of the images were undefined at $(1, 0)$, then ADD would still be $*$ (undefined) there. Also note that $[ADD(f, g)](0, 2) = *$, since $f(0, 2) = *$. This is implicit in the bound-matrix representation of the image f, since all values outside the bound matrix are assumed to be $*$.

Similar to the addition of images are the operations of multiplying images and finding the maximum and minimum of two images. These operations are also defined pointwise. Moreover, like addition, whenever one of the inputs is undefined, so is the output. *Multiplication* of two images f and g, denoted MULT (f, g), is defined by

$$[MULT(f, g)](i, j) = \begin{cases} f(i, j) \cdot g(i, j), & \text{if both inputs are defined at } (i, j) \\ *, & \text{if either input is undefined at } (i, j) \end{cases}$$

The block diagram corresponding to multiplication is

Example 4.21

Let f and g be the images given in Figure 4.31. Then

The *maximum* operator, MAX(f, g), compares two images in a pointwise manner and returns the maximum, or highest, value at each pixel. If either f or g is undefined at a particular pixel, then MAX(f, g) is likewise undefined there. Functionally,

$$[MAX(f, g)](i, j) = \max[f(i, j), g(i, j)]$$

unless either $f(i, j) = *$ or $g(i, j) = *$, in which case $[MAX(f, g)](i, j) = *$. MAX has the block diagram

Example 4.22

Using the same inputs as in Example 4.21 gives

$$f = \begin{pmatrix} 2 & 1 & 4 \\ 3 & * & * \end{pmatrix}_{0,\,1} \rightarrow \boxed{\text{MAX}} \rightarrow \begin{pmatrix} 2 & 4 \\ 3 & * \end{pmatrix}_{0,\,1}$$

$$g = \begin{pmatrix} 8 & * \\ -7 & 4 \\ 3 & * \end{pmatrix}_{0,\,2} \rightarrow$$

Note that

$$[\text{MAX}(f,\,g)](0,\,1) \,=\, \max(2,\,-7) \,=\, 2$$

and

$$[\text{MAX}(f,\,g)](0,\,2) \,=\, *, \qquad \text{since } f(0,\,2) \,=\, *$$

Similar to MAX is the *minimum* operator MIN defined by

$$[\text{MIN}(f,\,g)](i,\,j) \,=\, \min[f(i,\,j),\,g(i,\,j)]$$

unless either $f(i,\,j) \,=\, *$ or $g(i,\,j) \,=\, *$, in which case the value of $\text{MIN}(f,\,g)$ at $(i,\,j)$ is $*$ ($[\text{MIN}(f,\,g)](i,\,j)$ is undefined). The block diagram for MIN is defined in the customary manner:

$$f \longrightarrow \boxed{\text{MIN}} \longrightarrow \text{MIN}(f,\,g)$$
$$g \longrightarrow$$

Example 4.23

Once again using the inputs of Example 4.21,

$$\begin{pmatrix} 2 & 1 & 4 \\ 3 & * & * \end{pmatrix}_{0,\,1} \longrightarrow \boxed{\text{MIN}} \rightarrow \begin{pmatrix} -7 & 1 \\ 3 & * \end{pmatrix}_{0,\,1}$$

$$\begin{pmatrix} 8 & * \\ -7 & 4 \\ 3 & * \end{pmatrix}_{0,\,2} \longrightarrow$$

The operator MULT is binary in that it takes two inputs. Like ADD, MAX, and MIN, it takes inputs that are of the same type or *sort*. Both inputs are images. Not all multi-input operations take operands of the same sort. The next operation to be introduced is also a form of multiplication; however, although it is still binary, its inputs are of different types. SCALAR is an image operator that takes an image as one input and a real number as another. The *scalar multiplication* of an image f by a real number r is an image denoted by $\text{SCALAR}(r; f)$ and defined by

$$[\text{SCALAR}(r; f)](i, j) = r \cdot f(i, j)$$

unless $f(i, j) = *$, in which case $\text{SCALAR}(r; f)$ is also undefined ($*$). To put it simply, to find $\text{SCALAR}(r; f)$, multiply each gray value of f by r. Scalar multiplication in bound matrix algebra is analogous to the same-named operation in vector algebra, and it has the block diagram

Note the semicolon between r and f in the notation for scalar multiplication, which indicates that r and f are different sorts of entities.

Example 4.24

Letting f be as in Example 4.21,

The simplest image-to-image unary transformation is *subtraction*, or *negation*. It is defined pointwise by

$$[\text{SUB}(f)](i, j) = -f(i, j)$$

for every (i, j) in the domain of f. SUB has the block diagram

Example 4.25

$$\begin{pmatrix} * & 3 \\ 4 & 0 \\ -7 & 1 \end{pmatrix}_{0,0} \rightarrow \boxed{\text{SUB}} \rightarrow \begin{pmatrix} * & -3 \\ -4 & 0 \\ 7 & -1 \end{pmatrix}_{0,0} = \begin{pmatrix} \circledast & -3 \\ -4 & 0 \\ 7 & -1 \end{pmatrix}$$

The subtraction of f is nothing more than scalar multiplication of f by -1.

Unary *division*, or *reciprocation*, is also defined on an image f. It is defined by

$$[\text{DIV}(f)](i, j) = \begin{cases} \dfrac{1}{f(i, j)}, & \text{if } f(i, j) \text{ is real and not } 0 \\ *, & \text{if } f(i, j) = 0 \text{ or } f(i, j) = * \end{cases}$$

In other words, one divided by zero is, as usual, undefined.   The block diagram for reciprocation is

$$f \to \boxed{\text{DIV}} \to \text{DIV}(f)$$

Example 4.26

$$\begin{pmatrix} 1 & * \\ 0 & 2 \end{pmatrix}_{0,0} \to \boxed{\text{DIV}} \to \begin{pmatrix} 1 & * \\ * & \tfrac{1}{2} \end{pmatrix}_{0,0}$$

Among the most useful operators involving images is the *translation* operator TRAN.   This operator is trinary with three inputs, an image and two integers. Given an image f and two integer inputs i and j, $\text{TRAN}(f; i, j)$ is an image that is the same as f, but moved over i pixels to the right and up j pixels.   In terms of bound matrices, if $f = (a_{pq})_{rt}$, then

$$\text{TRAN}(f; i, j) = (a_{pq})_{r+i,t+j}$$

In full bound matrix format, if

$$f = \begin{pmatrix} a_{11} & a_{12} & \cdots & a_{1n} \\ & & & \\ & & & \\ & & & \\ a_{m1} & a_{m2} & \cdots & a_{mn} \end{pmatrix}_{r,t}$$

then

$$\text{TRAN}(f; i, j) = \begin{pmatrix} a_{11} & a_{12} & \cdots & a_{1n} \\ & & & \\ & & & \\ & & & \\ a_{m1} & a_{m2} & \cdots & a_{mn} \end{pmatrix}_{r+i,t+j}$$

Notice that no values a_{pq} change; only the location of the gray values change by a translate.   The block diagram for TRAN is given by

$$\begin{array}{c} f = (a_{pq})_{rt} \longrightarrow \\ i \quad\quad\quad \longrightarrow \\ j \quad\quad\quad \longrightarrow \end{array} \boxed{\text{TRAN}} \longrightarrow \text{TRAN}(f; i, j) = (a_{pq})_{r+i,\, t+j}$$

Translation can also be defined pointwise.   In reading the pointwise description of TRAN, keep in mind that i and j represent inputs, and u and v correspond to the coordinates of the pixel under consideration.   Pointwise,

$$[\text{TRAN}(f; i, j)](u, v) = f(u - i, v - j)$$

Pay particular attention to the minus signs in the argument for f.   The somewhat confusing situation of a minus sign on the variable for a right translation is similar to that for real–valued functions in calculus.

Example 4.27

Let

$$f = \begin{pmatrix} 3 & 4 \\ 1 & * \end{pmatrix}_{0,0}$$

The domain of f is given by $D_f = \{(0, 0), (1, 0), (0, -1)\}$. Applying translation with integer inputs 4 and 1 gives

$$
\begin{array}{c}
f \longrightarrow \\
4 \longrightarrow \boxed{\text{TRAN}} \longrightarrow h = \begin{pmatrix} 3 & 4 \\ 1 & * \end{pmatrix}_{4, 1} \\
1 \longrightarrow
\end{array}
$$

The domain of $h = \mathrm{TRAN}(f; i, j)$ is $D_h = \{(4, 1), (5, 1), (4, 0)\}$, with $h(4, 1) = 3$, $h(5, 1) = 4$, and $h(4, 0) = 1$. With inputs 4 and 1, the domain of the image has been shifted four pixels to the right and one pixel up. The gray values have remained unchanged in their relative positions. This might best be seen by writing h in the origin specification form:

$$h = \begin{pmatrix} * & * & * & * & * & 3 & 4 \\ \circledast & * & * & * & 1 & * & * \end{pmatrix}$$

Bound matrices can be rotated 90°, 180°, 270°, and 360° = 0°. A counterclockwise 90° *rotation* of f is denoted by $\mathrm{NINETY}(f)$. It is given in pointwise form by

$$[\mathrm{NINETY}(f)](i, j) = f(j, -i)$$

This means that if $f(3, 1) = 4$ then $[\mathrm{NINETY}(f)](-1, 3) = 4$. A 180° rotation of f is found by applying two 90° rotations in succession. To simplify notation, a composition of two 90° rotations is denoted by NINETY^2. In other words,

$$\mathrm{NINETY}^2(f) = \mathrm{NINETY}[\mathrm{NINETY}(f)]$$

Similarly, a 270° rotation is equal to NINETY^3, NINETY applied three times in succession. The respective block diagrams for NINETY, NINETY^2, and NINETY^3 are

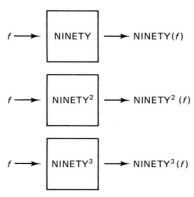

Example 4.28

Let

$$f = \begin{pmatrix} 3 & 2 \\ 1 & * \\ 5 & 2 \end{pmatrix}_{3,\,4} = \begin{pmatrix} * & * & * & 3 & 2 \\ * & * & * & 1 & * \\ * & * & * & 5 & 2 \\ * & * & * & * & * \\ \circledast & * & * & * & * \end{pmatrix} \begin{array}{l} \text{Rotate } f\ 90° \\ \text{with origin} \\ \text{as pivot} \end{array}$$

origin

Then

$$f \longrightarrow \boxed{\text{NINETY}} \longrightarrow \begin{pmatrix} 2 & * & 2 \\ 3 & 1 & 5 \end{pmatrix}_{-4,\,4} = \begin{pmatrix} 2 & * & 2 & * & * \\ 3 & 1 & 5 & * & * \\ * & * & * & * & * \\ * & * & * & * & * \\ * & * & * & * & \circledast \end{pmatrix}$$

This can be seen from a pointwise perspective by letting $h = \text{NINETY}(f)$. Then

$$h(-4, 4) = f(4, 4) = 2$$
$$h(-3, 4) = f(4, 3) = *$$
$$h(-2, 4) = f(4, 2) = 2$$
$$h(-4, 3) = f(3, 4) = 3$$
$$h(-3, 3) = f(3, 3) = 1$$
$$h(-2, 3) = f(3, 2) = 5$$

and

$$h(i, j) = *, \qquad \text{for all other } (i, j)$$

In general, if f is given by the m by n minimal bound matrix $(a_{pq})_{rt}$, then NINETY(f) will be given by an n by m bound matrix with first row, first column gray value located at $(-t, r + n - 1)$.

The rotation operator NINETY^2 is of particular importance. In terms of the domain D of an image f, NINETY^2 rotates D 180° around the origin. In precise terms, this means that (i, j) is an element of D if and only if $(-i, -j)$ is an element in the domain of NINETY$^2(f)$ (see Figure 4.32).

Bound matrices can also be *flipped*. There is a horizontal, a vertical, and two distinct diagonal flips (a 45° and a 135°). Only the 135° flip, denoted FLIP, will be discussed in detail. The others are obtained by using FLIP in conjunction with the rotation operation defined previously. Pointwise, FLIP is given by

$$[\text{FLIP}(f)](i, j) = f(-j, -i)$$

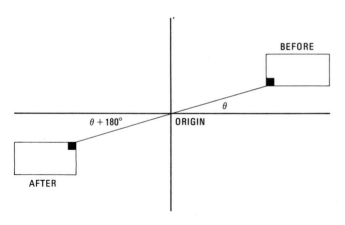

Figure 4.32.   180° rotation about origin

The block diagram for FLIP is

$$f \longrightarrow \boxed{\text{FLIP}} \longrightarrow \text{FLIP}(f)$$

Example 4.29

   Using the image f of Example 4.28,

$$\begin{pmatrix} 3 & 2 \\ 1 & * \\ 5 & 2 \end{pmatrix}_{3,\,4} \longrightarrow \boxed{\text{FLIP}} \longrightarrow \begin{pmatrix} 3 & 1 & 5 \\ 2 & * & 2 \end{pmatrix}_{-4,\,-3}$$

There are two salient points.   First, notice how the coordinates of the upper-left pixel have flipped both position and sign.   Second, notice that in matrix terms the output of FLIP is the transpose of the input.   (The rows and columns have reversed roles, the rows becoming the columns and the columns becoming the rows.)   Using these two facts, we can easily generate the outcome of FLIP if given a bound matrix input.

   Geometrically, the result of the preceding can be explained with the help of the 9 by 9 bound matrix in Figure 4.33.   In that representation, the image is thought to be rigidly fastened to the 135° line.   This line is then twisted 180° on its own axis.   This causes the upper-right elements to come out of the page and then occupy the lower-left position, the desired result being obtained in the process.
   The next two operations to be introduced in this section are similar to operators found in database algebras.   The first operator is the *selection* operator SELECT.   It is used for extracting part of an image from a given image $f = (a_{pq})_{rt}$. Intuitively, SELECT leaves entries within a specified *window* unchanged, and it *stars out* all entries outside this window.   To use the selection operator, the size and location of the window must be given.   More precisely, five inputs must be specified.   The first type of input to be specified is the image f; the next two inputs give the *size m* by n, $m, n \geq 1$, of the desired image $h = (b_{pq})_{r't'}$; and the final

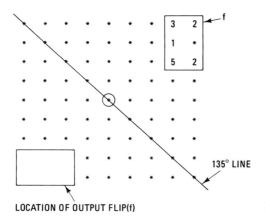

LOCATION OF OUTPUT FLIP(f)

Figure 4.33.   Reflection about 135° line

two inputs determine the location (r', t') in $Z \times Z$ of the first row, first column element b_{11} in the resulting image h.   By definition, $h(i, j) = f(i, j)$ for all points inside the window, for all (i, j) such that $r' \le i < r' + n$ and $t' - m < j \le t'$. For all other (i, j) in $Z \times Z$, $h(i, j) = *$.   The block diagram illustrating the operation SELECT$(f; m, n, r', t') = h$ is given by

$$f \longrightarrow$$
$$m \longrightarrow$$
$$n \longrightarrow \boxed{\text{SELECT}} \longrightarrow h = \text{SELECT}(f; m, n, r', t')$$
$$r' \longrightarrow$$
$$t' \longrightarrow$$

Example 4.30

Let

$$f = \begin{pmatrix} 3 & 7 & 5 & * \\ -2 & 4 & 1 & 3 \\ 0 & * & 8 & 2 \end{pmatrix}_{1, 1}$$

SELECT selects this portion of f.

Then

Input image $f \longrightarrow$

Output image $4 \longrightarrow$
is 4 by 2 $2 \longrightarrow$ $\boxed{\text{SELECT}} \longrightarrow h = \begin{pmatrix} 4 & 1 \\ * & 8 \\ * & * \\ * & * \end{pmatrix}_{2, 0}$

b_{11} element of $2 \longrightarrow$
output image is $0 \longrightarrow$
located at (2, 0)

The bound matrix resulting from the application of SELECT is 4 by 2 and has its b_{11} entry located at (2, 0).

Another important database-type operator in the bound matrix algebra is the *extension* operator EXTEND.   Whereas the selection operator extracts a smaller piece of an image from a given image, the extension operator takes two images and renders a larger image.   Rigorously, given images f and g, the extension

operator is defined by

$$[\text{EXTEND}(f, g)](i, j) = \begin{cases} f(i, j), & \text{if } f \text{ is defined at } (i, j) \\ g(i, j), & \text{elsewhere} \end{cases}$$

EXTEND(f, g) is obtained by *adjoining* to f that part of g which does not overlay f. The image f is called *dominant* since it is extended by using a *piece* of the *subordinate* image g. The block diagram for the extension operator is

It must be recognized that the extension operator is not commutative. In general, we do not have EXTEND(f, g) = EXTEND(g, f). Therefore, when using the block diagram, it is important to write the dominant input above the subordinate input.

Example 4.31

The following block diagram illustrates extension:

$$f = \begin{pmatrix} 4 & 5 & * \\ 3 & 7 & 8 \\ -2 & * & 5 \\ * & * & 3 \end{pmatrix}_{0, -3}$$

$$g = \begin{pmatrix} * & * & * & * \\ * & * & * & 3 \\ 4 & 5 & 8 & 9 \\ 2 & * & 1 & 3 \\ 5 & 0 & 1 & 1 \end{pmatrix}_{0, -3}$$

EXTEND

$$h = \begin{pmatrix} 4 & 5 & * & * \\ 3 & 7 & 8 & 3 \\ -2 & 5 & 5 & 9 \\ 2 & * & 3 & 3 \\ 5 & 0 & 1 & 1 \end{pmatrix}_{0, -3}$$

Notice that $h(0, -6) = 2$ since $f(0, -6) = *$ and $g(0, -6) = 2$. Additionally, $h(2, -6) = 3$ since $f(2, -6) = 3$, even though $g(2, -6) = 1$. Furthermore, $h(0, -7) = 5$ since $f(0, -7) = *$ and $g(0, -7) = 5$.

It is now appropriate to demonstrate the power of the operators thus far introduced. By using them in combination, a host of higher-level operators can be obtained. This is accomplished by composing the given operators to generate desired outputs.

As an illustration, consider the following block diagram:

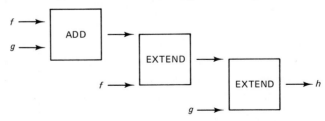

What is the output h? The ADD operator outputs an image that is the sum of f and g on their common domain $D_f \cap D_g$ and is undefined ($*$) elsewhere. This output is then used as the dominant input into an EXTEND, while f is used as the subordinate input. Hence ADD(f, g) is extended so that it equals f on the part of the domain of f that does not intersect the domain of g ($D_f - D_g$ in set-theoretic notation). This new output is then input into EXTEND as the dominant input, while g is used as the subordinate input. Hence the image is extended so that it equals g on $D_g - D_f$. The final output can be written as

$$h = \text{EXTEND} \, [\text{EXTEND}(\text{ADD} \, (f, g), f), g]$$

This new higher-level operator sums f and g on the intersection of their domains and leaves them unaltered elsewhere. It is given the name *extended addition* and denoted by EXTADD(f, g). It has the usual block diagram:

$$f \longrightarrow \boxed{\text{EXTADD}} \longrightarrow \text{EXTADD}(f, g)$$
$$g \longrightarrow$$

Example 4.32

Consider the bound matrices

$$f = \begin{pmatrix} 2 & 1 & 0 & 4 & * & * \\ 4 & 0 & 3 & -1 & * & * \\ 3 & 1 & -3 & 3 & * & * \\ ① & 2 & 5 & 2 & * & * \end{pmatrix}$$

and

$$g = \begin{pmatrix} * & * & * & * & * & * \\ * & * & 2 & 1 & 7 & 9 \\ * & * & 5 & -2 & 8 & 7 \\ ⊛ & * & 2 & 0 & 8 & 9 \end{pmatrix}$$

Then

$$\text{EXTADD}(f, g) = \begin{pmatrix} 2 & 1 & 0 & 4 & * & * \\ 4 & 0 & 5 & 0 & 7 & 9 \\ 3 & 1 & 2 & 1 & 8 & 7 \\ ① & 2 & 7 & 2 & 8 & 9 \end{pmatrix}$$

whereas

$$\text{ADD}(f, g) = \begin{pmatrix} * & * & * & * & * & * \\ * & * & 5 & 0 & * & * \\ * & * & 2 & 1 & * & * \\ ⊛ & * & 7 & 2 & * & * \end{pmatrix}$$

In addition to EXTADD, there are extended arithmetic binary operations for multiplication, maximum, and minimum. These are EXTMULT, EXTMAX, and EXTMIN, respectively. Like EXTADD, each performs the appropriate arithmetic operation on the intersection of the two input domains and leaves the inputs as they were elsewhere.

To this point, all the transformations introduced have been of a certain kind. Each has had at least one bound matrix for an input, and each has had a single bound matrix for its output. It is true that an operator may have had some auxiliary inputs of a different sort; nevertheless, it would not be inappropriate to characterize the operators thus far introduced as being *image-to-image operators*. Excluding the auxiliary inputs, which have thus far been either integers or real numbers, the input image data structure has been matched by the output data structure. In this section, three operators that are not image-to-image are discussed.

A bound matrix is a data structure consisting of a two-dimensional array together with four integers. By relative-address-type techniques, it can be changed to a three-dimensional array or, equivalently, a two-dimensional array consisting of absolute locations (i, j) together with a one-dimensional array consisting of real-valued gray levels $f(i, j)$. Throughout the remainder of this section the latter approach will be assumed, since from an intuitive standpoint it fits best with the structural operators to be defined.

Imagine two stacks called DOMAIN and RANGE. Each stack contains the same number of entries, the first containing ordered pairs (i, j) and the second containing real numbers (see Figure 4.34). Together the stacks implicitly contain a bound matrix, for if they were popped simultaneously, the corresponding words would form locations together with their gray values. One could logically go so far as to say that an image is a *pair of stacks* (DOMAIN, RANGE). It simply depends on one's point of view. Yet when the stacks are separated, each can be treated as an individual data structure, and its contents can be operated on independently of the other. Once such operations are completed, the stacks can once again be considered as a pair and a new image created, or the results of the independent operations can be output.

With the preceding in mind, the *creation* operator is defined. CREATE, as it will be called, takes an array consisting of real numbers or stars and an array of integer-ordered pairs (or, equivalently, a two-dimensional array of integers) and outputs a bound matrix. For each (i, j) in the array of ordered pairs, pixel (i, j) is given the corresponding value, be it a real number or a star, in the other array.

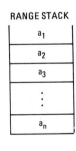

DOMAIN STACK   RANGE STACK

(i_1, j_1)	a_1
(i_2, j_2)	a_2
(i_3, j_3)	a_3
$\vdots$	$\vdots$
(i_n, j_n)	a_n

Figure 4.34. Decomposition of an image into stacks

All remaining pixels are given the value $*$. Except for the addressing techniques required to change a three-dimensional array to a bound matrix, the operation CREATE is purely *structural* in that it simply alters structure. Nevertheless, for logical reasons it needs to be specifically articulated. Moreover, from a low-level programming point of view or from an architectural perspective, it does involve an actual operation. The block diagram for CREATE is given by

$$D \longrightarrow \boxed{\text{CREATE}} \longrightarrow \text{CREATE}(D,\ R)$$
$$R \longrightarrow$$

where D is an array of ordered integer pairs, R is an array of real numbers or stars, and each array contains the same number of entries. A schematic is given in Figure 4.35. Keep in mind that the two input stacks are not considered a bound matrix until *joined* by CREATE. This point is crucial since the bound matrix results not only from the contents of the stacks but also from the ordering within the stacks. As long as the stacks remain independent, each can have its ordering permuted, and the output of CREATE depends on those orderings.

Example 4.33

Consider the two arrays

$$A = [(0,\ 0),\ (0,\ 1),\ (1,\ 0),\ (2,\ 0),\ (2,\ 1)]$$
$$B = [1,\ *,\ 0,\ 2,\ 6]$$

Then

$$\text{CREATE}(A,\ B) = \begin{pmatrix} * & * & 6 \\ 1 & 0 & 2 \end{pmatrix}_{0,1}$$

Just as two arrays of the appropriate types can be joined to form a bound matrix, a bound matrix can be *disjoined* to form two arrays. These operations, called DOMAIN and RANGE, collectively invert CREATE. DOMAIN takes an image input and yields an array of ordered pairs that make up the domain of

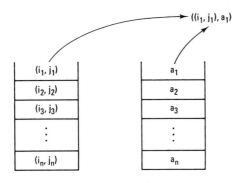

Figure 4.35. Creating image by popping stacks

the image.   RANGE takes an image and yields an array consisting of the gray values of the input image.   If f is the input image, their respective block diagrams are given by

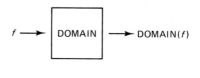

and

$$f \longrightarrow \boxed{\text{RANGE}} \longrightarrow \text{RANGE}(f)$$

It will be assumed that the data are taken from f and put into DOMAIN(f) and RANGE(f) in a compatible manner.   In other words, the bound matrix is *read* in both instances from top down and from left to right.   This uniformity of approach allows the exact image to be reconstructed by CREATE as long as the arrays DOMAIN(f) and RANGE(f) have not been transformed in any manner:

$$\text{CREATE [DOMAIN}(f), \text{RANGE}(f) \text{]} = f$$

Example 4.34

Let

$$f = \begin{pmatrix} 2 & 4 & 0 \\ * & 2 & 1 \end{pmatrix}_{1,1}$$

Then

$$\text{DOMAIN}(f) = [(1, 1), (2, 1), (2, 0), (3, 1), (3, 0)]$$

and

$$\text{RANGE}(f) = [2, 4, 2, 0, 1]$$

In Example 4.34, note that composing CREATE with the outputs DOMAIN(f) and RANGE(f) returns f.   But this is not usually what occurs in practice.   First, there might be a permutation of the elements in DOMAIN(f) or there might be an arithmetic operation performed on the gray levels in RANGE(f).   Second, a new stack might be popped simultaneously with DOMAIN(f) to form a new image. Whatever the case might be, the intention is to utilize these operators to go from the image world to the number or set world (RANGE and DOMAIN), and to go from the number world and set world back to the image world (CREATE).

As an illustration, suppose one wishes to *insert* a gray value r into the (i, j) location of a bound matrix f.   This is to be done whether or not a gray value is there already.   Whatever the given value of f at (i, j), its new value is to become r.   The operator INSERT is used to accomplish this end.   Therefore, INSERT is defined by

$$[\text{INSERT}(f; r; i, j)](u, v) = \begin{cases} r, & \text{if } u = i \text{ and } v = j \\ f(u, v), & \text{otherwise} \end{cases}$$

INSERT is a four-input operator. It requires an image, a real number, and two integers. Its block diagram is given by

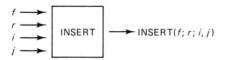

Let us now implement INSERT employing only the operators thus far introduced. The key is to utilize the image g, where

$$g = (r)_{i,j}$$

is the image with singleton domain $\{(i, j)\}$ and gray value r at (i, j). The image g needs to be created. INSERT can be implemented by the following block diagram:

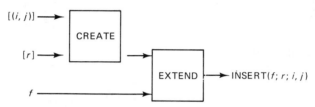

DOMAIN and RANGE take bound matrices to arrays (and hence to sets). However, RANGE can also be utilized to take a bound matrix to a real number. It does so, in the most trivial case, by taking a 1 by 1 bound matrix to an array of length 1 (which is logically equivalent to a real number).

We define a matrix-type multiplication on bound matrices that generalizes the usual multiplication of matrices. Let f be given by an m by n bound matrix $(a_{pq})_{rt}$, and let g be given by an n by k bound matrix $(b_{pq})_{r't'}$. Bound matrices f and g are said to be *compatible* (for matrix multiplication) if f is of size m by n and g is of size n by k. The *matrix multiplication* operator, denoted simply by X, is defined by $X(f, g) = h$, where h is the m by k bound matrix $(c_{pq})_{rt}$, with

$$c_{pq} = \sum_{i=1}^{n} a_{pi} b_{iq}$$

where $1 \le p \le m$ and $1 \le q \le k$. As usual, if either $a_{pi} = *$ or $b_{iq} = *$, then the product is $*$; moreover, if any term in the sum is $*$, then the result is $*$. The block diagram for bound matrix multiplication is given by

Example 4.35

Let

$$f = \begin{pmatrix} 3 & 4 \\ 7 & * \\ 5 & 1 \end{pmatrix}_{8,3} \quad \text{and} \quad g = \begin{pmatrix} 1 & 5 & 8 & 4 \\ * & 3 & 5 & 8 \end{pmatrix}_{2,5}$$

Since the bound matrices are compatible, the operator X can be employed.

$$\begin{matrix} f \longrightarrow \\ \\ g \longrightarrow \end{matrix} \boxed{ X } \longrightarrow \begin{pmatrix} * & 27 & 44 & 44 \\ * & * & * & * \\ * & 28 & 45 & 28 \end{pmatrix}_{8,3} = X(f, g)$$

Note two things. First, the formal method of arriving at the terms of the product is exactly similar to that utilized in normal matrix algebra, except here there is the stipulation regarding the manner in which stars are to be handled. Second, the position of the output matrix (the absolute location of c_{11}) is determined solely by the position of the first bound matrix in the product.

It should be noted that, as an operation on images, the operator X is not representation independent. In practice, this problem can be obviated by requiring the input images to be in minimal bound matrix format. Of course, as a binary operation on the collection of bound matrices, X requires no such restriction.

It was mentioned previously that the set-theoretic algebra of finite subsets of $Z \times Z$ is a subalgebra of bound matrix algebra. Consider the collection $\mathscr{C}$ of all bound matrices whose entries are either ones or stars. Every such bound matrix S can be identified with its domain. Specifically, if we consider the output of the operator DOMAIN as a set instead of as an array, and we let $\mathscr{F}$ denote the collection of all finite subsets of $Z \times Z$, then

$$\text{DOMAIN}: \mathscr{C} \underset{\text{onto}}{\overset{1-1}{\longrightarrow}} \mathscr{F}$$

Moreover, DOMAIN is a homomorphism relative to the binary operator

$$\vee = \text{EXTMAX}$$

on $\mathscr{C}$ and the union operator on $\mathscr{F}$, and also relative to the binary operator

$$\wedge = \text{MIN}$$

on $\mathscr{C}$ and the intersection operator on $\mathscr{F}$. To be precise, treating the output of DOMAIN as a set, for any $S, T \in \mathscr{C}$,

$$\text{DOMAIN}(S \vee T) = \text{DOMAIN}(S) \cup \text{DOMAIN}(T)$$

and

$$\text{DOMAIN}(S \wedge T) = \text{DOMAIN}(S) \cap \text{DOMAIN}(T)$$

Thus, DOMAIN is an isomorphism relative to both binary operations (EXTMAX is identified with union and MIN is identified with intersection), and we do not differentiate between a bound matrix in $\mathscr{C}$ and its domain.

Example 4.36

Let

$$S = \begin{pmatrix} 1 & 1 & * & * \\ * & \textcircled{1} & 1 & 1 \\ 1 & 1 & 1 & * \end{pmatrix}$$

and

$$T = \begin{pmatrix} 1 & 1 & * \\ 1 & \textcircled{1} & * \\ 1 & * & 1 \\ 1 & 1 & 1 \end{pmatrix}$$

Then

$$S \wedge T = \begin{pmatrix} 1 & 1 & * \\ * & \textcircled{1} & * \\ 1 & * & 1 \end{pmatrix}$$

and

$$S \vee T = \begin{pmatrix} 1 & 1 & * & * \\ 1 & \textcircled{1} & 1 & 1 \\ 1 & 1 & 1 & * \\ 1 & 1 & 1 & * \end{pmatrix}$$

Note that both homomorphism relations hold: (1) the domain of the EXTMAX output is equal to the union of the input domains, and (2) the domain of the MIN output is equal to the intersection of the input domains.

From the standpoint of digital image representation, a bound matrix in $\mathscr{C}$ is a *constant image*, in that it only takes on a single gray value. Such images will play a fundamental role in the morphological analysis of Section 8.4. Because constant images, elements in $\mathscr{C}$, can be identified with finite subsets of $Z \times Z$, they serve as a suitable model for two-valued (black and white) digital images. While it might at first glance seem preferable to model black-and-white images by using the gray values 1 and 0, such a modeling would result in bound matrices having three values, 1, 0, and $*$, and the identification with subsets of $Z \times Z$ would be destroyed. Intuitively, black-and-white images appear as subsets; thus, faithful modeling requires that the digital representation reflect this intuition.

EXERCISES FOR CHAPTER 4

4.1. Discuss the number of possible, and legal, positions involving the tower of Hanoi game when using 3 rings of distinct sizes.

4.2. For the tree given in Figure 2.5, use the back and front functions to perform a breadth-first search.

4.3. Repeat Exercise 4.2, except perform a depth-first search.

4.4. Draw a tree illustrating the operations constituting the quadratic formula.

4.5. Perform an inorder, preorder, and postorder traversal of the tree developed in Exercise 4.4.

4.6. Is a frame a special type of flat file?   Discuss.

4.7. Using STDS methodology, find
  a) $\{a, b, c\} \cap (a, b, c, d)$
  b) $\{\{a, b, c\}, (a, b), a\} \triangle ((a, b), a, \{a, b\})$
  c) $(a, b, c, d) \triangle (b, b, c, d)$

4.8. If the information at address 4 in Figure 4.23 is changed to read

rat	7	8

how does the corresponding linking in Figure 4.23 change?

4.9. For the lattice list structure in Example 4.16, how are $g(2, b)$ and $g(4, e)$ related? How are $g(2, b)$ and $g(3, c)$ related?

4.10. For the bound matrices f and g,

$$f = \begin{pmatrix} 2 & * \\ 3 & 1 \\ 4 & 0 \end{pmatrix}_{1,2} , \quad g = \begin{pmatrix} 3 & 5 & 1 \\ * & * & * \\ 2 & 2 & 1 \\ 3 & 1 & 4 \end{pmatrix}_{0,4}$$

determine the bound matrix resulting from the following operations:
(a) ADD(f, g)
(b) MULT(f, g)
(c) MAX(f, g)
(d) MIN(f, g)
(e) SCALAR$(3; f)$
(f) SUB(g)
(g) DIV(f)
(h) TRAN$(f; -1, -2)$
(i) NINETY(f)
(j) NINETY$^2(f)$
(k) NINETY$^3(f)$
(l) FLIP(f)
(m) SELECT$(f; 2, 2, 1, 1)$
(n) EXTEND(g, f)
(o) X(g, f)

4.11. Using the bound matrices f and g defined in Exercise 4.10, find:
  (a) EXTADD(f, g)
  (b) EXTMULT(f, g)
  (c) EXTMAX(f, g)
  (d) EXTMIN(f, g)
  (e) DOMAIN(f)
  (f) RANGE(f)

4.12. Using block diagrams involving the operators previously described, express the operation $h = $ DOMULT(f, g), where

4.13. Describe the following reflection operations in terms of block diagrams involving operators described in this chapter.
  (a) $g = $ HORREFLCT(f), where $g(i, j) = f(i, -j)$
  (b) $g = $ VERTREFLCT(f), where $g(i, j) = f(-i, j)$
  (c) $g = $ DIFLIP(f), where $g(i, j) = f(j, i)$

4.14. Explain and illustrate how, at times, nonminimal bound matrices might be easier to work with than ones that are minimal.

4.15. Let

Find $g = $ NINETY[FLIP(f)] and $h = $ FLIP[NINETY(f)]. Does $g = h$? Explain and describe the two outputs in terms of mirror images of the original image f.

4.16. Explain how EXTMIN can be found from the SUB and EXTMAX operations. Can the MIN operation similarly be found?

5

FINITE STATE
MACHINES

5.1 CLASSIFICATION OF AUTOMATA

Automata are abstract (mathematical) machines. They are employed to model both behavioral situations and intelligent systems, including game playing, human intelligence, machine processing, nervous system activity, and robotic motion systems.

Various types of automata are utilized in modeling this wide range of applications, and they are classified in several ways. One manner of classification is according to the complexity of the language used in communicating with them; however, the study of language complexity belongs properly to a course in formal language theory and will not be pursued here.

Automata can also be classified according to the ways in which they utilize language, of which there are basically three: they can accept, generate, or transform languages. Some automata can only "listen"; that is, they only accept or reject statements from the language employed. For such an *acceptor* automaton, the output is usually binary, perhaps the nod of a robot's head or the flashing of a light. Similar to the recognition scheme of Section 3.1, a string of symbols is either accepted or rejected solely on the basis of its syntax, independently of whether or not it is meaningful to an outside observer.

An automaton is called a *language generator*, or just a *generator*, if once it is started it emits a sequence of symbols from some language. To start the generator, a reset button is activated, at which point the internal mechanism goes to some initial state. The reset button may be triggered by touch, light, sound, or some other method. Once the machine is operative, the generation of the output is usually in response to a single pattern, called the *stimulus*. Thus, the input is binary: it either initiates output or it does not. The output of the generator may not make sense to an observer; however, it will be of the proper syntax and consistent with the architecture producing it. Different outputs may be initiated at different times by the stimulus. The set of all output sentences is called the *language generated by the automaton*. At first glance, it may appear odd that the same stimulus results in different outputs. However, the same is true for humans: a person might very well give drastically different responses to the same stimulus.

Some abstract machines operate as *transducers*: they translate or transform languages into others. Given a particular machine, the language involved must be of a structure compatible with the design of the machine. Such automata are often called *input–output* machines. The two previously discussed types of automata, acceptors and generators, are special types of transducers, the former being restricted to binary output and the latter to binary input.

A further method of classification is based on whether the automaton can produce varying outputs for the same input. If so, it is said to be *nondeterministic*, if not, then it is said to be *deterministic*. In general, generators are of the former type.

5.2 DETERMINISTIC FINITE-STATE MACHINES: TRANSDUCERS

Among the different classes of automata is one consisting of *finite-state machines* (*FSM*). In this section we will discuss a particular type of FSM known as a *deterministic FSM transducer*, which is defined as a sextuple

$$(Q, q_0, \Sigma, \Phi, f, g)$$

where

Q = nonempty finite set of *states*
$q_0 \in Q$ is called the *initial state*
Σ = nonempty finite set of *input symbols*
Φ = nonempty finite set of *output symbols*
f = *state transition function*,

$$f: Q \times \Sigma \rightarrow Q$$

g = *output function*,

$$g: Q \times \Sigma \rightarrow \Phi$$

A deterministic FSM transducer (or transducer, for short) can be represented in several ways: among these are strict mathematical representation, tables, and a generalized type of directed graph called a *Markov diagram*.

The mathematical description results from the specification of each entity in the defining sextuple. A more intuitive description is the *FSM state table* (see

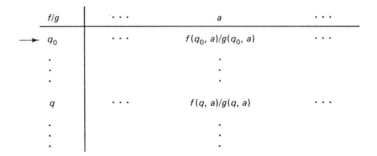

f/g	$\cdots$	a	$\cdots$
$\longrightarrow\ q_0$	$\cdots$	$f(q_0,\ a)/g(q_0,\ a)$	$\cdots$
$\vdots$		$\vdots$	
q	$\cdots$	$f(q,\ a)/g(q,\ a)$	$\cdots$
$\vdots$		$\vdots$	

Figure 5.1.   FSM state table

Figure 5.1).   Here the input elements (symbolized by a in the figure) are placed along the top and the states q in Q (sometimes called *old states*) are placed along the left.   In the tabular position corresponding to the row with state q and column with input a must appear two values: the *new state* $f(q, a)$ and the output $g(q, a)$. In the table, these take the form

$$f(q, a)/g(q, a)$$

Moreover, the unique initial state is specified by having an arrow pointing to its position on the left side of the state table.

In the Markov state diagram (see Figure 5.2), each node corresponds to a state of the machine and is so labeled.   Each directed arc indicates a transition between states and is labeled with the input a that causes the transition.   Adjacent to the a and separated from it by a slash is the appropriate output symbol b.   Thus,

$$q \xrightarrow{\ a/b\ } q'$$

means that

$$f(q, a) = q'$$

and

$$g(q, a) = b$$

The node for the initial state has an arrow pointing to it.

Example 5.1

Let

$$Q = \{q_0, q_1\}, \qquad \Sigma = \{0, 1\}, \qquad \Phi = \{e, d\}$$

Figure 5.2.   Markov state diagram for Example 5.1

q_0 be the initial state, and the transition and output functions be defined by

$$f(q_0, 0) = q_0$$

$$f(q_0, 1) = q_1$$

$$f(q_1, 0) = q_1$$

$$f(q_1, 1) = q_0$$

and

$$g(q_0, 0) = e$$

$$g(q_0, 1) = d$$

$$g(q_1, 0) = d$$

$$g(q_1, 1) = e$$

respectively. Then the corresponding finite state table is given by

	f/g	0	1
Old	q_0	q_0/e	q_1/d
States	q_1	q_1/d	q_0/e

and the Markov diagram is given in Figure 5.2. Given the input sequence

$$1\ 1\ 0\ 1\ 0\ 0\ 1$$

the corresponding output is found by beginning in the initial state and traversing the Markov diagram in accordance with the input symbols. The following table provides a walk-through trace:

Input		1		1		0		1		0		0		1	
State	q_0		q_1		q_0		q_0		q_1		q_1		q_1		q_0
Output		d		e		e		d		d		d		e	

A close look shows this tranducer to be a parity checker. When the automaton is presented with any finite string of 0's and 1's, it will ultimately output an e for even parity (an even number of 1's in the string) and a d for odd parity (an odd number of 1's in the string).

In the preceding example, only two states were required to build the parity-checking machine. This is because, aside from the initial state, only one other state is needed to remember that something different has occurred. In applications, states are utilized in remembering or storing information. The next example should make this more apparent.

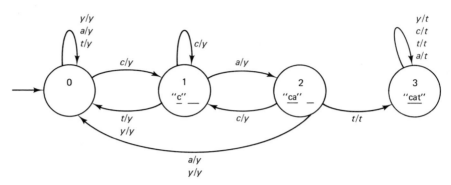

Figure 5.3.   Markov state diagram for recognition system

Example 5.2

Recall the word-recognition system given in Section 3.1.   There, if the word "cat" appeared in the input string, then the output changed from a string of y's to a string of t's, beginning with the t in "cat."   The corresponding Markov state diagram is illustrated in Figure 5.3.   A total of four states are required.   0 is the initial state and denotes that no part of the word "cat" has thus far been spelled.   Three other states are required to remember various parts in the spelling of "cat."   State 1 is used to note that a c has appeared thus far in the spelling; state 2 is used to remember that a ca has appeared; and, finally, state 3 represents the completed spelling of "cat."

5.3 BUILDING DETERMINISTIC FSM TRANSDUCERS

Besides a clock and power supply, FSM transducers can be built using only combinational logic in conjunction with memory devices such as flip-flops.   Among the various automata, FSMs are perhaps the most important, since they describe behavior involving finite memory storage, and, in practice, it is impossible to build machines that require infinite storage capacity.   An FSM transducer can be built utilizing a finite number of flip-flops whose state transitions are synchronized by clock pulses.

A popular methodology for building a deterministic FSM transducer employs the *Huffman sequential circuit model* illustrated in Figure 5.4.   As usual, we will ignore timing considerations in our discussion of the Huffman circuit.   In the Huffman model, the inputs $x_1, x_2, \ldots, x_n$ are obtained by encoding the inputs to the FSM.   Hence, each x_i is 0 or 1 valued.   The outputs $y_1, y_2, \ldots, y_m$ are also 0 or 1 valued and are found by encoding the outputs of the FSM.   The variables a_1, $a_2, \ldots, a_k$ are also 0 or 1 valued and are found by encoding the (old) states of the FSM; $A_1, A_2, \ldots, A_k$ comprise the corresponding coding for the next, or new states; thus

$$a_i(t) = A_i(t - 1)$$

Upon the reception of each clock pulse (not shown), the inputs x_i and the old state values a_j are entered into the combinational circuit, which consists of *and*,

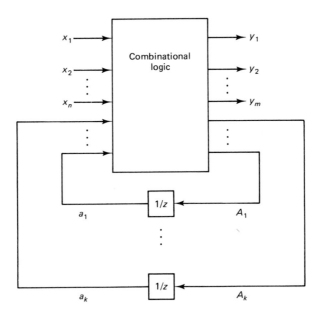

Figure 5.4. Huffman sequential circuit

or, and *not* gates.   In turn, this circuit produces outputs y_i and new states A_j. Each new state is then delayed one clock pulse and utilized as an old state for the ensuing clock cycle.   The process repeats ad infinitum.

The machine corresponding to the Huffman circuit is meant to operate on an (encoded) sequence of inputs.   Moreover, prior to the application of an input sequence to the machine, it is necessary to initialize the machine by starting the machine in the initial state q_0.   Thus, the values of $a_1, a_2, \ldots, a_k$ must initially be q_0 properly encoded.   The steps involved in building a machine based on utilization of the Huffman sequential model can be summarized as follows:

Step 1*: Based on the behavior of the desired system, represent it using a transition table of the FSM model.

Step 2: Remove redundant states, if any exist, to find an equivalent FSM.   (This step can be accomplished algorithmically by the use of *Moore minimization procedures*.)

Step 3*: Perform the state assignment; that is, encode (using 0 and 1) the entries in the transition table.

Step 4*: Write the appropriate logic; that is, express encoded output expressions in terms of input variables.

Step 5: Reduce the logic by the removal of redundancy through the use of Karnaugh maps (Section 2.5) or the Quine–McClusky method.

Step 6*: Build the machine on paper using *and*, *or*, and *not* gates together with $1/z$ delay elements as specified in Figure 5.4.

Essential steps in the methodology have been marked with an asterisk; the remaining steps are of lesser importance when using VLSI because they only involve a reduction of the number of logic gates. Step 3, which involves heuristic judgments, will be discussed shortly.

The number n of encoded inputs to the Huffman sequential circuit is given by

$$n = \lceil \log_2 \text{card}(\Sigma) \rceil$$

where Σ is the set of inputs to the FSM, $\text{card}(\Sigma)$ specifies the cardinality of the set concerned, and $\lceil \ \rceil$ denotes the upper ceiling function. Similarly,

$$m = \lceil \log_2 \text{card}(\Phi) \rceil$$

and

$$k = \lceil \log_2 \text{card}(Q) \rceil$$

where Φ and Q are the sets of output symbols and states, respectively. When encoding entries in the state table, it is prudent to use more 0's for those entries that occur most frequently. The intuition behind this convention will become evident shortly. Each entry in the table, that is, each entry of the form

$$f(q, a)/g(q, a)$$

will be represented in an encoded fashion. Whenever a 1 appears in the encoding of $f(q, a)$ or $g(q, a)$, a conjunction of the Boolean expressions representing the encodings of q and a should be formed, where, for a 1, the old state (or input) variable itself appears and, for a 0, the primed (complemented) variable appears. Each Boolean new state (or output) variable should be expressed as the disjunction of all the conjunctions of the Boolean expressions corresponding to state table entries having a 1 in the said variable bit. In forming the conjunction, instead of using the $\wedge$ symbol, a dot or simple concatenation is employed; correspondingly, when forming the disjunction, a + is used instead of $\vee$. A detailed example should help to make the entire procedure clear.

Example 5.3

Referring to Example 5.2, the state table associated with the Markov diagram in Figure 5.3 is given by

Old	f/g	Inputs			
		y	c	a	t
Old	$\longrightarrow 0$	$0/y$	$1/y$	$0/y$	$0/y$
states	1	$0/y$	$1/y$	$2/y$	$0/y$
	2	$0/y$	$1/y$	$0/y$	$3/t$
	3	$3/t$	$3/t$	$3/t$	$3/t$

Since the most frequently employed next state is 0, it gets encoded as 00.   States 3 and 1 are the two next most frequently employed next states and are therefore encoded as 10 and 01, respectively.   State 2, which is the least employed next state, is encoded 11.   The symbols are correspondingly encoded with reference to the frequency of their utilization.   The following tables provide a complete encoding of states and inputs.

States	Encoded states
0	0 0
1	0 1
2	1 1
3	1 0

Inputs	Encoded inputs
y	0 0
c	0 1
a	1 1
t	1 0

The encoded finite-state machine table is

		Encoded Inputs (uv)			
	f/g	0 0	0 1	1 1	1 0
Encoded	0 0	0 0/0 0	0 1/0 0	0 0/0 0	0 0/0 0
Old	0 1	0 0/0 0	0 1/0 0	1 1/0 0	0 0/0 0
States	1 1	0 0/0 0	0 1/0 0	0 0/0 0	1 0/1 0
(rs)	1 0	1 0/1 0	1 0/1 0	1 0/1 0	1 0/1 0
			RS/UV		

Boolean expressions are used in representing the encoded inputs, outputs, and states.   Let rs denote the 2-bit encoding of the old states, RS denote the encoded value of the new states, uv denote the encoding of the input, and, finally, UV denote the encoded value of the output.

The boolean variables R, S, U, and V are found in terms of r, s, u, and v from the encoded finite-state table.   To find R, determine every position among the 16 where the value of R is 1: these positions consist of the four in the bottom row, one in row 2, and one in row 3.   The position in the second row occurs in the third column, and, hence, the row position determines $rs = 01$, while the column position determines $uv = 11$.   To obtain $R = 1$ from these values, the logical expression in terms of r, s, u, and v must be $r'suv$.   Similarly, $R = 1$ when $rs = 11$ and $uv = 10$, which leads to the expression $rsuv'$.   Continuing through all six positions in the table where $R = 1$, we obtain

$$R = r'suv + rsuv' + rs'u'v' + rs'u'v + rs'uv + rs'uv'$$

where the disjunctions ($+$) simply mean that R will be 1 if at least one of the terms is 1-valued.   In a similar manner, we obtain expressions for S and U:

$$S = r's'u'v + r'su'v + r'suv + rsu'v$$

$$U = rsuv' + rs'u'v' + rs'u'v + rs'uv + rs'uv'$$

These expressions can be reduced by using Karnaugh maps to

$$R = r'suv + rsuv' + rs'$$

$$S = r'u'v + r'sv + su'v$$

$$U = rsuv' + rs'$$

Note that because the only outputs are y and t, V is never 1. A machine that produces the desired behavior can now be built; indeed, Figure 3.2 illustrates such a machine.

Earlier we noted that 0's should be used for those entries that occur most frequently in the state table. The reason for this should be clear from the preceding example: the more 1's, the more terms in the disjunctive expansions for R, S, and U, and, conversely, the more 0's, the less terms in the expansions. (See Section 6.5 for a fuller discussion of how to select an appropriate encoding to minimize bit transmission.)

5.4 DETERMINISTIC AND NONDETERMINISTIC AUTOMATA

Nondeterministic and deterministic acceptor-type automata are introduced in this section. Specifically, a *nondeterministic finite automaton* (*NFA*) is a sextuple

$$(Q, q_0, I, V, \delta, f)$$

where

Q = finite nonempty *set of states*
$q_0 \in Q$ is the *initial state*
I = finite nonempty set of *instructions* or *inputs*
$V = \{0, 1\}$ is the *valuation space*
δ = *delta* or *transition* function that governs whether or not (1 or 0) there is a transition from a given state q to another state q' utilizing a specific instruction; thus,

$$\delta: Q \times I \times Q \to V$$

f = *final state determination function*,

$$f: Q \to V$$

Nondeterministic finite automata are often represented graphically in much the same manner as transducers. A Markov diagram is utilized with circular nodes representing the states, an arrow points to the initial state, and *final states*, those states q for which $f(q) = 1$, are denoted by a double circle. In practice, final states are often employed to indicate the occurrence of noteworthy events. Intuitively, we might imagine that a "landing" in a final state causes a bell to ring, a light to go on, or the like. It might denote the combination that opens a safe, the winning or losing of a game, or the occurrence of some other final happening.

There exists an arrow from state q to state q', labeled with input a, if and only if

$$\delta(q, a, q') = 1$$

in which case a portion of the graph has the form

Here, q is called the *source*, or *originating state*, and q' is called the *destination state*. If

$$\delta(q, b, q') = 0$$

then no arrow labeled b is drawn from q to q'.

A *deterministic finite automaton* (*DFA*) is a special type of NFA. Specifically, it is an NFA such that, for any fixed state q and input a, there exists one and only one destination state q'; that is, q' is the unique state such that

$$\delta(q, a, q') = 1$$

for the given state q and input a. Deterministic automata are like deterministic FSM transducers, but without output. Moreover, every DFA is an NFA, but not conversely.

Example 5.4

Consider the nondeterministic automaton with two states and two instructions that is represented by the Markov diagram

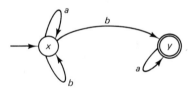

In this case,

$$Q = \{x, y\}$$

$$x = \text{initial state}$$

$$I = \{a, b\}$$

$$f(x) = 0 \text{ and } f(y) = 1; \text{ hence, only } y \text{ is a final state}$$

$$\delta(x, a, x) = \delta(x, b, x) = \delta(y, a, y) = \delta(x, b, y) = 1$$

and all other delta values are 0

This automaton is not deterministic since two arrows leave state x with the label b and also because there is no arrow leaving state y labeled with a b.

It should be emphasized that whenever a nondeterministic machine has two or more different destination states for a common source state and common instruction, then, just as in the case of a multiprocessor, each destination state is reached.

Nondeterministic automata can be employed in the recognition of patterns. In that direction, an NFA is said to *accept* the input string

$$s = s_1 s_2 \cdots s_n \in I^*$$

if there exists a sequence of states

$$q_0, q_1, q_2, \ldots, q_n \in Q$$

such that q_0 is the initial state, q_n is a final state, and

$$\delta(q_i, s_{i+1}, q_{i+1}) = 1$$

for $i = 0, 1, \ldots, n - 1$. Insofar as recognition is concerned, the acceptance of a string can be viewed as recognition of a pattern described by the string.

In Example 5.4, any string in I^* having at least one b is accepted because the last b in such a string will be utilized in forming

$$\delta(x, b, y) = 1$$

Nondeterministic automata can also be employed to build machines that solve problems and play games. The next example illustrates the manner in which this can be accomplished.

Example 5.5

Consider the Tower of Hanoi game described in Section 4.1 and suppose there are only two rings. Figure 5.5 shows an NFA that will correctly play the game. It is comprised of nine states, one of which is final, and the six instructions $s1$, $s2$, $s3$, $b1$, $b2$, and $b3$, where si means "move the small ring to peg number i," and bi means "move the large ring to peg number i." Each state denotes a distinct valid configuration, and each arrow is labeled with the proper move to change the source configuration into the destination configuration. For instance,

$$\delta(2, s2, 3) = 1$$

which is graphically depicted by

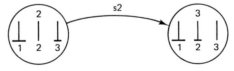

means "move the small ring to peg 2." Note that, while the automaton plays the game correctly, there is no guarantee that it will ever enter the final state.

In Figure 5.5, it can intuitively be seen that there exist three constellations,

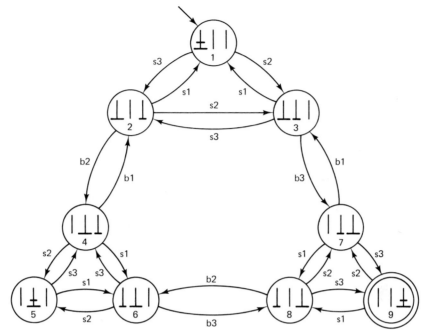

Figure 5.5. FSM for Tower of Honoi game

each comprised of three states. Each constellation is held together by moves of the small ring, and the constellations themselves are held together by moves of the large ring. Observations such as these are important if an automaton is desired that models the Tower of Hanoi game with more than two rings.

The automaton of Example 5.5 is not deterministic; however, it is possible to construct a DFA that plays the Tower of Hanoi game. This can be accomplished by the introduction of a single additional state, say state 10. The new automaton will have two final states, state 9, denoting a happy ending, and state 10, denoting any bad ending resulting from an illegal move. Each state will have six arrows leaving it, one for each distinct instruction, and all new arrows must point to state 10. Therefore, the new machine will have additional instructions such as

$$\delta(3, b2, 10) = 1$$

which results in the illegal configuration

$$|\pm|$$

It will also have other illegal instructions of the form

$$\delta(3, s2, 10) = 1$$

that are "self-loops" and represent "not allowed, or no-move-type" instructions.

Finally, state 10 will be *absorbing* in that, for each of the six instructions x,

$$\delta(10, x, 10) = 1$$

Like the recognition system discussed in Example 5.3, this new deterministic machine can be built using the Huffman sequential design.

Example 5.6

The magic 4 square puzzle game introduced in Section 4.1 can also be described utilizing a nondeterministic automaton. Indeed, there are several ways of modeling the situation. A particularly interesting model is one that leads to the nonconnected Markov diagram illustrated in Figure 5.6, where there are two separate constellations, neither of which can be reached from the other by any instruction. One constellation illustrates the real world, while the other provides a mirror-image reflected world that cannot be physically obtained without destroying the puzzle. The automaton has 24 states, 12 in each constellation. There are four instructions: d, u, r, and l, respectively denoting downward, upward, rightward, and leftward movement of the blank in the puzzle. For instance,

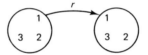

is a valid transition since moving the blank to the right yields the destination configuration. There are 24 states because that is the number of permutations of 4 entities. Of course, there cannot be valid instructions between certain pairs of states. For

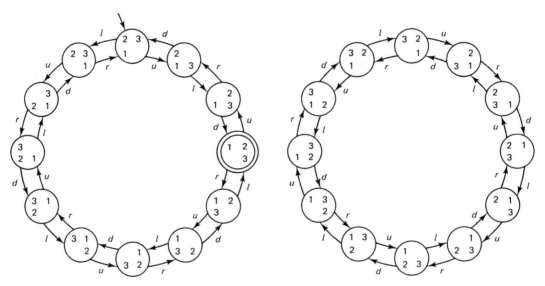

Figure 5.6.   FSM for magic 4 square puzzle

instance, there cannot be a valid instruction that takes the state

into the state

since these are reflections of one another.

5.5 STOCHASTIC AUTOMATA

Intelligent behavior is very often characterized by a lack of deterministic predictability. Given the same stimulus, an intelligent being might appear to act in varying ways. Of course, we might argue that the observer is just lacking sufficient information to pin down the stimulus–response relationship. Be that as it may, scientifically it is the observational model that is paramount, not speculation regarding this or that occult cause. The apparent uncertainty in behavior requires models that reflect that uncertainty. One way of achieving such a model is through the use of probability. In this section, we wish to explore a probabilistic state model.

Given an input (stimulus), a human who is in a certain state of being might enter any one of several states. Using a probabilistic model, each of these potential destination states can be assigned a transitional probability, which might be found by observing the human over some period of time, collecting data, and statistically reducing the data. (See Section 6.1 for a more in-depth discussion of the meaning of probabilities and their relation to observation.) By employing the estimated probabilities, a machine can be built that appears to simulate the behavior of the human (in certain situations). This machine might be an autonomous robot utilizing sensors and control surfaces in much the same manner as a human being.

A robot's brain consists of CPUs and memories. The problem is to construct an appropriate algebraic model, one that takes into account the observed uncertainty. One such model is the stochastic automaton, the definition of which is quite similar to the NFA discussed in the preceding section.

Mathematically, a *stochastic automaton* is a sextuple

$$(Q, q_0, I, V, \delta, f)$$

where

Q = finite nonempty set of states
$q_0 \in Q$ is the initial state

I = finite nonempty set of inputs or instructions
V = [0, 1] is the valuation space
δ = delta or transition function,

$$\delta: Q \times I \times Q \to V$$

f = the final state determination function,

$$f: Q \to V$$

and where it is required that for any fixed original state q and any fixed instruction a

$$\sum_{q' \in Q} \delta(q, a, q') = 1$$

This last requirement results from the fact that we interpret

$$\delta(q, a, q') = x$$

as meaning that x is the probability of the machine going from state q to state q' utilizing the instruction a and the sum of the probabilities must be 1.

A Markov diagram is utilized to provide a graphical representation of a stochastic automaton. As before, nodes are drawn as circles and labeled with the states of the automaton, and an arrow points to the initial state. Furthermore, directed line segments, each connecting two (not necessarily distinct) states, are labeled with both inputs and appropriate probabilities, in each case, the two being separated by a slash. For instance,

$$\delta(q, a, q') = x$$

is graphically represented by

If $\delta(q, a, q') = 0$, then no arrow is drawn from state q to q' utilizing instruction a. Finally, final states for these automata also occur with certain probabilities. A final state q that is certain is one for which

$$f(q) = 1$$

All other final states are not certain, and this is reflected in the definition by the fact that the valuation space, which is the codomain of the final state determination function, is the closed interval [0, 1]. Final states that occur with certainty are double circled; all others have the probability of being a final state labeled to the right of the name of the state and separated from it by a slash. If $f(q) = 0$, then no recording of the probability is given in the Markov diagram.

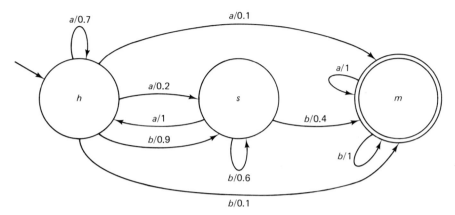

Figure 5.7.   Stochastic Markov state diagram describing robot behavior

Example 5.7

Let

$$Q = \{h, s, m\}$$

where h is the initial state, and

$$I = \{a, b\}$$

Figure 5.7 describes a stochastic automaton having Q as the set of states, I as the set of inputs, and final state determination function f defined by

$$f(h) = f(s) = 0$$
$$f(m) = 1$$

The delta function is defined to be zero on all triples except for the following:

$\delta(h, a, h) = 0.7$	$\delta(s, a, h) = 1$	$\delta(m, a, m) = 1$
$\delta(h, a, m) = 0.1$	$\delta(s, b, s) = 0.6$	$\delta(m, b, m) = 1$
$\delta(h, a, s) = 0.2$	$\delta(s, b, m) = 0.4$	
$\delta(h, b, s) = 0.9$		
$\delta(h, b, m) = 0.1$		

Note that

$$\sum_{q' \in Q} \delta(q, r, q') = 1$$

holds for each $r \in I$ and $q \in Q$.

When a stochastic machine is presented with a string of instructions, it goes from state to state with specified probabilities.   Prior to the presentation of an input string, the machine is usually reset so that it is in the initial state, awaiting the input of a string. We will now give a method for determining the probability of going from a given state, not necessarily the initial state, to another (not necessarily distinct) state based on the utilization of a string

$$a_1 a_2 \ldots a_n \in I^*$$

We define an extension of the transition function,

$$\delta': Q \times I^* \times Q \to V$$

in the following manner:

$$\delta'(q, \varepsilon, q') = \begin{cases} 1, & \text{if } q = q' \\ 0, & \text{otherwise} \end{cases}$$

where ε is the empty string. This means that if no instruction is given, then the machine remains in the current state. Next, for any input symbol in $a \in I$,

$$\delta'(q, a, q') = \delta(q, a, q')$$

Finally, for an arbitrary string of length $n > 1$,

$$\delta'(q, a_1 a_2 \ldots a_n, q')$$
$$= \sum_{q_1, \ldots, q_{n-1} \in Q} [\delta(q, a_1, q_1) \cdot \delta(q_1, a_2, q_2) \cdots \delta(q_{n-2}, a_{n-1}, q_{n-1}) \cdot \delta(q_{n-1}, a_n, q')]$$

The next example should help provide insight into the motivation behind the definition of δ'.

Example 5.8

Employing the automaton depicted in Figure 5.7, we find the probability of going from state h to state m by employing the program consisting of the two-instruction string ab. Since the input string is of length $n = 2$, according to the definition of the extension δ',

$$\delta'(h, ab, m) = \sum_{q_1 \in Q} \delta(h, a, q_1) \cdot \delta(q_1, b, m)$$

$$= \delta(h, a, h) \cdot \delta(h, b, m)$$

$$+ \delta(h, a, s) \cdot \delta(s, b, m)$$

$$+ \delta(h, a, m) \cdot \delta(m, b, m)$$

$$= (0.7 \times 0.1) + (0.2 \times 0.4) + (0.1 \times 1) = 0.25$$

Consequently, there is a 0.25 probability that, when in state h, if instructions a and b are given, the machine will go to state m.

If we look closely at the defining sum for $\delta'(h, ab, m)$ in this example, its meaning should be clear; to wit, we consider all paths from state h to state m where the first arrow is labeled a and the second is labeled b, we find the transition probability of each path by multiplying the probabilities of the two arrows comprising the path, and then we sum the probabilities of the paths. For those with some background in probability theory, this procedure is tantamount to assuming that the transition pairs forming the arrows are (probabilistically) independent and that the various paths are mutually disjoint. The general defining equation for δ', when employing a string of n input symbols, has the same interpretation, except that in the general case there are $n - 1$ possible intermediate states between q and q'.

We now consider an elementary case of robot behavior. Suppose a robot possesses three emotional states: state h is a happy state, state s is sad, and state m is mad. Given an input a, which we will take to mean the greeting "hello," the robot will go through an emotional transition. Supposing that he is in state h, a state of happiness, behaviorial observation has shown that 70% of the time he remains happy, 20% of the time he becomes sad, and 10% of the time he gets angry and goes to state m. Consequently, we model his "very humanlike" behavior by

$$\delta(h, a, h) = 0.7$$

$$\delta(h, a, s) = 0.2$$

$$\delta(h, a, m) = 0.1$$

Other behaviorial patterns can similarly be modeled.

It might be objected that a stochastic automaton model of the robot's emotional states is devoid of any mechanistic analysis of its transitions and that further study might reveal that other factors are present besides happiness, sadness, and anger. In fact, the objection is really no objection at all: since all observation is finite, and since the number of variables that constitute whatever behaviorial model is being employed is also finite, a finer analysis of the states and corresponding transition probabilities only results in a model revision that incorporates the new knowledge. Moreover, any mechanistic analysis will only provide approximate equational relations among the salient variables; it certainly will not supplant the observational (and thus statistical) basis of behaviorial description. Of course, the desirability of the stochastic automaton model itself might be questioned; however, this is simply a question of pragmatics and is only a matter of the degree to which the model gives satisfactory results.

To build a stochastic automaton, we can employ *Monte Carlo* statistical methods. Although the present exposition is certainly not the place for a detailed discussion of Monte Carlo methods, some intuition can be gained through Figure 5.8(a), where a circle is inscribed inside a unit square. Imagine that the figure is placed on a wall and a large number of darts is tossed randomly and without aim onto the square, the stipulation regarding lack of aim meaning that we expect the darts to distribute themselves *uniformly* (see Example 6.3) across the entire square. Recognizing that the area of the circle is $\pi/4$, whereas the area of the square is 1, if 1000 darts were tossed, we might expect that approximately $780 \cong \pi/4 \times 1000$ of them would fall inside the circle. Indeed, statistical verification bears out our supposition. Intuitively, the proportion of the areas is equal to the proportion of "hits" on the target.

At its roots, the Monte Carlo method stems from standing the preceding

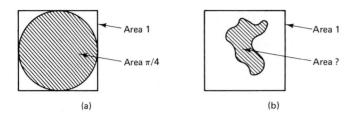

Figure 5.8.   Monte Carlo procedure

proportionality argument on its head.   In Figure 5.8(b), there is an irregular shape inside a unit square.   To estimate the area of the shape, we toss 1000 darts randomly, and without aim, onto the square.   If x darts fall inside the shape, we estimate the area of the shape to be $x/1000$.

In the construction of a stochastic automaton, a random-number generator is employed, its function being to produce probabilistic decisions.   Rules are specified, using the propositional calculus, that determine the next state based on the output of the random-number generator, which, in this scheme, is taking the place of a random dart thrower.   Although the actual details of implementation are somewhat involved, a simple example can be used to give the flavor of the methodology.

Example 5.9

Consider the previously discussed emotional robot and assume that its emotional states are described by the state diagram in Figure 5.7.   Internal to the robot is a random-number generator that outputs numbers x between 0 and 1.   Also stored within the robot's thinking system are rules that are functions of its states and inputs.   Although in a real robot these rules would be adaptive, changing in accordance with circumstances, in this example we will assume they are fixed.   Thus, corresponding to a present state of happiness, state h, and a greeting of "hello," input a, a valid set of rules would be:

Generate random number x:

If $0 \le x \le 0.7$, then go to state h
If $0.7 < x \le 0.9$, then go to state s
If $0.9 < x \le 1$, then go to state m

To conclude this section, let us reemphasize that the intent here is to model behavior through the utilization of a finite-state machine and that probabilistic transitions between states must reflect the observed tendencies of the behavior in question.   Even if expert knowledge is employed in the establishment of the set of states, the set of inputs, and the logical inference machinery, that knowledge will still involve uncertainty regarding the destination states resulting from a specific input being applied to a specific state.   As a consequence, some model of uncertainty, be it probabilistic, fuzzy, or some other, must be employed to formalize the expert's educated guesses, prognostications, and hunches.   Moreover, some statistical fusion of varying expert estimates will no doubt be required.   This is not a negative reflection on the expertise being solicited; rather, it is simply a recognition of the scientific epistemology, which, as we have said before, plays an a priori determining role in the design of artificially intelligent systems.

5.6 FUZZY AND LATTICE AUTOMATA

Whereas, in the last section, uncertainty was modeled by means of probability, in the current section a fuzzy approach will be employed, the differences essentially being the manners in which measures of certainty are manipulated and interpreted.

When an automaton in a given state is presented with an instruction, depending on the type of automaton, several courses of action might result. A deterministic automaton will transition to a unique destination state; a nondeterministic automaton will remain in the current state, transition to a unique destination state, or transition to several states simultaneously, the transition to each destination state being certain; and a stochastic automaton, like a DFA, will transition to a single destination state, the likelihood of any particular transition being specified by the relevant value of the transition function. In the case of stochastic automata, the transition probabilities indicate the perceived likelihoods associated with entering the various destination states: the closer the probability is to 1, the more likely the automaton is to enter the given state.

A fuzzy automaton is similar to a nondeterministic automaton in that several destination states may be entered simultaneously; however, it is also similar to a stochastic automaton in that there is a measure of the degree to which the automaton transitions between states, that measure being between 0 and 1.

Mathematically, a *fuzzy automaton* is a sextuple

$$(Q, q_0, I, V, \delta, f)$$

where

Q = nonempty finite set of states
$q_0 \in Q$ is the initial state
I = nonempty finite set of inputs
V = [0, 1] is the valuation space
δ = delta or transition function,

$$\delta \colon Q \times I \times Q \to V$$

f = the final state function,

$$f \colon Q \to V$$

Markov diagrams are used for representing fuzzy automata, and the notation is identical to that employed for stochastic automata.

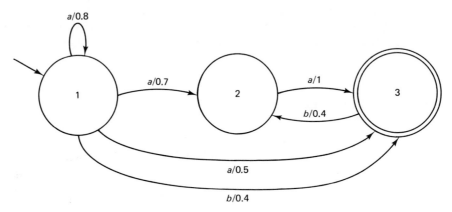

Figure 5.9. Fuzzy automaton

Example 5.10

Let $Q = \{1, 2, 3\}$, with 1 being the initial state, $I = \{a, b\}$, $f(3) = 1$, and $f(1) = f(2) = 0$. Moreover, suppose that

$$\delta(1, a, 1) = 0.8$$
$$\delta(1, a, 2) = 0.7$$
$$\delta(1, a, 3) = 0.5$$
$$\delta(1, b, 3) = 0.4$$
$$\delta(2, a, 3) = 1$$
$$\delta(3, b, 2) = 0.4$$

and that δ of every other triple is defined to be 0. This fuzzy automaton is illustrated in Figure 5.9. Notice that

$$\sum_{q' \in Q} \delta(3, b, q') = 0.4$$

There is no reason why this or any other similar sum should be 1. A fuzzy automaton need not be stochastic.

As in the case of stochastic automata, the transition function for a fuzzy automaton is extended to a function δ' on strings of instructions; however, instead of using sums of products, as in the stochastic setting, maxima of minima are employed. Specifically,

$$\delta': Q \times I^* \times Q \to V$$

and is defined as follows: For the empty string ε,

$$\delta'(q, \varepsilon, q') = \begin{cases} 1, & \text{if } q = q' \\ 0, & \text{otherwise} \end{cases}$$

for the singleton string $a \in I$

$$\delta'(q, a, q') = \delta(q, a, q')$$

and for the string $a_1 a_2 \ldots a_n \in I^*$,

$\delta'(q, a_1 a_2 \ldots a_n, q')$

$$= \bigvee_{q_1, \ldots, q_{n-1} \in Q} [\delta(q, a_1, q_1) \wedge \delta(q_1, a_2, q_2) \wedge \cdots \wedge \delta(q_{n-1}, a_n, q')]$$

where the cup ($\vee$) notation means that the maximum is being taken over all possible collections of $n - 1$ states in Q.

Before we discuss modeling considerations, an example will be provided to demonstrate the computational aspects of the extended transition function.

Example 5.11

Consider the fuzzy automaton given in Example 5.10 and illustrated in Figure 5.9. Suppose the automaton is in state 1 and receives the string input aa. Then the extended transition value to state 3 is given by

$$\delta'(1, aa, 3) = \bigvee_{q_1 \in Q} \delta(1, a, q_1) \wedge \delta(q_1, a, 3)$$

$$= [\delta(1, a, 1) \wedge \delta(1, a, 3)] \vee [\delta(1, a, 2) \wedge \delta(2, a, 3)] \vee [\delta(1, a, 3)$$

$$\wedge \delta(3, a, 3)]$$

$$= [0.8 \wedge 0.5] \vee [0.7 \wedge 1] \vee [0.5 \wedge 0]$$

$$= 0.5 \vee 0.7 \vee 0 = 0.7$$

In a similar manner,

$$\delta'(1, ab, 2) = 0.4$$

For a stochastic automaton, if $\delta(q, a, q') = x$, then x is the probability of transitioning from q to q' utilizing the instruction a, and the transition function is extended to δ' in a manner consistent with probabilistic reasoning. The interpretation of fuzzy automata transitioning is different. For instance, consider the automaton discussed in Examples 5.10 and 5.11. Originating in source state 1 and receiving the instruction a, the automaton reaches three destination states: state 1 is entered at level 0.8, state 2 is entered at level 0.7, and state 3 is entered at level 0.5. We will now present a physical problem that is modeled by this automaton.

Let each arrow in the Markov diagram of Figure 5.9 denote a wire over which current can flow only in the direction of the arrow. Moreover, imagine that the fuzzy values represent ampere load limits of circuit breakers that have been placed on all the arrows. Given an instruction string, a source state, and a destination state, the question is raised as to the maximum amperage that can be sent, in turn, through each circuit specified by the instruction string, starting at the source state and ending at the destination state. Since each individual connecting circuit is in series, its load limit is given by the minimum of the load limits of the arrows forming it. Now, suppose we wish to know if there is at least one multiarrow connection specified by the instruction string that will carry a given load. Then we desire the maximum of the minima just obtained, since, as long as the amperage remains beneath the threshold specified by that maximum, there is at least one arrow circuit from the source state to the destination state that will bear it. For instance (referring to Example 5.11), there are two two-arrow connections from states 1 to 3 using the instruction string aa:

$$1\text{-}a\text{-}1\text{-}a\text{-}3$$

and

$$1\text{-}a\text{-}2\text{-}a\text{-}3$$

Although the first cannot bear a load of 0.6, the second can. The fact that $\delta'(1, aa, 3) = 0.7$ guarantees that at least one connection possesses threshold 0.7.

A *lattice automaton* (or *L automaton*) is a generalization of a fuzzy automaton. In particular, an L automaton is defined exactly the same as a fuzzy automaton, except that the valuation space is a distributed lattice with units. The sup and inf operations are denoted by $\vee$ and $\wedge$, respectively, and the units are 0 and 1. As usual, for $x \in V$,

$$x \vee 0 = x = x \wedge 1$$
$$x \wedge 0 = 0$$

and

$$x \vee 1 = 1$$

Markov diagrams for L automata are drawn exactly as in the fuzzy case.

Example 5.12

Consider the L automaton with set of states

$$Q = \{1, 2, 3\}$$

with initial state 1, with

$$I = \{a, b\}$$

and with valuation space given by the lattice depicted in the Hasse diagram

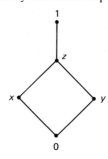

Assume that $f(1) = 0, f(2) = f(3) = 1,$

$$\delta(1, a, 1) = x$$
$$\delta(1, a, 2) = y$$
$$\delta(1, a, 3) = z$$
$$\delta(1, b, 3) = x$$
$$\delta(2, b, 1) = x$$
$$\delta(2, b, 3) = x$$
$$\delta(3, b, 3) = x$$

and δ is defined to be zero for all other tuples.   The Markov representation is given in Figure 5.10.

Unlike fuzzy automata, where V is totally ordered, certain transitions in general L automata need not be comparable.   For instance, in Example 5.12,

$$\delta(1, a, 1)$$

and

$$\delta(1, a, 2)$$

are not comparable.   Thus, all that is known about the destination states in this case is that state 3 is entered more readily than states 1 and 2, since

$$\delta(1, a, 1) \le \delta(1, a, 3)$$

and

$$\delta(1, a, 2) \le \delta(1, a, 3)$$

An extended transition function is defined for L automata in exactly the same manner as for fuzzy automata.   We need only remember that the symbols $\vee$ and $\wedge$ denote the sup and inf, respectively.

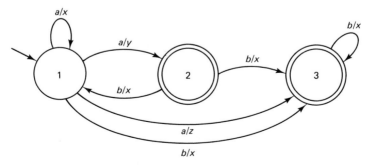

Figure 5.10.   Lattice automaton

Example 5.13

For the L automaton given in Example 5.12,

$$\delta'(1, ab, 3) = [\delta(1, a, 1) \wedge \delta(1, b, 3)] \vee [\delta(1, a, 2) \wedge \delta(2, b, 3)] \vee [\delta(1, a, 3)$$
$$\wedge\ \delta(3, b, 3)]$$
$$= [x \wedge x] \vee [y \wedge x] \vee [z \wedge x]$$
$$= x \vee 0 \vee x = x$$

EXERCISES FOR CHAPTER 5

5.1. Describe, using a Markov diagram, a deterministic finite state transducer that recognizes the words "cat" or "bat." Specifically, when given a string from $\Sigma = \{b, a, t, c\}$, the output 0 will be given for any input unless the word "cat" or the word "bat" has appeared, the output 1 will be given when a t is input for the first spelling of the word "cat," and a 1 will be output for all succeeding inputs, and, finally, a 2 will be output when a t is input for the first spelling of the word "bat," and a 2 will be output for all succeeding inputs. Note that whichever recognition word appears first will determine the eventual output of the machine. Thus, the output will be all 0's, a string of 0's followed by a string of 1's, or a string of 0's followed by a string of 2's.

5.2. Build a finite state machine that will recognize a single instance of both the words "bat" and "cat." This machine is similar to the machine described in Exercise 5.1 in that it outputs strings of 0's, 1's, and 2's. However, valid output sequences for this machine include 0's followed by 1's followed by 2's and 0's followed by 2's followed by 1's.

5.3. Build a Huffman sequential circuit for the machine described in Exercise 5.1.

5.4. Describe how to build a deterministic automaton for the magic four puzzle game described in Example 5.6.

5.5. How many states would be needed in a nondeterministic automaton that plays the magic nine puzzle game analogously to the one illustrated in Figure 5.7 for the magic four puzzle game?

5.6. For the stochastic automaton illustrated in Figure 5.8, find $\delta(h, bb, m)$.

5.7. Repeat Exercise 5.6, except interpret the machine as fuzzy.

5.8. Explain how a fuzzy automaton acts "more like" a multiple processor than a corresponding stochastic automaton.

5.9. For the Markov diagram illustrated in Figure 5.12, find $\delta(1, ab, 3)$ using the M_5 lattice, whose Hasse diagram is given in Figure 2.11(a).

6

DATA AND
ESTIMATION

6.1 MEASUREMENT

To this point in the text we have concerned ourselves with the presentation of
varied mathematical structures that can be employed to artificially simulate human
analytical thinking. In this chapter, we will change directions and pay attention
to the acquisition of data. Properly speaking, the study of data acquisition belongs
to the realm of statistics. However, our purpose is not to proceed with a course
on statistics or probability, but instead to provide some fundamental probabilistic
notions that are essential to any practical study of artificial intelligence. Indeed,
the collection of data and its compression into usable forms are basic functions of
intelligence. Furthermore, from a practical standpoint, the filtering of raw data
and the use of that filtered data in decision making are primary parts of any
automatic control system, whether that system be designed for the navigation of
an airplane, the sighting of an automatic weapon system, or the vision system of
a robot.

Imagine, if you will, a very accurate scale that is to be used to weigh some
object. Let X denote the outcome of any particular weighing. X is a measurement. Physically, an intelligent entity determines X by reading the position of a
needle on a meter (or by means of some other sensory task). Now suppose person
$P1$ is to observe person $P2$ reading the meter, and, moreover, suppose person $P1$
possesses knowledge concerning the weight of the object at hand. We wish to
raise the question as to what form $P1$'s knowledge might take.

First, $P1$ certainly cannot know the actual reading of the needle that will be observed by $P2$.   Not only is there experimental error due to the physical system represented by the scale, but there is also some question as to the current state of the object.   Even had $P1$ weighed the object 50 times and at each weighing obtained the same result, both the scale and the object may not now be the same.   Indeed, since there is no way of experimentally verifying an "exact" weight of the object, the entire notion of exactness is meaningless.   It is only through observational verification that the logical symbols are given meaning.   To write the sentence "$w = 7.233$" and to mean by it that there is an identity, one would have to have means of verification.   This, of course, is functionally impossible, since the sentence would mean that all methods of verification that are humanly possible would result in the same identity.   Indeed, what if we were to utilize a scale accurate to eight decimal places?   Would we really expect a reading of 7.23300000?   The point is this: the measurement X can have no deterministic meaning in the scientific epistemology.   Then what type of knowledge can person $P1$ possess?

Essentially, he or she can have predictive knowledge.   Although we will not go into a detailed theory of statistical epistemology, the essence of the matter, at least from a pragmatic engineering perspective, is fairly easy to grasp.   What is known of the measurement X is that it will vary between 0 and infinity.   Moreover, person $P1$, based on reliable prior observation of X, can very likely make statements regarding the likelihood that X will fall in some interval.   If he or she uses a scale from 0 to 1, 0 being impossibility and 1 being certainty, then a statement of the following form might be reasonable: "the likelihood of X being between 7.232 and 7.234 is 0.75."   Letting P denote likelihood (or, more properly, probability), the statement can be written symbolically as

$$P[7.232 < X < 7.234] = 0.75$$

Intuitively, we might interpret the foregoing equality as meaning that $P1$ expects that, if he or she were to observe $P2$ weighing the object some number of times, then 75% of those weighings would lie between 7.232 and 7.234.   But beware: such an interpretation, while naively correct, can lead to all sorts of problems, not the least of which being that $P1$ plans to observe only one instance of the measurement X.

Our goal in this chapter is to give some sense to probability statements such as the preceding one and to give some insight into problems relating to the manner in which measurements such as X can be employed to guide the future behavior of a system and to make adaptations within the decision-oriented intelligence apparatus guiding the system.   Throughout, our presentation will remain essentially heuristic, leaving the mathematical details to courses in probability and statistics.   Those having some background in these areas should pay attention to the manner in which statistical considerations affect control decisions.

Given a measurement X to be performed, we would like to be able to make statements of the sort previously noted.   In general, what can be said about the probability of X being in some range of values, where our notion of probability is that it gives some measure of belief?   Using 0 as total disbelief and 1 as total belief, we wish to be able to make probability statements of the form

$$P[a < X < b]$$

Given that X satisfies certain mathematical constraints, it is possible to make such statements.   Moreover, if X represents a measurement involving continuous change, such as weight or velocity, then very often the probabilistic behavior of X can be described graphically.   Indeed, for a continuous measurement X, it is always possible to find some function $f(x)$ such that the aforementioned probability is given by the area under the curve of $f(x)$ between the points a and b.   Mathematically,

$$P[a < X < b] = \int_a^b f(x) \, dx \tag{1}$$

(see Figure 6.1).   In the parlance of probability theory, X is known as a *random variable* and $f(x)$ is called its *density*.   Before proceeding, let it be clear that we are in no way claiming that it is necessarily easy to find a density to describe the behavior of the random variable.   What we are saying, however, is that if $f(x)$ is known then our predictive knowledge is complete.   This last statement is paramount: if predictive knowledge is all that we can possess, then full knowledge of the probabilistic behavior of X is full scientific knowledge of the physical situation, at least insofar as that situation manifests itself in the measurement X.

It is important to recognize that not simply any function can serve as a density for a random variable (measurement).   Two requirements are obvious.   First, since probabilities must be nonnegative, so must $f(x)$ be nonnegative, else the integral might be negative.   Second, since it is obvious that X must fall somewhere between $-\infty$ and $+\infty$, the total integral of $f(x)$ must be 1:

$$\int_{-\infty}^{+\infty} f(x) \, dx = P[-\infty < X < +\infty] = 1$$

A fact of fundamental importance for both theory and application is that any function that is both nonnegative and possesses total integral 1 is the density for some random variable; that is, given such a function, it is possible to find a random variable X whose density is the given function.

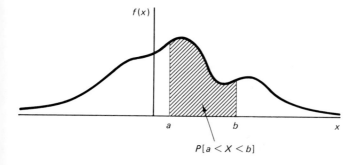

Figure 6.1.   Probability density

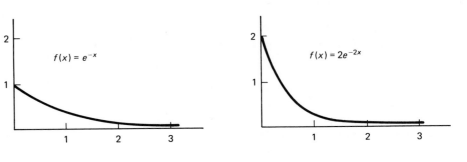

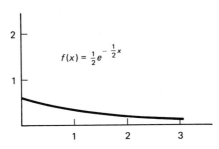

Figure 6.2. Exponential density

Example 6.1

Consider the exponential function

$$f(x) = \begin{cases} be^{-bx}, & \text{if } x \geq 0 \\ 0, & \text{if } x < 0 \end{cases}$$

where b is a positive constant. Then $f(x)$ is both nonnegative and possesses total integral 1. It is known as the *exponential* density, and any random variable that has $f(x)$ as a density is said to be *exponentially distributed*. Note that the exponential density is actually a family of densities, a different one results for each possible value of b. Figure 6.2 illustrates several members of the family.

Now suppose we consider the case $b = 2$. If X possesses this density, then probability information regarding X can be found by integration. For instance, the probability that X falls between 1 and 3 is given by

$$P[1 < X < 3] = \int_1^3 2e^{-2x}\, dx = e^{-2} - e^{-6} = 0.133$$

Example 6.2

The *Gaussian*, or *normal*, density is defined by the function

$$f(x) = \frac{1}{\sqrt{2\pi}\sigma}\, e^{-\frac{1}{2}\left(\frac{x-\mu}{\sigma}\right)^2}$$

where μ and σ are parameters that generate the Gaussian family. Referring to Figure 6.3, where several possible Gaussian densities are drawn, we see that the density is

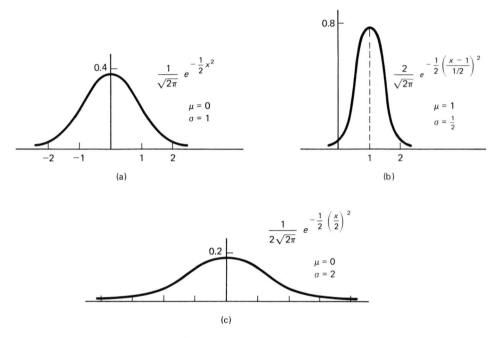

Figure 6.3.   Gaussian density

centered at μ and that σ determines the *spread* of the curve: the greater σ, the wider the curve, the smaller σ, the narrower the curve. In subsequent sections of the current chapter, we will see the significance of these notions.

The Gaussian density in Figure 6.3(a) is of particular interest. It is called the *standard normal* density, and for it $\mu = 0$ and $\sigma = 1$. Most statistics books contain integral tables for this density. For instance, if X possesses a standard normal density, then

$$P[-1.96 < X < 1.96] = \frac{1}{\sqrt{2\pi}} \int_{-1.96}^{1.96} e^{-\frac{1}{2}x^2} \, dx = 0.95$$

where the value 0.95 has been obtained from a table. Intuitively, if X possesses a standard normal density, then the measurements fall on the x axis and tend to center about zero. Moreover, for any particular occurrence of X, the probability that X falls between plus and minus 1.96 is 0.95.

Example 6.3

The *uniform* density on the interval $[a, b]$ is constant on $[a, b]$ and 0 elsewhere. To make its total integral equal to 1, it takes the constant value $1/(b - a)$ on $[a, b]$. Figure 6.4 gives the uniform density on the interval $[0, 2]$.

Imagine tossing a dart onto the interval $[a, b]$ in such a manner that the tosses distribute themselves uniformly over the interval. It should be clear that the appropriate probability model is the uniform density; indeed, if $[x, y]$ and $[u, v]$ are two

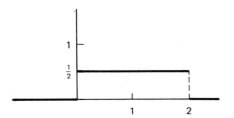

Figure 6.4. Uniform density

subintervals of $[a, b]$ of equal length, then

$$P[x < X < y] = P[u < X < v] = \frac{y - x}{b - a}$$

At this point we would like to briefly describe one manner in which we might attempt to find a density for a measurement X. Imagine taking the object to be measured (weighed) and performing a number of measurements, say $x_1, x_2, \ldots, x_{100}$. Suppose all the measurements fall between 7.230 and 7.240. Let us partition the interval [7.230, 7.240] into ten nonoverlapping subintervals, each of length 0.001. Calling these intervals $I_1, I_2, \ldots, I_{10}$, suppose that the number of measurements in I_j is given by w_j, for $j = 1, 2, \ldots, 10$. For sake of discussion, suppose the values of the w_j are given by the numbers in Figure 6.5. Using these values, each called a *frequency*, we can plot a standard histogram (bar graph) to visually depict the number of occurrences in each subinterval. In Figure 6.6, this bar graph is drawn in conjunction with a continuous curve that tends to approximate it.

If we think about the matter from a frequency perspective, it is clear that the proportion of observed measurements in subinterval I_j is given by $w_j/100$. We might then be tempted to say that $P[X \in I_j] = w_j/100$. In other words, based on past experience, we infer some probability statement.

Although we do not wish to open up a Pandora's box of epistemological fuzziness, let us note that making such a probability statement based on past

I_1	2
I_2	4
I_3	4
I_4	10
I_5	20
I_6	30
I_7	15
I_8	8
I_9	3
I_{10}	4

Figure 6.5. Frequency table

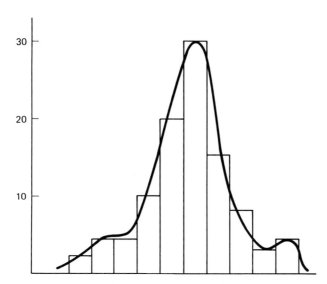

Figure 6.6. Frequency histogram

observations involves an inductive leap.   There is no logical reason to conclude that any number of past observations, no matter how large the number, yields definitive probabilistic knowledge about future measurements.   Indeed, even supposing a coin is fair (the probability of a head and tail both equaling 1/2), it is still possible that we might observe 50 heads in a row.   Nonetheless, we customarily employ past observations to make probabilistic statements regarding future measurements.   This is the scientific method, and at its deepest it involves the aforementioned inductive leap.   From an experimental perspective, it is just the wariness regarding this leap that drives us to find experimental conditions that are as close to repeatable as possible.   From the point of view of artificial intelligence, this leap must be confronted when we attempt to weight the importance of new data that seem to be at odds with parameters in the system that have been derived from past observations.

Returning to the situation depicted in Figure 6.6, we see that, after a suitable rescaling of the x axis so that the base of each rectangle is of length 1, the approximate number of past observations between two points a and b can be found by finding the integral under the curve $f(x)$ between a and b.   Suppose now we go a step further and reinterpret the frequency histogram.   Instead of plotting the actual frequencies, change the scale on the y axis to represent the relative frequencies $w_j/100$.   Then the integral of $f(x)$ from a to b gives the approximate percentage of observations between a and b.   If we then make the inductive leap discussed previously and call this percentage the probability that X will fall (in the future) between a and b, we then have

$$P[a < X < b] \approx \int_a^b f(x)\, dx$$

which looks just like equation (1).

Put simply, we utilize the continuous representation of the frequency histogram, which is computed from past observations, to be the density for the random variable X: probability statements concerning measurements to be made are predicated on observations of phenomena whose behavior we believe to be much the same as that of X. Moreover, we make the implicit assumption that the distribution of the past measurements reflects the distribution of future measurements, in the sense that the distribution of the observed data, as reflected in the frequency histogram, can serve as a reasonable quantitative predictor of probability statements concerning the random measurement X.

6.2 MOMENTS

Although the density of a random variable contains all probabilistic information regarding the random variable (and is therefore sometimes called the *law* of the random variable), it is convenient to compress that information into some discrete collection of parameters. If the information contained in those parameters is sufficient for the purpose at hand, then we can simply utilize them (or some subcollection of them) as our temporary characterization of the random variable. In this section we will briefly discuss the moments of a random variable. These are the most commonly employed parameters, and, moreover, they are relatively easy to work with.

Given a random variable X with associated density $f(x)$, we define the *expected value* of X by

$$E[X] = \int_{-\infty}^{+\infty} xf(x)\, dx$$

Geometrically, the expected value of X is the center of mass of its density. As such, it gives a *measure of central tendency* of the random variable. Intuitively, if we employ the frequency model given in the previous section, $E[X]$ gives a value about which the occurrences of X tend to center. Other measures of central tendency are utilized in statistics; however, for profound mathematical reasons, the expected value is the most important, and it is the only one we will pursue. When used as a measure of central tendency, $E[X]$ is often called the *mean* of X and denoted by the Greek letter μ.

Example 6.4

Consider the exponential density introduced in Example 6.1. Then

$$E[X] = \int_{0}^{+\infty} xbe^{-bx}\, dx = \frac{1}{b}$$

where the integral can be evaluated by means of integration by parts. From the point of view of mass, $1/b$ is the point on the x axis that represents the center of mass of the area under the defining exponential curve.

Example 6.5

Although we will not go through the mathematical details, it can be shown that the expected value of the Gaussian density with parameters μ and σ is given by μ. This result is geometrically obvious from the symmetry of the curve. There is a point of possible notational confusion here: generally, μ denotes the mean, and for the Gaussian density, the parameter that ultimately is the mean is also denoted μ.

Example 6.6

For the uniform density on the interval $[a, b]$,

$$E[X] = \frac{b + a}{2}$$

the midpoint of the interval, which is also obviously the center of mass.

More generally, we define the kth *moment*, $k = 1, 2, 3, \ldots$, of the random variable X to be the expected value of the kth power of X:

$$m_k = E[X^k] = \int_{-\infty}^{+\infty} x g_k(x) \, dx$$

where $g_k(x)$ is a density for the random variable X^k. Notice the subtle point here: if X denotes a measurement, then X^k is also a measurement, and it is a fundamental principle of probability theory that X^k, as a random phenomenon, possesses a density that can be obtained from the density of X (albeit, perhaps not easily). As a random variable, the expected value of X^k can be computed as any other expected value, $E[X^k]$ giving the center of mass of its density $g_k(x)$.

Fortunately, we need not go through the difficulty of finding the density of the random variable X^k. Indeed, it is a basic theorem from probability theory that

$$E[X^k] = \int_{-\infty}^{+\infty} x^k f(x) \, dx$$

where $f(x)$ is the density for the original random variable X. In other words, the kth moment can be evaluated directly from the original density.

Example 6.7

The kth moment of the exponential density is given by

$$E[X^k] = \int_0^{+\infty} x^k b e^{-bx} \, dx$$

For any value of k, the integral can be evaluated by applying integration by parts k times. For instance, two applications of integration by parts yields

$$E[X^2] = \int_0^{+\infty} x^2 b e^{-bx} \, dx = 2/b^2$$

Example 6.8

Let us compute the kth moment for the uniform density:

$$E[X^k] = \frac{1}{b - a} \int_a^b x^k \, dx$$

$$= \frac{1}{b - a} \frac{x^{k+1}}{k + 1} \Big|_a^b$$

$$= \frac{b^{k+1} - a^{k+1}}{(k + 1)(b - a)}$$

Now suppose we have two random variables X and Y. If we take both measurements and add the results, we get a new quantity $X + Y$. But this, too, is a random quantity. More generally, if a and b are real numbers, the linear combination $aX + bY$ is also a random variable. One of the most important properties of the expected value operator is that it is *linear:*

$$E[aX + bY] = aE[X] + bE[Y]$$

Once again, note that we can find a center of mass without recourse to actually determining the density itself, in this instance that density being the density of the sum of the random variables. In terms of the compression of information, the linearity of E allows us to manipulate the compressed information (the expected value) directly. Indeed, in that sense, the expected value operation represents a transform technique where the inputs are functions (densities) and the transforms are simply real numbers.

Example 6.9

Suppose X and Y are both normally distributed, (i.e., each possesses a Gaussian density) and suppose $E[X] = \mu_x$ and $E[Y] = \mu_y$. Then

$$E[X + Y] = E[X] + E[Y] = \mu_x + \mu_y$$

More generally, suppose $X_1, X_2, \ldots, X_n$ are n Gaussian random variables with $E[X_i] = \mu_i$, for $i = 1, 2, \ldots, n$. Then

$$E[X_1 + X_2 + \cdots + X_n] = \mu_1 + \mu_2 + \cdots + \mu_n$$

Another collection of parameters closely associated with the moments is the collection of *central moments.* These are defined, for $k = 1, 2, 3, \ldots$, by

$$m_k' = E[(X - \mu)^k] = E[(X - E[X])^k] = \int_{-\infty}^{+\infty} (x - \mu)^k f(x) \, dx$$

The most commonly employed of these central moments is the second, which is known as the *variance* of X. Using the general definition of central moments, we obtain for the variance

$$\text{Var}[X] = m_2' = E[(X - \mu)^2] = \int_{-\infty}^{+\infty} (x - \mu)^2 f(x)\, dx$$

Using the linearity of E, we obtain the very useful relation

$$\begin{aligned}
\text{Var}[X] &= E[X^2 - 2\mu X + \mu^2] \\
&= E[X^2] - 2\mu E[X] + E[\mu^2] \\
&= m_2 - 2\mu^2 + \mu^2 = m_2 - \mu^2
\end{aligned} \qquad (2)$$

where we have used the fact that the expected value of a constant (in this instance μ^2) is the constant itself.   In words, the variance is known once the mean and the second moment are known.

Example 6.10

Using the formula for the variance given in equation (2), it is easy to find the variances of the exponential and uniform densities from the respective expected values (found in Examples 6.5 and 6.6) and the respective second moments (found in Examples 6.7 and 6.8).   For the exponential density, we have

$$\text{Var}[X] = m_2 - \mu^2 = 2b^{-2} - b^{-2} = b^{-2}$$

For the uniform density, after a little bit of algebraic manipulation, we obtain

$$\begin{aligned}
\text{Var}[X] &= \frac{b^3 - a^3}{3(b - a)} - \frac{(b + a)^2}{4} \\
&= \frac{(a - b)^2}{12}
\end{aligned}$$

A very important variance is that of the Gaussian density.   If X is Gaussian with parameters μ and σ, then $\text{Var}[X] = \sigma^2$.

If we look at the definition of the variance, we see that it is given by the expected value of the square of the difference between the random variable and its mean.   This difference, too, is random and is graphically depicted in Figure 6.7.   If we think in terms of prediction, it seems to make qualitative sense that a good value to predict for any future occurrence of the random variable is its

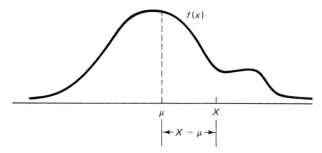

Figure 6.7.   Distance to mean

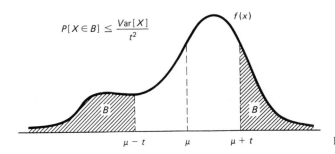

Figure 6.8. Chebyshev inequality

expected value. (We will quantify this statement in Section 6.4.) If this is so, then the random quantity $(X - \mu)^2$ is a nonnegative quantity that measures the degree to which X differs from the expected measurement and $\text{Var}[X]$ gives the expected value of the square of the difference between X and its predicted value. It should be intuitively clear that the variance gives a measurement of the degree to which the mass of the density is dispersed along the x axis: the greater the dispersion of the density, the greater the variance, and vice versa. For this reason, the variance is also called the *dispersion*.

The preceding remarks are quantified in the following theorem, which is known as *Chebyshev's inequality* and is one of the most celebrated results in probability theory.

Theorem 6.1.   For any $t > 0$, $P[|X - \mu| \geq t] \leq \text{Var}[X]/t^2$.

In words, the probability that X differs absolutely from its mean by greater than t is less than or equal to its variance divided by t^2 (see Figure 6.8).

Other moments can also be graphically interpreted, but we leave that to a text on statistics. Let us just reemphasize the point that there is a great deal of information contained within the moments and that in many situations it is easier to work with the moments of a random variable than directly with the density.

6.3 JOINT MEASUREMENTS AND CONDITIONING

In many situations we are confronted by more than one measurement at a time, and very often the measurements are related. For instance, if we consider X to be the distance of a rocket from its launch site and Y to be its momentum, then surely X and Y are not "independent" of each other: knowledge of one gives knowledge of the other. To what extent there is a correlation between the measurements depends on the physical system determined by the rocket and the earth, and also on the type of sensors involved in making the relevant measurements. Keep in mind that, even though we have a degree of deterministic knowledge concerning the rocket–earth system, that knowledge being in the form of differential equations, ultimately our knowledge is probabilistic. Not only do the dif-

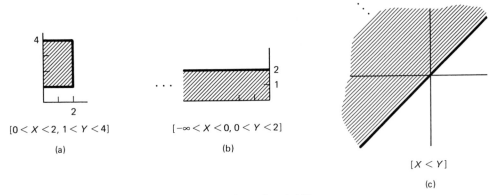

Figure 6.9. Planar regions of probability statements

ferential equations only represent a mathematical description of the most salient features of the system, but there is inherent variability in the sensor measurements.

In general, any two measurements X and Y, when considered simultaneously, determine a point in the xy plane. Consequently, *joint* probability statements about them must be of the form

$$P[(X, Y) \in B]$$

where B is some set in the plane. For instance, we might consider the following probabilities:

$$P[0 < X < 2, 1 < Y < 4]$$
$$P[-\infty < X < 0, 0 < Y < 2]$$
$$P[X < Y]$$

Figure 6.9 gives the planar regions determined by each of the preceding statements.

Just as a single continuous random variable has its law defined by a function of one variable, joint random variables have their law described by a function $f(x, y)$ of two variables. Analogously to the single-variable case, we have the following properties applying to the joint density $f(x, y)$ of two random variables:

1. $f(x, y) \geq 0$

2. $\displaystyle\int_{-\infty}^{+\infty}\int_{-\infty}^{+\infty} f(x, y)\, dy\, dx = 1$

3. $\displaystyle P[(X, Y) \in B] = \iint_{B} f(x, y)\, dy\, dx$

Once again the density must be somehow experimentally determined.

Example 6.11

For $x \geq 0$ and $y \geq 0$, let

$$f(x, y) = 2e^{-(x+2y)}$$

and let $f(x, y) = 0$ otherwise. Then $f(x, y)$ is nonnegative and its total integral is 1:

$$\int_0^{+\infty} \int_0^{+\infty} 2e^{-(x+2y)}dy \, dx = 1$$

Suppose X and Y are a pair of random variables with density $f(x, y)$. Then, for any region B in the xy plane,

$$P[(X, Y) \in B] = \iint_B 2e^{-(x+2y)}dy \, dx$$

the computation of which will involve the evaluation of a double integral. For instance, if B is the region

$$\{(x, y): 0 < x < 2, 1 < y < 4\}$$

depicted in Figure 6.9(a), then we obtain

$$P[0 < X < 2, 1 < Y < 4] = 2 \int_0^2 e^{-x} \int_1^4 e^{-2y} \, dy \, dx$$

$$= 2 \left(-e^{-x} \Big|_0^2 \right)\left(-\frac{1}{2} e^{-2y} \Big|_1^4 \right)$$

$$= (1 - e^{-2})(e^{-2} - e^{-8})$$

Given two random variables X and Y, it is possible to obtain all probabilistic knowledge about each individually if we know the joint density. In other words, full joint knowledge yields full individual knowledge. Specifically, we can find the individual densities according to the following relations:

$$f_X(x) = \int_{-\infty}^{+\infty} f(x, y) \, dy$$

$$f_Y(y) = \int_{-\infty}^{+\infty} f(x, y) \, dx$$

where f_X and f_Y denote the *marginal* densities of the individual (or marginal) random variables. In words, the marginal densities are found by "integrating out" the other variable. For our purposes here, it should simply be recognized that marginal information is fully obtainable from full information regarding the behavior of the random variables jointly.

Example 6.12

Consider the joint density given in Example 6.11. The marginal density $f_X(x)$ is given, for $x \geq 0$, by

$$f_X(x) = \int_0^{+\infty} 2e^{-(x+2y)} \, dy$$

$$= 2e^{-x} \int_0^{+\infty} e^{-2y} \, dy$$

$$= 2e^{-x} \left(-\frac{1}{2} e^{-2y} \Big|_0^{+\infty} \right)$$

$$= e^{-x}$$

which is an exponential density with $b = 1$. Similarly, integrating out x will leave the marginal density of the random variable Y, which is also an exponential density, but with $b = 2$:

$$f_Y(y) = 2e^{-2y}$$

for $y \geq 0$, and $f_Y(y) = 0$ for $y < 0$.

Example 6.13

As in the one-random-variable case, we can consider uniformly distributed joint random variables. Here, there exists a region A of area a in the plane and the joint density is defined to be $1/a$ on A and 0 elsewhere. Because the density is a constant, for any set B in the plane,

$$P[(X, Y) \in B] = \frac{1}{a} \text{AREA}(B \cap A)$$

Now consider the region A of area 1/3 depicted in Figure 6.10. The marginal density for X is given by

$$f_X(x) = \int_{-\infty}^{+\infty} f(x, y) \, dy = 3 \int_0^{x^2} dy = 3x^2$$

for $0 < x < 1$. It is 0 elsewhere (which makes sense intuitively since the pair falls within the square $[0, 1] \times [0, 1]$ with probability 1). The marginal density for Y is

$$f_Y(y) = \int_{-\infty}^{+\infty} f(x, y) \, dx = 3 \int_{\sqrt{y}}^1 dy = 3(1 - y^{1/2})$$

for $0 < y < 1$ and 0 elsewhere.

Our main concern is the extraction of information about one random variable when given information about the behavior of another. This leads us to the problem of *conditioning*. Individually, our probabilistic knowledge about the variable Y in the pair (X, Y) is contained within its density. However, suppose we

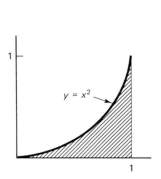

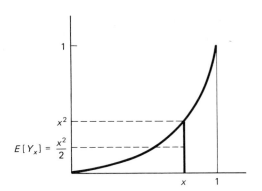

Figure 6.10. Support region of uniform joint density

Figure 6.11. Conditional mean

have in hand a measurement of X: What can be said *conditionally* about Y, given that we know the outcome (measurement) of X?

Going back to the example of the rocket, the measurement of the position and momentum at a given instant of time involves jointly distributed random variables X and Y. However, if we should have a "fix" on X, certainly that should reduce the variability of the measurement of Y. Put another way, since the physical laws governing the variables are not independent of one another, any restriction in the variability of one variable should result in a corresponding restriction of the variability of the other. From the perspective of data acquisition for autonomous systems, conditioning is perhaps the most fundamental of all probabilistic notions. The filtering of raw data to provide knowledge-based input data for the logico-mathematical apparatus comprising the intelligence of the system depends substantially on the concept of conditioning.

Without going through the mathematical details, which are somewhat involved, we will proceed through a specific example, using heuristic arguments to deduce the relevant notions. We consider the uniform joint density of Example 6.13, whose support region is depicted in Figure 6.10. As we found in that example, the marginal densities are given by $f_X(x) = 3x^2$, $0 < x < 1$, and by $f_Y(y) = 3(1 - y^{1/2})$, $0 < y < 1$. Now suppose we fix the value of x between 0 and 1. In other words, suppose we are observing the random variable Y under the condition that X has a priori the observed value x. Then Y must fall on the line depicted in Figure 6.11. Moreover, since the original pair was assumed to be uniformly distributed over the support region, we can intuitively conclude that this conditional observation of Y will be uniformly distributed along the line $X = x$. Calling this new conditional variable Y_x and denoting its density by $f(y|x)$, we see that Y_x can fall between 0 and x^2. Hence,

$$f(y|x) = 1/x^2 \qquad \text{for } 0 < y < x^2$$

Notice that the density for the conditional observation of Y given x depends on x. Moreover, note that the conditional density is derived (in this instance, heuristically) from the original joint density.

   We can get an idea of what is happening by simply imagining a dart falling uniformly randomly in the support region of Figure 6.10, and imagining two sensors, $S1$ observing the distance from the y axis and $S2$ observing the distance from the x axis. In general there is a correlation between the readings of the two sensors. Because of that correlation, a fixed reading on the first sensor tells us something about the reading on the second sensor.   In the problem at hand, the conditional density $f(y|x)$ gives a distribution of the probability mass relating to the sensor $S2$, given that we have an initial reading on the sensor $S1$.   The straight marginal density for the unconditioned measurement Y simply gives the distribution of the probability mass for the sensor $S2$ independent of any prior knowledge concerning a reading on $S1$.

   To continue, let us now determine the expected value of the conditional random variable Y_x.   By the definition of expected value, it must be given by

$$E[Y_x] = \int_{-\infty}^{+\infty} yf(y|x) \, dy$$

Intuitively, the *conditional expectation* gives the center of mass of the conditional density (see Figure 6.11).   Consequently, from simple geometry we can deduce its value to be $x^2/2$, precisely the midpoint of the darkened line in Figure 6.11. Notice that this expectation depends on the a priori observed value of x.   As such, the conditional expectation is itself a random phenomenon: it measures the center of mass of a density which depends on the outcome of a nondeterministic trial, the outcome of the random variable X.

   Since $E[Y_x]$ is a random quantity dependent on the random variable X, it too has an expected value.   Intuitively, where should its central tendency lie given that the observation from sensor $S1$ can vary along the x axis between 0 and 1? Although we do not intend to pursue these matters much further, let us simply note that the expected value of the conditional expectation of Y given $X = x$ is equal to the unconditioned expected value of Y itself:

$$E[E[Y_x]] = E[Y]$$

This rather strange expression is a basic result in the theory of estimation.   Heuristically, it says that we can determine the mean of the marginal random variable Y by "averaging" the conditional means that have resulted from observation of sensor $S2$ given fixed readings on sensor $S1$.

   Before concluding this section, we would like to return to the problem of the rocket that was mentioned at the beginning.   Let us suppose, for simplicity, that the rocket is moving linearly and thus possesses only a single position component, say X.   Moreover, suppose we have a device for measuring its momentum Y. Since both X and Y are random variables, certainly our desire is to minimize the variances of each. In general, these variances depend on the joint density and can be computed by means of the marginal densities. In effect, by reasoning such as that relating to Chebyshev's inequality (Theorem 6.1), a statement of the form

$$P[|X - \mu_X| < t, |Y - \mu_Y| < t]$$

which gives the probability that both variables will be within t of their respective means, can be bounded by variability considerations. From a practical point of view, the smaller the individual variances of X and Y, the greater the accuracy of the joint measurement and, concomitantly, the greater our confidence that any given joint measurement (X, Y) gives a good fix on the location and momentum of the rocket. As $\text{Var}[X]$ and $\text{Var}[Y]$ decrease to zero, our certainty relative to our observations increases. From a pragmatic standpoint, of course, these variances can never be reduced to zero, since any such attempt comes up against the limits of the sensors. Nevertheless, better engineering and better intelligence in the system can, at least so it seems, produce ever smaller variances.

6.4 ESTIMATION

Perhaps no topic is more important to the physical implementation of autonomous systems than the theory of statistical estimation. Generally, our desire is to estimate the value of a particular random phenomenon by means of the observation of a related phenomenon. Due to physical constraints on the sensors, it is often impossible to record the desired data; rather, we must estimate these data on the basis of data from observations of related measurements. From this brief description it should be evident that conditional expectation will play a role in the estimation.

   To begin, we introduce the notion of correlation between random variables. Suppose that two jointly distributed random variables X and Y have means μ_X and μ_Y, respectively. We know (Section 6.2) that the expected value of $X + Y$ is the sum of the expected values. Let us now examine the variance of the sum. Writing the variance in terms of the second moment and the mean, we have

$$\begin{aligned}
\text{Var}[X + Y] &= E[(X + Y)^2] - (\mu_X + \mu_Y)^2 \\
&= E[X^2] + E[Y^2] + 2E[XY] - \mu_X^2 - \mu_Y^2 - 2\mu_X\mu_Y \qquad (3)\\
&= \text{Var}[X] + \text{Var}[Y] + 2(E[XY] - \mu_X\mu_Y) \\
&= \text{Var}[X] + \text{Var}[Y] + 2\text{Cov}[X, Y]
\end{aligned}$$

where $\text{Cov}[X, Y]$ is called the *covariance* of X and Y and is defined by

$$\text{Cov}[X, Y] = E[XY] - \mu_X\mu_Y$$

Note that, just as $X + Y$ defines a random variable resulting from the addition of X and Y, XY is a random variable resulting from the multiplication of X and Y. In sum, the variance of a sum of random variables is not the sum of the variances; it is the sum plus twice the covariance.

The covariance, which is an important quantity in its own right, can be found directly from the formula

$$E[XY] = \int_{-\infty}^{+\infty} \int_{-\infty}^{+\infty} xyf(x, y) \, dy \, dx$$

where $f(x, y)$ is the joint density of the variables. It also satisfies the following fundamental theorem:

Theorem 6.2.   Given the joint random variables X and Y,

$$\text{Cov}[X, Y]^2 \leq \text{Var}[X] \, \text{Var}[Y]$$

Moreover, there is equality if and only if Y can be written linearly in terms of X, that is, if and only if there exist real numbers a and b such that

$$Y = aX + b$$

If we define the *correlation coefficient* for X and Y by

$$\text{Cor}[X, Y] = \frac{\text{Cov}[X, Y]}{\sqrt{\text{Var}[X] \, \text{Var}[Y]}}$$

then, according to Theorem 6.2, the correlation always varies between -1 and $+1$, with a value near to $+$ or -1 meaning that there is a high degree of linearity between the variables. If $\text{Cor}[X, Y] = 0$, the variables are said to be *uncorrelated*. It is important to note that if the random variables are uncorrelated then equation (3) for the variance of a sum becomes

$$\text{Var}[X + Y] = \text{Var}[X] + \text{Var}\{Y\}$$

In words, the variance of a sum of uncorrelated random variables is the sum of the variances.

Before proceeding, we note that the square roots of the variances, which appear in the definition of the correlation coefficient, are called the *standard deviations* of the respective random variables. In many statistical situations, the standard deviation is employed instead of the variance. The accepted notation for the standard deviation is the Greek letter sigma (σ). Just like μ is used to represent the mean of the Gaussian density as well as a general mean, note, too, that σ serves similar double duty, it being commonly written as the standard deviation parameter for the Gaussian density.

Example 6.14.

Consider the uniformly jointly distributed random variables given in Example 6.13. Then

$$E[XY] = \int_0^1 \int_0^{x^2} 3xy \ dy \ dx = \int_0^1 (3/2)x^5 \ dx = \tfrac{1}{4}$$

Moreover, using the marginal densities that were found in Example 6.13,

$$\mu_x = \int_0^1 3x^3 \ dx = \tfrac{3}{4}$$

and

$$\mu_y = \int_0^1 3y(1 - y^{1/2}) \ dy = 3 \int_0^1 (y - y^{3/2}) \ dy = \tfrac{3}{10}$$

Hence,

$$\text{Cov}[X, Y] = \tfrac{1}{4} - (\tfrac{3}{4})(\tfrac{3}{10}) = \tfrac{1}{40}$$

To find the correlation coefficient, we need both of the variances for the marginal densities. These can be obtained by finding the second moments m_{x2} and m_{y2} for X and Y, respectively. We have

$$m_{x2} = \int_{-\infty}^{+\infty} x^2 f_X(x) \ dx$$

$$= 3 \int_0^1 x^4 \ dx = \tfrac{3}{5}$$

and

$$m_{y2} = 3 \int_0^1 y^2 (1 - y^{1/2}) \ dy = \tfrac{1}{7}$$

Using the fact that the variance is equal to the second moment minus the square of the mean, the respective variances are

$$\text{Var}[X] = \tfrac{3}{5} - \tfrac{9}{16} = \tfrac{3}{80}$$

and

$$\text{Var}[Y] = \tfrac{1}{7} - \tfrac{9}{100} = \tfrac{37}{700}$$

Putting the preceding quantities into the formula for the correlation coefficient yields

$$\text{Cor}[X, Y] = 0.562$$

Example 6.15

Suppose X is any random variable and we define the random variable Y by $Y = 2X + 3$, which simply means that, whatever the measurement X, Y is found directly in terms of X. According to Theorem 6.2, the absolute value of the correlation coefficient must be 1.

We are now ready to turn to the problem of *estimation:* given an observation of a random variable X, how can we best use that information to estimate a random variable Y that we have not observed? Like most problems in statistics, there is, hidden in the question, a more primary question regarding what is to be meant by the notion of *best*. Probably the most common approach, and the one we will follow herein, is to define the best estimate in the following manner. We look for that function of X, say $g(X)$, which itself will be a random variable, that will minimize the expected value of the square of the error: the best estimate is the random variable $g(X)$ that minimizes

$$E[(Y - g(X))^2]$$

If we can find such a $g(X)$, it is called the *best mean-square (MS) estimate* of Y. Intuitively, the best MS estimate is the one that utilizes the observed data X in a manner that minimizes our expectation (in the mean-square sense) of error.

As a simple illustration, suppose we wish to estimate Y by a constant. Then we must ask what number c gives a minimum value for the quantity $E[(Y - c)^2]$. To find this best estimate, we expand the MS error to obtain

$$E[Y^2] - 2cE[Y] + c^2$$

If we differentiate this expression with respect to c and set the derivative equal to zero to find the minimum, we easily discover that the minimum MS error is given by $c = E[Y]$, the mean of the random variable. (This result was hinted at in Section 6.2.) In the absence of any information about a random variable, save its own probabilistic description, the best MS estimate is given by the expected value.

Let us now consider the general case where X is observed and some function $g(X)$ is desired that will give the best MS estimate of Y. We have the following theorem:

Theorem 6.3.   Given two random variables X and Y, the best mean-square estimate for Y in terms of X is given by the conditional expectation $E[Y_x]$.

Intuitively, Theorem 6.3 is just what might be expected. It says that, in the presence of an observation $X = x$, our best estimate is the expected value of Y_x, given the information that $X = x$. After all, in the case where there are no a priori observations, we choose $E[Y]$, the center of mass of the density for Y. According to Theorem 6.3, in the presence of the observation $X = x$, we choose the center of mass of the conditional density $f(y|x)$.

To further illustrate the notion of conditional expectation as it applies to a best estimate, we consider the case of *independent* random variables. Intuitively, X and Y are independent if knowledge of one gives no added information regarding the other. Mathematically, it turns out that the condition for X and Y to be independent is that their joint density equal the product of the marginal densities:

$$f(x, y) = f_X(x)f_Y(y)$$

An immediate result of independence is that the expected value of the product is equal to the product of the expected values:

$$E[XY] = E[X]E[Y]$$

Indeed,

$$E[XY] = \int_{-\infty}^{\infty} \int_{-\infty}^{\infty} xyf(x, y)\, dy\, dx$$

$$= \int_{-\infty}^{\infty} \int_{-\infty}^{\infty} xyf_X(x)f_Y(y)\, dy\, dx$$

$$= \left(\int_{-\infty}^{\infty} xf_X(x)\, dx \right)\left(\int_{-\infty}^{\infty} yf_Y(y)\, dy \right)$$

$$= E[X]E[Y]$$

Since the covariance is given by $E[XY]$ minus the product of the marginal means, it is immediate that whenever X and Y are independent the covariance is 0, and hence so is the correlation coefficient. In sum, independent random variables are uncorrelated. (The converse is not true.) More than that, for independent random variables, the conditional density $f(y|x)$ equals the marginal density for Y, $f_Y(y)$. Consequently, the corresponding centers of mass are identical for all observations $X = x$ and the conditional expectation $E[Y_x]$ is equal to the expectation $E[Y]$ for all x, the net effect being that the best MS estimate given an observation of X is the same as the best MS estimate given no a priori observations of the random variable X.

Example 6.16.

Consider the joint density $f(x, y)$ given in Example 6.11. The marginals were found in Example 6.12, and it is immediate that $f(x, y) = f_X(x)f_Y(y)$, so the corresponding random variables X and Y are independent. As a consequence, the conditional densities are given by

$$f(y|x) = f_Y(y) = 2e^{-2y}$$

for $y \geq 0$, and

$$f(x|y) = f_X(x) = e^{-x}$$

for $x \geq 0$. Moreover, the conditional expectations of Y given $X = x$ and X given $Y = y$ are equal to the unconditioned expectations $E[Y] = \frac{1}{2}$ and $E[X] = 1$, respectively.

Example 6.17

We will present a very practical sensor-related problem in estimation. Although the supporting details are beyond the scope of the present text, the problem, together with the fundamentals of its solution, can be given.

Figure 6.12 depicts a situation where there is a source sending a signal, which

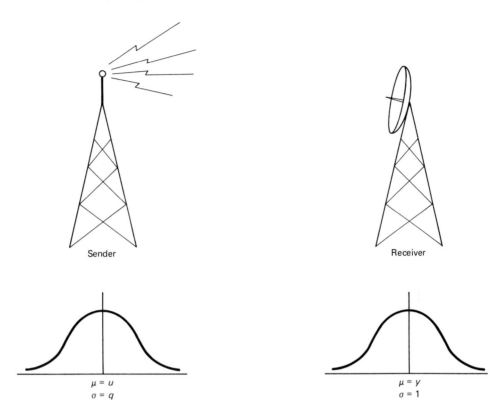

Figure 6.12.   Transmission system

consists of a single numerical value, and a receiver receiving the transmitted signal. The person at the receiving end knows from experience that Y, the value of the signal sent, is normally distributed with mean $\mu = u$ and standard deviation $\sigma = q$.   Moreover, if the signal transmitted has value y, then the received value X is normally distributed with mean y and a fixed standard deviation independent of y, which, for the sake of simplicity, we will assume to be 1.   In other words, the received signal is treated as a random phenomenon; however, its expected value is equal to the actual transmitted signal.   From a modeling standpoint, the receiver realizes that he or she will be receiving a signal that has been distorted and therefore bases his or her estimate of the transmitted signal on both the actual instrument reading and a priori knowledge concerning the sender's tendencies.

Now, given that the receiver records the datum $X = x$, what is the best MS estimate of Y, the value sent.   According to Theorem 6.3, the answer must be the conditional expectation of Y given $X = x$, which can be shown to be given by

$$E[Y_x] = \frac{u + xq^2}{1 + q^2} = \frac{1}{1 + q^2} u + \frac{q^2}{1 + q^2} x$$

where the 1 occurs due to our assumption concerning the standard deviation of X.

Note the form of the result: If q is near zero, meaning the variation of the sender's signal is negligible, then the actual recorded value of X is essentially disregarded in the estimate. On the other hand, if q is very large, meaning that the a priori knowledge regarding the sender does not reveal a concentrated probability mass, then the first addend is near zero, while the second is near x, and the estimate is essentially the same as the recorded value x. In any event, the estimate is a weighted average of the mean of the sender's signals and the actual value recorded.

From a practical data-processing perspective, the methodology of Example 6.17 is fundamental. It represents a model of estimation amidst uncertainty. Intuitively, given that data are not received with certainty, especially outside rigidly controlled environments, we attempt to utilize a priori knowledge in conjunction with actual observations to temper those observations. Such behavior is profoundly characteristic of animal intelligence: in the presence of observations that conflict with past experience, past experience is not disregarded; rather, it is brought to bear in the decision process along with the new information.

Similar estimation techniques are employed extensively in autonomous control systems. Data are *filtered* before being used, the purpose being to remove unwanted *noise* that is obscuring the desired information. Such filtering procedures are an essential part of any adaptive system and, ipso facto, of adaptive robotic systems.

Although we will not pursue this specific matter any further, it is possible to generalize the entire discussion and try to find the best estimate of Y given observations of a collection of random variables $X_1, X_2, \ldots, X_n$. Indeed, we often have numerous observations to work with, and, needless to say, we desire to use all the information that is available.

Although the foregoing theory is both elegant and intuitive, there are often difficulties in employing it directly. As a result, rather than try to discover the best MS estimate among all possible functions of a single observation or a collection of observations, we look for the best solution among some special class of functions of the observations. The most commonly employed class is the collection of *linear estimates* derived from the observations. For instance, given the observation X, what is the best MS estimate of the form $aX + b$, where a and b are real numbers? To solve this problem, we have to minimize the quantity

$$E[(Y - (aX + b))^2]$$

Without going through the details, let us simply note that the solutions for a and b that give the minimum are

$$a^* = \frac{\text{Cov}[X, Y]}{\text{Var}[X]}$$

and

$$b^* = E[Y] - a^* E[X]$$

Moreover, using the estimate $a^*X + b^*$ results in an MS error given by

$$e^* = \text{Var}[Y](1 - \text{Cor}[X, Y]^2)$$

Several points are immediate. First, if X and Y are uncorrelated, which means there is no linear relation between them, then $a^* = 0$ and the best linear estimate for Y is simply $E[Y]$, which is always the best MS estimate in the presence of no relevant observations. Furthermore, if $\text{Cor}[X, Y] = 1$, then the covariance is simply the product of the standard deviations, and

$$a^* = \frac{\sigma[Y]}{\sigma[X]}$$

$$b^* = E[Y] - \frac{\sigma[Y]}{\sigma[X]} E[X]$$

where $\sigma[X]$ and $\sigma[Y]$ denote the standard deviations of X and Y, respectively. Most significantly, $e^* = 0$, which should be expected, since, according to Theorem 6.2, whenever the correlation coefficient is zero, the variables are exactly linearly related.

Example 6.18

Consider the jointly uniformly distributed random variables given in Example 6.13. Suppose we wish to obtain the best linear MS estimate of Y in terms of X. Using the information of Example 6.14, we have

$$a^* = \frac{1/40}{3/80} = 2/3$$

$$b^* = 3/10 - (2/3)(3/4) = -1/5$$

and

$$e^* = (0.053)(1 - 0.316) = 0.036$$

The best MS linear estimator for Y in terms of X is $(2/3)X - 1/5$.

As with the case of general mean-square estimation, we can find the best linear MS estimator given a number of observations, say $X_1, X_2, \ldots, X_n$. In this situation, we attempt to find constants $a_1, a_2, \ldots, a_n$, and b for which the MS error

$$E[(Y - (a_1X_1 + a_2X_2 + \cdots + a_nX_n + b))^2]$$

is minimized (see Section 6.8).

In any event, it should be remembered that finding the overall best MS estimate will always give at least as good an estimation as one that is best over some subcollection of functions of the observation random variables. In this direction, let us just note that, if X and Y are both Gaussian, then the best linear MS estimate of Y given X agrees with the overall best MS estimate.

As has been illustrated above, especially in Example 6.17, the purpose of estimation is to give a best prediction of the value of one variable by means of an observation of one or more others. We do not simply wish to register raw data; instead, we wish to weigh new data in terms of our expectation. Such judgments are certainly part and parcel of intelligence. All forms of intelligence possess operational control systems. These systems rely on data, and new data are measured in terms of the old.

6.5 ENTROPY

Essential to the real-time implementation of robotic systems is the efficient transmission of data internally within the system and externally to and from other systems. In the present section we will introduce the notion of entropy and explain its importance relative to the efficient transmission of binary-encoded data.

Thus far we have concentrated on continuous random variables, ones that represent measurements on continuous scales. For these, probability statements of the form $P[a < X < b]$ can be described by means of an appropriate density. But what of measurements that are *discrete*, for instance, counting the number of successful trials of an experiment that has been run some fixed number of times? In such circumstances, the random variable can only take on discrete values.

More generally, suppose the random variable X can take on the values x_1, $x_2, \ldots, x_n$. We would like to be able to make probability statements of the form $P[X = x_i]$, for $i = 1, 2, \ldots, n$. For continuous random variables, the probability of attaining any specific value is 0; however, in the discrete case, it is precisely the probabilities of the possible outcomes that are important. Of course, this means that we cannot represent probability statements as integrals of densities. Nonetheless, the situation is similar in that the probability that X falls between a and b is equal to the *sum* of the probabilities $P[X = x_i]$ such that $a < x_i < b$:

$$P[a < X < b] = \Sigma \; \{P[X = x_i]: a < x_i < b\}$$

Note that now we must pay attention to the inequality sign; indeed,

$$P[a \leq X < b] = \Sigma \; \{P[X = x_i]: a \leq x_i < b\}$$

$$= P[a < X < b] + P[X = a]$$

where $P[X = a]$ is nonzero if and only if a is a possible outcome for X.

In line with the foregoing discussion, we define the *density* of a discrete random variable to be the *point mass function*

$$f(x_i) = P[X = x_i]$$

for $i = 1, 2, \ldots, n$, where the x_i are the possible values of X. Consequently, for real a and b, $a < b$,

$$P[a < X < b] = \sum_{a < x_i < b} f(x_i)$$

Example 6.19

Imagine tossing a single coin and letting X be the number of heads. Then there are two possible values for the measurement, 0 and 1. As in the continuous case, the density must be found by some statistical method, and, ultimately, the assignment of the values $f(0) = P[X = 0]$ and $f(1) = P[X = 1]$ must be based on past observations. For the moment, let us assume that $f(0) = \frac{2}{3}$ and $f(1) = \frac{1}{3}$. Then all possible probability statements can be answered based on these values; for instance,

$$P[-2 < X < \tfrac{1}{2}] = P[X = 0] = f(0) = 2/3$$

and

$$P[1/4 < X \le 1] = P[X = 1] = f(1) = 1/3$$

Now suppose the same coin is tossed m times. Then X can take on any value in the set

$$\{0, 1, 2, \ldots, m\}$$

If we assume that each toss of the coin, or *trial*, has equal probability, then, based on the probabilities 1/3 and 2/3 for a single toss, it can be shown that a reasonable density for the new *compound experiment* is given by

$$f(k) = P[X = k] = \frac{m!}{k!(m - k)!}\,(1/3)^k(2/3)^{m-k}$$

For instance, if $m = 3$ (i.e., the coin is tossed three times), then X, the number of heads obtained, can take on the value 0, 1, 2, or 3, and the discrete density is given by

$$f(0) = P[X = 0] = \frac{3!}{0!3!}\,(1/3)^0(2/3)^3 = 1 \times 1 \times 8/27 = 8/27$$

$$f(1) = P[X = 1] = \frac{3!}{1!2!}\,(1/3)^1(2/3)^2 = 3 \times 1/3 \times 4/9 = 12/27$$

$$f(2) = P[X = 2] = \frac{3!}{2!1!}\,(1/3)^2(2/3)^1 = 3 \times 1/9 \times 2/3 = 6/27$$

$$f(3) = P[X = 3] = \frac{3!}{3!1!}\,(1/3)^3(2/3)^0 = 1 \times 1/27 \times 1 = 1/27$$

(See Figure 6.13 for a graph of f.) Note that the sum of all the probabilities is 1, which is analogous to the total integral of a continuous density being 1.

The situation described in the second part of Exercise 6.19 occurs commonly in probability modeling: a given trial is repeated some number, say m, times, on each trial there are two possible outcomes, and the individual outcome probabilities remain constant throughout the m trials. Such trials are termed *Bernoulli* trials. If we call the two possible outcomes on a given trial *success* and *failure*, S and F, if we let the probability of a success be p and the probability of a failure be $q = 1 - p$, and if the random variable X denotes the number of successes, then a

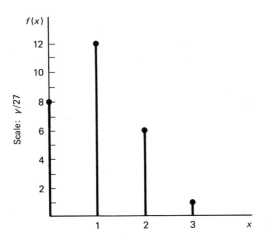

Figure 6.13. Discrete density function

density that appropriately models the experiment is given by

$$f(k) = P[X = k] = \frac{m!}{k!(m - k)!} \, p^k q^{m-k}$$

for $k = 0, 1, 2, \ldots, m$. $f(k)$ is known as the *Bernoulli* or *binomial* density. In Example 6.19, we had $m = 3$, $p = 1/3$, and $q = 2/3$. Note that we must have $p + q = 1$.

Consider a discrete random variable X with density $f(x_i)$, for $i = 1, 2, \ldots, n$. Looking at the density in Figure 6.13, we see that, as mentioned above, f looks like a point mass function that we might obtain in physics. Indeed, whereas in the continuous case the probability mass is distributed in some manner along the extent of the x axis, in the discrete case the mass is quantized at discrete points situated on the axis. Taking the physical analogy as our cue, we see that the notion of a moment (Section 6.2) has a corresponding interpretation in the discrete case. Instead of defining the center of mass as though the mass were distributed continuously along the x axis, we define the center of mass of the point masses in the usual summation manner:

$$E[X] = \sum_{i=1}^{n} x_i f(x_i)$$

As in the continuous case, $E[X]$ is called the *expected value* or *mean* of the random variable. Also, as in that case, general moments can be analogousy defined; however, we will not pursue the matter here.

Example 6.20

Let X be the Bernoulli random variable of Example 6.19, with $m = 3$ and $p = 1/3$. Then

$$E[X] = 0 \times 8/27 + 1 \times 12/27 + 2 \times 6/27 + 3 \times 1/27 = 1$$

Looking at Figure 6.13, we can see that $E[X]$ gives the physical center of the point mass distribution.

In general, it can be shown that for a Bernoulli density with m trials and p being the probability of a successful trial,

$$E[X] = mp.$$

Now suppose we once again consider a situation where X can take on two values, say 0 and 1, and suppose $f(1) = p$ and $f(0) = q$. The fact that the phenomenon measured by X is random guarantees that an observer faces *uncertainty* in his observation of X. As has been noted previously, this uncertainty is inherent in the measurement process. Nonetheless, depending on the phenomenon to be observed, the degree of uncertainty may vary. For instance, if $p = 0.99$ and $q = 0.01$, then the observer "feels" less uncertain than if the probabilities were given by $p = 0.6$ and $q = 0.4$. Proceeding heuristically, it seems as though his or her uncertainty would be maximized if the probabilities were equal ($p = q = 1/2$) and minimized if one of the probabilities were zero ($p = 0$ and $q = 1$, or $p = 1$ and $q = 0$). Of course, in the latter case, there appears to be *certainty* in that the observation is based on conditions that are apparently deterministic.

Suppose, more generally, a random variable X can taken on the n values x_1, $x_2, \ldots, x_n$, with corresponding density values (probabilities) $f(x_i) = p_i$, for $i = 1$, $2, \ldots, n$. Intuitively, at least, it appears that the uncertainty of observation is increased when the probabilities p_i are more alike than when one or two of them carry most of the probability mass.

A formalization of the notion of uncertainty evoked by a random variable is the measure of entropy: for a discrete random variable with n possible outcomes, we define the *entropy* of X to be the quantity

$$H[X] = -\sum_{i=1}^{n} p_i \log_2 p_i$$

$$= \sum_{i=1}^{n} p_i \log_2 \frac{1}{p_i}$$

where the convention is adopted that $p_i \log_2 p_i = 0$ whenever $p_i = 0$. Although we will not go through the mathematical details, $H[X]$, which is also called the *uncertainty* of X, satisfies the following properties:

1. $H[X] \geq 0$, and $H[X] = 0$ if and only if one of the probabilities equals 1 and the others are 0.
2. Maximum entropy is obtained when all the p_i are the same, that is, when the possible outcomes of the random variable are *equally likely*.
3. If the random variables X and Y possess n and m equally likely outcomes, respectively, with $n < m$, then

$$H[X] < H[Y]$$

That is, maximum entropy increases as the number of possible outcomes increases.

Surely, the preceding three properties agree with our intuitive notion of uncertainty.

Example 6.21

Suppose the random variable X possesses the discrete density

$$f(0) = \tfrac{1}{8}$$

$$f(1) = \tfrac{1}{4}$$

$$f(2) = \tfrac{1}{8}$$

$$f(3) = \tfrac{1}{2}$$

Then

$$H[X] = 1/8 \log_2 8 + 1/4 \log_2 4 + 1/8 \log_2 8 + 1/2 \log_2 2 = 7/4$$

If we consider a random variable Y with the same possible outcomes, but having equally likely outcomes, the entropy would be maximized (for the case of four outcomes) and we would have $H[Y] = 2$.

Our immediate interest is the coding of information. Specifically, if a random variable X is observed, and each possible outcome is to be given a binary code of 0's and 1's, then how can the expected number of transmitted bits be minimized? Before proceeding with the analysis of this question, we make one proviso: no code corresponding to a specific outcome of the random variable may be obtained from the code of a distinct outcome by simply adding more 0's and 1's. For instance, if 001 is the code of an outcome, then 00110 cannot be the code of a different outcome. Such a code is called a *prefix* code. The adoption of the prefix convention is motivated by our desire to avoid errors in transmission that might occur due to concatenation.

Suppose we consider the random variable X of Example 6.21, and suppose we encode the four possible outcomes into binary form. Then, keeping in mind the restriction regarding the concatenation of bits, we might have the code

$$0 \rightarrow 1$$

$$1 \rightarrow 01$$

$$2 \rightarrow 001$$

$$3 \rightarrow 000$$

Now let B denote the random variable that counts the number of bits in the encoding. B has three possible outcomes, 1, 2, and 3. Moreover,

$$P[B = 1] = P[X = 0] = f(0) = 1/8$$

$$P[B = 2] = P[X = 1] = f(1) = 1/4$$

$$P[B = 3] = P[X = 2] + P[X = 3] = f(2) + f(3) = 1/8 + 1/2 = 5/8$$

Therefore, the expected value of B is given by

$$E[B] = 1 \times 1/8 + 2 \times 1/4 + 3 \times 5/8 = 5/2$$

Now, suppose we take into account the various probabilities of X in the coding procedure and assign longer bit codes to the less likely occurrences. Then we might rearrange the preceding encoding in the following manner:

$$
\begin{align}
0 &\to 001 \\
1 &\to 01 \\
2 &\to 000 \\
3 &\to 1
\end{align}
\tag{4}
$$

In this case, the expected number of bits is $E[B] = 7/4$, and the new code results in more efficient transmission.

The question naturally arises as to the manner in which we can obtain an encoding with minimal expected value $E[B]$. The following theorem helps to answer this question.

Theorem 6.4.   Suppose X is a random variable with possible outcomes x_1, $x_2, \ldots, x_n$ and corresponding probabilities $p_1, p_2, \ldots, p_n$, and suppose we encode the possible outcomes of X in such a manner that x_i has k_i bits comprising its code. If B is the random variable that counts the number of transmitted bits, then the expected value of B is at least equal to the entropy of X; that is,

$$E[B] \geq H[X]$$

or, written out,

$$\sum_{i=1}^{n} k_i p_i \geq - \sum_{i=1}^{n} p_i \log_2 p_i$$

Example 6.22

Once again consider the random variable of Example 6.21. We saw there that its entropy is $H[X] = 7/4$. Consequently, the code given in (4) is optimal, because, according to Theorem 6.4, $H[X]$ represents a lower bound for all possible expected numbers of bit transmissions and, in (4), $E[B] = 7/4$.

While it is usually impossible to find a code that actually attains the minimum possible expected value $H[X]$, it is always theoretically possible to find a code such that $E[B]$ is within 1 of $H[X]$.

6.6 FAULT-TOLERANT SYSTEMS

To make an autonomous system less prone to overall system failure, very often systems are designed so that they will continue to function even when several components fail. This *fault tolerance* is achieved by the judicious utilization of replicated components: when a particular component fails, a duplicate assumes its function. The issue to be addressed in this section is the knowledgeable employment of redundancy for the purpose of fault tolerance. It is presupposed that mechanisms are in place that detect and isolate failed components.

Practically speaking, due to the current decrease in price and the concomitant miniaturization of VLSI components, replication of circuitry is certainly feasible, both from engineering and cost-effectiveness standpoints. As a result, fault-tolerant computers are becoming ever more popular. The ultimate benefit of fault-tolerant systems includes an increase in the life expectancy of the system, as well as a decrease in expected down time. Indeed, the *mean time before failure (MTBF)* of a fault-tolerant system is greater than the MTBF for the "same system" implemented without redundancy.

Let X be a nonnegative random variable representing the lifetime of a system and $f(x)$ be its density, which, in the present situation, is also called the *failure density*, or *failure frequency*. When obtained from data, $f(x)$ is a histogram representing the probabilities of the system lasting specified durations of time. The *reliability function R* is defined by

$$R(t) = \int_t^{+\infty} f(x)\, dx, \qquad t \geq 0$$

and, according to the fundamental theorem of calculus, has the property that

$$\frac{dR(t)}{dt} = -f(t)$$

whenever the derivative exists. From the perspective of probability,

$$R(t) = P[X > t]$$

the probability that the system functions for a time greater than t. Moreover, $R(0) = 1$, $R(+\infty) = 0$, and $R(t)$ is monotonically decreasing.

Systems are sometimes compared on the basis of their reliability functions, the one with the greater reliability function being judged the better. This method of comparison is sometimes difficult since at certain times one reliability function may be greater while at other times the situation might be reversed (see Figure 6.14). More often than not, the MTBF, $\bar{t}$, is used as a measure of reliability, where

$$\bar{t} = \int_0^{+\infty} R(t)\, dt$$

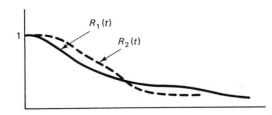

Figure 6.14. Nonordering of reliability functions

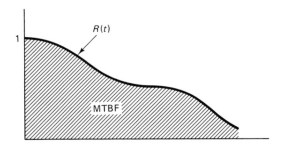

Figure 6.15.   MTBF as area under reliability function

(see Figure 6.15).   A straightforward integration by parts shows that

$$\bar{t} = \int_0^{+\infty} t f(t)\, dt$$

and so the MTBF is a true average; specifically, it is the expected value of system life (i.e., the average life of the system).   The reliabilities of two systems are often compared on the basis of which possesses the greater MTBF, the one with the greater MTBF being judged superior.

Example 6.23

Consider two systems possessing exponential reliability, the first system having reliability

$$R(t) = e^{-\lambda_1 t}, \qquad \lambda_1 > 0$$

and the second

$$R(t) = e^{-\lambda_2 t}, \qquad \lambda_2 > 0$$

The MTBF of the first system is

$$\bar{t}_1 = \int_0^{+\infty} e^{-\lambda_1 t}\, dt = \frac{1}{\lambda_1}$$

Similarly,

$$\bar{t}_2 = \frac{1}{\lambda_2}$$

If $\lambda_1 > \lambda_2$, then $\bar{t}_2 > \bar{t}_1$, and conversely.   The quantities λ_1 and λ_2 are called *failure rates*.   Thus, the larger the failure rate, the smaller the average life, and conversely.

In many systems, components are utilized in a series configuration (see Figure 6.16), the result being that the failure of a single component causes the entire system to fail.   If the components have independent failures, then the reliability of the entire series configuration is the product of the individual reliabilities $R_i(t)$:

$$R(t) = \prod_{i=1}^{n} R_i(t)$$

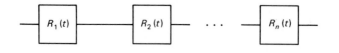

$$R(t) = \prod_{i=1}^{n} R_i(t)$$

Figure 6.16. Series system

Since $0 \le R_i(t) \le 1$ for each i, it follows that

$$R(t) \le R_i(t)$$

and the reliability of the entire system is less than or equal to the reliability of each single component.   The only way to improve the reliability of a system is to increase the reliability of the individual components or to add extra components in an astute manner, or to do both.

Replicated components are often added using parallel structures, as in Figure 6.17.   In this redundant configuration, even though only a single component is needed to perform the desired task, n components are nevertheless employed, each performing the identical task.   A total of $n - 1$ faults, or failures, can be tolerated for components organized in this manner.   Should the component failures be mutually independent, then, employing standard probabilistic methods, the reliability of the total parallel configuration, $R(t)$, can be found in terms of the reliabilities of the individual components:

$$R(t) = 1 - \prod_{i=1}^{n} (1 - R_i(t))$$

Rewriting this expression as

$$(1 - R_j(t)) \prod_{i \ne j} (1 - R_i(t)) = 1 - R(t)$$

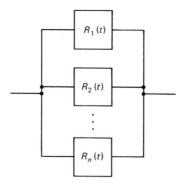

$$R(t) = 1 - \prod_{i=1}^{n} (1 - R_i(t))$$

Figure 6.17. Parallel system

gives, for any particular j,

$$1 - R_j(t) \geq 1 - R(t)$$

since $0 \leq 1 - R_i(t) \leq 1$. Therefore,

$$R(t) \geq R_j(t)$$

for any j. Thus, the reliability of a parallel system is greater than or equal to the reliability of any of its components.

Example 6.24

Based on a larger MTBF, which computer system, A or B, illustrated in Figure 6.18 is more reliable? Component failures are assumed to be independent, and the reliabilities of all components in both systems are assumed to be equal and to continuously fall off linearly until time 3, and to zero out thereafter; that is,

$$R_{\text{mem}}(t) = R_{\text{CPU}}(t) = \left(1 - \frac{t}{3}\right)I_{[0,3)}(t)$$

where $I_{[0,3)}$ is the indicator function for the interval $[0, 3)$. Thus, both reliability functions equal $1 - t/3$, for $0 \leq t < 3$, and 0, for $t \geq 3$. Based on the diagrams in Figure 6.18, system B is comprised of two computers in parallel, where redundancy exists at a high level, and system A incorporates redundancy at a low level—a better feature. Of course, system A is more complicated in that each CPU has access to either memory. The reliability of the two memories in parallel is

$$R_1(t) = 1 - \left(1 - \left(1 - \frac{t}{3}\right)I_{[0,3)}(t)\right)^2$$

$$= \left(1 - \frac{t^2}{9}\right)I_{[0,3)}(t)$$

and the same reliability function holds for the two CPUs in parallel. Since these subsystems are in series, these reliabilities are multiplied together to give the reliability of the overall system A. Thus,

$$R_A(t) = \left(1 - \frac{t^2}{9}\right)^2 I_{[0,3)}(t)$$

The corresponding MTBF is

$$\bar{t}_A = \int_0^3 \left[1 - \frac{2t^2}{9} + \frac{t^4}{81}\right] dt = \frac{8}{5}$$

As for system B, each computer consists of a memory and a CPU in series. Hence, each possesses reliability

$$R_2(t) = \left(1 - \frac{t}{3}\right)^2 I_{[0,3)}(t)$$

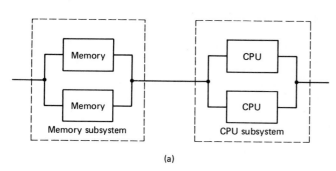

(a)

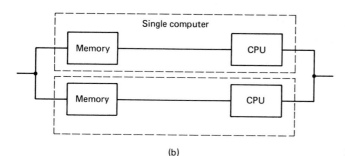

(b)   **Figure 6.18.**   Reliability networks

Since the whole system consists of two computers in parallel, the reliability of system B is

$$R_B(t) = 1 - (1 - R_2(t))^2$$
$$= 2R_2(t) - R_2^2(t)$$

and so the MTBF for system B is

$$\bar{t}_B = \int_0^3 \left[1 - \frac{4t^2}{9} + \frac{4t^3}{27} - \frac{t^4}{81} \right] dt = \frac{7}{5}$$

Thus, system A is more reliable based on a larger MTBF. Note that the MTBF of a single computer (comprised of a CPU and memory in series) is 1.

Several other configurations are used in fault-tolerant systems. In particular, the (n, m) structure consists of n identical independent components, of which m or more are required for the system to be up. If workload warrants at least five computers to be working at all times and as a safety precaution seven computers are employed, then this would be a $(7, 5)$ system. Two failures can be tolerated. The reliability $R(t)$ of an (n, m) system can be found in terms of the reliability $p(t)$ of any individual component: since we require m successful components, we sum up the individual probabilities of $m, m + 1, \ldots,$ and n successful components, and each of these is given by the appropriate binomial density.   Thus,

$$R(t) = \sum_{k=m}^{n} \frac{n!}{k!(n-k)!} p(t)^k (1 - p(t))^{n-k}$$

Observe that an $(n, 1)$ system is a parallel configuration of n identical components, and an (n, n) system is a series combination of n identical components.

Example 6.25

Four modules are available for an application where three modules are needed, each module having reliability

$$p(t) = e^{-\lambda t}$$

Assuming a $(4, 3)$ configuration, the reliability of the system is

$$R(t) = \sum_{k=3}^{4} \frac{4!}{k!(4-k)!} p^k (1 - p)^{4-k}$$

$$= e^{-4\lambda t} + 4e^{-3\lambda t}(1 - e^{-\lambda t})$$

$$= 4e^{-3\lambda t} - 3e^{-4\lambda t}$$

The MTBF of the system is $\bar{t} = \dfrac{7}{12\lambda}$.

6.7 DECISION THEORY

Suppose we know that a random variable X possesses a density from a certain family (i.e., its law is uniform, exponential, Gaussian, or some other well-studied family).   However, suppose we do not know precisely which member of the family it is.   For instance, if X is exponential, we know that its density is of the form be^{-bx}, for $x \geq 0$, but we do not know the specific value of the parameter b.   What is needed is an *estimate* of b.   As a second instance, suppose we know that X is Gaussian.   Then there are two parameters, μ and σ, to estimate.   Of course, it might be that we know μ and wish to estimate σ, or, conversely, that we know σ and wish to estimate μ.

For the sake of simplicity, we will assume that the random variable X possesses a density with a single unknown parameter θ, and we will write that density as $f(x; \theta)$ to indicate that it is θ we desire to estimate.   We consider the *parametric estimation problem:* Given a collection of observations of the random variable, say $x_1, x_2, \ldots, x_n$, what is the "best" estimate of θ?   Note the similarity to the estimation problem considered in Section 6.4.   Once again we are trying to find a "best" estimate, and, consequently, we will have to specify a "best" criterion.   Whereas in Section 6.4 we were trying to find a function $g(X)$ to estimate another random variable Y, here we are trying to find a function of the observations $x_1, x_2, \ldots, x_n$ that best estimates the unknown parameter θ.   This function, known as a *decision function*, or *estimation rule*, takes the form $d(x_1, x_2, \ldots, x_n)$, and its value is taken as the estimate of θ.

To check the goodness of the estimate, we define a *loss function* $L(\theta, d)$ to measure the error of the estimate: the greater the loss, the worse the estimate. In general, the actual goodness criterion arrived at will depend on the choice of loss function. Two typical loss functions are the *absolute loss*

$$L(\theta, d) = |\theta - d(x_1, x_2, \ldots, x_n)|$$

and the *quadratic loss*

$$L(\theta, d) = (\theta - d(x_1, x_2, \ldots, x_n))^2$$

Example 6.26

Suppose X possesses an exponential density with unknown parameter b:

$$f(x; b) = be^{-bx}$$

for $x \geq 0$, and $f(x; b) = 0$, elsewhere. Using our intuition and our past experience in computing averages, we might observe the random variable four times (take four measurements), compute the average of the four observations, and take that average as an estimate of the mean of X. Since the mean is $1/b$, we could then estimate b by the reciprocal of the observed average. For instance, if we were to obtain the four observations 3, 2, 4, and 3, the average of the four is $\bar{x} = 3$. Setting $\bar{x} = 1/b$, the true mean of the random variable, we obtain the estimate $b = 1/3$. Using a quadratic loss function, the loss is then given by

$$L(b, d(x_1, x_2, x_3, x_4)) = L(b, 4/(x_1 + x_2 + x_3 + x_4))$$

$$= L(b, 1/3) = (b - 1/3)^2$$

If the true value of b is 1/2, then the quadratic loss is 1/36.

To this point, we have considered the loss based on a fixed collection of observed values. However, to measure the worth of an estimation rule, we must consider its accuracy over all possible outcomes of the n observations. After all, we do not know beforehand the values of these observations. As a consequence, the estimation rule takes the form

$$d = d(X_1, X_2, \ldots, X_n)$$

and is a function of the random variables X_j, $j = 1, 2, \ldots, n$, where each X_j is identically distributed with the underlying random variable X; that is, each X_j possesses the same density, $f(x; \theta)$, as X. Since the loss function depends on θ and d, it, too, must be a random variable. Therefore, to judge the efficacy of the decision function d, we define the *risk function* R by taking the expected value of the loss function (relative to the random variables $X_1, X_2, \ldots, X_n$):

$$R(\theta, d) = E[L(\theta, d)]$$

$$= E[L(\theta, d(X_1, X_2, \ldots, X_n))]$$

For quadratic loss, we obtain the risk function

$$R(\theta, d) = E[(\theta - d)^2]$$

Supposing, for instance, that there are two observations to be taken, then, in the quadratic case,

$$R(\theta, d) = \int_{-\infty}^{+\infty} \int_{-\infty}^{+\infty} (\theta - d(x_1, x_2))^2 \, f(x_1, x_2; \theta) dx_1 \, dx_2$$

where $f(x_1, x_2; \theta)$ is the joint density for the observation random variables X_1 and X_2. Generalization to n observations is immediate; however, for the sake of simplicity, we will restrict our attention to two observations. Note that we must continue to keep the parameter θ denoted in the density, since it remains unknown. As a result, the risk function is a function of θ.

Given two decision functions, d_1 and d_2, we would like to declare which one is "better" on the basis of which one provides minimum risk. The problem, of course, is that the corresponding risk functions depend on the actual value of θ. If

$$R(\theta, d_1) \leq R(\theta, d_2)$$

for all possible θ, then the choice between the decision functions is clear; d_1 is better than d_2 (see Figure 6.19). In practice, such a clear-cut choice is very rare.

A very common criterion of goodness results from choosing between two decision functions based on which possesses the minimum maximum risk: d_1 is *better* than d_2 if the maximum value, over all θ, of the risk function $R(\theta, d_1)$ is less than the maximum value, over all θ, of the risk function $R(\theta, d_2)$; that is,

$$\max_\theta R(\theta, d_1) < \max_\theta R(\theta, d_2)$$

(see Figure 6.20). To arrive at a notion of the "best" estimation rule, we take that decision function d such that the maximum of its risk function is less than or equal to the maxima of all risk functions for the estimation rules in some given class C. In other words, we define "best" in terms of the minimum maximum of the risk functions in some predetermined class C of decision functions. As a result,

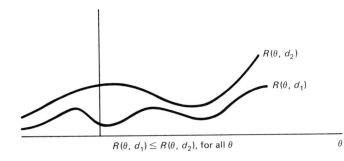

$R(\theta, d_2)$

$R(\theta, d_1)$

$R(\theta, d_1) \leq R(\theta, d_2)$, for all θ

θ

Figure 6.19. Full pointwise ordering between risk functions

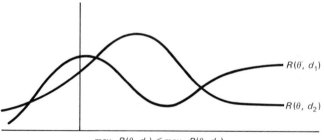

$\max_\theta R(\theta, d_1) < \max_\theta R(\theta, d_2)$

Figure 6.20. Minimax ordering of risk functions

bestness is relative to some class of possible choices, not necessarily all possible choices. Rigorously, using the criterion just stated, $\overline{d}$ is called the *minimax decision function*, or the *minimax estimation rule*, in the class C of decision functions if

$$\max_\theta R(\theta, \overline{d}) = \min_{d \in C} \max_\theta R(\theta, d)$$

At first sight, the minimax criterion might appear somewhat abstruse; however, notice that it allows us to determine bestness on the basis of a numerical value. We could choose other criteria; however, we will content ourselves with the minimax criterion.

Example 6.27

Suppose X possesses a Gaussian density with unknown mean μ and known variance 1. Then its density is given by

$$f(x; \mu) = \frac{1}{\sqrt{2\pi}} e^{-\frac{1}{2}(x - \mu)^2}$$

We will utilize only a single observation of the random variable in order to make an estimation of μ. Moreover, we will choose the estimation rule from the class of decision functions $C = \{cX\}$. In other words, if we wish to use an estimate for μ of the form cx, where x is the observed value and c is a constant, which choice of c provides the best estimation rule? Once again, we will employ a quadratic loss function. To begin, we find the risk function, which in this instance is given by

$$R(\mu, d) = \int_{-\infty}^{+\infty} (\mu - cx)^2 \frac{1}{\sqrt{2\pi}} e^{-\frac{1}{2}(x - \mu)^2} \, dx$$

$$= \int_{-\infty}^{+\infty} (\mu^2 - 2c\mu x + c^2 x^2) \frac{1}{\sqrt{2\pi}} e^{-\frac{1}{2}(x - \mu)^2} \, dx$$

$$= \mu^2 - 2c\mu^2 + c^2(1 + \mu^2)$$

$$= c^2 + \mu^2(c - 1)^2$$

The minimax choice for c will be the one for which the maximum of this function of μ is minimum. Note that, unless $c = 1$, the risk function has no maximum. Thus, we choose $c = 1$, and the best (minimax) decision function in the class C is given by $d(x) = x$ or, in terms of the random variable, $d(X) = X$.

Although we could go further and unify the mean-square error methodology of Section 6.4 and the parametric theory of the present section by introducing the notion of Bayesian estimation, we will leave that to a text in statistical theory. Our main purpose here has been to introduce the concepts of decision, loss, and risk. While we have focussed our attention on parametric estimation, it should be recognized that the loss-function approach to statistical decision making can also be employed in problems of detection, a subject we will not pursue.

6.8 DISCRETE WIENER FILTER

At the conclusion of Section 6.4, we mentioned finding the best linear MS estimator of the random variable Y given the n observations $X_1, X_2, \ldots, X_n$:

$$X = a_1 X_1 + a_2 X_2 + \cdots + a_n X_n + b$$

where $a_1, a_2, \ldots, a_n$ and b are constants. In artificial-intelligence applications, we are often concerned with the special case $b = 0$. We desire to estimate Y based on sensor readings, the X_i, and the problem is to find the *weights*, or *gains*, that result in the best linear MS estimate. The overall process plays a key role in learning systems, where the weights *adapt* to the desired response Y, which is often called the *training signal*.

Let e denote the *error* $Y - X$:

$$e = Y - X$$

If

$$X = \begin{pmatrix} X_1 \\ X_2 \\ \cdot \\ \cdot \\ \cdot \\ X_n \end{pmatrix}$$

and

$$W = \begin{pmatrix} a_1 \\ a_2 \\ \cdot \\ \cdot \\ \cdot \\ a_n \end{pmatrix}$$

then

$$e = Y - X'W = Y - W'X$$

where the prime denotes the matrix transpose.

The best MS estimate is found by minimizing

$$E[e^2] = E[Y^2] + W'E[XX']W - 2E[YX']W$$

with respect to W. Denote the second-order moment matrix by R; that is,

$$R = E[XX'] = R'$$

R is called the *autocorrelation matrix* for X. Next, let

$$P = E[YX]$$

P is called the *cross-correlation vector*. Then

$$E[e^2] = E[Y^2] + W'RW - 2P'W$$

This average error is easy to minimize with respect to W if the matrix R is positive definite. In this case, R^{-1} exists and, since $P'W = W'P$,

$$\begin{aligned} E[e^2] &= E[Y^2] + W'RW - 2P'W + P'R^{-1}P - P'R^{-1}P \\ &= E[Y^2] + (P'R^{-1} - W')R(R^{-1}P - W) - P'R^{-1}P \end{aligned} \tag{5}$$

The middle summand is a nonnegative scalar; hence, if it is set equal to 0, the error $E[e^2]$ is minimized. Thus, the best MS estimate is given by the weight vector

$$W = R^{-1}P$$

Example 6.28

Suppose X_1, X_2, and Y are both independent and uniformly distributed on $[0, 1]$. Due to independence, $E[X_1X_2] = E[X_1]E[X_2]$ and $E[YX_i] = E[Y]E[X_i]$ for $i = 1$ and 2. Using the results of Examples 6.6 and 6.8 in conjunction with equation (2), we obtain

$$R = \begin{pmatrix} E[X_1^2] & E[X_1X_2] \\ E[X_1X_2] & E[X_2^2] \end{pmatrix} = \begin{pmatrix} 1/3 & 1/4 \\ 1/4 & 1/3 \end{pmatrix}$$

and

$$P = \begin{pmatrix} 1/4 \\ 1/4 \end{pmatrix}$$

Therefore,

$$W = \begin{pmatrix} 48/7 & -36/7 \\ -36/7 & 48/7 \end{pmatrix} \begin{pmatrix} 1/4 \\ 1/4 \end{pmatrix} = \begin{pmatrix} 3/7 \\ 3/7 \end{pmatrix}$$

and the best linear MS estimate (with $b = 0$) of Y is given by

$$X = 3/7X_1 + 3/7X_2$$

Now suppose that at each instant of time i, $i = 1, 2, 3, \ldots,$ a vector of random variables

$$X_i = \begin{pmatrix} X_{i1} \\ X_{i2} \\ \cdot \\ \cdot \\ \cdot \\ X_{in} \end{pmatrix}$$

is given along with a training random variable Y_i, and that a constant weight vector

$$W_i = \begin{pmatrix} w_{i1} \\ w_{i2} \\ \cdot \\ \cdot \\ \cdot \\ w_{in} \end{pmatrix}$$

is to be found such that

$$E[e_i^2] = E[(Y_i - X_i'W_i)^2]$$

is minimized.   From the previous discussion, if

$$R_i = E[X_iX_i']$$

is positive definite, and if

$$P_i = E[Y_iX_i]$$

then

$$W_i = R_i^{-1}P_i$$

provides the weights for the the best mean-square estimate at time i.   Moreover, if it is assumed that the statistics do not change over time, that is,

$$R_i = R_j$$

and

$$P_i = P_j$$

for all i and j, then

$$W_i = R^{-1}P$$

for all i, where R and P are the common values of R_i and P_i, respectively.   (For those with a background in stochastic processes, a sufficient condition for the constancy of the statistics over time is wide sense stationarity.)   The solution so obtained is called the *discrete Wiener filter*.   By equation (5),

$$E[e_i^2] = E[Y_i^2] - P'R^{-1}P$$

for any i.   Given the constancy of the statistics, the second-order moments do not depend on the time i, and we can write

$$E[e_i^2] = E[e^2]$$

and

$$E[Y_i^2] = E[Y^2]$$

Several important applications, including noise cancellation and some learning models, involve the observation of random vectors having the same second-order statistics.   More often than not, however, both R and P are unknown.   In such circumstances, the Wiener filter, as given above, cannot be employed, and more sophisticated methods must be used.

EXERCISES FOR CHAPTER 6

6.1. Find the third and fourth moments of the exponential density.

6.2. Suppose X possesses an exponential density with $b = 3$.   Find
(a) $P(1 < X < 4)$
(b) $P(1 < X < \infty)$
(c) $P(-2 < X < 1)$

6.3. Let

$$f(x) = cxe^{-4x}$$

for $x \geq 0$ and $f(x) = 0$ for $x < 0$.   Find c so that $f(x)$ is a density (so that its integral from 0 to ∞ is 1).   Then, assuming that X possesses the density $f(x)$, find
(a) $E[X]$
(b) $E[X^2]$
(c) $\text{Var}[X]$
(d) $P(0 < X < 1)$

6.4. Let $f(x)$ possess the graph given in Figure 6.21.   Find a through d of Exercise 6.3.

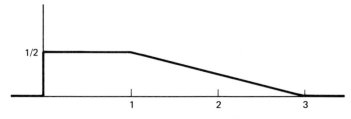

Figure 6.21.   Density for Exercise 6.4

6.4. Let

$$f(x, y) = ce^{-(3x + 5y)}$$

for (x, y) in the first quadrant and let $f(x, y) = 0$ otherwise. Find c so that $f(x, y)$ is a density, and, supposing that X and Y possess $f(x, y)$ as their joint density, find

(a) $P(0 < X < 2, 1 < Y < \infty)$

(b) $P(X < Y)$

(c) $f_X(x)$ and $f_Y(y)$

6.5. Suppose X and Y are uniformly jointly distributed over the shaded region in Figure 6.22.

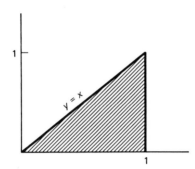

Figure 6.22.

Find

(a) $f_X(x)$ and $f_Y(y)$

(b) $f(y|x)$

(c) $E[Y_x]$

(d) $E[XY]$

(e) $\text{Var}[X]$ and $\text{Var}[Y]$

(f) $\text{Cov}[X, Y]$

(g) $\text{Cor}[X, Y]$

Show that $E[E[Y_x]] = E[Y]$.

6.6. Repeat Exercise 6.6 except employ the shaded region in Figure 6.23.

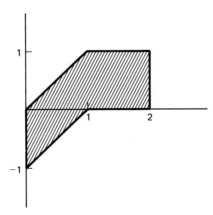

Figure 6.23.

6.7. In general, the conditional density $f(y|x)$ is defined by

$$f(y|x) = \frac{f(x, y)}{f_X(x)}$$

Employing this definition, repeat Exercise 6.5 for the density found in Exercise 6.4.

6.8. Find the best linear MS estimate of Y in terms of X for the joint random variables of Exercise 6.5.

6.9. Repeat Exercise 6.8 for the random variables given in Exercise 6.6.

6.10. Let X denote the number of heads obtained on tossing a coin 5 times, where the probability of a head on any given toss is $p = 3/4$. Graph the discrete density $f(x)$ for X and find
(a) $P(1 < X \le 4)$
(b) $P(X \ne 5)$
(c) $E[X]$

6.11. For a discrete random variable with possible outcomes $x_1, x_2, \ldots, x_n$, we define the kth moment by

$$m_k = E[X^k] = \sum_{j=1}^{n} x_j^k f(x_j)$$

and the variance is given by equation (2). Find the variance of the random variable given in Exercise 6.10.

6.12. Find the entropy of the random variable given in 6.10.

6.13. Suppose X, Y, and Z are discrete random variables with 3, 4, and 5 equally likely outcomes, respectively. Find the entropy of each of the random variables.

6.14. Consider the encoding

$$0 \to 00000$$
$$1 \to 1$$
$$2 \to 01$$
$$3 \to 001$$
$$4 \to 00001$$
$$5 \to 0001$$

If the relative frequencies of the symbols 0, 1, 2, 3, 4, and 5 are governed by the random variable in Exercise 6.10 and B is the random variable that counts the number bits transmitted for a single symbol, find $E[B]$. Find the encoding that minimizes $E[B]$.

6.15. Consider the discrete random variable X with density given by

$$f(1) = f(2) = f(6) = 1/10$$
$$f(3) = f(4) = 2/5$$

and

$$f(5) = 3/10$$

Find a proper binary encoding of the symbols 1 through 6 that minimizes $E[B]$, where B is the number of transmitted bits per symbol.

6.16. Suppose that each component of the system depicted in Figure 6.24 possesses reliability function $(1 - t)I_{[0, 1]}(t)$.   Find the MTBF of the system.

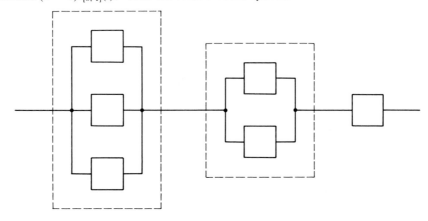

Figure 6.24.

6.17. Repeat Exercise 6.16, except let each component possess reliability

$$p(t) = (1 - t^2)I_{[0, 1]}(t)$$

6.18. Repeat Exercise 6.16 for the system of Figure 6.25.

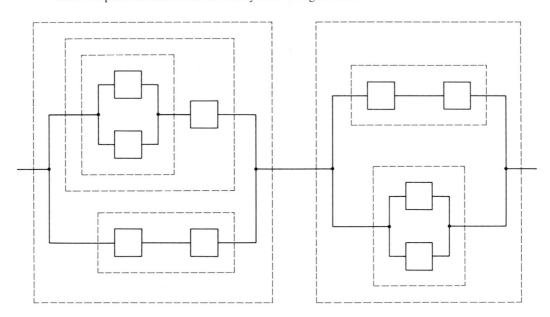

Figure 6.25.

6.19. Assuming that three CPUs are required out of five available, each possessing reliability

$$p(t) = e^{-\lambda t}$$

find the reliability function and the MTBF of the system.

6.20. Suppose a random variable is uniformly distributed over an interval of length 1; however, we do not know the precise interval. In such a situation, its density would be given by

$$f(x; b) = I_{[b, \, b \, + \, 1]}(x)$$

Since the mean of the random variable is $b + 1/2$, a good estimation rule for b, given two observations X_1 and X_2, would be

$$d(X_1, X_2) = \frac{X_1 + X_2 - 1}{2}$$

(Why?)   Find the risk function for quadratic loss.

6.21. Repeat Example 6.28, except employ random variables X_1, X_2, X_3, and Y that are both independent and uniformly distributed on $[0, 1]$.

6.22. The Poisson density is a discrete density defined by

$$f(k) = e^{-\lambda}\lambda^k/k!$$

for $k = 0, 1, 2, \ldots$ and parameter $\lambda > 0$. If the random variable X possesses a Poisson density, then it can only attain nonnegative integral values. Show the Poisson density is a legitimate density by showing that

$$\sum_{k=0}^{\infty} f(k) = 1$$

Show $E[X] = \text{Var}[X] = \lambda$ (see Exercise 6.11).

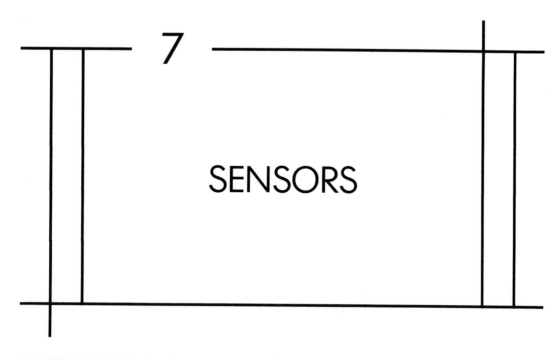

7

SENSORS

7.1 SENSORS FOR HUMANS AND ROBOTS

Human beings possess several senses, each a consequence of the brain's ability to receive and react to stimuli. Sensors, in the form of bodily organs and associated nerves, enable humans to receive signals corresponding to the several senses: sight, touch, taste, smell, and sound. Other senses may exist, but these five are the ones commonly agreed upon. To lay the groundwork for the subsequent discussion of artificial sensors, a brief and intuitive description of the bodily sensors utilized for observation of the environment will be given.

The sense of sight is enabled by vision sensors existing within the eye that are sensitive to light from a luminous source. Bodies that are not self-luminous can be observed by means of reflected light. Light passes through the cornea, a transparent, refracting surface within the eye, and then through the crystalline lens. The latter can change shape to provide variable focal length, thus allowing bodies to be seen at varying distances. An image is produced on the retina, which is located in the back part of the eye. Attached to the retina are a great many (125 million) photo receptors that send signals to the sight center of the brain. Under normal conditions, the eye is most sensitive to yellow-green light, less sensitive to blue and red light, even less sensitive to violet light, and essentially insensitive to infrared and ultraviolet light.

The sense of touch mainly provides information regarding texture, pressure, and temperature and is facilitated by nerve endings in the skin, which send signals to the touch center of the brain.   Sensitivity to touch varies throughout the body and is a function of the density of nerve endings present at certain locations.

Taste is produced by the chemical stimulation of taste buds, as well as by the mucous membrane on the upper side of the tongue and upper part of the mouth. Taste buds contain endings of nerve filaments that convey impulses to the taste center of the brain.   Four primitive tastes, or a combination of these, can be sensed.   The four are sweet, sour, salty, and bitter.

Sensors for smell exist in humans in the form of olfactory cells located in the mucous membrane of the upper portion of the nasal cavity.   These cells have the ability to distinguish between different molecular structures of substances possessing (causing) different odors.   Nerve fibers attached to these cells send signals to the scent and odor cavity of the brain.

Sound sensors are located within the ears.   Sound waves enter the outer ear and travel to the ear drum, which forms a boundary to the middle ear.   Three bones in the middle ear transmit sound vibrations from the eardrum to the oval window, which in turn transmits vibrations to the inner ear.   There, located at different positions within the cochlea, are a variety of nerve terminals sensitive to various frequencies of sound.   Signals from these terminals are sent to the brain to be interpreted as different sounds.

Robots can be equipped with sensors similar to those possessed by humans, thereby enabling them to probe the environment similarly to humans.   Several sensors, somewhat like eyes, can be used for creating images.   Charge-coupled devices, intuitively explained in Section 7.3, are perhaps most like human eyes. It is through their ability to sense light that these devices enable robots to see. Robots can also "see" by means of frequencies outside the human visual spectrum (see Figure 7.1).   They can utilize radio frequencies by employing radar and sound by employing sonar.

In *active* sonar systems, the robot transmits acoustic energy, signals associated with the transmitted energy are reflected by the object, and these are observed by the sonar receiver.   The technique is similar to that used by ultrasound devices in most medical institutions.   *Passive* sonar systems simply contain receivers that listen (much like ears).   For instance, sources of acoustic energy in the ocean are often detected through the utilization of passive sonar sensors.

As opposed to a human being, a robot has the capacity to possess large numbers of sensors, the exact makeup of the sensor configuration depending on the tasks it is set to accomplish.   Besides those mentioned previously, there are infrared sensors that sense heat to manufacture an image, there is computer axial tomography, where x-rays are used to create an image, and there are NMR (nuclear magnetic resonance) imaging devices that utilize magnetism for image creation. More generally, there exists a sensor that can detect waveforms in each frequency range illustrated in Figure 7.1.   In the next section, we will discuss sensors that allow a robot to sense linear and angular acceleration.   Although we could go on, the point should be clear: the capacity of an autonomous system to observe its environment is virtually limitless, being bounded only by the limits of human technology.

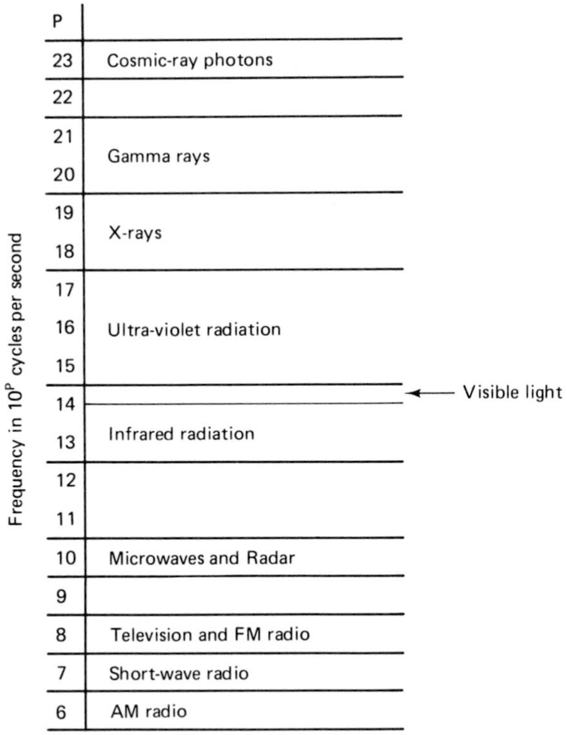

P		
23	Cosmic-ray photons	
22		
21	Gamma rays	
20		
19	X-rays	
18		
17	Ultra-violet radiation	
16		
15		
14		← Visible light
13	Infrared radiation	
12		
11		
10	Microwaves and Radar	
9		
8	Television and FM radio	
7	Short-wave radio	
6	AM radio	

Frequency in 10^P cycles per second

Figure 7.1 Frequency content of waveforms

7.2 ACCELEROMETERS

Accelerometers are nonradiating autonomous sensors utilized in measuring acceleration. They are employed in numerous applications, such as determining the velocity and position of a robot. They can also be used in place of sound to provide a signature indicative of grinding and vibration-type noises. For instance, assembly-line robots can employ acceleration profiles to identify malfunctioning products at various stages of partial assembly. We will be especially concerned with the use of accelerometers for robotic navigation.

We begin with the case of a single accelerometer. Consider the robot illustrated in Figure 7.2, which can travel only along a straight line starting from point zero. An accelerometer pointing in the direction of the motion can be employed to determine the robot's acceleration $a(t)$. If, initially, at time zero, the robot is at rest at location $x = 0$ and possesses initial velocity $v_0 = 0$, then the velocity at time t is

$$v(t) = \int_0^t a(u) \, du$$

and the total distance traveled by the robot is

$$x(t) = \int_0^t v(u) \, du$$

Figure 7.2 Robot limited to straight line motion

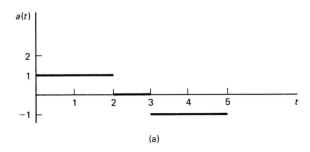

(a)

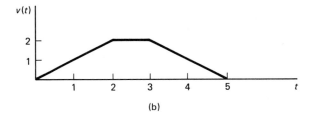

(b)

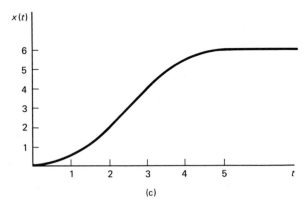

(c)

Figure 7.3 Acceleration, velocity, and distance

In actuality, the velocity and distance are calculated digitally by a computer utilizing numerical approximations to the preceding integrals.

As an illustration, if the accelerometer senses acceleration in accordance with Figure 7.3(a), the corresponding velocity and distance functions are those given in Figures 7.3(b) and (c), respectively. Thus, the distance traveled at time $t = 5$ is $x(5) = 6$, and the robot remains at rest thereafter.

Robotic applications restricted to straight-line motion are not uncommon; for instance, linear probes can be used to enter a human body or to enter the ground in search of minerals, water, or oil.

A robot whose motion is restricted to a curve might also employ an accelerometer; however, in this case, while the velocity and distance are found as in the linear situation, the quantity $x(t)$ is the distance measured along the curve from some prespecified starting point.

A simple accelerometer can be constructed using a mass attached to a spring as in Figure 7.4. Such a sensor might only be half the size of a piece of chalk. When it is accelerated, the spring is either elongated or compressed, depending on the direction of the acceleration. For instance, acceleration of the sensor case in the direction of the arrow causes the spring to compress, which in turn causes the pointer on the mass to point to a number on the ruled base that is indicative of the acceleration. The number is converted into digital representation, and an approximation to the double integral is performed digitally, the result being the position of the accelerometer (and hence the robot of which it is a part).

More generally, for a robot whose motion is in two or three dimensions, two or three accelerometers are respectively required. In two dimensions, the sensing axes of the instruments must not be collinear. In fact, the accelerometers are often mounted orthogonally in order to maximize the sensitivity of the instruments to the acceleration. In three dimensions, the three sensors must be mounted so that they are not coplaner, and, analogously to the two-dimensional situation, they are usually mounted as an orthogonal triad.

For three-dimensional applications, the orthogonal accelerometer triad will usually be positioned in a set of gimbals. These are similar to, but more complicated than those employed to hold globes of the earth. They are mechanical devices that prevent the triad from rotating. Thus, if the accelerometers are initially oriented so that their sensing axes are parallel to the positive x, y, and z coordinate axes, then the respective axes will remain parallel throughout the entire

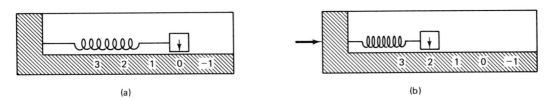

(a)   (b)

Figure 7.4 Simple accelerometer

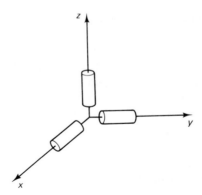

Figure 7.5 Triad of accelerometers

mission (see Figure 7.5). Intuitively, it can be imagined that the triad is homogeneously immersed in a liquid so that as the container is continuously rotated it appears to the eye that the triad does not move. In actuality, of course, there is friction and, as a result, the triad moves ever so slightly; indeed, this occurs even with almost perfect gimbals. To remedy the problem, an error-control system is employed (see Figure 7.6). Additional sensors, called *gyroscopes*, are used to

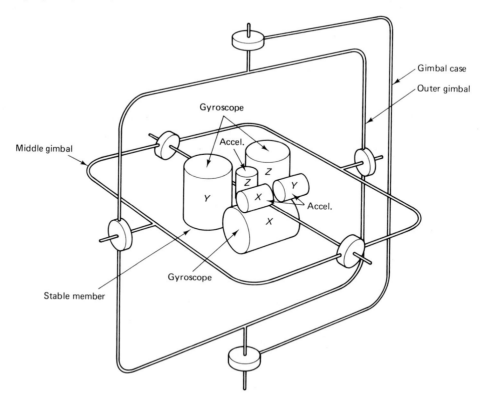

Figure 7.6 Error control system using gyroscopes

sense angular rotation.   The rotation information is sent back to motors on the gimbals, which maintain the triad in its original orientation.   Thus, the accelerometers do not rotate.

Why the great effort to maintain the orientation of the accelerometer triad as the robot moves?   The answer is straightforward: we desire the location of the robot in the given coordinate system; that is, we need the x, y, and z distances. If the accelerometers were to rotate along with the robot and the integrations were then performed, the outputs would be of no value; however, if the accelerometers remain in the fixed orientation and the integrations are performed, then the x, y, and z distances are obtained, and the exact location of the robot is specified.

The role of the computer in determining the location of the robot is many faceted.   Not only does it numerically perform the double integrations to convert accelerations into distances, but it also corrects errors in the accelerometers.   These errors are found by applying statistically designed tests on the system prior to its actual use.   This phase is called *calibration* and will not be discussed herein.   It entails the determination of an inverse model of the sensors, and that model is utilized in the computer to ascertain best estimates of the actual accelerations. The methodology is somewhat related to the information fusion to be discussed in Section 7.4.

The computer might also be employed in an overall control mode.   In such

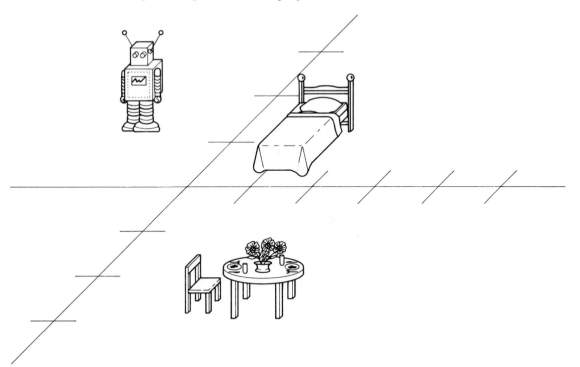

Figure 7.7   Autonomous navigation of robot using guidance laws

a situation, rules are prestored in the robot's brain. For instance, a schedule comprised of *guidance laws* might be utilized. These may take the following form: at time $t = 1$, the robot should be located at $x = 1$, $y = 1$, and $z = 0$; at time $t = 2$, it should be located at $x = 2$, $y = -3$, and $z = 0$; and so on (see Figure 7.7). The robot navigates autonomously to ensure that the schedule is carried out.

7.3 RADAR AND CHARGE-COUPLED DEVICES

Radar (radio detection and ranging) utilizes both a transmitter and a receiver and is employed in the detection of distance, or range. Radio waves, in the form of electromagnetic radiation, are broadcast by the transmitter. When these are interrupted by a target, some of the energy is reflected back and is detected by the receiver. The reflected pattern, called the *echo*, is compared with the transmitted (*target*) signal, and, if they compare favorably, the target's distance is found by means of a clock, the difference in time between the reception of the echo and the transmission of the original energy being proportional to the distance. Since the velocity of the radio wave is equal to that of light (approximately 1000 feet per microsecond), if it takes 20 microseconds for the energy to reach the target and return to the receiver, then it can be concluded that the distance to the target is 10,000 feet.

The method by which the time t between the emission of the transmitted signal f and the reception of the return signal g is calculated involves correlation techniques. Suppose the original signal is transmitted at time $x = 0$ and is a unit-height pulse of energy lasting one unit in time:

$$f(x) = I_{[0,1]}(x)$$

the characteristic function for the interval $[0, 1]$ [see Figure 7.8(a)]. The transmitted signal is reflected from the target and the reflection becomes the received signal. If there were no noise, then this signal would be an identical copy of the transmitted signal, only delayed in time, as is illustrated in Figure 7.8(b). However, in practice there is both noise and possible target motion; thus, the received signal will look more like the one given in Figure 7.8(c). Consequently, in practice the time t is found by finding a translated version of the original signal, $f(x - t)$, such that the integral

$$\int_{-\infty}^{+\infty} g(x)f(x - t)\, dx$$

is maximized. A computer performs the numerical evaluation of the integral for various realistic values of t, and the t that gives the largest value is chosen. This technique for finding the time, and therefore the desired range, is called the *correlation* method, and it is a special type of *matched filter* recognition procedure. When the noise is not significant, as is the case in Figure 7.8(c), the method works rather well.

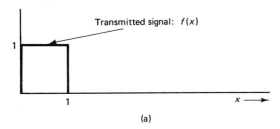

(a)

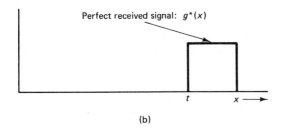

(b)

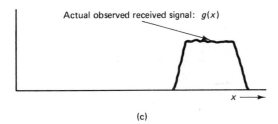

(c)

Figure 7.8 Transmitted and observed signals

Example 7.1

Let the transmitted signal be $f(x) = I_{[0,1]}(x)$, which is illustrated in Figure 7.8(a), and consider an idealized situation in which the received signal is $g(x) = I_{[10,11]}(x)$. Clearly, the elapsed time is $t = 10$; however, we will find this value by the correlation methodology. Specifically, t must be found so as to maximize

$$A = \int_{-\infty}^{+\infty} I_{[10,11]}(x)I_{[0,1]}(x - t) \, dx$$

$$= \begin{cases} 0, & \text{if } t \le 9 \\ \int_{10}^{1+t} dx, & \text{if } 9 < t \le 10 \\ \int_{t}^{11} dx, & \text{if } 10 < t \le 11 \\ 0, & \text{if } 11 \le t \end{cases}$$

$$= (t - 9)I_{(9,10]}(t) + (11 - t)I_{(10,11)}(t)$$

which is maximized at $t = 10$ (see Figure 7.9).

Figure 7.9 Correlation function

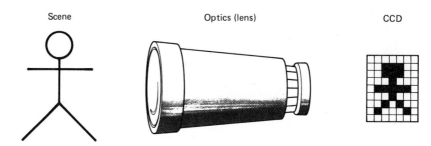

Figure 7.10 Optical system with CCD

Not only can radar be used for finding distance, it can also be employed for determining target velocity.   In addition, several radar devices exist for the creation of images.

A *charge-coupled device* (*CCD*) is a self-scanning image-creation apparatus consisting of an array of photodetectors.   Each detector is situated at a given position and accumulates electrical charge proportional to the incident light intensity at the position.   The charge is read out and employed as a measure of the gray value at the position.   To create the image, some optical device is used to expose the CCD to a scene of interest, and the resulting gray values contain the

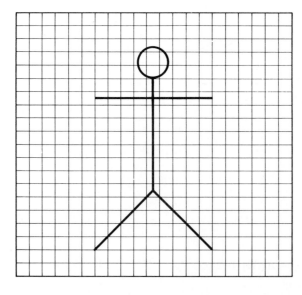

Figure 7.11 Projected scene on CCD

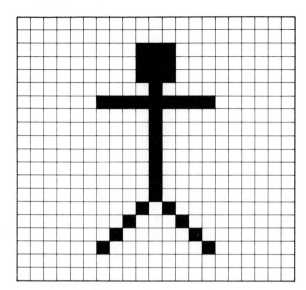

Figure 7.12 Digitized image

information revealed by the exposure. At present, a postage-stamp-sized CCD can be employed to create an image consisting of approximately 1000 by 1000 picture elements. Figure 7.10 provides an illustration of a lens being used to project a scene onto a CCD; Figure 7.11 shows an enlarged version of the projected scene; and Figure 7.12 illustrates the resulting black-and-white image.

7.4 FUSION OF SENSOR INFORMATION

Intelligent systems must function when too many data are present, as well as when too few data are present. Often, in the latter case, the full amount of data is used and this is supplemented with heuristic information. In the former case, the entirety of the data cannot be employed directly since, in most cases, it will be contradictory in nature and must be filtered prior to utilization by the computer.

Example 7.2

Consider the problem of measuring the length of a rod. Suppose three independent measurements are taken by three distinct measuring devices of similar accuracy: $x_1 = 67$, $x_2 = 63$, and $x_3 = 62$. The measurements must be *fused* into a single value called an *estimate*. One choice for the length might be the sample mean

$$\bar{x} = \frac{x_1 + x_2 + x_3}{3} = 64$$

In terms of the concepts of Section 6.7, the sample mean is found my employing the estimation rule

$$\overline{X} = d(X_1, X_2, X_3) = \frac{X_1 + X_2 + X_3}{3}$$

and $\bar{x} = 64$ is simply a particular value taken on by the estimation rule for a certain set of sensor readings.

In that "the length of a rod" is a quantity that is manifested solely in a process of measurement, it is, from a scientific perspective, a random variable X (see Section 6.1). We do not employ the estimation rule $\bar{X}$ to "find X;" indeed, due to the inherent randomness of X, such a notion is absolutely meaningless. Instead, the three sensor measurements give us an instance of the estimation rule, and we employ that instance as an estimate of the mean of X. In sum, length is not a deterministic quantity and when we employ a number to represent it, the number is actually an estimate of the mean of the length.

One of the reasons that the sample mean is so often employed is that, "on average," it yields the expected value of the random quantity for which it is being used as an estimate. Mathematically, $E[\bar{X}] = E[X]$. Generally, any estimation rule whose expected value is the expected value of the random variable it is estimating is said to be *unbiased*. In addition, among all unbiased estimation rules that are formed by taking a weighted average of the individual measurements, the *linear* unbiased estimators, the sample mean is best relative to the quadratic loss function.

Consider a robot that moves in a planar world. Two accelerometers are required for autonomous navigation; however, suppose the robot is using three accelerometers in order to obtain better, "more accurate" estimates of its true acceleration. The three accelerometers are assumed to be positioned in the plane of motion as illustrated in Figure 7.13, and it is also assumed that gimbals are being utilized to prevent rotation of the accelerometers. Referring to the figure, we denote the outputs of the accelerometers by u, v, and w; these measurements of acceleration result from the motion of the robot in the plane.

Now, if acceleration exists only in the x direction and is of magnitude x, then $u = x$, $v = 0$, and

$$w = x \cos 45° = (0.707)x$$

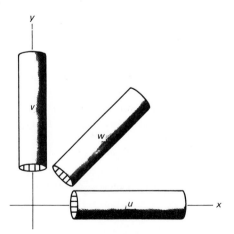

Figure 7.13   Redundant system

On the other hand, if acceleration exists only in the y direction and is of magnitude y, then $u = 0$, $v = y$, and $w = (0.707)y$.

In practice, there are accelerations in both the x and y directions, but these are unknown; only the readings u, v, and w are available, and the true components of the acceleration must be estimated on the basis of the readings. The following equation relates the true acceleration components, denoted x and y, with the observed accelerations u, v, and w:

$$\begin{pmatrix} u \\ v \\ w \end{pmatrix} = \begin{pmatrix} 1 & 0 \\ 0 & 1 \\ \frac{1}{\sqrt{2}} & \frac{1}{\sqrt{2}} \end{pmatrix} \begin{pmatrix} x \\ y \end{pmatrix}$$

This matrix equation is of the form $z = Ab$, with z called the *observation vector*, A the *system*, or *design matrix*, and b the *state vector*. The *pseudoinverse* of the design matrix,

$$A^+ = (A'A)^{-1}A'$$

(A' denoting the transpose of A) can be employed to determine an estimate of the state vector, the estimate being given by

$$b = A^+z$$

This vector estimate yields componentwise estimates of the desired x and y accelerations:

$$\begin{pmatrix} x \\ y \end{pmatrix} = \frac{1}{4}\begin{pmatrix} 3 & -1 & \frac{2}{\sqrt{2}} \\ -1 & 3 & \frac{2}{\sqrt{2}} \end{pmatrix} \begin{pmatrix} u \\ v \\ w \end{pmatrix}$$

or

$$x = \frac{3}{4}u - \frac{1}{4}v + \frac{1}{2\sqrt{2}}w$$

and

$$y = -\frac{1}{4}u + \frac{3}{4}v + \frac{1}{2\sqrt{2}}w$$

These equations are programmed into the computer and allow the three inputs u, v, and w to be processed in place of a two-input system. As previously mentioned, the estimated values of x and y in this case would be more accurate than a two-input system. The rationale for the methodology is based on statistical considerations. For those with a background in statistics, the following points should be noted regarding the pseudoinverse methodology.

1. A least-squares best estimate is obtained.

2. If the sensors are independent with average error zero and possess equal degrees of accuracy, then a best linear unbiased estimate results; in particular, the pseudoinverse solution for x and y possesses minimal variance.
3. If, additionally, the sensor errors are normally distributed, the pseudoinverse solution is also the maximum-likelihood solution.

A disadvantage associated with the use of an extra accelerometer, besides the cost, is the added computation necessary to convert the three sensor readings into two estimates. Nonetheless, the benefit of utilizing extra sensors includes both superior accuracy and higher reliability. Regarding the latter, should a single accelerometer fail, the fault can be isolated and the software reconfigured so that the output of the failed sensor is not utilized in the processing. This process is called *reconfiguration management*, and it requires additional sensors for the detection and isolation of accelerometer failures. Sensors used for the detection of inadequately functioning equipment are often called *built-in test equipment*, or *BITE*.

Consider the robot with three accelerometers discussed previously. If sensor u fails, and BITE is employed in detecting and isolating the failure, then the appropriate reconfiguration of the system equation is

$$\begin{pmatrix} v \\ w \end{pmatrix} = \begin{pmatrix} 0 & 1 \\ \dfrac{1}{\sqrt{2}} & \dfrac{1}{\sqrt{2}} \end{pmatrix} \begin{pmatrix} x \\ y \end{pmatrix}$$

Inversion yields

$$\begin{pmatrix} x \\ y \end{pmatrix} = \begin{pmatrix} -1 & \sqrt{2} \\ 1 & 0 \end{pmatrix} \begin{pmatrix} v \\ w \end{pmatrix}$$

Figure 7.14 illustrates the intelligent reconfiguration automatically implemented by the robot in question. From the diagram, it can be seen that a single failure can be tolerated; more than one failure brings the robotic system down. From a reliability point of view, this is a (3, 2) system. Moreover, if a single accelerometer has a reliability function $p(t)$, then the reliability function of the entire system is given by

$$R(t) = p^3(t) + 3p^2(t)(1 - p(t))$$
$$= 3p^2(t) - 2p^3(t)$$

(see Section 6.6). A nonredundant system with only two accelerometers has reliability function

$$R^*(t) = p^2(t)$$

If

$$p(t) = e^{-\lambda t} I_{[0,\infty)}(t)$$

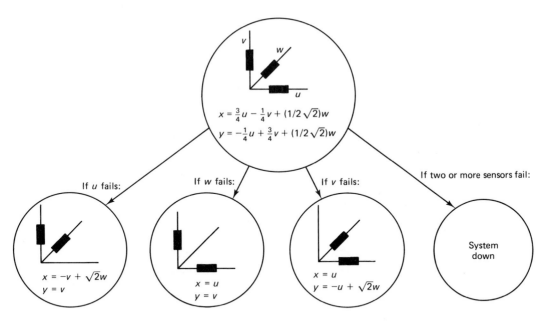

Figure 7.14   Estimates using reconfiguration management

then the MTBF for the $(3, 2)$ system is

$$\bar{t} = \frac{5}{6\lambda}$$

whereas the MTBF for the nonredundant system is

$$\bar{t}^* = \frac{1}{2\lambda}$$

7.5 ROBOTIC CONTROL SYSTEMS

A robotic system is often classified as a closed-loop control system. Such a system is characterized in part by the fact that the input is a function of the output. Figure 7.15 illustrates a block diagram of a simple closed-loop control system. The physical process to be controlled in a closed-loop system is called the *plant*. Sensors are used in measuring the response of the plant, and response signals are processed by the computer and are subsequently compared to *guidance laws* that characterize the desired response. The difference signal is computed by subtracting the computer-modified sensor response from the desired response. This signal is computer compensated and then used to generate commands to the control surfaces in order to drive the difference signal to zero. Several control loops, like the one illustrated in Figure 7.15, might be employed in a robotic system.

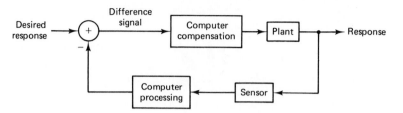

Figure 7.15   General control loop

Consider a robot surveyor designed to study the landscape illustrated in Figure 7.16. It is equipped with several sensors, including accelerometers, radar, and a CCD, and is preprogrammed to go to some (absolute) location, point p, in the xy plane, and, once there, locate certain landmarks and record the distances from these to the point p.

The various sensors help the robot in the performance of its task. For instance, the accelerometers are instrumental in enabling the robot to locate point p (see the control loop in Figure 7.17). More specifically, a trajectory going from

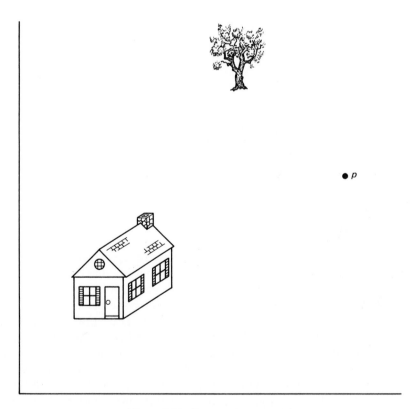

Figure 7.16   Scene to be surveyed

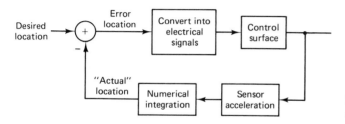

Figure 7.17   Control loop for position determination

the initial location of the robot, say (0, 0), to point p may be given in the form of a function of time or as a table.   If the robot is at the desired location, it stays fixed; if not, the error is computed and then converted into electrical signals that drive control surfaces.   Thus, the robot moves in the desired direction (the one that tends to zero out the error).   In the correction process, accelerometers sense the acceleration of the robot, and this is integrated twice to obtain the "actual" location of the robot (see Section 7.2).   This location is subtracted from the desired location, and the resulting error distance is used in driving the system.   The cycle is repeated until the error distance is zero.   Ultimately, the robot maneuvers to location p (see Figure 7.18).   Once there, using the CCD, it looks to find designated landmarks.   In the process, it utilizes image-processing algorithms, perhaps some of those discussed in Chapter 8.   Once the landmarks, say the tree and the house, are detected, the ranges, $\sqrt{2}$ and 2, respectively, are found by means of radar measurements.   Thus, the robot has completed its task.

7.6 COMMUNICATION OF KNOWLEDGE

Stored knowledge is of little value if it cannot be utilized, and utilization requires communication.   The data, or operations on the data, that constitute the knowledge must be transmitted by a control surface (*transmitter*) and received by sensors (*receivers*) that are sensitive to the transmitted signals.

To facilitate a timely and accurate transmission of information, a communication system like the one illustrated in Figure 7.19 is often employed.   Many steps

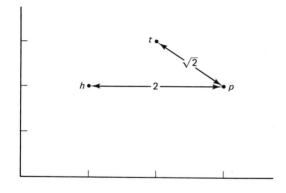

Figure 7.18   Radar range measurements for surveying

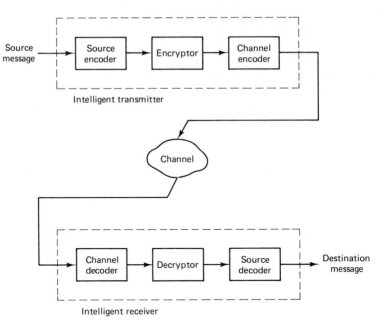

Figure 7.19   Communication system

within the transmitter and receiver blocks have not been portrayed.   For instance, operations that convert energy from one form to another do not involve intelligent operations on strings of information and therefore have been omitted.   Note that, for each block in the transmitter, there is a corresponding block in the receiver that performs an inverse operation.   We will now briefly describe the operations depicted by the blocks.

Source encoding is a string-compression technique that removes irrelevancies and redundancy from a message.   A source encoder converts a given string of information into another (usually shorter) string.   Numerous source encoding techniques exist for the compression of information that is in the form of images, text, instructions, and the like.   These methods include block transform coding, block or sequential multipath coding, and sequential predicate coding.   Strict redundancy-reduction techniques are also available.   Some source-encoding techniques are invertible, whereas some are not.   In the former case, the method is also said to be *reversible*; in the latter, it is called *irreversible*.

A simple example of source encoding is the Morse code, where letters, such as *e, t, a, o, n, i, r, s,* and *h,* that are used with high frequency in English text are encoded using relatively few dots and dashes, and letters that are used rarely, such as *j, k, q, x,* and *z,* are represented with relatively long strings of dots and dashes.

The well-known *Huffman coding procedure* uses a *coding tree* to produce a binary (0 and 1) code.   The Huffman procedure presupposes that the frequency of occurrence of the source symbols is known, and one of its purposes is to produce variable-length opcodes to maximize execution performance in various computer architectures. A binary tree (see Figure 7.20) is drawn by first labeling the leaves with the probabilities of the symbols involved, the labeling being done so that the corresponding probabilities are listed from smallest to largest. The other nodes of the tree are formed by combining two minimum probability nodes, labeling the resulting node with the sum of the probabilities, and then proceeding inductively until the root node is labeled with probability 1. Note that higher-probability nodes are always placed on top, and nodes that have been combined cannot be combined again. To obtain the encoding of the symbols, start from the root, label each left branch 0 and each right branch 1, and trace a path from the root to each symbol. The string of 0's and 1's from the root to the symbol is the *codeword* for the symbol. The significance of the method is that the average length of the strings obtained will be close to the entropy (see Section 6.5).

Example 7.3

Assume that the instructions to the robot ROBY, along with their relative frequencies of occurrence, are given by

Command	Frequency
Go	0.1
Come	0.1
Pickup	0.5
Giveme	0.2
Help	0.1

The appropriate coding tree is given in Figure 7.20. Note that whenever two symbols possess the same probability an arbitrary decision is made. Table 7.1 gives the encoded commands, together with the expected number of bits per command. The expected number of bits is 2, and the entropy is

$$H = -[0.3 \log_2 0.1 + 0.2 \log_2 0.2 + 0.5 \log_2 0.5]$$

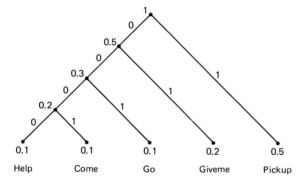

Figure 7.20   Huffman coding tree

TABLE 7.1   INSTRUCTION ENCODING.

Command	Encoding	Frequency	Number of Bits Times Frequency
Go	001	0.1	0.3
Come	0001	0.1	0.4
Pickup	1	0.5	0.5
Giveme	01	0.2	0.4
Help	0000	0.1	0.4
		Expected number of bits =	2.0

Instructions to ROBY are decoded using the same binary tree.   For instance, if the command string

$$1\ 0\ 0\ 1\ 0\ 0\ 0\ 1\ 0\ 1\ 0\ 0\ 0\ 0$$

is transmitted and received, it is interpreted as

Pickup   Go   Come   Giveme   Help

No spaces are required between commands, since no codeword is a prefix to another: the Huffman code is a *prefix code*.   Thus, it is always possible to uniquely partition a command string.   In the illustration at hand, we have the partition

1   001   0001   01   0000

Pickup   Go   Come   Giveme   Help

While source encoding is beneficial for improving time and memory loading of systems, it is of little benefit in protecting data in computer and communication systems.   To begin with, there must be protection against unauthorized access to the system.   Lists authorizing specific users, along with the type and degree of use, need be kept.   For instance, the type of use might be WRITE, READ, or USE.   Certain programs in computers can be written into and hence modified as well as read.   Other programs can only be read.   Still others cannot even be read: such a program, a random-number generator being an example, can only be used for the purpose for which it was written.   The degree of access involves a hierarchy of trust, as well as need to know.   It should be recognized that a degree of use determination is not a simple matter, since information not explicitly present in a database can often be deduced from existent data.   A case in point is where a priori known correlations exist.   Finally, data security requires guidelines and approvals regarding access to communication channels.

Among the ways for ensuring data security is *encryption*, which is an invertible transformation technique that involves the conversion of original strings of information, called *plaintext*, into new strings, called *cryptograms*, the latter intended to be unintelligible to those lacking system authorization.   The cryptograms are transmitted and, upon reception, are inverted by a *deciphering transform*, the inversion producing the original text that was to be transmitted.

Two fundamental operations are employed in the construction of an encryption transformation: transposition, whereby symbols in the original string are permuted, and substitution, whereby symbols in the original string are replaced by symbols from a different alphabet. Control of the type of substitutions and transpositions is achieved by the use of a *key*. Knowledge of the key is shared by both the encryption and deciphering devices.

Example 7.4

Suppose the original message to be encrypted consists of the following sequence of commands to ROBY:

Pickup   Gohelp   Giveme

One way of producing a transposition transform is by using an *interleaving* technique, whereby the first letters in each word are grouped as a new "word," the second letters in each word are grouped as a new "word," and so on. Listing the original word as rows in a matrix format facilitates the procedure. Thus, we write

pickup

gohelp

giveme

and the columns are utilized as the transmitted signals. The resulting cryptogram is

pgg   ioi   chv   kee   ulm   ppe

Upon reception, if the key is known, these words are rewritten as the columns in a matrix format, and the rows are read to retrieve the original text.

Example 7.5

An illustration of a substitution cypher applied to the commands to ROBY given in Example 7.4 consists of the cryptogram

pockap   guhilp   govimi

Here, each vowel in the text has been replaced by the next, or successor vowel, using the key given by the directed-type graph

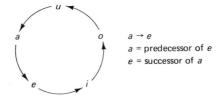

Upon reception of the cryptogram, the plaintext is obtained by replacing each received vowel by its predecessor.

The final stages of Figure 7.19 to be discussed are channel encoding and decoding, the purpose of which are to increase reliability and accuracy through the introduction of controlled redundancy in the form of word, or partial word, re-dundancy. Among the common error-control procedures employed are loop-echo check, detect retransmit, and forward error correction (FEC).

In the *loop-error* check method, each character in a transmitted string is sent back to the source and compared. If there is a match, nothing is done; if there is not a match, then the original character is retransmitted and the procedure continues. In addition to the cost in terms of time, this procedure is highly sus-ceptible to false-alarm errors.

Detect–retransmit procedures involve the use of redundant bits employed only to detect an error. If an error is detected, a retransmission is performed. Unlike the loop-echo check procedure, each word is not retransmitted, only those that have been observed to be in error.

A simple detect–retransmit technique is the *constant-ratio code* (also known as the *m out of n code*, with $n > m > 0$). Here, n binary bits are utilized as the string of symbols to be transmitted. Every valid word must contain m ones, the others being zeros. If a string of symbols is received that does not contain m ones, a retransmission of the string is performed. This technique makes use of the assumption that, should an error in transmission occur, there is a high likelihood that only one bit will be altered and only scant likelihood that two or more bits will be altered. The method recognizes syntactical, but not semantic errors.

Example 7.6

Consider the constant-ratio code with $n = 6$ and $m = 4$. In this case, there are

$$\frac{6!}{2!4!} = 15$$

valid commands that can be transmitted; there are $2^6 = 64$ distinct signals that might be received signals. If

$$x = 1\,1\,0\,1\,0\,1$$

is transmitted and if

$$y = 1\,0\,0\,1\,0\,1$$

is received, a retransmission would be performed since only three ones appear in y. On the other hand, if

$$z = 1\,0\,1\,1\,0\,1$$

is received, then no retransmission would occur and the wrong information would be utilized.

Both channel encoding methods thus far described require sensors and ac-tivators at both the source and destination sites. *Forward error-correction (FEC)* methods are more "intelligent" in that they do not require receivers and transmitters at both channel ends; rather, they use redundant (*parity*) symbols to detect and correct errors, and there is no need to retransmit the original signal. As many parity symbols are employed as are required to reduce error rates and guarantee certain throughput levels. FEC is self-contained: it is not radiating, and thus there is no need for a reverse channel as in the two previous methods.

Two principal FEC codes are tree codes and block codes. Tree codes involve variable-length strings and make use of trees for the encoding of messages (similar to the Huffman coding tree illustrated in Figure 7.20).

In block codes, a message word consisting of k symbols is given. The channel encoder generates $n - k$ parity symbols and forms a codeword comprised of the original message concatenated with the parity symbols. The codeword is transmitted and a string of n symbols is received. The structure of the received word is utilized in ascertaining whether or not an error occurred during the transmission. If this is the case, the structure also indicates changes to be made in the received signal, thereby providing an estimate of the true transmitted signal. The following example should help to clarify some of these notions.

Example 7.7

Consider commands to ROBY that consist of elements in the alphabet $\{h, r, p, t\}$. For instance, h might stand for "help," r for "rush," and so on. Messages in this example are only $k = 1$ symbol long, and parity will be produced by replicating the message two times and concatenating this with the message to form the codeword. Thus, codewords are strings of length $n = 3$. If the message is "help," then the codeword hhh is transmitted. Whenever a received signal consists of three identical symbols from the alphabet, the symbol serves as an estimate of the transmitted message; whenever the received signal does not contain three identical symbols from the alphabet, a transmission error is detected. If it happens that two symbols in the received word are identical, then the replicated symbol serves as an estimate, albeit, a less certain one, of the original message. Finally, if no two symbols agree, the procedure fails.

We close this section by noting that several algebraic structures can be utilized in the development of well-known channel encoding techniques. Groups, vector spaces, rings, and fields can be profitably employed in the production of group codes, linear block codes, cyclic codes, and BCH codes, respectively.

7.7 EXPERT SYSTEMS: AN EXPERT SOUND ROBOT

The autonomous action of the robot arm in Section 1.10 depended on both data from the sensors and inference rules that facilitated closed-loop control based on the sensor information. In an uncomplicated universe such as the block world, the inference rules can be constructed directly from the geometry of the environment: their formation requires no expert knowledge regarding the interaction of the robot arm and its limited sphere of activity. Because such a system involves a program that utilizes a logical calculus that operates on a set of facts and rules, it is called a *knowledge-based system*.

Now consider the problem of isolating a malfunction in the engine of an automobile. Here, the environment is much more complex. Besides the engine proper, which consists of the block (including the crank, camshaft, and piston assembly) and the cylinder head (including the rocker arm and valve assembly), there are also separate fuel, electrical, coolant, ignition, exhaust, and antipollution systems. To troubleshoot such a complex hierarchical system requires knowledge in several areas: (1) overall system design, (2) subsystem designs, (3) control functions between systems, (4) the performance relationships between the various subsystems, and (5) expert knowledge as to symptoms and the related causal connections. Consequently, if we wish to design an autonomous troubleshooting system, the knowledge base must not only contain design facts and inference rules based on the design, but, to be efficient, it must contain rules based on the manner in which an expert would interpret malfunction-related symptoms, the latter to be registered by appropriate sensors. It is the incorporation of inference rules based on expert knowledge that results in an *expert system*.

The notion of an expert system is not new. For some time, technical manuals have included *if–then* diagrams to assist technicians in fault diagnosis. Indeed, the amateur automobile hobbyist can purchase commercially any number of troubleshooting diagrams to assist in repairing a car. What the amateur might lack, however, is the expert knowledge required for the recognition of sound-, sight-, touch-, smell-, and taste-based symptoms. Moreover, troubleshooting diagrams are usually incomplete in that they do not include all the possible causal interconnections between the subsystems. For instance, a variation in the ignition system can result in performance loss due to carburation; hence, a correction of the ignition timing can necessitate a change in the fuel–oxygen mixture. Finally, and perhaps most problematic, is the nondeterminism of the symptom–fault relation. The same symptom, or complex of symptoms, can result from numerous faults (or combination of faults). As a result, a troubleshooting diagram requires valuations to point the search in directions that are more likely to be fruitful. The source of these valuations might be an analysis of statistical data pertaining to fault analysis of the particular engine under consideration, or it might be based on heuristically obtained likelihoods or order relations elicited from experts. Ultimately, of course, the degree of nondeterminism is a function of sensor-related expertise, as that expertise pertains to the engine system design. Whereas a periodic noise of a certain frequency might indicate any of several malfunctions, perhaps an associated vibration might reduce the number of possibilities or even pinpoint the malfunction precisely. In any event, a deterministic logical calculus is certainly not sufficient for the analysis of sensor information in terms of a rule–fact knowledge base.

While the expert system concept is not new, when the terminology *expert system* is employed, we usually are referring to a computer-implemented, knowledge-based inference system. The introduction of this type of system is relatively recent. Even here, however, the term *expert system* does not usually refer to a truly autonomous system. Although the computer may give advice on the location of a fault, such advice, of necessity, leads to some sort of test to see if the hypothesized malfunction is actually the cause of the problem. Such a test might involve the simple use of test equipment, the replacement of a suspect part, or a detailed statistical analysis of overall system functioning. Only when testing is completed do we know whether or not the proposed fault hypothesis is verified, another *secondary* hypothesis must be checked, or new sensor information must be fed into the system due to the fact that the given hypothesis has only provided a partial remedy. An expert system can only be judged fully autonomous when all diagnosis, testing, and repair are accomplished without human intervention.

To illustrate the knowledge–logic–sensor interplay required in an expert system, we will consider the design of an expert sound robot, one that makes its decisions based on sound sensors. In the design of the expert sound robot, to be called ROBY, actual sound information is represented in the database in some mathematical form, for instance, utilizing its spectral content. Based on the opinion of human experts or statistical analysis, functioning modalities associated with different sound representations in the database are also recorded. The database containing the sound information might be stochastic or fuzzy, and it is a principal ingredient in the diagnostic expert (ROBY).

The internal workings of ROBY are simplistically illustrated in Figure 7.21. The sound sensor senses the desired data and provides a mathematical representation as illustrated in the figure. The mathematical representation is then compared with representations stored in the database. Once a match (to a desired degree of confidence) is obtained, the corresponding fault is reported by ROBY.

Similar techniques can be employed for diagnostic testing in the automated production of a machine. Specifically, expert sound robots can be stationed at various stages along an assembly line (see Figure 7.22). As the machine goes

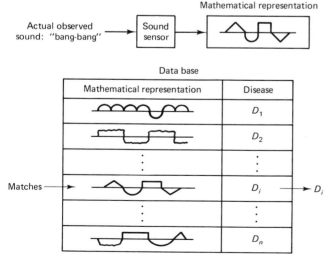

Figure 7.21   Observed and database signals

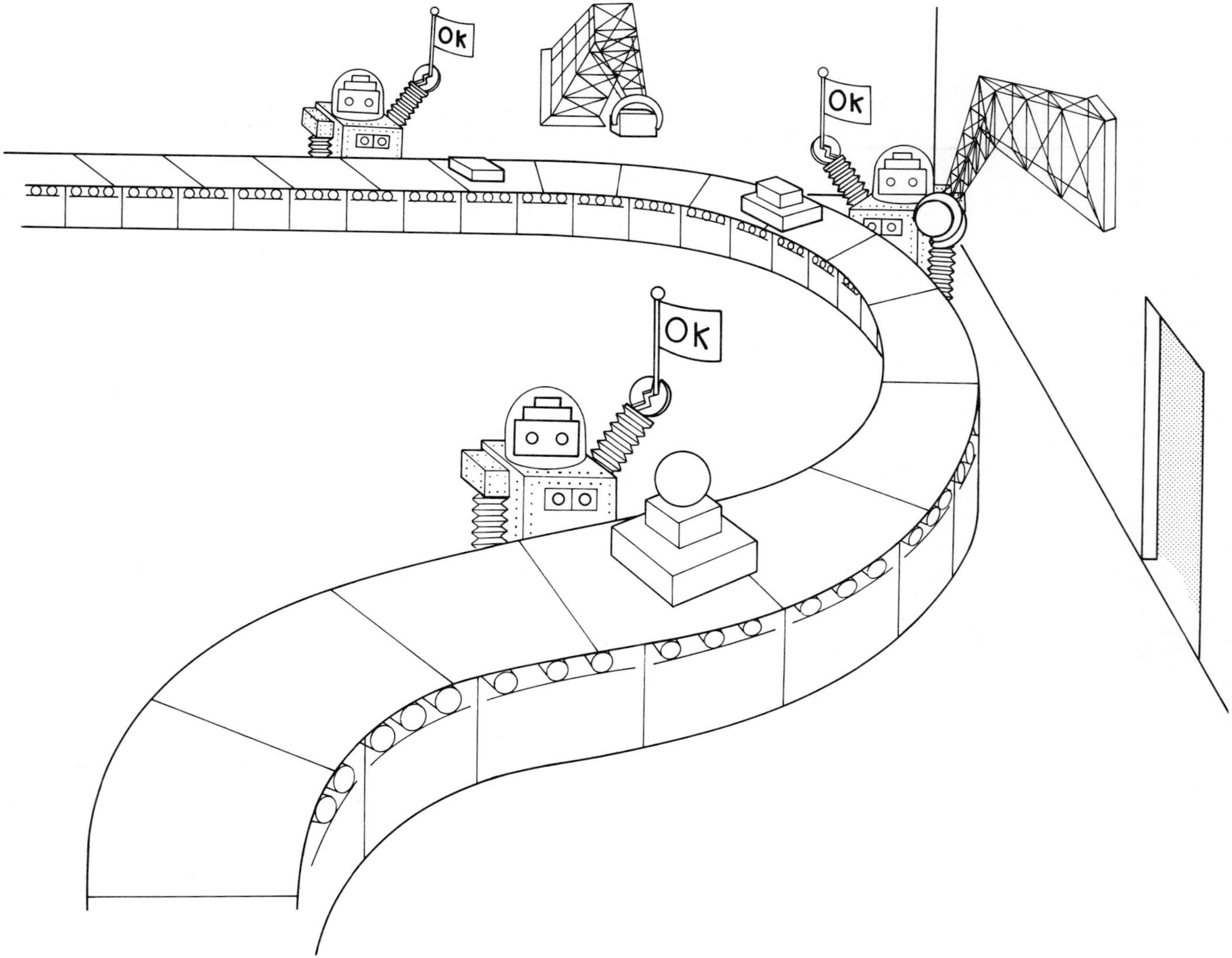

Figure 7.22 Expert sound robots on assembly line

through each (higher) level of assembly, a robot listener makes a judgment as to the overall condition of the machine at that particular stage of development. Each robot must be an expert on the proper sound that the partially assembled machine (at the given stage) should make. If all is well, the machine continues its journey to the next assembly stage; if not, the machine is "pulled" and the fault is corrected. In an ideal diagnostic system, the sound robot not only discovers the existence of a fault, but also pinpoints the problem.

A severe shortcoming of the expert listening robot for the assembly line is that ambient and other noise will usually contaminate the sound from the machine under observation. Consequently, a sound signature will often be obtained that is not recognizable or, perhaps even worse, is matched with an incorrect stored signal in the database.

Several modifications of the robot system can be made to prevent this difficulty. A reverberant chamber can be employed to accentuate self-noise while simultaneously blocking out ambient noise. A serious difficulty with such chambers, besides the cost, might be the extra handling required to position the machine within the chamber and the consequent interruption of the natural flow of the assembly line.

An alternative to the reverberant chamber is the use of accelerometers to sense vibrations in place of sound sensors, such as microphones. If the accelerometers are judiciously placed so that there exists a high correlation between the acceleration profiles and the sound profiles constituting the knowledge base, then this type of system will function adequately. Among the difficulties with this approach is the large amount of front-end processing that is required. This includes the necessity of converting sound profiles into corresponding acceleration profiles and conversely. Two other potential problems are the sensitivity of acceleration profiles to position and the possible lack of correlation between the acceleration and sound profiles.

Perhaps the best method for the removal of background noise is adaptive noise cancellation, the fundamental structure of which is given in Figure 7.23. The basic idea is to utilize two (or more) microphones (sensors), the primary and the secondary. The primary sensor is situated near the object under scrutiny and is

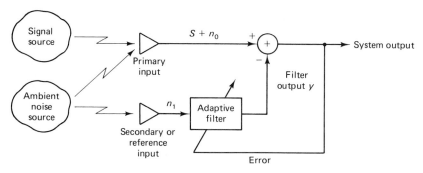

Figure 7.23   Adaptive noise cancellation

utilized to recognize the sound made by the object, corrupted of course by the unavoidable and unpredictable ambient noise. The signal recorded by this sensor constitutes the primary input. The second sensor is located so that it essentially senses only the ambient noise. Its recorded signal is the secondary input. The intuitive principle behind interference canceling techniques is to subtract the secondary signal from the primary signal, thereby removing the noise in the primary signal.

While the preceding noise-cancellation methodology appears rather straightforward, it is far from so. Both the ambient and object noise are random phenomena. Consequently, the noise removal requires the use of stochastic processes and will not be pursued herein. Generally, the filtering of random data, such as the sensed noise just discussed, involves somewhat sophisticated probabilistic notions and for that reason belongs properly to the study of stochastic processes. Nevertheless, let us emphasize most strongly that stochastic filtering is indeed a fundamental aspect of artificially intelligent systems.

EXERCISES FOR CHAPTER 7

7.1. Describe benefits and shortcommings of active sonar systems and compare these with passive sonar systems.

7.2. If an accelerometer outputs acceleration

$$a(t) = tI_{[0,2]}(t) + (4 - t)I_{(2,4)}(t)$$

what are the corresponding velocity and distance profiles?

7.3. Verify that the correlation function $A(t)$ illustrated in Figure 7.9 is obtained utilizing the transmitted signal $f(x)$ and the perfect received signal $g^*(x)$ given in Figure 7.8.

7.4. Find an estimate of the state vector b using the pseudoinverse formula if

$$b = \begin{pmatrix} x \\ y \end{pmatrix}$$

and

$$\begin{pmatrix} 2 \\ 0 \\ 1.1 \end{pmatrix} = \begin{pmatrix} 1 & 1 \\ 1 & -1 \\ 0 & 1 \end{pmatrix} b$$

7.5. Referring to Figure 7.13, if the accelerometer w now points $180°$ from what is illustrated in the diagram, then what are the pseudoinverse estimates of the accelerations x and y?

7.6. Utilizing the configuration explained in Exercise 7.5, draw a reconfiguration management diagram similar to the one provided in Figure 7.14.

7.7. Referring to Figure 7.13, let an additional independent accelerometer, say w', be introduced in the diagram and assume that it operates $180°$ opposite of w. What is the reliability of this four-accelerometer configuration?   How does this answer compare with a (4, 2) system?

7.8. Use the Huffman encoding scheme to encode the independent instructions to ROBY that are given, together with their relative frequencies of occurrence, in the following table?

Command	Frequency
Go	0.1
Come	0.1
Pickup	0.4
Giveme	0.2
Help	0.1
Speak	0.1

7.9. In a constant-ratio code with $n = 8$ and $m = 5$, how many valid commands can be transmitted?   How many possible received signals are there?

7.10. Explain why the adaptive noise cancellation technique, as intuitively explained herein, might present difficulties.

8

COMPUTER VISION SYSTEMS AND IMAGE PROCESSING

8.1 IMAGE RECOGNITION

Computer vision is an area of artificial intelligence and robotics that has generated significant interest in the last 20 years. Given a mathematical representation of an image, which in the digital case will be a bound matrix (see Section 4.8), we wish to extract information from the image that can be employed in a decision procedure. The image itself may result from any number of different kinds of sensors. These sensors may utilize an optical technique, such as in a camera, they may sense heat, as with infrared sensors, they may sense illumination, as in synthetic aperture radar (SAR), or they might involve x-rays, as in tomographical medical imaging. Although each particular sensing technique may possess its own requirements insofar as imaging methodology is concerned, the scope of that methodology is not constrained by the demands of any specialized technology. The purpose of image processing continues to be the extraction of information upon which intelligence-type procedures can be implemented. In a fully autonomous AI system, these procedures lead to a decision, which in turn leads to some sort of robotic action.

Perhaps the best way to understand the problems and goals that constitute the subject of image processing is to reflect on our own human vision system. Although visual sensation, object recognition, and the decision for action seem almost instantaneous, the complexity of the process is to this day beyond full comprehension. Imagine a batter awaiting the pitch that will momentarily arrive from the mound.   In a fraction of a second, a stringent real-time constraint, the following must be accomplished:

1. Visual sensors, the batter's eyes, must *sense* the reflected light coming from the ball.

2. This purely physical sensory data must be organized into an *image*; the image must be *created*.

3. The image must be *cleaned up*; it must be preprocessed so as to yield an image that is not distorted by the act of sensation.   The image must be *restored* to some "perfect" image that, by experience, the batter believes it to be. For example, he expects a ball to be coming toward him, and he must restore the image so that *noisy* interference such as light or fog do not result in something other than a ball.

4. The image is *enhanced* so that the ball stands out more starkly from the background.

5. The enhanced image is *segmented*; the ball is cut from the rest of the image except insofar as the background is necessary to determine the speed and trajectory of the ball.

6. Fundamental *features* of the image are *selected* and perhaps computed. *Compression* takes place in that extraneous information, that which is not required for the task at hand (hitting the ball), is filtered out and removed from further processing by the brain.

7. The position and internal data of the batter himself are *registered* and *linked* to the image.   The complexity of this step is extreme in that the new knowledge concerning the image must be combined with the batter's self-knowledge of himself, including his own inertial system.

8. The total image must be *classified*; for example, the type of pitch, such as a curve ball, fast ball, or slider, must be determined.

9. A *decision*, or a complex of decisions, must be made, for example, to swing or not to swing, where to swing, and how hard to swing.

To fully appreciate the enomity of the task faced by any vision system, one should recognize that each of these stages consists of numerous substages, all to be accomplished in less than a second!

To begin with, let us consider a specific approach to the construction of a computer vision system.   Since an imitation of human intelligence is a stated goal, it is most natural to view the automated vision system as some sort of replication of our own human vision system.   Indeed, the attitude we adopt in framing mathematical categories relating to image intelligence naturally results from reflection on those categories which occur naturally within ourselves.   Image understanding, as we simulate it in logicomathematical systems, is bound to employ categories that are defined in terms of shape, texture, orientation, edge demarcation, area, length, and relative position, to name a few.

The human vision system is not passive. The brain takes the raw sensory data and transorms it into percepts which correspond to mental conceptual categories. The "real" image, if such a thing can even be given meaning, is not a subject of mental analysis. It is the percepts formed by the brain which form the material upon which conceptual analysis is performed. Any data that do not conform to the requirements of perceptual organization cannot be processed.

Even when data are organized into perceptions, judgments made by the brain are sometimes internally contradictory. For instance, consider the images in Figure 8.1. It is well known that most people conclude, on first viewing them, that line L_1 is longer than line L_2; however, measurement soon "proves" otherwise. Here we are presented with two contradictory judgments. Although we tend to make the decision that L_1 and L_2 have the same length, we do so in the realization that we are choosing one decision process over another. Even a simple categorical parameter such as length presents perceptual anomalies.

In sum, the sequence of steps running from the initial data collection to the final decision procedure is both long and strewn with pitfalls. The arsenal of mathematical tools necessary for traversing each path is substantial. Moreover, there are many paths, each one leading from a different source to different decision requirements.

Figure 8.2 provides a course breakdown of the stages involved in an image recognizer system. It is certainly not exhaustive of all possibilities, nor are the particular blocks necessarily distinct. Moreover, any individual system may only employ some subcollection of the delineated stages.

The raw data are gathered by an imaging sensor or collection of sensors. The resulting image, which must be created from the data (Figure 8.2, block A), may be Euclidean (continuous) or digital. In the first case, it is represented by some continuously changing level of gray, as in an everyday photograph. If digital processing is to be performed, the image must be digitized: the continuously changing levels of gray, which are represented (in the two-dimensional case) by a function $F(x, y)$ of two real variables, must be approximated by a function $f(i, j)$ of two integer variables. This approximation will no doubt lose some of the quantitative characteristics of the Euclidean image, since $f(i, j)$ is a course replica of $F(x, y)$. The digitized image $f(i, j)$ is said to be a *sampled version* of $F(x, y)$. At once we are confronted by the troublesome sampling problem: the digital image is defined only on a grid within the domain of the image; so how fine a grid is necessary in order not to lose a significant quantity of information? The answer depends upon both the methodology that is eventually to be applied to the digital image and the

Figure 8.1 Two lines of equal length

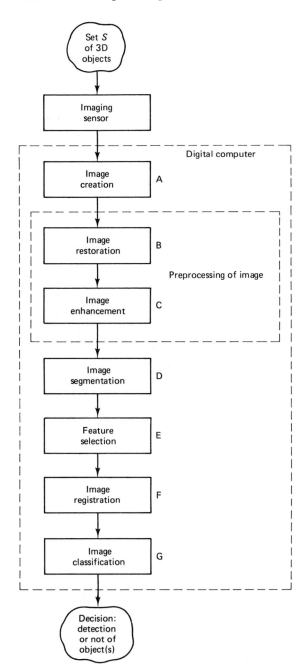

Figure 8.2 Some stages for image recognition systems

fineness of the ultimate decision process.   Figure 8.3 gives a digitization of a signal $f(t)$ (a function of one real variable).

A problem closely related to digitization is quantization.   Given that the range values of both $F(x, y)$ and the digitized version $f(i, j)$ are real numbers, and given that we wish to utilize a discrete range for computer implementation of image processing algorithms, what scale do we choose for the representation of the gray values $f(i, j)$?   Any choice of a uniform discrete scale will require the alteration of actual gray values at the grid points (i, j).   Not only must the direct mathematical representation obtained from the sensor be sampled on a grid, but also the gray values at the sample points must be altered.   Figure 8.4 gives a quantization of a signal.

Once the incoming data have been formed into an image, it will most likely have to be restored or cleaned up (Figure 8.2, block B).   Restoration involves the filtering out of noise, the correction of sensor bias, and perhaps the alteration of the originally created image into one that is more compatible with what is expected. It is at this stage that image processing closely parallels the perception formation inherent in human mental perceptual processes.

Consider the image in Figure 8.5.   At first glance, it appears to be a circle. However, even if we were to grant that the circular part were perfect, there is a tiny hole in it.   In effect, the brain restores the image to one to which its perceptual categories are most responsive.   It has filtered out the noise (the hole) and has interpreted the actual image to be one that it "expects."   If the observer happens to have astigmatism, corrective lenses could be used to correct "sensor" bias.

From the perspective of intelligence, the restoration stage is crucial.   A computer vision system cannot be passive.   More than that, it cannot consist solely of an inference system and a knowledge base.   It must be endowed with heuristics.

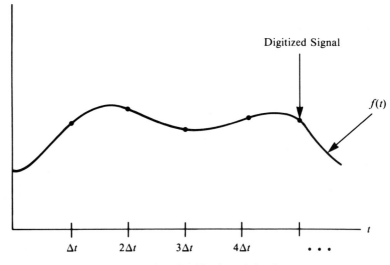

Figure 8.3   Digitization of signal

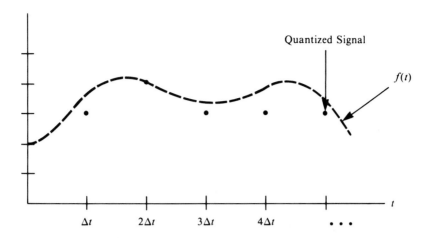

Figure 8.4   Quantization of digitized signal

Its design must be categorical so that it can constitute images that are compatible with its purpose, and its algorithms must be adaptive so that they can be upgraded through the application of statistical techniques.   Restoration must be "smart."

An image may be enhanced prior to further processing (Figure 8.2, block C). That is, features that are of special interest to the problem at hand might be emphasized so that they are more distinctive.   For instance, edges of objects within the image might be singled out or darkened.   Or the background might be eliminated or whitened.   Indeed, as is common, the entire image may be transformed into one that is black and white.

Sometimes it is profitable to segment an image into mutually exclusive pieces that are more amenable to later processing and recognition (Figure 8.2, block D). Curves or shapes of interest might then be located.

In terms of intelligence processing, block E of Figure 8.2 is paramount.   Here features of the image are selected, and it is upon these features, and not on the

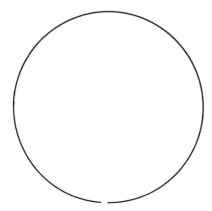

Figure 8.5   Circle with hole

image or enhanced image itself, that decision processing operates. Features are parameters that can be obtained geometrically, statistically, or through the use of transform techniques. The selected features represent those aspects of the image that we believe to be useful for characterization. The methodology for feature parameter construction is as extensive as that of the mathematical apparatus that can be brought to bear on the image. The features may involve parameters such as boundary length or area from geometry, Fourier coefficients from projection theory, moments from statistics, size distributions from morphology, or some combination of these together with a host of others. Indeed, it is common to consider a feature vector, that is, a collection of feature parameters, rather than simply a single feature.

Since the sensor itself does not represent an absolute frame of reference, its relevant aspects, such as velocity and attitude, must be registered (Figure 8.2, block F). Thus, just as a human observer must take him- or herself into account, so too must the attributes of the sensor be accounted for.

Once a feature vector has been judiciously selected and the parameters computed, the vector can be compared to some archetypal vector in the knowledge base to see whether the parameters are sufficiently close to make an identification based upon the features under consideration (Figure 8.2, block G). A categorical decision must be made as to what features are to be utilized and what norming operation is to be employed in the comparison. These decisions must be made prior to any actual feature calculation. Should there be no archetypal vector forms in the knowledge base corresponding to the observational feature vector under consideration, no decision can be made. On the other hand, if there are vector forms present in the knowledge base which correspond to the given feature vector, then classification can take place. That is, based on the feature vector of the observed image and a comparison of it with vectors in the knowledge base, the image can be classified. Notice that this classification is inherently uncertain. It is highly unlikely that a perfect match will be obtained and, even if it were, some uncertainty would still remain. Nevertheless, we must depend on the features we have chosen. Based on them, a detection decision must be made which, in the end, may be no decision at all.

Figures 8.6(a) through (d) give a visual indication of the manner in which an original image, Figure 8.6(a), can be processed to give varying outputs.

The preceding analysis of a typical image recognizer system leads us to consider four levels of transformations that appear in image processing:

Level 0   Image representation
Level 1   Image-to-image transformations
Level 2   Image-to-parameter transformations
Level 3   Parameter-to-decision transformations

We will consider each level in turn.

(a)

(b)

(c)

(d)

Figure 8.6 Image with various processing styles

Level 0 consists of digitization and quantization transformations. Suppose $F(x, y)$ is a real-valued function of two real variables. Then a digitizing operation $F \to f$, where f is a real-valued function on a square grid of lattice points in R^2, the Euclidean plane, is a level 0 transformation. Similarly, a quantization of the range of f to yield a function f_0 whose range is some equally spaced discrete subset of R would also be a level 0 transformation.

We might also wish to invert a digitization, that is, construct a Euclidean image from one that is digital. A reconstruction of this type goes to the heart of the sampling problem: what is the relationship between the original Euclidean image and the reconstructed image if no intermediate processing has occurred? More generally, suppose that the Euclidean image is processed by means of transformations that output only Euclidean images, and that a digitization of the original image is processed by digital analogues of the Euclidean processes. If a Euclidean image is constructed from the final output of the digital processing, what is its relationship to the final output of the Euclidean processing? Figure 8.7 provides a schematic of this more general digitization problem. Suffice it to say that the problem is one of the most profound in image processing.

Level 1 transformations are those that take images as inputs and yield an image output that is of the same type as the input images (i.e., continuous goes to continuous and digital goes to digital). Although there might be auxiliary real-number or vector inputs, the operations are essentially image to image. It is at level 1 that most processing takes place. Restoration, enhancement, segmentation, and some types of feature selection (see Figure 8.2) are level 1 operations. It is these operations that are most commonly associated with image processing in the everyday world. However, while it is possible to use entire images in the classification problem, proceeding in such a manner is not likely to be fruitful, at least

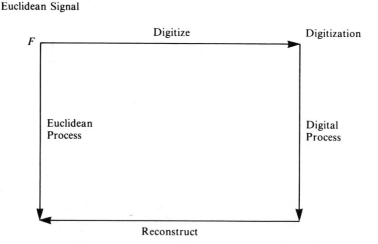

Figure 8.7   Commutative diagram for digitization

in a real-time situation.   Accordingly, we must concern ourselves with level 2 operations.

Level 2 operations involve the production of feature parameters.   Consequently, these operations are image to parameter.   Since it is the feature parameters that are utilized in the eventual intelligence processing, the mathematical properties satisfied by the parameters are of supreme importance.   Not only must we know how they behave in and of themselves, but it is also useful to know the extent to which a specific set of parameters characterizes a particular problem.   Furthermore, a couple of important questions present themselves: Is there some number of parameters that jointly prove sufficient for identification given some criterion that must be met? and Is there some parameter or set of parameters that is best for the task relative to some measure of goodness?

Decision takes place at level 3, where some sort of logic, in the form of rules, is employed to render a judgment.   The decision process can utilize propositional, predicate, fuzzy, or any other formal calculus, and it will be applied to the feature parameters resulting from level 2 operations.

In the remainder of this chapter, we will briefly discuss some methodologies that are commonly employed for the extraction of information from images.   The emphasis will be on level 1 and level 2 transformations.   Our intention is to illustrate some methodologies while at the same time providing some insight into the general problems inherent in the processing of images and the construction of a computer vision system.

8.2 THRESHOLDING AND FILTERING

One of the most useful methods for extracting a figure or a feature of particular interest from an image is to apply the method of thresholding.   The *threshold* operator produces a black and white image in which the object of interest is black and the background is white.   It does so by producing a *binary* image, one where there are only two gray values, 0 (white) and 1 (black).   (There might also be stars but these are not affected by thresholding.)   Numerous variants of the operator are in use; nevertheless, the essential methodology can be demonstrated with one underlying definition.

Consider the image f given by the bound matrix in Figure 8.8 and sketched in Figure 8.9.   In both figures the gray-level quantization runs from 0 through 8, where 0 represents white and 8 represents black.   To *threshold* the image f at the value 7 is to *white out* (set the value equal to 0) all pixels with a gray value less than 7 and to *blacken* (set the value equal to 1) all pixels with a gray value greater than or equal to 7.   The resulting image (Figure 8.10) has only two gray values, 0 and 1, where a dash (—) has been used in place of the numeral 0 to make the resulting image more distinguishable to the human eye.   The letter H is clearly discernible in the thresholded image.   It is important to note that, whereas the dashes are part of the image and denote the gray value 0, the stars (*) are not in

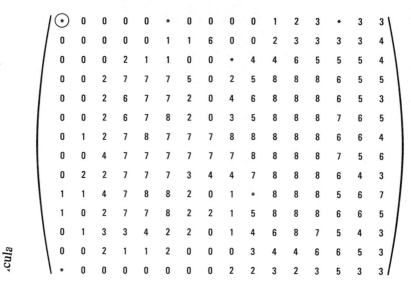

$$\begin{pmatrix}
\circledast & 0 & 0 & 0 & 0 & * & 0 & 0 & 0 & 0 & 1 & 2 & 3 & * & 3 & 3 \\
0 & 0 & 0 & 0 & 0 & 1 & 1 & 6 & 0 & 0 & 2 & 3 & 3 & 3 & 3 & 4 \\
0 & 0 & 0 & 2 & 1 & 1 & 0 & 0 & * & 4 & 4 & 6 & 5 & 5 & 5 & 4 \\
0 & 0 & 2 & 7 & 7 & 7 & 5 & 0 & 2 & 5 & 8 & 8 & 8 & 6 & 5 & 5 \\
0 & 0 & 2 & 6 & 7 & 7 & 2 & 0 & 4 & 6 & 8 & 8 & 8 & 6 & 5 & 3 \\
0 & 0 & 2 & 6 & 7 & 8 & 2 & 0 & 3 & 5 & 8 & 8 & 8 & 7 & 6 & 5 \\
0 & 1 & 2 & 7 & 8 & 7 & 7 & 7 & 8 & 8 & 8 & 8 & 8 & 6 & 6 & 4 \\
0 & 0 & 4 & 7 & 7 & 7 & 7 & 7 & 7 & 8 & 8 & 8 & 8 & 7 & 5 & 6 \\
0 & 2 & 2 & 7 & 7 & 7 & 3 & 4 & 4 & 7 & 8 & 8 & 8 & 6 & 4 & 3 \\
1 & 1 & 4 & 7 & 8 & 8 & 2 & 0 & 1 & * & 8 & 8 & 8 & 5 & 6 & 7 \\
1 & 0 & 2 & 7 & 7 & 8 & 2 & 2 & 1 & 5 & 8 & 8 & 8 & 6 & 6 & 5 \\
0 & 1 & 3 & 3 & 4 & 2 & 2 & 0 & 1 & 4 & 6 & 8 & 7 & 5 & 4 & 3 \\
0 & 0 & 2 & 1 & 1 & 2 & 0 & 0 & 0 & 3 & 4 & 4 & 6 & 6 & 5 & 3 \\
* & 0 & 0 & 0 & 0 & 0 & 0 & 0 & 2 & 2 & 3 & 2 & 3 & 5 & 3 & 3
\end{pmatrix}$$

Figure 8.8 Letter H hidden in image

the domain of the image and starred pixels are not involved in the thresholding operation. They are invariant.

The fundamental thresholding operation is a binary operation. The inputs are an image f and a real number t. The output is a pure black and white image without intermediate gray values. Notationally, the thresholded image is denoted

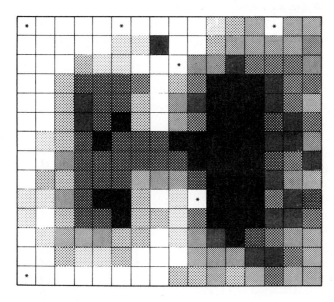

Figure 8.9 Picture of letter H in image

by THRESH($f; t$).   It is a binary image and is defined by

$$[\text{THRESH}(f \; ; \; t)](i, j) = \begin{cases} 1, & \text{if } f(i, j) \geq t \\ 0, & \text{if } f(i, j) < t \\ *, & \text{if } f(i, j) = * \end{cases}$$

The block diagram is given by

$$f \longrightarrow \boxed{\qquad \text{THRESH} \qquad} \longrightarrow \text{THRESH}(f; t)$$
$$t \longrightarrow$$

Much can be learned about thresholding in particular, and image processing in general, by studying THRESH(f; 7) as it has been applied to the image f in Figure 8.10.   First note the stars.   These occur at pixels where the sensor has yielded no information.   Starred pixels are not in the domain of the image any more than pixels that are outside the representing bound matrix.

Second, note the two white (zero-valued) pixels at the upper left of the letter H in the thresholded image of Figure 8.10.   These originally had the gray value 6, a fairly dark value, but were whitened due to the choice of 7 as the threshold input.   Overall it can be seen that the right side of the image f is darker than the left side.   This seeming distortion might be due to sensor bias, reflected light, or garbled data transmission, to name a few possibilities.

Analogous to the loss of two pixels in the letter H on the left, there are six extra black pixels on the right.   Whereas the lost pixels on the left could be recovered by thresholding at $t = 6$, all but one on the right could be removed by

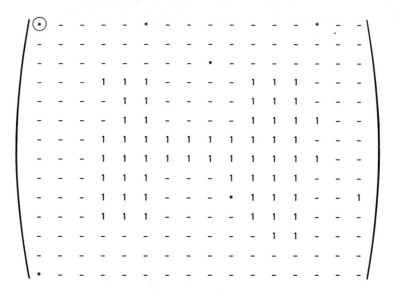

Figure 8.10   THRESH(f;7)

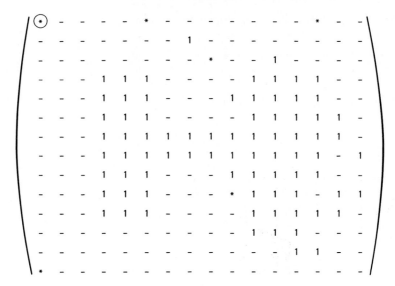

Figure 8.11   THRESH(f;6)

thresholding at $t = 8$. However, the input $t = 7$ appears to be best. Figures 8.11 and 8.12 give the results of thresholding by 6 and 8, respectively. The lower figure creates excess distortion by the inclusion of too many pixels on the right, while the higher figure results in too few pixels on the left.

Even for the apparent best choice of threshold input, the letter H is not output in perfect form. While there are many reasons for such inexactness, some of which

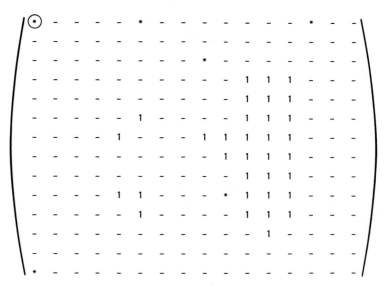

Figure 8.12   THRESH(f;8)

have been pointed out, the phenomenon of fuzzy demarcation is inherent to image processing. Very often gray values appear extreme, in the sense that an intelligent observer would likely conclude that they are out of place in the picture. Such gray-value readings are referred to as *noise*, a term borrowed from signal processing. Noise is a fact of life in image analysis, and its removal is a central problem.

Consider the image f of Figure 8.8 and the subsequent thresholded images of Figures 8.10, 8.11, and 8.12. Those pixels of THRESH(f; 7) that appear to be missing from the letter H in Figure 8.10 might be termed noisy, since an intelligent observer would likely guess the figure in the image to be H. The excess black values on the right would also be classified as noise. In Figure 8.11, the amount of noise might even result in no identification of the figure. Finally, in Figure 8.12 the choice of too great a threshold could easily lead to the conclusion that the image contains the letter I, and that those blackened pixels toward the left are noise due to sensor distortion, interference, or some other unexplained phenomenon.

To give two of the most important properties of the threshold operator, it is necessary to introduce an order relation regarding images defined on the same domain. One says that image g is *less than or equal to* image h if g and h have the same domain, and, for any pixel (i, j) in the common domain, the gray value of g is less than or equal to the gray value of h, or, in functional notation, $g(i, j) \leq h(i, j)$. The notation for the order relation is $g \leq h$. For example, $g \leq h$ in Figure 8.13. Intuitively, every pixel of g is lighter than the corresponding pixel of h.

Given this order relation, the threshold operator satisfies the following properties:

1. $g \leq h$ implies THRESH(g; t) $\leq$ THRESH(h; t)(increasing monotonicity relative to input image).
2. $t \leq s$ implies THRESH(g; s) $\leq$ THRESH(g; t)(decreasing monotonicity relative to input threshold).

Property 1 says that *thresholding* a lighter image *results* in a lighter image. Property 2 states that *thresholding* the same image by a higher threshold *results* in a lighter image.

Another commonly employed operation in image processing is smoothing. Intuitively, *smoothing* refers to any image-to-image operation that tends to flatten the input image by leveling off rapidly fluctuating gray values. In this text, the term will apply to a particular type of averaging operation that is often used to improve the image by reducing the level of noise in the image.

$$g = \begin{pmatrix} 0 & * & 3 & 7 \\ 2 & 2 & 1 & * \\ 1 & 1 & 0 & 3 \end{pmatrix}_{3,2} \qquad h = \begin{pmatrix} 1 & * & 3 & 7 \\ 3 & 5 & 5 & * \\ 1 & 4 & 4 & 4 \end{pmatrix}_{3,2}$$

Figure 8.13   Ordered images

We must now introduce the concept of a *neighborhood*. In general, a neighborhood of a pixel (i, j) is simply a collection of pixels containing (i, j). However, whenever the term is employed, reference will invariably be being made to some predetermined collection of pixel elements. For example, the *square neighborhood* of (i, j), denoted by SQUARE(i, j), refers to (i, j) together with the pixels immediately above, immediately below, at the sides, and at the corners. In coordinate notation,

$$\begin{aligned}\text{SQUARE}(i, j) = \{&(i, j), (i + 1, j), (i - 1, j), (i, j + 1),\\ &(i, j - 1), (i + 1, j + 1), (i - 1, j - 1),\\ &(i + 1, j - 1), (i - 1, j + 1)\}\end{aligned}$$

Pictorially, SQUARE(i, j) is given by

$(i - 1, j + 1)$	$(i, j + 1)$	$(i + 1, j + 1)$
$(i - 1, j)$	(i, j)	$(i + 1, j)$
$(i - 1, j - 1)$	$(i, j - 1)$	$(i + 1, j - 1)$

While many other neighborhoods are utilized, only SQUARE will be specifically named.

Associated with the notion of neighborhood is the concept of a *mask*. A mask is a two-dimensional array of real numbers, one of which will be referred to as the *center*. In Figure 8.14, M is a mask with value $\frac{1}{2}$ at the center.

In fact, a mask is nothing but a bound matrix containing the origin within its domain. Hence it is an image! The reason for introducing the new terminology is the special use to which these particular images will be put. Given a neighborhood, a mask of the same shape can be placed over the neighborhood to *weight* the pixels within it. For example, the preceding mask can be associated with SQUARE(i, j) in such a manner. The intent here is to create a weighting schema that will be utilized in the definition of certain image operations.

The operator SMOOTH will assign to each pixel in an image a weighted average of the gray values in some predefined neighborhood containing the pixel. By doing this, each resulting gray value will tend to be less differentiated from its neighbors than it was originally. The net effect will be an image that is flattened. Rapidly oscillating highs and lows will be mediated. As a result, high-frequency salt-and-pepper noise, a type composed of isolated high-intensity gray-value fluc-

$$M = \begin{pmatrix} \frac{1}{32} & \frac{3}{32} & \frac{1}{32} \\ \frac{3}{32} & \left(\frac{1}{2}\right) & \frac{3}{32} \\ \frac{1}{32} & \frac{3}{32} & \frac{1}{32} \end{pmatrix}$$

Figure 8.14 Image used as a mask

tuations, will be attenuated. However, an unwanted side result will be the blurring of contrast within the image. The distinguishability of features that result from substantial differences in the gray values of surrounding pixels will be reduced.

The operator SMOOTH is a binary operator in that it has two inputs: (1) an image f and (2) a mask M. However, the mask is of a particular type in that its entries must be nonnegative and they must sum to 1. Such a mask will be called an *averaging mask* since its role is to define a weighted average. The mask M of Figure 8.14 is such a mask. SMOOTH is defined by

$$[\text{SMOOTH}(f; M)](i, j) = \sum_{(u, v) \in N} M_{ij}(u, v) \times f(u, v)$$

where N is the neighborhood corresponding to the mask M when the center of M is placed over the pixel (i, j), $M_{ij}(u, v)$ is the mask value at the pixel (u, v) after M has been centered at (i, j), and $f(u, v)$ is the gray value of the image f at (u, v). Intuitively, the value of SMOOTH$(f; M)$ at the pixel (i, j) is the weighted average, the weights given by M, over the M-shaped neighborhood of (i, j), the neighborhood center. The stipulation is made that, if any of the terms of the sum defining SMOOTH$(f; M)$ at (i, j) have a term $f(u, v)$ that is undefined $[f(u, v) = *]$, then SMOOTH will be star valued (undefined) at (i, j).

Example 8.1

Let M be the mask of Figure 8.14 and f be the image given by the bound matrix

$$f = \begin{pmatrix} 0 & 0 & 0 & 0 & 0 & 0 & 0 \\ * & 0 & 0 & 0 & 0 & 0 & 0 \\ 0 & 0 & 8 & 8 & 8 & 0 & 0 \\ 0 & 0 & 8 & 8 & 8 & 0 & 0 \\ 0 & 0 & 8 & 8 & 8 & 0 & 6 \\ 0 & 0 & 0 & 6 & 0 & 6 & 0 \\ 0 & 0 & 6 & 0 & 6 & 0 & 6 \end{pmatrix}_{-3,3}$$

Assuming a gray-scale quantization of 0 through 8, it can clearly be seen that there is a black square in the middle of the image. It can also be seen that there is some high-frequency noise (the 6's) in the lower-right corner of the image. To compute SMOOTH$(f; M)$, the mask is successively placed over the pixels in the domain of f. (The value of SMOOTH must be $*$ at every pixel for which f is undefined, since a $*$ appears in the sum defining SMOOTH in such a situation.) For instance, recalling that the upper-left entry of the bound matrix is situated at $(-3, 3)$, we can see that $f(1, -1) = 8$ and that, when f is restricted to SQUARE$(1, -1)$, the square neighborhood about $(1, -1)$, the restricted portion of f takes the form

$$f' = \begin{pmatrix} 8 & 8 & 0 \\ 8 & 8 & 0 \\ 6 & 0 & 6 \end{pmatrix}_{0,0}$$

According to the definition of SMOOTH, the gray values of f' are multiplied times

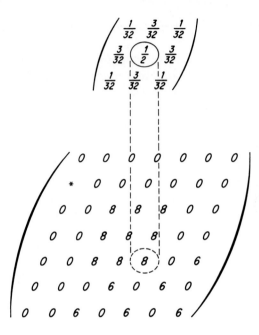

Figure 8.15 Use of mask in smooth

the corresponding values of M and the sum is taken.   As a result

$$[\text{SMOOTH}(f;\ M)](1,\ -1) = (\tfrac{1}{32} \times 8) + (\tfrac{3}{32} \times 8) + (\tfrac{1}{32} \times 0)$$
$$+ (\tfrac{3}{32} \times 8) + (\tfrac{1}{2} \times 8) + (\tfrac{3}{32} \times 0)$$
$$+ (\tfrac{1}{32} \times 6) + (\tfrac{3}{32} \times 0) + (\tfrac{1}{32} \times 6)$$
$$= 6\tfrac{1}{8}$$

Pictorially, we can view the mask M over f as in Figure 8.15.

Proceeding with the calculation for the remaining pixels in the domain of f, we obtain the following bound matrix for SMOOTH$(f;\ M)$:

$$
\begin{pmatrix}
* & * & * & * & * & * & * \\
* & * & 1 & 1\tfrac{1}{4} & 1 & \tfrac{1}{4} & * \\
* & * & 5\tfrac{3}{4} & 6\tfrac{3}{4} & 5\tfrac{3}{4} & 1 & * \\
* & 1\tfrac{1}{4} & 6\tfrac{3}{4} & 8 & 6\tfrac{3}{4} & 1\tfrac{7}{16} & * \\
* & 1 & 5\tfrac{15}{16} & 7\tfrac{5}{16} & 6\tfrac{1}{8} & 2\tfrac{1}{8} & * \\
* & \tfrac{7}{16} & 2\tfrac{1}{8} & 4\tfrac{5}{8} & 2\tfrac{11}{16} & 3\tfrac{13}{16} & * \\
* & * & * & * & * & * & *
\end{pmatrix}_{-3,\ 3}
$$

There are two points to notice. First, the outer columns and rows of the image have been lost because the mask centered at these pixels must contain star-valued pixels. There is also a loss of gray values at $(-2, 1)$ and $(-2, 2)$ resulting from the intrusion of a $*$ value at $(-3, 2)$ of the original image. Although in this instance the loss of information does not seem crucial, a repeated use of SMOOTH would eventually decimate the square figure.

The second point concerns the behavior of SMOOTH in terms of flattening. The noisy pixels have had their gray values substantially reduced, but at the cost of a less clear demarcation between the square in the center of the image and its background. The problem can perhaps best be illustrated by applying THRESH to both f and $SMOOTH(f; M)$. If THRESH is applied to f with threshold $t = 7$, then the square is extracted perfectly. However, with the threshold value lowered only to $t = 6$, THRESH applied to the smoothed image yields

$$\text{THRESH[SMOOTH}(f;M);6] = \begin{pmatrix} * & - & - & - & - \\ * & - & 1 & - & - \\ - & 1 & 1 & 1 & - \\ - & - & 1 & 1 & - \\ - & - & - & - & - \end{pmatrix}_{-2,2}$$

where the bound matrix has been put in minimal form. While the smoothing operation has eliminated noise, it has also altered the content of the image beyond recognition. We might argue that there is no need to smooth since the square is clearly delineated with a threshold value of 7. However, suppose the original threshold value had been 6. In other words, suppose we did not know the figure to begin with (the actual situation confronted in practice). Then an original threshold at 6 would have yielded a noisy binary image:

$$\text{THRESH}(f; 6) = \begin{pmatrix} - & - & - & - & - & - & - \\ * & - & - & - & - & - & - \\ - & - & 1 & 1 & 1 & - & - \\ - & - & 1 & 1 & 1 & - & - \\ - & - & 1 & 1 & 1 & - & 1 \\ - & - & - & 1 & - & 1 & - \\ - & - & 1 & - & 1 & - & 1 \end{pmatrix}_{-3,3}$$

In other words, thresholding at $t = 6$ would have made recognition impossible, but so would have smoothing by M and then thresholding at $t = 6$.

Example 8.1 illustrates the hurdle one faces when attempting to apply SMOOTH. In return for a flattening of high-frequency noise, there is a loss of sharpness within the image. However, the problem goes well beyond the specific operator being discussed.

SMOOTH is an example of a class of operators known as space-invariant, moving-average filters. The output image generated by SMOOTH is constructed by taking weighted averages over varying portions of the input image. Hence the term *average* is most appropriate. However, even when a similar procedure is used without employing an averaging mask, the same terminology is applied. Regarding the *space-invariant* phraseology, this relates to the constancy of the mask. The same mask is used for each gray-level computation. To be precise, a space-invariant moving-average filter is an operator of the following form:

$$[\text{FILTER}(f; M)](i, j) = \sum_{(u, v) \in N} [\text{TRAN}(M; i, j)](u, v) \times f(u, v)$$

where $\text{TRAN}(M; i, j)$ is the mask M translated so that its center lies at (i, j), and N is the domain of the translated mask. As with SMOOTH, the stipulation is made that all terms in the defining sum must be defined or else the output is $*$ (undefined). If M happens to be an averaging mask, then the preceding definition coincides with the definition of SMOOTH.

SMOOTH can be considered to be a *low-pass filter* in that it attenuates high frequencies (rapidly fluctuating gray values). To be a bit more precise, a low-pass filter transmits with relatively little alteration an input image that fluctuates slowly with respect to pixel changes, but it levels out an input image that fluctuates rapidly with respect to such changes. On the other hand, a *high-pass filter* has the reverse effect. It alters little a rapidly fluctuating input image but accentuates changes in a slowly changing image. Each type has its advantages and drawbacks. A low-pass filter reduces high-frequency noise at the cost of blurring contrast.

Example 8.2

Consider the mask M and the image f given, respectively, by

$$M = \begin{pmatrix} 0 & -1 & 0 \\ -1 & \circledast & -1 \\ 0 & -1 & 0 \end{pmatrix}$$

and

$$f = \begin{pmatrix} 0 & \dot{0} & 0 & 0 & 0 & 0 & 0 \\ 0 & 1 & 1 & 1 & 1 & 1 & 0 \\ 0 & 1 & 2 & 2 & 2 & 1 & 0 \\ 0 & 1 & 2 & 2 & 2 & 1 & 0 \\ 0 & 1 & 2 & 2 & 2 & 1 & 0 \\ 0 & 1 & 1 & 1 & 1 & 1 & 0 \\ 0 & 0 & 0 & 0 & 0 & 0 & 0 \end{pmatrix}_{-3,3}$$

Filtering f by using M yields

$$\text{FILTER}(f; M) = \begin{pmatrix} 6 & 4 & 4 & 4 & 6 \\ 4 & 10 & 9 & 10 & 4 \\ 4 & 9 & 8 & 9 & 4 \\ 4 & 10 & 9 & 10 & 4 \\ 6 & 4 & 4 & 4 & 6 \end{pmatrix}_{-2,2}$$

Assuming the gray-scale quantization to run from 0 to 31, it might be difficult to distinguish the square of gray value 2 in the middle of f. Not only would it be difficult for the eye to detect, but a threshold parameter t would have to be chosen in the range $1 < t \leq 2$, a very small range considering the gray range of 0 to 31. Filtering with the mask M has increased the contrast between the 3 by 3 square and its surrounding pixels. Notice, however, the seemingly noisy pixels at the corners of the image and the new gray-level variation introduced into the square. The square has been more markedly revealed at the cost of some loss of intensity uniformity and the introduction of some noise. The full impact of the dilemma is demonstrated by filtering f with the mask N, where

$$N = \begin{pmatrix} 0 & -2 & 0 \\ -2 & \textcircled{10} & -2 \\ 0 & -2 & 0 \end{pmatrix}$$

In this case we obtain

$$\text{FILTER}(f; N) = \begin{pmatrix} 6 & 2 & 2 & 2 & 6 \\ 2 & 8 & 6 & 8 & 2 \\ 2 & 6 & 4 & 6 & 2 \\ 2 & 8 & 6 & 8 & 2 \\ 6 & 2 & 2 & 2 & 6 \end{pmatrix}_{-2,2}$$

Filtering with N has introduced enough noise to destroy the figure of the square. Indeed, thresholding with $t = 6$ gives

$$\text{THRESH[FILTER}(f; N); 6] = \begin{pmatrix} 1 & - & - & - & 1 \\ - & 1 & 1 & 1 & - \\ - & 1 & - & 1 & - \\ - & 1 & 1 & 1 & - \\ 1 & - & - & - & 1 \end{pmatrix}_{-2,2}$$

while thresholding with $t = 7$ yields

$$\text{THRESH [SMOOTH}(f; M); 6] = \begin{pmatrix} * & -- & - & - & - \\ * & - & 1 & - & - \\ - & 1 & 1 & 1 & - \\ - & - & 1 & 1 & - \\ - & - & - & - & - \end{pmatrix}_{-2,2}$$

Example 8.2 has once again shown the problematic nature of space-invariant, moving-average filters. The situation can be improved somewhat by removing the requirement of space invariance. Instead of utilizing a single mask and translating it to the pixel at which it is needed, one can define a collection of masks, each to be used at a specific pixel or set of pixels within the image domain. For example, if the sensor equipment is such that one portion of the image is usually noisy while the rest is not, we need only smooth on the noisy portion while leaving the rest of the image alone.

To facilitate the operator FILTER, we introduce the level 2 operator DOT. This new operator is defined as follows:

1. If f and g have a common domain D, then

$$\text{DOT}(f, g) = \sum_{(u, v) \in D} f(u, v) \times g(u, v)$$

2. If f and g do not have the same domain, then

$$\text{DOT}(f, g) = * \quad \text{(is undefined)}$$

Example 8.3

Consider images f, g, and h defined, respectively, by

$$f = \begin{pmatrix} 1 & 3 & 4 \\ 2 & 1 & 0 \end{pmatrix}_{2,0}, \qquad g = \begin{pmatrix} 1 & * & 2 \\ 5 & 3 & 1 \end{pmatrix}_{2,0}, \qquad h = \begin{pmatrix} 2 & 1 & 0 \\ 5 & 1 & 6 \end{pmatrix}_{2,0}$$

Then $\text{DOT}(f, g) = *$ since $(3, 0)$ is in the domain of f but not in the domain of g. On the other hand,

$$\text{DOT}(f, h) = (1 \times 2) + (3 \times 1) + (4 \times 0)$$
$$+ (2 \times 5) + (1 \times 1) + (0 \times 6) = 16$$

To compute the value of $\text{FILTER}(f; M)$ at pixel (i, j), simply "place the center of the mask over (i, j)" and apply DOT to the translated mask and that portion of f that lies beneath it. This will produce the defining sum for $[\text{FILTER}(f; M)](i, j)$.

8.3 GRADIENT-TYPE EDGE DETECTION

The organization of visual sensory data into patterns is an integral part of human perception. Very often these patterns consist of regions defined by some form of homogeneity with respect to the data. This homogeneity might result from the existence of regions having constant, or essentially constant, gray levels. It might also result from textural properties of regions within the overall image. In either event, it might be possible to segment the image according to a definable homogeneic characteristic. For example, in thresholding, an effort is made to segment the image into *figure and ground* by a judicious choice of threshold value. In doing so, we are considering the degree of darkness, in a bilevel sense, as a measure of homogeneity. If an image happens to contain two figures within it that are both measurably darker than the background, thresholding can detect both of them. However, if one is darker than the background while the other is lighter, then the single application of a simple operator such as THRESH will not detect both. In general, the situation is far more complex than simply the occurrence of two gray-level homogeneous figures.

Figure 8.16 gives an image f together with a pictorial representation. The letter E is discernible to the eye in the picture; however, it would not be discovered by a thresholding operation. The eye is sensitive to the local contrast between dark and light. It discerns the E due to such contrast. On the other hand, an operator such as THRESH takes a global view of the gray-level variation. The image of Figure 8.16 has an *illumination gradient*; it is darker on the top and lighter on the bottom. Hence it is not receptive to a global thresholding. Yet this is precisely the situation often encountered in practice. Although it might be feasible to obtain uniform illumination in a restricted setting such as a laboratory or factory, it is not so feasible in a natural setting. Thresholding might still play a role under

$$
f = \begin{pmatrix}
7 & 7 & 7 & 6 & 7 & 6 & 7 & 7 & 5 \\
7 & 9 & 9 & 9 & 9 & 9 & 9 & 9 & 6 \\
6 & 9 & 8 & 9 & 8 & 8 & 9 & 8 & 6 \\
6 & 8 & 8 & 8 & 6 & 6 & 6 & 5 & 6 \\
5 & 9 & 8 & 8 & 6 & 6 & 5 & 5 & 6 \\
5 & 7 & 8 & 8 & 5 & 5 & 5 & 5 & 6 \\
5 & 7 & 7 & 8 & 7 & 8 & 7 & 5 & 5 \\
4 & 7 & 7 & 7 & 7 & 7 & 7 & 5 & 4 \\
4 & 7 & 6 & 7 & 4 & 5 & 5 & 4 & 5 \\
4 & 6 & 6 & 6 & 4 & 4 & 4 & 3 & 4 \\
3 & 6 & 5 & 6 & 3 & 3 & 2 & 3 & 3 \\
3 & 5 & 5 & 6 & 6 & 5 & 5 & 5 & 3 \\
2 & 5 & 4 & 5 & 6 & 5 & 4 & 4 & 2 \\
2 & 2 & 1 & 1 & 2 & 2 & 2 & 1 & 2
\end{pmatrix}_{2,\,6}
$$

(a)

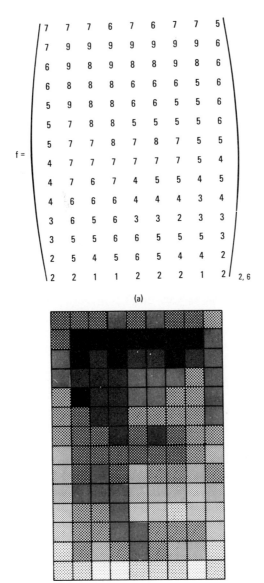

(b)

Figure 8.16   Image with hidden letter E

the latter circumstances, but it must certainly be preceded by some other type of processing.

It is through the use of *edge-detection* techniques that local contrast differences can be determined. Intuitively, an edge is a zone of demarcation between two regions that differ according to some measure of homogeneity. If we consider local gray-level intensity as such a measure, then the letter E in Figure 8.16 differs from its ground accordingly.   If we focus our attention on gray level and ignore texture, then an edge may occur in essentially two ways:

1. As the border between two differing regions, each region being homogeneous with regard to some homogeneity criterion.
2. As a thin, dark *arc* on a light background, or a thin, light arc on a dark background.

The intent here is to input an image and output another image, the latter being a thin figure that represents the edge of whatever object lies within the input image.

The term *thin* must be taken in a relative sense when dealing with edges. While the border between two regions might be representable as a *curve* of single pixels, it might also be a region of transition.   Indeed, such a situation is quite common.   Imagine a dark figure against a light background where there is some thin region of gray-level gradation between them.   Even though this region of gradation might be several pixels wide, it might still be termed an *edge*.   Indeed, it would appear so to the human eye.   In other words, while the intent in edge detection is the formation of "stick figures" that represent the borders of homogeneous regions, sufficient latitude in terminology must be allowed to include "wide" edges.   It is for this reason that the term *curve* is not used interchangeably with the term *edge*.   Whereas the former is precisely defined, the latter is used somewhat loosely.

If two adjacent regions exist within an image that differ substantially with respect to gray level at the edge between them, then the computation of a rate of change with respect to gray level can help to determine the edge.   What is required is a difference operator that measures the rate of change of gray levels.   The value of this operator will be zero on constant domains within the image and vary according to the rate of gray-level fluctuation elsewhere.   For those who have had a course in calculus, a *difference operator* is a digital analogue of a differential operator.

The simplest such operators measure the digital rate of gray-level change in either the horizontal or vertical direction.   These are the *partial difference operators*.   The first measures the rate of gray level change in the *x* direction, and the second measures the rate of gray-level change in the *y* direction.   They are the digital analogues of the partial derivative operators from calculus.   They are defined respectively by

$$[DX(f)](i, j) = \begin{cases} f(i, j) - f(i - 1, j), & \text{if } f \text{ is defined at} \\ & (i, j) \text{ and } (i - 1, j) \\ *, & \text{otherwise} \end{cases}$$

and

$$[DY(f)](i, j) = \begin{cases} f(i, j) - f(i, j - 1), & \text{if } f \text{ is defined at} \\ & (i, j) \text{ and } (i, j - 1) \\ *, & \text{otherwise} \end{cases}$$

At each pixel, DX yields the difference between the gray level at the pixel and the gray level at the adjacent pixel to the left, while DY yields the difference between the gray level at the pixel and the gray level at the adjacent pixel beneath. DX is useful for the location of vertical edges and DY is useful for the location of horizontal edges.   The block diagram for DX is given by

$$f \longrightarrow \boxed{\text{DX}} \longrightarrow \text{DX}(f)$$

DY has a similar block diagram.

Example 8.4

Let

$$f = \begin{pmatrix} * & 4 & 4 & 1 & 0 & 1 \\ 4 & 5 & 4 & 1 & 1 & 2 \\ 5 & 4 & 5 & 2 & 1 & 2 \\ 6 & 6 & 6 & 2 & 3 & 2 \\ 6 & 7 & 6 & 3 & 3 & * \\ 7 & 7 & 7 & 3 & 4 & 4 \\ 8 & 7 & 7 & 4 & 4 & 5 \end{pmatrix}_{0,\,6}$$

Application of the partial difference operator DX gives the output

$$\text{DX}(f) = \begin{pmatrix} * & * & 0 & -3 & -1 & 1 \\ * & 1 & -1 & -3 & 0 & 1 \\ * & -1 & 1 & -3 & -1 & 1 \\ * & 0 & 0 & -4 & 1 & -1 \\ * & 1 & -1 & -3 & 0 & * \\ * & 0 & 0 & -4 & 1 & 0 \\ * & -1 & 0 & -3 & 0 & 1 \end{pmatrix}_{0,\,6}$$

Some illustrations of how the gray values of the output have been calculated are

$$[\text{DX}(f)](1, 5) = 5 - 4 = 1$$

$$[\text{DX}(f)](2, 5) = 4 - 5 = -1$$

$$[\text{DX}(f)](3, 5) = 1 - 4 = -3$$

$$[\text{DX}(f)](5, 2) = *, \qquad \text{since } f(5, 2) = *$$

$$[\text{DX}(f)](0, 0) = *, \qquad \text{since } f(-1, 0) = *$$

For the same f, DY gives

$$\text{DY}(f) = \begin{pmatrix} * & -1 & 0 & 0 & -1 & -1 \\ -1 & 1 & -1 & -1 & 0 & 0 \\ -1 & -2 & -1 & 0 & -2 & 0 \\ 0 & -1 & 0 & -1 & 0 & * \\ -1 & 0 & -1 & 0 & -1 & * \\ -1 & 0 & 0 & -1 & 0 & -1 \\ * & * & * & * & * & * \end{pmatrix}_{0,\,6}$$

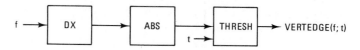

Figure 8.17   Block diagram of VERTEDGE

Much can be learned about the use of difference operators in image processing by examining the outputs in Example 8.4.   For instance, DX has revealed a vertical edge.   In terms of absolute value, the greatest differences show up in the fourth column of the bound matrix representing DX(f).   These differences, which happen to be negative, result from the contrast of dark to light in the original image f that occurs between the third and fourth columns of the bound matrix representing f. The negativity of these extreme values results from the left-to-right shift of dark-to-light intensity.

Since the occurrence of an edge does not depend on the direction of the contrasting intensities, DX should be used in conjunction with the absolute value operator ABS and the thresholding operator THRESH to produce the desired thin figure.   The edge is then represented in a black and white image.   In other words, the edge-detection operator associated with DX is defined by the block diagram in Figure 8.17.   In the sequel it will be denoted by VERTEDGE.   It requires two inputs, an image and a threshold value t.   Applied to the preceding image f with threshold value $t = 3$, VERTEDGE outputs the image

$$VERTEDGE(f;\ 3) = \begin{pmatrix} * & * & - & 1 & - & - \\ * & - & - & 1 & - & - \\ * & - & - & 1 & - & - \\ * & - & - & 1 & - & - \\ * & - & - & 1 & - & * \\ * & - & - & 1 & - & - \\ * & - & - & 1 & - & - \end{pmatrix}_{0,\ 6}$$

The edge has been detected even though there is an obvious illumination gradient running top to bottom and light to dark.

The application of DY has produced no edge.   This can be seen by the application of a detection sequence analogous to the one for DX.   This sequence will be denoted HOREDGE and is given by the same block diagram as that for VERTEDGE except DY is used instead of DX.   Nevertheless, DY does give some useful information regarding the image f of Example 8.4.   All gray values of DY(f) are less than or equal to zero except for one.   This results from a process of increasing darkness as the pixels go from the top down.   DY has revealed the illumination gradient!

A severe problem with any partial difference approach to edge detection is the extreme sensitivity of partial difference operators to noise.   Indeed, consider the insertion of a single noise pixel into the image f that we have been discussing.

For example, suppose $f(4, 4) = 9$, instead of $f(4, 4) = 1$, as originally given. Such a change would produce a third row of the output bound matrix for DX as follows:

$$* \quad -1 \quad 1 \quad -3 \quad 7 \quad -7$$

Therefore, the output of VERTEDGE would be

$$\begin{pmatrix}
* & - & 1 & - & - \\
- & - & 1 & - & - \\
- & - & 1 & 1 & 1 \\
- & - & 1 & - & - \\
- & - & 1 & - & * \\
- & - & 1 & - & - \\
- & - & 1 & - & -
\end{pmatrix}_{1,6}$$

Hence the vertical edge would be distorted and an improper stick figure would result. With any significant degree of high-frequency noise, the output image would be of no use. To remedy this sensitivity to high-frequency noise, it is often necessary to smooth an image prior to a partial difference transformation.

Both partial difference operators DX and DY suffer from a dependence on directionality. DX can detect vertical edges and DY can detect horizontal edges. This can be a serious weakness when the desire is to detect *curved* edges, such as the boundary of a circular disk or of an ellipse.

Figure 8.18 gives an image and four edge images computed from it:

(a) Image f
(b) ABS[DX(f)]
(c) ABS[DY(f)]
(d) VERTEDGE(f; 3), which results from thresholding (b) at $t = 3$
(e) HOREDGE(f; 3), which results from thresholding (c) at $t = 3$

The image f represents the digitization of some elliptical shape consisting of similar gray values on a light background. Yet neither the application of DX or DY produces an edge that is elliptical. The application of DX reveals the edge pieces that tend to run vertically, while the application of DY reveals those that tend to run horizontally. Since the major axis of the ellipse lies horizontally, the edge tends to lie horizontally, and therefore DY reveals more than does DX.

To obtain a reasonable edge for the elliptical figure in image f by the use of DX and DY, it is necessary to utilize the difference operators in conjunction with one another so that the resulting operator is independent of directionality. To accomplish this end, we introduce a new operator, the *digital gradient*. The gradient is a different sort of image operator in that it has a single input image and two output images. Given an image f, GRAD(f) is defined by

$$\text{GRAD}(f) = [\text{DX}(f), \text{DY}(f)]$$

$$\text{(a)} \quad f = \begin{pmatrix}
- & - & - & - & 1 & - & - & - & - & - & - \\
- & 1 & 1 & - & 4 & 4 & 4 & - & - & 1 & - \\
- & - & 4 & 4 & 4 & 3 & 4 & 4 & 3 & - & 1 \\
- & 4 & 3 & 4 & 4 & 4 & 4 & 4 & 4 & 4 & - \\
- & 3 & 4 & 4 & 3 & 4 & 4 & 3 & 4 & 3 & - \\
- & - & 4 & 4 & 4 & 4 & 4 & 4 & 4 & - & 1 \\
- & 1 & - & - & 4 & 4 & 3 & - & 1 & - & - \\
1 & - & - & - & - & - & - & - & - & - & 1
\end{pmatrix}_{2,\,4}$$

$$\text{(b)} \quad ABS[DX(f)] = \begin{pmatrix}
* & - & - & - & 1 & 1 & - & - & - & - & - \\
* & 1 & - & 1 & 4 & - & - & 4 & - & 1 & 1 \\
* & - & 4 & - & - & 1 & 1 & - & 1 & 3 & 1 \\
* & 4 & 1 & 1 & - & - & - & - & - & - & 4 \\
* & 3 & 1 & - & 1 & 1 & - & 1 & 1 & 1 & 3 \\
* & - & 4 & - & - & - & - & - & - & 4 & 1 \\
* & 1 & 1 & - & 4 & - & 1 & 3 & 1 & 1 & - \\
* & 1 & - & - & - & - & - & - & - & - & 1
\end{pmatrix}_{2,\,4}$$

$$\text{(c)} \quad ABS[DY(f)] = \begin{pmatrix}
- & 1 & 1 & - & 3 & 4 & 4 & - & - & 1 & - \\
- & 1 & 3 & 4 & - & 1 & - & 4 & 3 & 1 & 1 \\
- & 4 & 1 & - & - & 1 & - & - & 1 & 4 & 1 \\
- & 1 & 1 & - & 1 & - & - & 1 & - & 1 & - \\
- & 3 & - & - & 1 & - & - & 1 & - & 3 & 1 \\
- & 1 & 4 & 4 & - & - & 1 & 4 & 3 & - & 1 \\
1 & 1 & - & - & 4 & 4 & 3 & - & 1 & - & 1 \\
* & * & * & * & * & * & * & * & * & * & *
\end{pmatrix}_{2,\,4}$$

$$\text{(d)} \quad VERTEDGE(f;\,3) = \begin{pmatrix}
* & - & - & - & - & - & - & - & - & - & - \\
* & - & - & - & 1 & - & - & 1 & - & - & - \\
* & - & 1 & - & - & - & - & - & - & 1 & - \\
* & 1 & - & - & - & - & - & - & - & - & 1 \\
* & 1 & - & - & - & - & - & - & - & - & 1 \\
* & - & 1 & - & - & - & - & - & - & 1 & - \\
* & - & - & - & 1 & - & - & 1 & - & - & - \\
* & - & - & - & - & - & - & - & - & - & -
\end{pmatrix}_{2,\,4}$$

Figure 8.18 Image with several associated edge images

$$
\text{(e)}\quad \text{HOREDGE}(f; 3) = \begin{pmatrix}
- & - & - & - & 1 & 1 & 1 & - & - & - & - \\
- & - & 1 & 1 & - & - & - & 1 & 1 & - & - \\
- & 1 & - & - & - & - & - & - & - & 1 & - \\
- & - & - & - & - & - & - & - & - & - & - \\
- & 1 & - & - & - & - & - & - & - & 1 & - \\
- & - & 1 & 1 & - & - & - & 1 & 1 & - & - \\
- & - & - & - & 1 & 1 & 1 & - & - & - & - \\
* & * & * & * & * & * & * & * & * & * & *
\end{pmatrix}_{2,\,4}
$$

Figure 8.18   Continued

In other words, $GRAD(f)$ is an *ordered pair* of images, where the notation [,] is used to denote an ordered pair. In a sense, $GRAD(f)$ is a two-vector in which each component is an image. Several norms will be developed for this vector. Each gives a measure for the degree of overall change of gray level at the pixel at which $GRAD(f)$ is being evaluated.

Given a vector $V = (x, y)$, there are three very common ways of defining the *norm*, or magnitude, of the vector. The first is called the l_∞-norm. It is given by

$$
\|V\|_\infty = \max\{|x|, |y|\}
$$

The second is the l_1-norm. It is given by

$$
\|V\|_1 = |x| + |y|
$$

Finally, there is the l_2-norm, or the usual vector magnitude utilized in elementary calculus. It is given by

$$
\|V\|_2 = (x^2 + y^2)^{1/2}
$$

Each of the three preceding norms can be applied to the gradient vector (DX, DY). The result is three different measures of the magnitude of the gradient (three different measures of the magnitude of the bidirectional gray-value change). In other words, each norm leads to an operator that has a single input image and a single output image, where each pixel of the output image has as its gray value the appropriate gradient magnitude at the corresponding input pixel.

The l_∞-norm leads to the operator GRADMAG0 defined by the block diagram

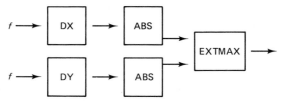

The diagram follows exactly the definition of the l_∞-norm, except that an extended maximum is taken at the end. This is done so that most of the stars resulting from

the application of DX and DY are filled in. Applied to the image f of Figure 8.18, GRADMAG0 yields the output of Figure 8.19(a). In a manner analogous to the application of the partial difference operators, clarity is gained by thresholding the output of GRADMAG0. The result is the edge detector we will call GRADEDGE0. The output of GRADEDGE0 for the image f and the threshold value $t = 3$ is given in Figure 8.19(b).

The l_1-norm leads to the operator GRADMAG1 defined by the block diagram

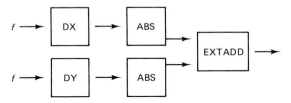

This diagram follows directly from the definition of the l_1-norm. Applied to the image f of Figure 8.18, GRADMAG1 outputs the image of Figure 8.19(c). Once again the gradient magnitude operator output must be thresholded. The result is the edge detector we will refer to as GRADEDGE1. For the image f that we have been considering, GRADEDGE1$(f; 3)$ = GRADEDGE0$(f; 3)$. In general, this is not so. It happens to be so in this case for the threshold value $t = 3$. It should be obvious from looking at the output images GRADMAG0(f) and GRADMAG1(f) that another threshold value might give differing outputs.

Finally, the l_2-norm leads to the operator GRADMAG2 defined by the block diagram

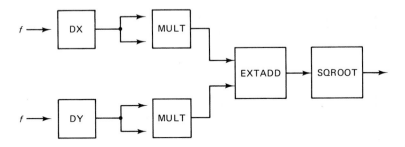

In this diagram, SQROOT is an operator that outputs at each pixel the square root of the corresponding input pixel gray value. The edge detector GRADEDGE2 is obtained by thresholding the output of GRADMAG2. Figure 8.19(d) gives the output GRADMAG2(f) for the input f of Figure 8.18. Once again, thresholding at $t = 3$ gives the image of Figure 8.19(b).

It is possible to view the three preceding gradient edge-detection schemes from a general perspective. We begin this by reexamining the partial difference operators DX and DY. Consider the masks

$$G1 = (-1 \quad \text{①})$$

(a) GRADMAG0(f) = $\begin{pmatrix} - & 1 & 1 & 0 & 3 & 4 & 4 & - & - & 1 & - \\ - & 1 & 3 & 4 & 4 & 1 & - & 4 & 3 & 1 & 1 \\ - & 4 & 4 & - & - & 1 & 1 & - & 1 & 4 & 1 \\ - & 4 & 1 & 1 & 1 & - & - & 1 & - & 1 & 4 \\ - & 3 & 1 & - & 1 & 1 & - & 1 & 1 & 3 & 3 \\ - & 1 & 4 & 4 & - & - & 1 & 4 & 3 & 4 & 1 \\ 1 & 1 & 1 & - & 4 & 4 & 3 & 3 & 1 & 1 & 1 \\ * & 1 & - & - & - & - & - & - & - & - & 1 \end{pmatrix}_{2,\,4}$

(b) GRADEDGE0(f; 3) = $\begin{pmatrix} - & - & - & - & 1 & 1 & 1 & - & - & - & - \\ - & - & 1 & 1 & 1 & - & - & 1 & 1 & - & - \\ - & 1 & 1 & - & - & - & - & - & - & 1 & - \\ - & 1 & - & - & - & - & - & - & - & - & 1 \\ - & 1 & - & - & - & - & - & - & - & 1 & 1 \\ - & - & 1 & 1 & - & - & - & 1 & 1 & 1 & - \\ - & - & - & - & 1 & 1 & 1 & 1 & - & - & - \\ * & - & - & - & - & - & - & - & - & - & - \end{pmatrix}_{2,\,4}$

(c) GRADMAG1(f) = $\begin{pmatrix} - & 1 & 1 & - & 4 & 5 & 4 & - & - & 1 & - \\ - & 2 & 3 & 5 & 4 & 1 & - & 8 & 3 & 2 & 2 \\ - & 4 & 5 & - & - & 2 & 1 & - & 2 & 7 & 2 \\ - & 5 & 2 & 1 & 1 & - & - & 1 & - & 1 & 4 \\ - & 6 & 1 & - & 2 & 1 & - & 2 & 1 & 4 & 4 \\ - & 1 & 8 & 4 & - & - & 1 & 4 & 3 & 4 & 2 \\ 1 & 2 & 1 & - & 8 & 4 & 4 & 3 & 2 & 1 & 1 \\ * & 1 & - & - & - & - & - & - & - & - & 1 \end{pmatrix}_{2,\,4}$

(d) GRADMAG2(f) = $\begin{pmatrix} - & 1 & 1 & - & 3.2 & 4.1 & 4 & - & - & 1 & - \\ - & 1.4 & 9 & 4.1 & 4 & 1 & - & 5.7 & 3 & 1.4 & 1.4 \\ - & 4 & 4.1 & - & - & 1.4 & 1 & - & 1.4 & 5 & 1.4 \\ - & 4.1 & 1.4 & 1 & 1 & - & - & 1 & - & 1 & 4 \\ - & 4.2 & 1 & - & 1.4 & 1 & 1 & 1.4 & 1 & 3.2 & 3.2 \\ - & 1 & 5.7 & 4 & - & - & 1 & 4 & 3 & 4 & 1.4 \\ 1 & 1.4 & 1 & - & 5.7 & 4 & 3.2 & 3 & 1.4 & 1 & 1 \\ * & 1 & - & - & - & - & - & - & - & - & 1 \end{pmatrix}_{2,\,4}$

Figure 8.19   GRADMAG images associated with image in Figure 8.18

and

$$G2 = \begin{pmatrix} ① \\ -1 \end{pmatrix}$$

If we apply the moving-average filter operator FILTER to an image f with input mask $G1$, we obtain at each pixel in the domain of f the output gray value

$$[\text{FILTER}(f; G1)](i, j) = [(-1) \times f(i-1, j)] + [1 \times f(i, j)]$$
$$= f(i, j) - f(i-1, j)$$
$$= [\text{DX}(f)](i, j)$$

Likewise,

$$[\text{FILTER}(f; G2)](i, j) = [\text{DY}(f)](i, j)$$

Hence both partial difference operators can be viewed as filters. Moreover, the first filter measures change in the x direction and the second measures change in the y direction. We refer to the two filters as *gradient filters*.

Once the filtering has been accomplished, one of three norms is applied to the resulting gradient vector. But these norms can be applied to any input image vector, whether or not the components result from filtering. Hence we can consider three norm operators on input image pairs:

1. MAXNORM(f, g)
2. ONENORM(f, g)
3. TWONORM(f, g)

These image norms are defined pixelwise by the vector norms, $\|V\|_\infty$, $\|V\|_1$, and $\|V\|_2$. TWONORM is known as the *root sum square* norm. Depending on heuristic considerations, one of the images, GRADMAG0, GRADMAG1, or GRADMAG2, is employed. The resulting image is thresholded to produce a binary edge image. The entire process is depicted in Figure 8.20, where the operation NORM refers to one of the three previously described magnitude operators.

Of note in Figure 8.20 is the role played by $G1$ and $G2$. These masks determine the gradient measuring to be implemented by the filtering operations. The two filters output a gradient pair, which is then normed and thresholded. We

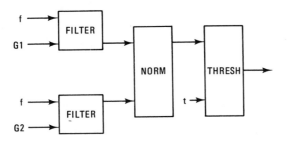

Figure 8.20 Gradient-type edge detector

could obtain a different edge-detection scheme by varying the input masks $G1$ and $G2$. The masks chosen thus far are those defined by the partial difference operators DX and DY. Others are possible.

Consider the *Prewitt masks* given by

$$P1 = \begin{pmatrix} -1 & 0 & 1 \\ -1 & (0) & 1 \\ -1 & 0 & 1 \end{pmatrix}$$

and

$$P2 = \begin{pmatrix} 1 & 1 & 1 \\ 0 & (0) & 0 \\ -1 & -1 & -1 \end{pmatrix}$$

The first Prewitt mask is a variant of the difference operator DX. It is different in that change is measured on both sides of the pixel at which the measure is being taken. It also differs in that the Prewitt gradient measure at pixel (i, j) is affected by the x direction changes one pixel above and one pixel below. This *spreading* of the measure makes the measure less sensitive to noise. The second Prewitt mask is a variant of the difference operator DY. Similar comments apply.

Whereas the usual gradient is defined by

$$\text{GRAD}(f) = [\text{FILTER}(f; G1), \text{FILTER}(f; G2)]$$

the *Prewitt gradient* is given by

$$\text{PREWITT}(f) = [\text{FILTER}(f; P1), \text{FILTER}(f; P2)]$$

In terms of pixel gray values, assuming that all relevant gray values are defined,

$$[\text{FILTER}(f; P1)](i, j) = f(i + 1, j + 1) + f(i + 1, j) + f(i + 1, j - 1)$$
$$- f(i - 1, j + 1) - f(i - 1, j) - f(i - 1, j - 1)$$

and

$$[\text{FILTER}(f; P2)](i, j) = f(i - 1, j + 1) + f(i, j + 1) + f(i + 1, j + 1)$$
$$- f(i - 1, j - 1) - f(i, j - 1) - f(i + 1, j - 1)$$

If, in the edge-detection scheme of Figure 8.20, the Prewitt masks $P1$ and $P2$ are utilized instead of the partial difference masks $G1$ and $G2$, then the three possible output images of NORM will be called PREWMAG0, PREWMAG1, and PREWMAG2, depending on whether the l_∞-norm, the l_1-norm, or the l_2-norm is applied. We will refer to the corresponding outputs of THRESH as PREWEDGE0, PREWEDGE1, and PREWEDGE2. It is helpful to note that we are using the numeric designations 0, 1, and 2 in a fashion consistent with the norming technique applied to the usual gradient GRAD.

Figure 8.21 gives an image f, the image f filtered with respect to both Prewitt masks, and the edge-detection images obtained by finding the three different norms of the Prewitt gradient. Recall that FILTER is obtained by placing the center of the mask over the appropriate pixel and then applying DOT. If all pixels of f under the fitted mask have defined gray values, the output of DOT is defined; otherwise, it is undefined. For instance,

$$[\text{FILTER}(f; P1)](4, -2) = \text{DOT}\left[\begin{pmatrix} -1 & 0 & 1 \\ -1 & 0 & 1 \\ -1 & 0 & 1 \end{pmatrix}_{3, -1} \begin{pmatrix} 4 & 4 & 4 \\ 0 & 4 & 4 \\ 0 & 0 & 3 \end{pmatrix}_{3, -1}\right]$$

$$= -4 + 4 + 4 + 3 = 7$$

Figure 8.21 also gives the thresholded image $\text{PREWEDGE0}(f; 7)$, which has been obtained by using $t = 7$ and applying THRESH to $\text{PREWMAG0}(f)$. Similar thresholded results are obtainable for PREWEDGE1 and PREWEDGE2.

Closely akin to the Prewitt edge detectors are the Sobel edge detectors. These are also produced by the detection scheme of Figure 8.20, the difference being the use of the *Sobel masks* $S1$ and $S2$ in place of the Prewitt masks. The Sobel masks are given by

$$S1 = \begin{pmatrix} -1 & 0 & 1 \\ -2 & \boxed{0} & 2 \\ -1 & 0 & 1 \end{pmatrix}$$

and

$$S2 = \begin{pmatrix} 1 & 2 & 1 \\ 0 & \boxed{0} & 0 \\ -1 & -2 & -1 \end{pmatrix}$$

The *Sobel gradient* is given by

$$\text{SOBEL}(f) = [\text{FILTER}(f; S1), \text{FILTER}(f; S2)]$$

Due to the similarity between the Sobel masks and the Prewitt masks, we will leave the associated gradient edge-detection operators to the exercises. As with the gradient and the Prewitt gradient, there will be three gradient magnitude images and three corresponding edge images.

Many other such gradient-type edge detectors can be created by simply utilizing the scheme of Figure 8.20. We have introduced only the most common. The use of larger masks tends to reduce the effect of noise while spreading the region of detection. Although the first effect is beneficial, the latter might lead to an increased incidence of false detection.

$$(a) \quad f = \begin{pmatrix} - & - & 3 & 4 & 4 & 4 & 4 & 4 & 4 \\ - & - & - & 4 & 4 & 4 & 4 & 4 & 4 \\ - & - & - & - & 4 & 4 & 4 & 4 & 4 \\ - & - & - & - & - & 3 & 4 & 4 & 4 \\ - & - & - & - & - & - & 4 & 4 & 4 \\ - & - & - & - & - & - & - & 4 & 4 \end{pmatrix}_{0,\,0}$$

$$(b) \quad \text{FILTER}(f; P1) = \begin{pmatrix} * & * & * & * & * & * & * & * & * \\ * & 3 & 8 & 9 & 4 & - & - & - & * \\ * & - & 4 & 8 & 7 & 4 & 1 & - & * \\ * & - & - & 4 & 7 & 8 & 5 & - & * \\ * & - & - & - & 3 & 8 & 9 & 4 & * \\ * & * & * & * & * & * & * & * & * \end{pmatrix}_{0,\,0}$$

$$(c) \quad \text{FILTER}(f; P2) = \begin{pmatrix} * & * & * & * & * & * & * & * & * \\ * & 3 & 7 & 7 & 4 & - & - & - & * \\ * & - & 4 & 8 & 9 & 5 & 1 & - & * \\ * & - & - & 4 & 8 & 8 & 4 & - & * \\ * & - & - & - & 3 & 7 & 7 & 4 & * \\ * & * & * & * & * & * & * & * & * \end{pmatrix}_{0,\,0}$$

$$(d) \quad \text{PREWMAG0}(f) = \begin{pmatrix} 3 & 8 & 9 & 4 & - & - & - \\ - & 4 & 8 & 9 & 5 & 1 & - \\ - & - & 4 & 8 & 8 & 5 & - \\ - & - & - & 3 & 8 & 9 & 4 \end{pmatrix}_{1,\,1}$$

$$(e) \quad \text{PREWMAG1}(f) = \begin{pmatrix} 6 & 15 & 16 & 8 & - & - & - \\ - & 8 & 16 & 16 & 9 & 2 & - \\ - & - & 8 & 15 & 16 & 9 & - \\ - & - & - & 6 & 15 & 16 & 8 \end{pmatrix}_{1,\,1}$$

Figure 8.21   Image with associated Prewitt edge images

$$(f) \quad \text{PREWMAG2}(f) = \begin{pmatrix} 4.2 & 10.6 & 11.4 & 5.7 & - & - & - \\ - & 5.7 & 11.3 & 11.4 & 6.4 & 1.4 & - \\ - & - & 5.7 & 10.6 & 11.3 & 6.4 & - \\ - & - & - & 4.2 & 10.6 & 11.4 & 5.7 \end{pmatrix}_{1, -1}$$

$$(g) \quad \text{PREWEDGE0}(f; 7) = \begin{pmatrix} - & 1 & 1 & - & - & - & - \\ - & - & 1 & 1 & - & - & - \\ - & - & - & 1 & 1 & - & - \\ - & - & - & - & 1 & 1 & - \end{pmatrix}_{1, -1}$$

Figure 8.21 Continued

8.4 MORPHOLOGY AND THE SEARCH FOR STRUCTURE

It is common practice in both image and signal processing to operate on an image in such a manner as to produce a new structure to "replace" the original image. This new structure might be the result of a transform technique, or it might simply be a set of *feature* measurements taken on the image. In either case, given an image f, we arrive at a transformed structure $\mathcal{T}(f)$, where the specific transformation employed depends upon the goals we have in mind.

The information revealed by the transformation depends upon the mathematical properties it possesses. So, too, does the amount of the information lost in the transformation process—for instance, if no information is lost, then the process is invertible. It might also be that the process preserves certain fundamental mathematical operations, as in the case of linear transformations. Any significance regarding the preservation of information or mathematical structure is relative to the intent of the investigator.

In pattern recognition, the problem is classification. If an operation $\mathcal{T}$ results in a satisfactory recognizer system, then all else is of little interest. For example, if a filter reduces noise to acceptable levels, then whether the filter is linear or not may be of no consequence.

The genesis of the morphological methodology lies in the search for structure within an image. The underlying strategy in the description of structure is to understand the textural or geometric properties of an image by probing the microstructure of the image with various forms. The intent is to approach image processing from the vantage point of human perception by deriving quantitative measures of natural perceptual categories, thereby exploiting whatever inherent congruences exist between image structure and ordinary human recognition. Necessarily, such an approach must break free of the classical linear-space framework that has so long dominated applied mathematics. Nevertheless, the method is well suited to eventual integration into an artificial intelligence schema: for a computer vision system to yield image-based decisions resembling those that result from direct human understanding, the categories upon which that system operates must correspond well to native human perceptual categories, whether or not the ensuing mathematical apparatus happens to be one that has served well for other classes of problems.

In searching for a given pattern within an image, a person perceives the image through the filter of his or her own motivation.   Sensory data are not passively received and acted upon by analytic intelligence; rather they are organized by the brain into *percepts*, and it these percepts that are the raw material for analysis. To employ engineering terminology, we might loosely refer to the act of perception (i.e., of rendering data into percepts) as a form of data compression.   Such compression involves a choice, prior to sensory reception, as to what manner the compression is to take place in and what end it serves.   In addition to this sensory organization, higher level filtering must take place in order to search for desired patterns.

The elaboration of structure, which is, after all, the intent of image processing, involves an analysis of the relationships between the component parts of whatever object is under investigation.   While it might be argued that structure inheres within an image, it certainly cannot be maintained that inherent structure is measurable, or even perceivable, while remaining outside the categories of human perception and conception.   Consequently, those relationships which comprise (perceived) image structure are imposed on the image by intelligence and do not exist independently of intelligence.   In the words of G. Matheron, the founder of morphological image processing,

> In general, the structure of an object is defined as the set of relationships existing between elements or parts of the object.   In order to experimentally determine this structure, we must try, one after the other, each of the possible relationships and examine whether or not it is verified.   Of course, the image constructed by such a process will depend to the greatest extent on the choice made for the system of relationships considered as possible.   Hence, this choice plays a priori a constitutive role (in the Kantian meaning) and determines the relative worth of the concept of structure at which we arrive.

Thus, only those aspects of the image which conform to some predetermined set of relational categories are relevant, and in that sense the image engineer's choice of these categories *constitutes*, or frames, the image.   For practical morphological image processing, this means that the type of filtering or probing of an image depends upon the particular knowledge desired.   Once the image is constituted in terms of the relational base of this desired knowledge, other characteristics of the image are no longer accessible.   However, if the base is well chosen relative to one's aims, the other characteristics are irrelevant.

The morphological approach is generally based on the probing of a two-valued image by some predetermined geometric shape known as a *structuring element*. Essentially, the manner in which the structuring element fits into the image is studied.   To begin with, we discuss two-valued Euclidean images, which are subsets of the Euclidean plane.

Consider the image S sketched in Figure 8.22.   From the figure, a square of the size shown will fit into S if its center is placed at (1, 2), but not if its center is situated at (3, 1).   It should be clear that the manner in which the square fits into S as it is moved about the plane is a reflection of the relationship between the geometric structure of S and that of the square.

Morphological operations can be employed for many purposes, including edge detection, segmentation, and enhancement of images.   From the morphological operations, an entire class of *morphological filters* can be constructed that can often be used in place of the standard linear filters.   Whereas linear filters sometimes distort the underlying geometric form of an image, morphological filters leave much of that form intact.   Finally, many useful feature parameters can be generated morphologically.

Besides dealing with the usual set-theoretic operations of union and intersection, morphology depends extensively on the translation operation.   Given an image (subset) A in R^2, the *translation* of A by the point x in R^2 is defined by

$$A + x = \{a + x: a \in A\}$$

where the plus sign inside the set notation refers to vector addition.   Considering x to be a vector in the plane, $A + x$ is A translated along the vector x.   This can be seen pictorially in Figure 8.23; the following example illustrates the definition of translation arithmetically.

Example 8.5

Let $A = \{(0, 0), (1, 0), (0, 1), (1, 1), (2, 2)\}$ and $x = (3, 1)$.   Then $A + x = \{(3, 1), (4, 1), (3, 2), (4, 2), (5, 3)\}$ (see Figure 8.24).

Note that the point z is in the translated set $A + x$ if and only if there exists

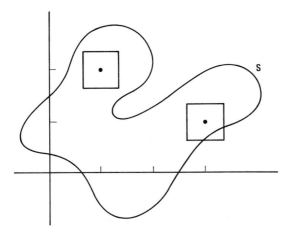

Figure 8.22   Image with structuring elements

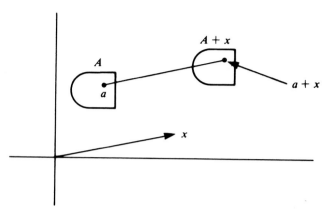

Figure 8.23   Translation of Euclidean image

some point a' in A such that $z = a' + x$. Also, because vector addition is commutative, we can write $x + A$ interchangeably with $A + x$.

Two fundamental operations are utilized in the morphological analysis of binary images. We first consider *Minkowski addition*. Given two images A and B in R^2, we define the Minkowski sum $A \oplus B$ set-theoretically as

$$A \oplus B = \bigcup_{b \in B} A + b$$

$A \oplus B$ is constructed by translating A by each element of B and then taking the union of all the resulting translates.

Example 8.6

Let A be the unit disk centered at (2, 2) and let $B = \{(4, 1), (5, 1), (5, 2)\}$. Then $A \oplus B$ is the union of the sets $A + (4, 1)$, $A + (5, 1)$, and $A + (5, 2)$. A, B, and $A \oplus B$ are depicted in Figure 8.25.

Example 8.7

This time, let A be the unit disk centered at $a = (\frac{3}{2}, 3)$ and let B be the closed line segment running from $b_1 = (\frac{5}{2}, 1)$ to $b_2 = (\frac{9}{2}, 2)$. Then $A + b_1$ is the unit disk centered at (4, 4) and $A + b_2$ is the unit disk centered at (6, 5). The Minkowski addition $A \oplus B$, depicted in Figure 8.26, consists of the union of all unit disks having centers on the line segment running from (4, 4) to (6, 5).

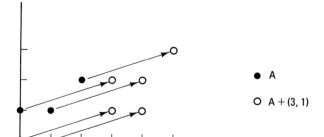

● A

○ A + (3, 1)

Figure 8.24   Translation of a discrete image

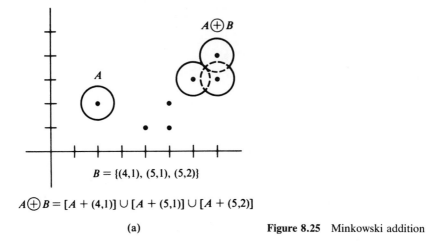

$$B = \{(4,1),\ (5,1),\ (5,2)\}$$

$$A \oplus B = [A + (4,1)] \cup [A + (5,1)] \cup [A + (5,2)]$$

(a)   **Figure 8.25**   Minkowski addition

The second fundamental morphological operation is *Minkowski subtraction*. Given images A and B in R^2, we define the Minkowski difference

$$A \ominus B = \bigcap_{b \in B} A + b$$

In this operation, A is translated by every element of B and then the intersection is taken.

Example 8.8

Consider the 3 by 2 rectangle A in Figure 8.27. Let $B = \{(4, 0), (5, 1)\}$. Then $A \ominus B$ is the intersection of the translates $A + (4, 0)$ and $A + (5, 1)$. That is, $A \ominus B$ is the 2 by 1 rectangle depicted in Figure 8.27.

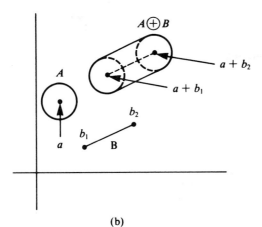

(b)   **Figure 8.26**   Minkowski addition

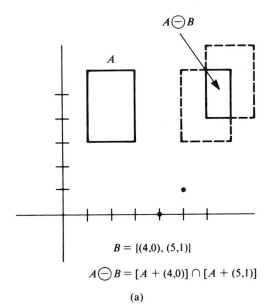

$$B = \{(4,0), (5,1)\}$$

$$A \ominus B = [A + (4,0)] \cap [A + (5,1)]$$

(a)   **Figure 8.27**   Minkowski subtraction

Example 8.9

Let A be the rectangle given in Figure 8.28 and let B be the unit segment emanating at the origin and making a 45° angle with the horizontal axis.   Then one end point of B is $(0, 0)$ and the other is $(\sqrt{2}/2, \sqrt{2}/2)$. $A \ominus B$ is the intersection of all the translates $A + b$ such that b lies on the segment B.   This intersection is the shaded region in the figure.

A fundamental property of Minkowski subtraction involves the "fitting" of the 180° rotation of the image B.   Let $-B = \{-b: b \in B\}$, where $-b$ is the scalar multiple of the vector b by -1.   Thus, $-B$ is simply B rotated 180° around the origin (see Figure 8.29).

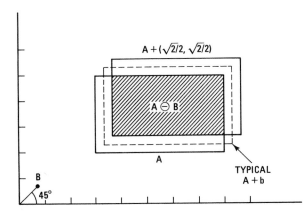

Figure 8.28   Minkowski subtraction of line segment from rectangle

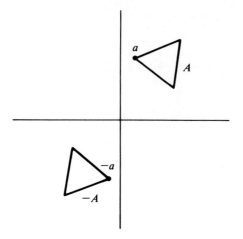

Figure 8.29 Reflection operation

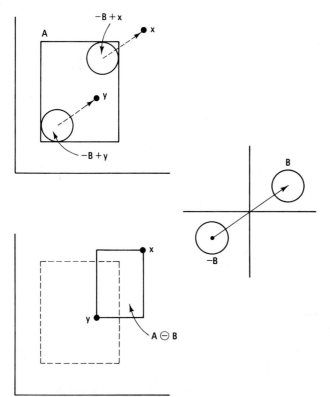

Figure 8.30 Minkowski subtraction by fitting

Theorem 8.1. $A \ominus B = \{x: -B + x \subset A\}$.

According to Theorem 8.1, $A \ominus B$ can be found by first rotating B 180° around the origin and then finding all points x such that the translate by x of that rotated image is a subimage (subset) of A.   Figure 8.30 demonstrates this "fitting" procedure.   Note that the output image $A \ominus B$ is *not* necessarily a subimage of the original image A; we are assured that $A \ominus B$ is a subimage of A only if B contains the origin.

Since $-(-B) = B$, Theorem 8.1 can be rewritten in the form

$$A \ominus (-B) = \{x: B + x \subset A\}$$

In other words, the direct fitting of B without rotating it by 180° is the Minkowski subtraction of A by $-B$.   Using this direct fitting technique, we define the *erosion* of A by B to be $\mathscr{E}(A, B) = A \ominus (-B)$.   When A is eroded by B, the latter is called a *structuring element*.   If $B = -B$, the erosion is equal to the Minkowski subtraction; otherwise the two are related by the preceding definition.

Eroding an image by a structuring element B has the effect of "shrinking" the image in a manner determined by B.   In Figure 8.31, B is a closed disk centered at the origin.   As such, it is symmetric, and hence $\mathscr{E}(A, B) = A \ominus B$.   In any event, notice the manner in which erosion by the circular surface of the disk has shrunk the original image.   This effect can also be seen in Figure 8.28, where $A \ominus B = \mathscr{E}(A, -B)$.

Corresponding to the erosion operation is the operation of *dilation*, which is defined simply as Minkowski addition: $\mathscr{D}(A, B) = A \oplus B$.   Here again, B is called a structuring element.   Dilation has the effect of "expanding" an image (see Figure 8.32).

Besides the fundamental morphological operations of Minkowski addition and subtraction, two other operations play a central role in image analysis.   These two secondary operations, called the *opening* and the *closing*, are respectively defined by

$$O(A, B) = [A \ominus (-B)] \oplus B$$

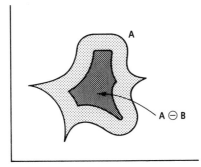

Figure 8.31   Erosion as shrinking

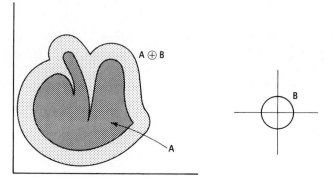

Figure 8.32 Dilation as expansion

and

$$C(A, B) = [A \oplus (-B)] \ominus B$$

Employing erosion and dilation terminology, we have

$$O(A, B) = \mathfrak{D}[\mathcal{E}(A, B), B]$$

and

$$C(A, B) = \mathcal{E}[\mathfrak{D}(A, -B), -B]$$

The opening and the closing are illustrated in Figures 8.33 and 8.34, respectively. In both figures, one should pay particular attention to the composite manner in which the final output is obtained. Moreover, note that in both cases $-B = B$.

A close examination of Figure 8.33 reveals that the original image has been

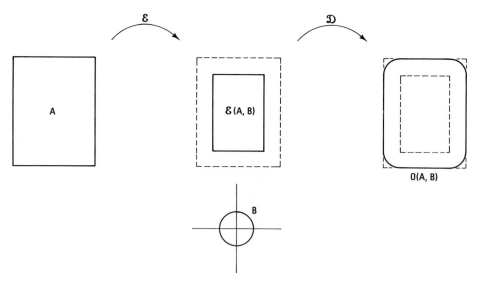

Figure 8.33 Opening in terms of dilation and erosion

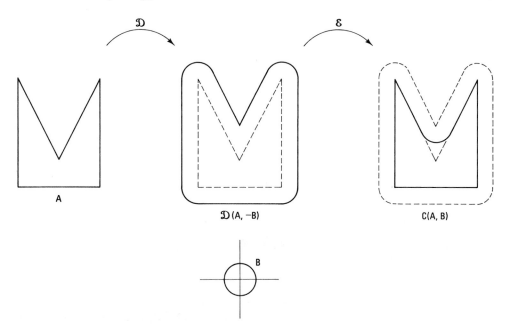

Figure 8.34   Closing in terms of dilation and erosion

smoothed.   That is, the output $O(A, B)$ is similar to the input except that the corners have been rounded from the inside.   This smoothing effect is a result of the definition of the opening together with the shape of the structuring element. Intuitively, $O(A, B)$ is obtained from A in this instance by "rolling the ball" B about the inside of the image.   The next theorem gives a rigorous set-theoretic characterization of this "fitting" property.   It states that the opening of A by B is obtained by taking the union of all translates of B that fit into A.   Figure 8.35 gives an illustration of the result when the structuring element is not symmetric with respect to the origin.

Theorem 8.2. $O(A, B) = \cup \{B + x: B + x \subset A\}.$

The output $O(A, B)$ in Figure 8.33 appears to be the result of rolling B about the inside of A.   On the other hand, the output $C(A, B)$ in Figure 8.34 appears to result from rolling B around the outside of A.   This inside–outside *duality* between the opening and closing is formalized in the next identity, which states that the closing is equal to the complement of the opening of the complement:

$$C(A, B) = O(A^c, B)^c$$

Together with Theorem 8.2, this says that the closing can be obtained (in the case of a disk B) by rolling the ball (really, the surface of B) about the outside of A— in other words, open A^c and then complement.

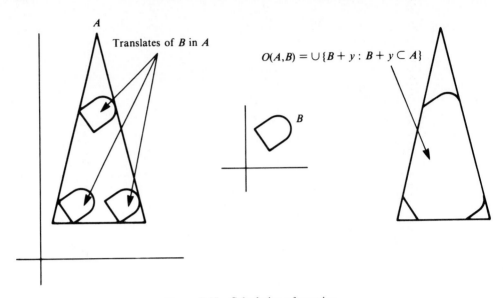

Figure 8.35   Calculation of opening

Applying Theorem 8.2, we can easily obtain a pointwise chararcterization of the opening, namely, a point z is in $O(A, B)$ if and only if there exists some translate $B + x$ of B such that $z \in B + x \subset A$ (see Figure 8.36).

Before proceeding, it is important to note that in employing dilation and erosion, the position of the structuring element in the plane affects the output. By contrast, the relation of the origin to the structuring template (element) is of no importance in employing the opening or the closing.

The next theorem gives the most fundamental algebraic properties of the opening. These properties are essential, for both theoretical and practical reasons, to the morphological methodology. The first states that opening an image produces

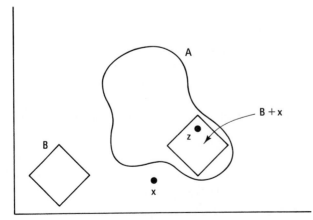

Figure 8.36   Pointwise characterization of opening

an output that is a subimage of the original image. The second says that, given a fixed structuring element, the opening is an increasing image-to-image mapping in the first variable. The third states that successive openings by the same structuring element do not alter the image after the primary application.

Theorem 8.3.   The opening satisfies:

(*i*) $O(A, B)$ is a subimage of A (antiextensivity)
(*ii*) If A_1 is a subimage of A_2, then $O(A_1, B)$ is a subimage of $O(A_2, B)$ (increasing monotonicity)
(*iii*) $O[O(A, B), B] = O(A, B)$ (idempotence)

The properties of the opening specified in Theorem 8.3 play a key role in the use of the opening for the construction of morphological filters. As mentioned previously, opening by a disk can have a smoothing effect: the opening acts as a filter, the exact result being dependent on the shape of the structuring template. According to Theorem 8.3, this filter, $O(\cdot, B)$, produces a subimage, is increasing, and is idempotent. Put succinctly, it filters in a manner that behaves quite well with respect to geometry.

As an example, consider the image A shown in Figure 8.37. It represents a rectangle on a background distorted by noise. Opening A by the disk B has produced a fairly clean copy of the rectangle.

Theorem 8.4 is the dual of Theorem 8.3; it states the corresponding algebraic properties of the closing.

Theorem 8.4.   The closing satisfies:

(*i*) A is a subimage of $C(A, B)$ (extensivity)
(*ii*) If A_1 is a subimage of A_2, then $C(A_1, B)$ is a subimage of $C(A_2, B)$ (increasing monotonicity)
(*iii*) $C[C(A, B), B] = C(A, B)$ (idempotence)

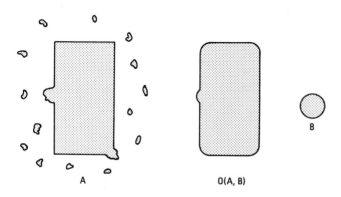

A   O(A, B)

Figure 8.37   Rectangle on noisy background

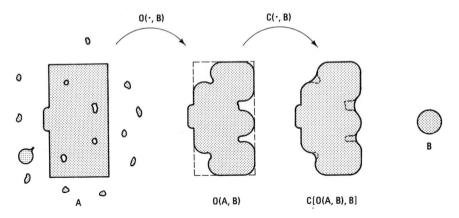

Figure 8.38 Filtering of rectangle in noisy image

To illustrate Theorem 8.4, consider image *A* of Figure 8.38. This time the image is noisy throughout, not just over the background. To clean it up, we apply the filter $C[O(\cdot, B), B]$. We first open by the disk *B* and then close by the same disk. This composite operation gets rid of the exterior noise, but leaves the rectangle unacceptably altered. To remedy the situation, we filter *A* by using the smaller disk *D* in Figure 8.39, again following an opening by a closing. This time, except for the large circular spot on the left, the rectangle is left essentially intact. Indeed, because the circular spot is so large, we might hesitate to call it noise: more than likely, it possesses some significance in the image.

Having introduced the fundamental Euclidean morphological operations, we now proceed to the digital case, which is, of course, our main concern. The setting will be the collection of constant $(1-*)$ images, since, as has been discussed in Section 4.9, it is these that best digitally model the algebra of subsets of the plane.

First, a bit of notation: if $S_1, S_2, \ldots$ are constant images, then $\bigvee_k S_k$ denotes

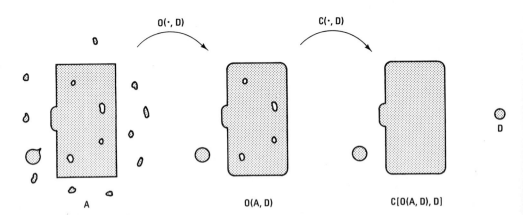

Figure 8.39 Alternative filtering of rectangle in noisy image

the image that is 1 on the union of the domains of the S_k and is undefined elsewhere; similarly, $\wedge_k S_k$ denotes the image that is 1 on the intersection of the domains of the S_k and is undefined elsewhere.   Pixelwise, we have

$$\left[\bigvee_k S_k\right](i,j) = \begin{cases} 1, & \text{if there exists at least one } k' \text{ for which } S_{k'}(i,j) = 1 \\ *, & \text{if } S_k(i,j) = * \text{ for all } k \end{cases}$$

and

$$\left[\bigwedge_k S_k\right](i,j) = \begin{cases} 1, & \text{if } S_k(i,j) = 1 \text{ for all } k \\ *, & \text{if there exists at least one } k' \text{ for which } S_{k'}(i,j) = * \end{cases}$$

In practice, the collection of images $\{S_k\}$ will be finite, and in that case the operations $\bigvee_k$ and $\bigwedge_k$ simply reduce to finite iterations of EXTMAX ($\vee$) and MIN($\wedge$), respectively.

Example 8.10

Let

$$S_1 = \begin{pmatrix} ① & 1 & * \\ 1 & 1 & 1 \end{pmatrix}$$

$$S_2 = \begin{pmatrix} ① & 1 & 1 \\ 1 & * & * \end{pmatrix}$$

$$S_3 = \begin{pmatrix} 1 & 1 \\ ⊛ & 1 \\ 1 & 1 \end{pmatrix}$$

$$S_4 = \begin{pmatrix} ① & 1 & 1 & 1 \\ 1 & * & * & 1 \end{pmatrix}$$

Then

$$\bigvee_{k=1}^{4} S_k = \begin{pmatrix} 1 & 1 & * & * \\ ① & 1 & 1 & 1 \\ 1 & 1 & 1 & 1 \end{pmatrix}$$

and

$$\bigwedge_{k=1}^{4} S_k = \begin{pmatrix} ⊛ & 1 \\ 1 & * \end{pmatrix}$$

Note that we could write these outputs as $S_1 \vee S_2 \vee S_3 \vee S_4$ and $S_1 \wedge S_2 \wedge S_3 \wedge S_4$, respectively.

In the digital setting, *Minkowski addition*, or *dilation*, is defined by

$$S \boxplus E = \bigvee_{(i,j) \in D_S} \text{TRAN}(E; i, j)$$

where D_S denotes the domain of S.   Notice the correspondence between the digital definition and the Euclidean one.   The domain of $S \boxplus E$ equals the union of the domains of the translates $\text{TRAN}(E; i, j)$.

As in the Euclidean case, the image E in $S \boxplus E$ plays the role of a template. If E is represented by a bound matrix, as it will be in practice, then the center of the template is the pixel of the bound matrix that is located at the origin. The Minkowski sum is found by placing the center of the template over each of the activated pixels of S and then taking the union of all the resulting copies of E, produced by using the translation operation. As in the Euclidean case, E is referred to as a structuring element. If the origin is contained in E, then the original image S will be a subimage of $S \boxplus E$.

Example 8.11

Consider the two images S and E, where

$$S = \begin{pmatrix} * & 1 & * & 1 & * \\ * & 1 & 1 & * & 1 \\ \circledast & 1 & 1 & 1 & * \end{pmatrix} \quad \text{and} \quad E = \begin{pmatrix} 1 & * \\ 1 & \textcircled{1} \end{pmatrix}$$

The domain of S is

$$D_S = \{(1, 2), (1, 1), (1, 0), (2, 1), (2, 0), (3, 2), (3, 0), (4, 1)\}$$

The translation operation should be used eight times (once for each element in D_S). We first use it to move the center of E to $(1, 0)$. Thus the translation of E by $(i, j) = (1, 0)$ yields the image

$$\text{TRAN}(E; 1, 0) = \begin{pmatrix} 1 & * \\ \textcircled{1} & 1 \end{pmatrix}$$

This shows that $S \boxplus E$ must have a 1 at $(0, 0)$, $(1, 0)$, and $(0, 1)$. Also,

$$\text{TRAN}(E; 1, 2) = \begin{pmatrix} 1 & * \\ 1 & 1 \\ * & * \\ \circledast & * \end{pmatrix}$$

Thus $S \boxplus E$ must have a 1 at $(0, 2)$, $(0, 3)$, and $(1, 2)$. When the additional six translations have been formed and the union has been taken, the resulting image is the Minkowski addition:

$$S \boxplus E = \begin{pmatrix} 1 & * & 1 & * & * \\ 1 & 1 & 1 & 1 & * \\ 1 & 1 & 1 & 1 & 1 \\ \textcircled{1} & 1 & 1 & 1 & * \end{pmatrix}$$

Note that E has value 1 at the origin and hence S is a subimage of the dilation. (It is recommended that the reader also form the image E on cellophane or some other transparent material and overlay translates of this image on S to visually obtain $S \boxplus E$ (see Figure 8.40).

As in the case of Euclidean dilation, digital dilation $S \boxplus E$ results in a "larger" image than S wherein the "small" holes of S have been filled in a manner

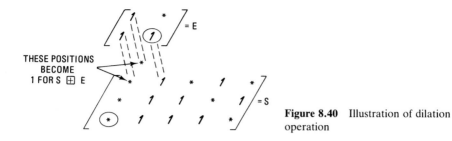

THESE POSITIONS
BECOME
1 FOR S ⊞ E

Figure 8.40   Illustration of dilation operation

depending on the size and shape of the structuring element E.   Figure 8.41 shows an image S and its dilation by the structuring element

$$E = \begin{pmatrix} 1 & 1 \\ ① & 1 \end{pmatrix}$$

A black-and-white drawing has been employed to depict the 1–* digital model. Specifically, if (i, j) is activated, then the pixel square with center (i, j) is colored black; however, if (i, j) is deactivated, the square is colored white.   The net result is a black figure on an infinite white background.

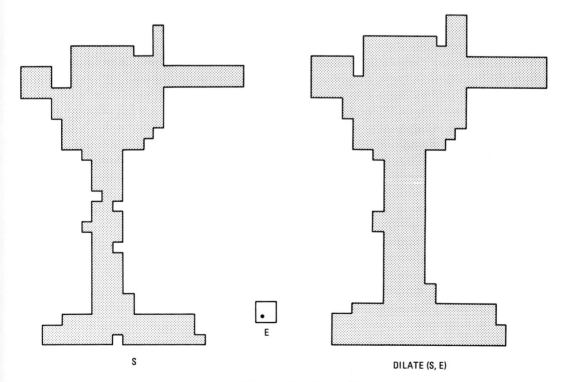

S   E   DILATE (S, E)

Figure 8.41   Digital dilation

The block diagram for dilation is

$$S \rightarrow \boxed{\text{DILATE}} \longrightarrow S \boxplus E$$
$$E \rightarrow$$

In accordance with this diagram, we shall often employ the notation DILATE(S, E) in place of $S \boxplus E$.

When inputs S and E are finite images, DILATE is a macro-operator relative to the primitives of Section 4.9. It can be implemented through the linking of TRAN, EXTMAX, and DOMAIN. The block diagram specification of this linkage is given in Figure 8.42, where each arrow running from the DOMAIN box to a TRAN box is interpreted as a single ordered pair (i, j) from DOMAIN(S), and where the output of the TRAN box in question is TRAN(E; i, j). Since our main interest is with finite images, because only these are amenable to machine processing, the restriction on the specification of Figure 8.42 regarding the finiteness of the inputs is of no practical concern. Consequently, DILATE has been effectively implemented in terms of just three primitives.

As in the Euclidean case, digital Minkowski subtraction and erosion are related by a 180° rotation of the structuring element. Due to the identification of a constant $(1-*)$ image with its domain, for such images we will often write $-S$ instead of NINETY^2(S). In any event, what is important is that the domain of NINETY^2(f) is $\{(-i, -j): (i, j) \in D_f\}$.

We define the *Minkowski subtraction $S \boxminus E$* by

$$[S \boxminus E](i, j) = \begin{cases} 1, & \text{if TRAN}(-E; i, j) \vee S = S \\ *, & \text{otherwise} \end{cases}$$

where it should be noted that $T \vee U = U$ if and only if T is a subimage of U. As

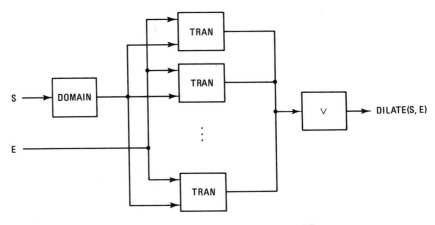

Figure 8.42   Block diagram of DILATE

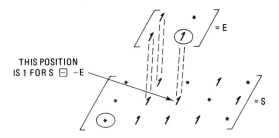

Figure 8.43   Illustration of erosion operation

in the Euclidean case, we are usually concerned with the *erosion*, ERODE(*S*, *E*) = *S* ⊟ (−*E*).   Pixelwise,

$$[\text{ERODE}(S, E)](i, j) = \begin{cases} 1, & \text{if TRAN}(E; i, j) \vee S = S \\ *, & \text{otherwise} \end{cases}$$

Erosion yields a "smaller" image than the original.   As in the Euclidean case, the erosion of an image will be a subimage of the original if the origin is an activated pixel of the structuring element.

Like dilation, the erosion of *S* by *E* can be described intuitively by template translation, and it is again advised that a physical model be employed to help see this (see Figure 8.43).   The template is moved across the image *S*.   If, for a given pixel, say (i, j), the translated copy of *E*, TRAN($E; i, j$), is a subimage of *S*, then (i, j) is activated in the erosion; otherwise (i, j) is given the value ∗ in the eroded image.   From this description it should be clear that erosion eliminates those parts of the image that are small in comparison to the structuring element.   The manner of the elimination is of course highly dependent on the shape of the element.

Example 8.12

Consider Example 8.11 again.   TRAN(E; 1, 2) is certainly not a subimage of *S*. Therefore, (1, 2) will not be activated in the eroded image.   On the other hand,

$$\text{TRAN}(E; 2, 1) = \begin{pmatrix} * & 1 & * \\ * & 1 & 1 \\ \circledast & * & * \end{pmatrix}$$

is a subimage of *S*.   Hence, (2, 1) will be activated in ERODE(*S*, *E*) = *S* ⊟ (−*E*). When all translations are checked, we obtain

$$\text{ERODE}(S, E) = \begin{pmatrix} * & * & 1 & * \\ \circledast & * & 1 & 1 \end{pmatrix}$$

As in the Euclidean case, Minkowski subtraction can be defined in terms of the intersection operator MIN(∧) as follows:

$$S \boxminus E = \bigwedge_{(i,j) \in \text{DOMAIN}(E)} \text{TRAN}(S; i, j)$$

Since $\text{ERODE}(S, E) = S \boxminus (-E)$, a corresponding formulation of erosion is

$$\text{ERODE}(S, E) = \bigwedge_{(i,j)\in\text{DOMAIN}(E)} \text{TRAN}(S; -i, -j)$$

$$= \bigwedge_{(i,j)\in\text{DOMAIN}[\text{NINETY}^2(E)]} \text{TRAN}(S; i, j)$$

Example 8.13

Let

$$S = \begin{pmatrix} 1 & 1 & 1 & * \\ 1 & 1 & 1 & * \\ * & 1 & * & 1 \\ \circledast & 1 & 1 & 1 \end{pmatrix}$$

and

$$E = \begin{pmatrix} * & 1 \\ \textcircled{1} & 1 \end{pmatrix}$$

There are three translations of S by pixels in the domain of E: $\text{TRAN}(S; 0, 0) = S$,

$$\text{TRAN}(S; 1, 0) = \begin{pmatrix} * & 1 & 1 & 1 & * \\ * & 1 & 1 & 1 & * \\ * & * & 1 & * & 1 \\ \circledast & * & 1 & 1 & 1 \end{pmatrix}$$

and

$$\text{TRAN}(S; 1, 1) = \begin{pmatrix} * & 1 & 1 & 1 & * \\ * & 1 & 1 & 1 & * \\ * & * & 1 & * & 1 \\ * & * & 1 & 1 & 1 \\ \circledast & * & * & * & * \end{pmatrix}$$

Application of $\wedge = \text{MIN}$ to the three translates yields

$$S \boxminus E = \begin{pmatrix} * & 1 & 1 \\ * & . & * & 1 \\ * & * & * \\ \circledast & * & * \end{pmatrix}$$

The block diagram for erosion is given by

$$S \longrightarrow \boxed{\text{ERODE}} \longrightarrow \text{ERODE}(S, E)$$
$$E \longrightarrow$$

A block diagram specification of ERODE in terms of primitive operations that employs the preceding MIN formulation is given in Figure 8.44. Figure 8.45 gives the erosion of the image S in Figure 8.41 by the structuring element E of the same figure.

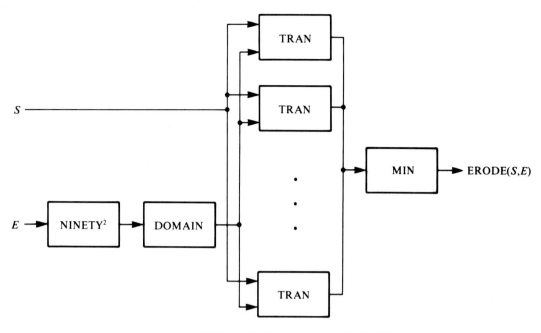

Figure 8.44   Block diagram of ERODE

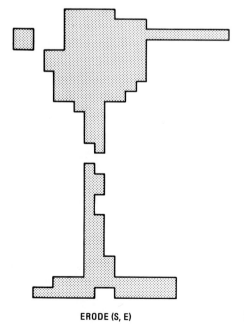

ERODE (S, E)   **Figure 8.45**   Digital erosion

The digital opening and closing are defined analogously to the definitions of the corresponding Euclidean operators; that is,

$$\text{OPEN}(S, E) = [S \boxminus (-E)] \boxplus E = \text{DILATE}[\text{ERODE}(S, E), E]$$

and

$$\text{CLOSE}(S, E) = [S \boxplus (-E)] \boxminus E = \text{ERODE}[\text{DILATE}(S, -E), -E]$$

Comments concerning the manner in which the Euclidean opening and closing affect the input image apply without material alteration to the digital versions of the same operators.   Figure 8.46 gives black-and-white interpretations of the opening and closing of image S of Figure 8.41 by the structuring element E of that same figure.

The respective block diagrams of OPEN and CLOSE are

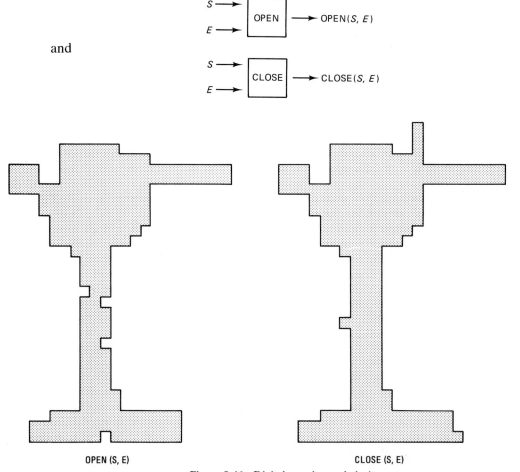

OPEN (S, E)   CLOSE (S, E)

Figure 8.46   Digital opening and closing

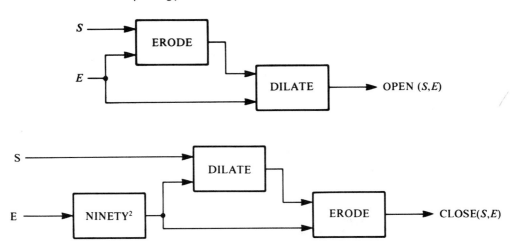

Figure 8.47   Block diagram of OPEN/Block diagram of CLOSE

The block diagram specifications for OPEN and CLOSE result directly from their respective definitions in terms of DILATE and ERODE.   These are given in Figure 8.47.

In a form similar to Theorem 8.2, the opening can be represented as an extended maximum (union) of fitted translates of the structuring element:

$$\text{OPEN}(S, E) = \bigvee \{\text{TRAN}(E; i, j): \text{TRAN}(E; i, j) \vee S = S\}$$

Example 8.14

Consider the image S and the structuring element E of Example 8.11.   There are three translations of E that fit into S: $\text{TRAN}(E; 2, 0)$, $\text{TRAN}(E; 3, 0)$, and $\text{TRAN}(E; 2, 1)$. These are precisely the translations that yielded the erosion given in Example 8.12. The extended maximum of these translations gives the opening:

$$\text{OPEN}(S, E) = \begin{pmatrix} * & 1 & * & * \\ * & 1 & 1 & * \\ \circledast & 1 & 1 & 1 \end{pmatrix}$$

The key to the morphological feature analysis of images is the method of successively filtering and then measuring the residues.   The particular method of filtering may vary (although it is customarily erosion or opening, or some related variant); but the methodology is essentially fixed, with the measure, at least in the digital case, being the number of activated pixels in the residue (see Figure 8.48). Here, we will only consider the method of filtering by opening with successively increasing linear structuring elements.

Consider the structuring elements $H(k)$ and $V(k)$, where $H(k)$ is a horizontal string of k activated pixels with the origin at the extreme left of the string, and $V(k)$ is a vertical string of k activated pixels with the origin at the base of the string

Figure 8.48 Block diagram illustration of parameter extraction

(see Figure 8.49).   Given a constant image S, consider the mappings

$$k \rightarrow \text{OPENS}(S, V(k))$$

and

$$k \rightarrow \text{OPENS}(S, H(k))$$

for $k = 1, 2, 3, \ldots$.   These mappings are known as *linear digital granulometries*. Since opening by larger sets causes ever greater filtering, the granulometries are decreasing functions of k in that

$$\text{OPEN}(S, V(1)) \supset \text{OPEN}(S, V(2)) \supset \text{OPEN}(S, V(3)) \supset \cdots$$

and

$$\text{OPEN}(S, H(1)) \supset \text{OPEN}(S, H(2)) \supset \text{OPEN}(S, H(3)) \supset \cdots$$

Moreover, since we are starting with finite images, after some value of k the null image will result in each case.

What is of interest is the two mappings that are derived by composing the cardinality function CARD, which counts the number of elements in a set, together with the preceding granulometries.   To be precise, we shall successively open with linear structuring elements and record the number of activated pixels in each case. Due to the decreasing nature of the granulometries, the resulting functions will also be decreasing and will reach 0 for some finite value of k.   Formally, we define the functions

$$\Psi_V(k) = \text{CARD}[\text{OPEN}(S, V(k))]$$

and

$$\Psi_H(k) = \text{CARD}[\text{OPEN}(S, H(k))]$$

where CARD simply counts the number of activated pixels.   Note that we have taken a slight liberty with the preceding definitions.   To be strictly accurate, CARD

$$V(k) = \begin{pmatrix} 1 \\ \cdot \\ \cdot \\ \cdot \\ \cdot \\ 1 \\ \textcircled{1} \end{pmatrix} \qquad H(k) = (\ \textcircled{1} \ \ 1 \ \ldots \ 1)$$

Figure 8.49 Two structuring elements

counts the elements in the domain of an image and, therefore, $\Psi_V(k)$ is actually the output of the following block diagram:

$$S \longrightarrow \boxed{\text{OPEN}} \longrightarrow \boxed{\text{DOMAIN}} \longrightarrow \boxed{\text{CARD}} \longrightarrow \psi_v(k)$$
$$V(k) \longrightarrow$$

A similar remark holds for $\psi_H(k)$. In the sequel, we will continue to take the liberty of writing CARD of an image to mean the cardinality of the domain. In any event, the functions $\psi_V(k)$ and $\psi_H(k)$ satisfy the schema of Figure 8.48.

Example 8.15

Let S be given by

$$S = \begin{pmatrix} \circledast & 1 & 1 & 1 & * & * & 1 & * & 1 & 1 \\ 1 & 1 & 1 & * & * & * & 1 & 1 & 1 & 1 \\ 1 & 1 & 1 & * & * & * & 1 & 1 & 1 & 1 \\ 1 & * & 1 & * & * & * & 1 & * & 1 & * \\ 1 & 1 & 1 & 1 & * & * & 1 & * & 1 & * \\ 1 & 1 & 1 & 1 & * & * & 1 & * & 1 & * \\ * & 1 & 1 & 1 & * & * & * & * & 1 & * \end{pmatrix}$$

By taking successive openings, first horizontally and then vertically, we find

$$k = \quad 1 \quad 2 \quad 3 \quad 4 \quad 5 \quad 6 \quad 7 \quad 8$$

$$\psi_H(k) = 40 \quad 30 \quad 28 \quad 16 \quad 0 \quad 0 \quad 0 \quad 0$$

$$\psi_V(k) = 40 \quad 39 \quad 37 \quad 25 \quad 25 \quad 20 \quad 14 \quad 0$$

For instance, $\psi_V(6) = 20$ since there are 20 activated pixels in the image

$$\text{OPEN}(S, V(6)) = \begin{pmatrix} \circledast & * & 1 & * & * & * & 1 & * & 1 & * \\ * & * & 1 & * & * & * & 1 & * & 1 & * \\ * & * & 1 & * & * & * & 1 & * & 1 & * \\ * & * & 1 & * & * & * & 1 & * & 1 & * \\ * & * & 1 & * & * & * & 1 & * & 1 & * \\ * & * & 1 & * & * & * & 1 & * & 1 & * \\ * & * & 1 & * & * & * & * & * & 1 & * \end{pmatrix}$$

In Example 8.15, it is clear that $\psi_V(k)$ is less affected by small values of k than is $\psi_H(k)$. This means that opening by $H(k)$ has a great filtering effect than opening by $V(k)$ for this example. Intuitively, there is a greater distribution of linear size in the vertical direction than in the horizontal direction. Indeed, measurement of a granulometry yields a measurement of the extent to which activated pixels are clustered relative to the shape of the structuring element.

It is common practice to normalize the functions $\psi_H(k)$ and $\psi_V(k)$ so that the resulting functions are distributions in the probabilistic sense. We define

$$\Phi_H(k) = 1 - \frac{\psi_H(k)}{\psi_H(1)} = 1 - \frac{\text{CARD}[\text{OPEN}(S, H(k))]}{\text{CARD}(S)}$$

and

$$\Phi_V(k) = 1 - \frac{\psi_V(k)}{\psi_V(1)} = 1 - \frac{\text{CARD}[\text{OPEN}(S, V(k))]}{\text{CARD}(S)}$$

The functions $\Phi_H(k)$ and $\Phi_V(k)$ are monotonically increasing, have leftmost value 0, and become 1 for some finite value of k. Moreover, by defining $\Phi(x)$ to be $\Phi(k)$ for any value x greater than $k - 1$ and less than or equal to k, a step function is obtained that is continuous from the left. As a result, the functions $\Phi_H(k)$ and $\Phi_V(k)$, called *size distributions*, are distributions in the usual sense. Figure 8.50 provides the graphs for the size distributions resulting from the image in Example 8.15.

Once again referring to Example 8.15, it should be noted that the granulometry $k \rightarrow \text{OPEN}(S, H(k))$ can be looked on as a *sieving process*. For each value of k, only those horizontal strings remain whose length is at least equal to k. The action is like a sequence of sieves; at each stage too small particles slide through the mesh of the sieve and are lost. In considering the distribution $\Phi_H(k)$, we are computing the percentage of the original mass that is contained in the particles of linear horizontal size greater than $k - 1$; the mass contained in smaller horizontal lengths is filtered and discarded.

With regard to sieving, the idempotence property is of particular interest. $\text{OPEN}[\text{OPEN}(S, E), E] = \text{OPEN}(S, E)$ shows that the repeated use of the same-sized sieve accomplishes nothing.

Although we have restricted ourselves to linear granulometries, others can be constructed using different-shaped structuring elements. Because we are uti-

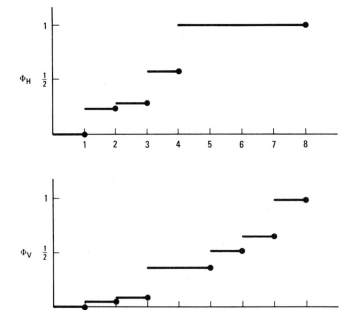

Figure 8.50   Size distributions

lizing a square grid structure, most relevant granulometric properties can be extracted by using either $H(k)$, $V(k)$, or a combination of the two. However, other parameterized families are certainly possible.

The behavior of size distributions, in that it is dependent on texture, is not describable in elementary geometric terms. Interpretation depends on not only the quantitative techniques described previously, but also on a deep understanding of the particular branch of science to which the techniques are to be applied.

In a second direction, we should take note of the difficulties inherent in the use of the size distributions as image features from which to recognize an image as belonging to a certain class. For example, suppose we wish to classify an image taken from a slide of human liver tissue as displaying evidence of pathology. It may be that the size distribution computed from a slide of healthy tissue is quite different from that computed from a slide of pathological tissue; however, there must be some listing of tissue size distributions in the database, and we must have a quantitative measurement technique to apply to the experimental distribution as it relates to the a priori functions stored in memory. This problem is characteristic of image classification based on the derivation of feature parameters through the quantitative analysis of empirical data.

8.5 SKELETON

One way in which images are characterized is by the employment of various *thinning* methodologies. In these, a figure is replaced by a *thin* representative of itself. The purpose of such a procedure is twofold. First, it yields a less complex figure that might be used as an archetype for classification purposes. Second, if in later processing the new image containing only the thin figure can be used in place of the original image, then memory load requirements are reduced.

There are many thinning algorithms; however, we will concentrate on the well-known *skeleton* or *medial axis* algorithm. To help to explain the intent, we will consider the skeleton of a set in the Euclidean plane. The Euclidean skeleton of a set S is defined in the following manner. For each x in S, let $D(x)$ denote the largest disk centered at x such that $D(x)$ is a subset of S. Then x is in the skeleton of S if there does not exist a disk D_1, not necessarily centered at x, such that D_1 properly contains $D(x)$ and such that D_1 is contained in S. For example, consider the isosceles triangle in Figure 8.51(a). The skeleton is drawn in dark lines. Note that, whereas the point x lies in the skeleton, since $D(x)$ cannot be included in a larger disk still within the triangle [Figure 8.51(b)], the point w does not lie in the skeleton, since $D(w)$ is a subset of the disk D', which is itself a subset of the triangle [Figure 8.51(c)].

Figure 8.52 gives a good indication of some of the intuitive notions concerning the Euclidean skeleton. While the skeleton gives a decent replication of the shape of a figure that is already somewhat thin [Figure 8.52(a)], it is far less appropriate when applied to a *thick* figure [Figure 8.52(b)]. Moreover, different geometric

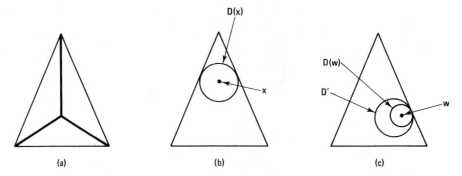

Figure 8.51   Determining skeleton for isosceles triangle

figures may possess the same skeleton [Figures 8.52(c) and (d)].   Perhaps most importantly, the skeleton is extremely sensitive to noise.   An infinitesimal distortion of the original shape can result in a vastly altered skeleton.   For instance, in Figures 8.52(e) and (f), notice how the removal of a tiny section of the figure results in a drastically changed skeleton.

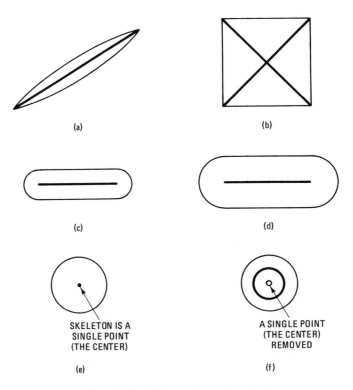

Figure 8.52   Skeleton for various pictures

In proceeding to a digital definition of the skeleton, we are immediately confronted with the impossibility of finding an exact analogue to a Euclidean disk. While there are several ways to give a digital version of Euclidean disks, we shall content ourselves with the collection of "square disks" given in Figure 8.53. Each of these is a constant image, or template, in which the origin is near the center of the domain. One might legitimately argue that a proper extension of the disk notion would require that we omit the even-numbered digital disks D_2, D_4, D_6, ..., since for these the center of the template is not a true center in the sense of symmetry. If we were to do this, the resulting thinning procedure would often result in skeletons that were not sufficiently thin. In any event, note that for the even-numbered disks the center has been defined in a consistent fashion.

The definition of the digital skeleton can now be stated in a manner analogous to the corresponding Euclidean definition. Let T be a constant image (pixel values 1 or $*$). For any pixel (i, j) in the domain of T, the maximal disk for (i, j), MAXDISK(i, j), is the highest-numbered disk D_k, translated so that its new center is at (i, j), such that TRAN$(D_k; i, j)$ is a subimage of T. The skeleton of T, SKEL(T), is a constant image (1's and $*$'s) such that a pixel lies within the domain of SKEL(T) if and only if its maximal disk is not a proper subimage of any other translated disk that is itself a subimage of T. Intuitively, (i, j) is in the digital skeleton if and only if its maximal disk is not a proper subset of some other disk lying within T.

$$D_1 = \begin{pmatrix} \textcircled{1} \end{pmatrix}$$

$$D_2 = \begin{pmatrix} 1 & 1 \\ \textcircled{1} & 1 \end{pmatrix}$$

$$D_3 = \begin{pmatrix} 1 & 1 & 1 \\ 1 & \textcircled{1} & 1 \\ 1 & 1 & 1 \end{pmatrix}$$

$$D_4 = \begin{pmatrix} 1 & 1 & 1 & 1 \\ 1 & 1 & 1 & 1 \\ 1 & \textcircled{1} & 1 & 1 \\ 1 & 1 & 1 & 1 \end{pmatrix}$$

$$D_5 = \begin{pmatrix} 1 & 1 & 1 & 1 & 1 \\ 1 & 1 & 1 & 1 & 1 \\ 1 & 1 & \textcircled{1} & 1 & 1 \\ 1 & 1 & 1 & 1 & 1 \\ 1 & 1 & 1 & 1 & 1 \end{pmatrix}$$

etc.

Figure 8.53 Square disks of increasing size

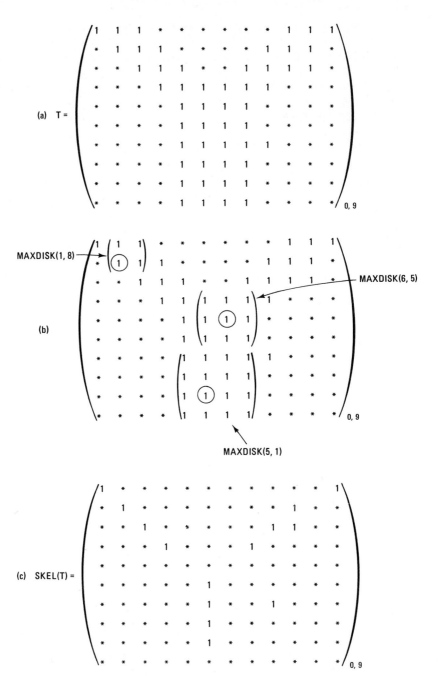

Figure 8.54 Image and associated skeleton image

Example 8.16

Referring to image T of Figure 8.54(a), the maximal disk for the pixel (1, 8) is given by

$$\text{MAXDISK}(1, 8) = \begin{pmatrix} 1 & 1 \\ 1 & 1 \end{pmatrix}_{1,9}$$

This is schematically indicated in Figure 8.54(b).   Also shown is the illustration of the maximal disks

$$\text{MAXDISK}(5, 1) = \begin{pmatrix} 1 & 1 & 1 & 1 \\ 1 & 1 & 1 & 1 \\ 1 & 1 & 1 & 1 \\ 1 & 1 & 1 & 1 \end{pmatrix}_{4, 3}$$

and

$$\text{MAXDISK}(6, 5) = \begin{pmatrix} 1 & 1 & 1 \\ 1 & 1 & 1 \\ 1 & 1 & 1 \end{pmatrix}_{5, 6}$$

Pixels (1, 8) and (5, 1) lie in the domain of the skeleton of T, but pixel (6, 5) does not.   This latter claim follows from the fact that the domain of MAXDISK(6, 5) lies properly within the domain of $\text{TRAN}(D_4; 5, 4)$, which is itself a subimage of T.

Finally, Figure 8.54(c) gives the skeleton SKEL(T).   Assuming the underlying image to be the letter Y, the skeleton gives a fairly good replication.   Unfortunately,

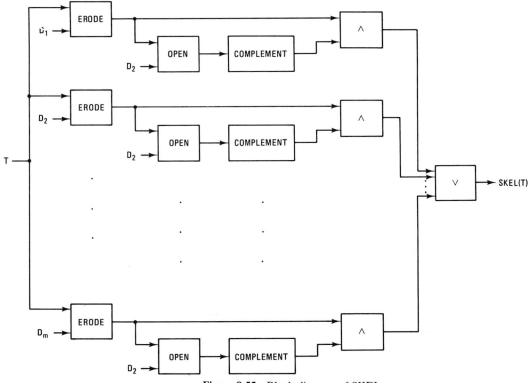

Figure 8.55   Block diagram of SKEL

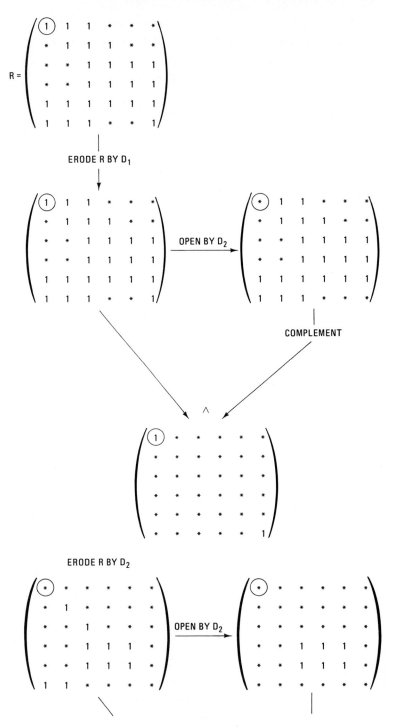

Figure 8.56 Walk-through for SKEL operation

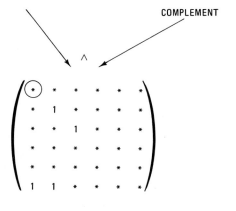

ERODE R BY D_3

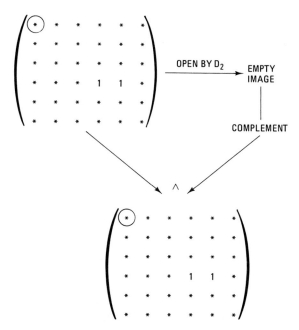

APPLY ∨ = EXTMAX TO THE THREE OUTPUT IMAGES

$$SKEL(R) = \begin{pmatrix} \textcircled{1} & * & * & * & * & * \\ * & 1 & * & * & * & * \\ * & * & 1 & * & * & * \\ * & * & * & 1 & 1 & * \\ * & * & * & * & * & * \\ 1 & 1 & * & * & * & 1 \end{pmatrix}$$

Figure 8.56   Continued

the pixel (8, 3), which appears to be affected by noise, results in an extraneous activated pixel in the skeleton. Moreover, the skeleton is not *connected*. The fifth row of the bound matrix contains no activated pixels. As a result, the top section of the letter Y is separated from the bottom section. Such connectivity problems are common for the skeleton.

At this point, we wish to provide the implementation of the operator SKEL in terms of basic morphological operations used in conjunction with elemental set-theoretic bound matrix operations. This implementation is given in Figure 8.55. In that figure, the number m is given by the minimum between the number of rows and columns of the minimal bound matrix for T. In essence, the block diagram of Figure 8.55 works by finding the skeleton pixels that have maximal disk of edge length 1, then those with maximal disk of edge length 2, and so on. It then takes the set-theoretic union of those pixel classes.

Figure 8.56 provides a walk-through of the first three branches of Figure 8.55 with input image R. For the remaining branches, $k = 4, 5$, and 6, the first erosion yields the empty image. This will usually be the case for values of k near to the value m unless the minimal bound matrix consists of mostly activated pixels, with all deactivated pixels near the outer edge of the matrix. Notice also that the image $S \wedge T^c$ is the image whose activated pixels are those contained in the domain of S minus (set-theoretic subtraction) the domain of T.

8.6 A DYNAMIC PROGRAMMING TECHNIQUE FOR LOCAL FEATURE MATCHING

There are numerous techniques for the construction of boundary-type images; for instance, the gradient-type edge-detection methodologies discussed in Section 8.3 might be employed. Very often, rather than possessing reliable information concerning the entire boundary, we only possess partial boundary information. This loss of information can occur at several stages in a computer vision system. Observation of an entire image might not be possible due to occlusion, noise, or inaccuracy within a portion of the sensor field. Poor restoration, enhancement, or segmentation techniques might also account for information loss in terms of missing or false boundary segments. Under such circumstances, feature-matching recognition techniques based on global properties of the image are often of little use; on the other hand, local feature extraction and matching techniques can prove beneficial in the context of partial information. Searching is performed in a sequential manner until the maximum degree of matching is achieved.

Local features are associated with only part of the object, in this case, pieces of the boundary. Such features are not sensitive to distortion or loss of information on other parts of the boundary. A partition of the entire boundary into n segments results in n feature vectors, each obtained by employing some specific feature-generation methodology. Many methods, such as the Fourier techniques of Section

8.9, are available that provide significant compression, while at the same time faithfully preserving information.

In the classification stage, features of observed boundary segments are compared with stored libraries of boundary segment features belonging to known images. Two boundary segments, one observed and one stored, are declared to be similar when their associated *feature vectors* are "close." In the dynamic programming methodology to be presented shortly, inter- and intradistance tables are utilized in systematically determining similar and dissimilar boundary segments. While a number of measures of closeness might be employed, we will restrict our attention to the *Chebyshev*- or supremum-type norm for feature vector comparison. Insofar as the overall string of features (corresponding to the collection of boundary segments) is concerned, in Section 8.7 we will introduce the Levenshtein distance.

Throughout the section it will be assumed that the images under discussion are polygonal boundary-type images that can be represented using nonoverlapping, connected straight-line segments that form a simple closed curve in the plane. Images of this type are called *line-drawing-type* images (see Figure 8.57). Vertices for such images occur at each intersection of two distinct line segments.

A polygonal boundary image is oriented; that is, it possesses an inside and an outside. If such an image is traversed by going in a counterclockwise fashion about the straight-line segments constituting the image, then the inside of the image will always remain on the left and the outside will always remain on the right.

We will now present an illustrative local feature methodology based on the counterclockwise traversal of the image. At each vertex we will record the outside angle resulting from the intersection of the corresponding line segments. Note that this angle will be the difference between 2π and the interior angle. Assuming there are n vertices, labeled $v_1, v_2, \ldots, v_n$, where the first vertex is chosen arbitrarily, we will denote the exterior angle at v_i by a_i. Moreover, standing at vertex v_i and looking toward the interior of the image, we will let l_i and r_i denote the respective lengths of the line segments to our left and right, and we will denote

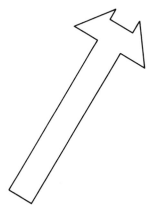

Figure 8.57 Line-drawing-type image

the two-segment boundary piece corresponding to v_i by x_i. The local feature vectors $\mathcal{F}(x_i)$, for $i = 1, 2, \ldots, n$, are defined by

$$\mathcal{F}(x_i) = \begin{pmatrix} l_i \\ a_i \\ r_i \end{pmatrix}$$

Treating each boundary piece x_i as an image, $\mathcal{F}(x_i)$ can be considered as a feature vector for x_i.

As an example of the methodology, consider the triangle in Figure 8.58(a). There are three boundary pieces x_1, x_2, and x_3, each possessing a vertex v_i and a feature vector $\mathcal{F}(x_i)$ consisting of three components. The feature vectors for x_1, x_2, and x_3 are illustrated in Figures 8.58(b), (c), and (d), respectively. Two other line-drawing-type images, together with their associated local feature vectors, are illustrated in Figures 8.59 and 8.60.

In general, observed feature vectors must often be compared to those stored in memory in a manner that is independent of the size, location, and orientation of the observed image. Due to these requirements, a self-consistent normalization based on intrinsic properties of the observed image must be employed in order to bring it into a standard form that allows comparison with the archetypes in the database.

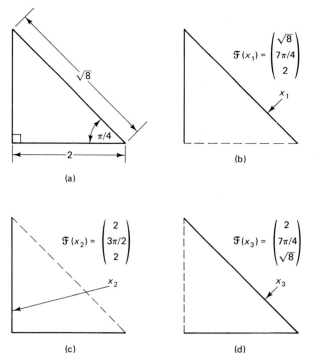

Figure 8.58 Image and boundary pieces

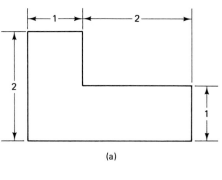

(a)

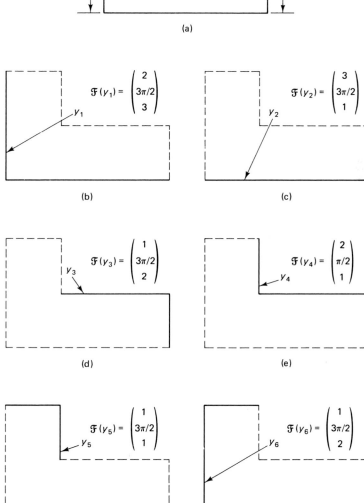

(b)

$$\mathcal{F}(y_1) = \begin{pmatrix} 2 \\ 3\pi/2 \\ 3 \end{pmatrix}$$

(c)

$$\mathcal{F}(y_2) = \begin{pmatrix} 3 \\ 3\pi/2 \\ 1 \end{pmatrix}$$

(d)

$$\mathcal{F}(y_3) = \begin{pmatrix} 1 \\ 3\pi/2 \\ 2 \end{pmatrix}$$

(e)

$$\mathcal{F}(y_4) = \begin{pmatrix} 2 \\ \pi/2 \\ 1 \end{pmatrix}$$

(f)

$$\mathcal{F}(y_5) = \begin{pmatrix} 1 \\ 3\pi/2 \\ 1 \end{pmatrix}$$

(g)

$$\mathcal{F}(y_6) = \begin{pmatrix} 1 \\ 3\pi/2 \\ 2 \end{pmatrix}$$

Figure 8.59 Image and boundary pieces

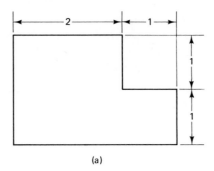

(a)

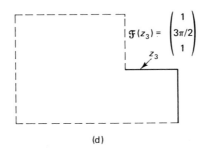

(b)

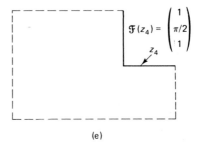

(c)

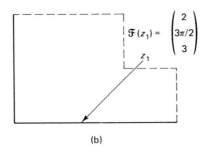

(d)

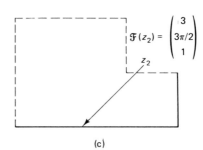

(e)

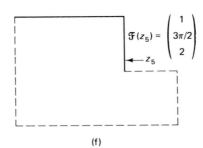

(f)

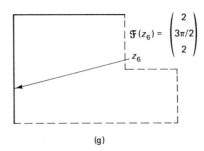

(g)

Figure 8.60   Image and boundary pieces

Insofar as the feature vectors $\mathcal{F}(x_i)$ are concerned, each is independent of both translation and rotation of the observed image. Scale factor invariance can readily be achieved with appropriate normalization; however, this will not be pursued since the required manipulations cannot be accomplished practically without the aid of a computer.

It should be noted that the local features $\mathcal{F}(x_i)$ are not invariant under reflection of the entire image. The feature vector of a specific vertex v_i is related to the corresponding vertex of the reflected image by the relation

$$\begin{pmatrix} l \\ a \\ r \end{pmatrix} \longrightarrow \begin{pmatrix} r \\ a \\ l \end{pmatrix}$$

Because of the simplicity of the foregoing relation, with only a slight modification, invariance under reflection could be achieved.

To compare local features, we will employ the following distance criterion: given two boundary pieces x_i and y_j from two, not necessarily distinct, images, the distance between the boundary pieces is defined to be

$$\rho(x_i, y_j) = \max(|l_{x_i} - l_{y_j}|, |a_{x_i} - a_{y_j}|, |r_{x_i} - r_{y_j}|)$$

Distance tables can be formed to display the distances between two corresponding sequences of boundary pieces, each of which is found by traversing a line-drawing-type figure in a counterclockwise manner. Sequences are compared piece by piece, and a table is constructed by listing the first sequence of boundary pieces across the top, the second sequence along the left-hand side, and the appropriate distances between corresponding entries in the table itself. In practice, the first sequence of boundary pieces comes from a library of prestored archetypal images, whereas the second represents the observed image. Recognition is achieved when the distances between corresponding boundary pieces are close to zero. Provided that the boundary-piece sequences have the same starting vertex, when there is a match, the main diagonal of the table will have entries close to zero. Tables 8.1 through 8.6 give inter- and intrapiece distance tables for the images of Figures 8.58, 8.59, and 8.60. Note that different tables result if different starting vertices are selected. Actual matching can be accomplished by dynamically checking comparisons for various starting vertices.

TABLE 8.1 DISTANCE TABLE

	y_1	y_2	y_3	y_4	y_5	y_6
x_1	1	1	1.82	3.9	1.82	1.82
x_2	1	1	1	3.14	1	1
x_3	0.78	1.82	0.82	3.9	1.82	1

TABLE 8.2 DISTANCE TABLE

	z_1	z_2	z_3	z_4	z_5	z_6
x_1	1	1	1.82	3.9	1.82	0.82
x_2	1	1	1	3.14	1	0
x_3	0.78	1.82	1.82	3.9	0.82	0.82

TABLE 8.3 DISTANCE TABLE

	z_1	z_2	z_3	z_4	z_5	z_6
y_1	0	2	2	3.14	1	1
y_2	2	0	2	3.14	2	1
y_3	1	2	1	3.14	0	1
y_4	3.14	3.14	3.14	1	3.14	3.14
y_5	2	2	0	3.14	1	1
y_6	1	2	1	3.14	0	1

TABLE 8.4 DISTANCE TABLE

	y_1	y_2	y_3	y_4	y_5	y_6
y_1	0	2	1	π	2	1
y_2	2	0	2	π	2	2
y_3	1	2	0	π	1	0
y_4	π	π	π	0	π	π
y_5	2	2	1	π	0	1
y_6	1	2	0	π	1	0

TABLE 8.5 DISTANCE TABLE

	z_1	z_2	z_3	z_4	z_5	z_6
z_1	0	2	2	π	1	1
z_2	2	0	2	π	2	1
z_3	2	2	0	π	1	1
z_4	π	π	π	0	π	π
z_5	1	2	1	π	0	1
z_6	1	1	1	π	1	0

TABLE 8.6   DISTANCE TABLE

	x_1	x_2	x_3
x_1	0	0.828	0.828
x_2	0.828	0	0.828
x_3	0.828	0.828	0

8.7 LEVENSHTEIN DISTANCE: A DISSIMILARITY MEASUREMENT FOR STRINGS

Given two strings x and y, we would like a measure of the dissimilarity between them. This would allow us, for example, to compare the similarity of two polygonal boundary images, each comprised of a string of boundary pieces. One such measure, the *Levenshtein distance*, is defined as the smallest number of editing operations that are required to derive string y from string x. It is denoted by $d(x, y)$. The permissible editing operations are the insertion, deletion, and substitution of letters. Small values of $d(x, y)$ indicate string similarity, whereas large values indicate dissimilarity.

Given the strings

$$x = x_1 x_2 x_3 \ldots x_n$$

and

$$y = y_1 y_2 y_3 \ldots y_m$$

a distance ρ' between letters x_i and y_j must be defined. For convenience, we will use

$$\rho'(x_i, y_j) = \begin{cases} 0, & \text{if } x_i = y_j \\ 1, & \text{if } x_i \neq y_j \end{cases}$$

The Levenshtein algorithm is then given recursively:

1. Let $\delta(i, 0) = i, i = 0, 1, \ldots, n$.
2. Let $\delta(0, j) = j, j = 0, 1, \ldots, m$.
3. For $i = 1, 2, \ldots, n$ and $j = 1, 2, \ldots, m$, let

$$\delta(i, j) = \min[\delta(i - 1, j) + 1, \delta(i, j - 1)$$
$$+ 1, \delta(i - 1, j - 1) + \rho'(x_i, y_j)]$$

4. $d(x, y) = \delta(n, m)$.

Example 8.17

Let

$$x = a \quad b \quad a \quad b \quad a$$

and

$$y = a \quad a \quad b \quad b \quad a \quad a$$

The letter distance ρ' defined above yields the following distance table for distances between letters in the strings x and y:

ρ'	$y_1 = a$	$y_2 = a$	$y_3 = b$	$y_4 = b$	$y_5 = a$	$y_6 = a$
$x_1 = a$	0	0	1	1	0	0
$x_2 = b$	1	1	0	0	1	1
$x_3 = a$	0	0	1	1	0	0
$x_4 = b$	1	1	0	0	1	1
$x_5 = a$	0	0	1	1	0	0

Using the distances $\rho'(i, j)$, the intermediate distance function δ is found in a forward-chaining-type sequential manner. Intermediate distances are found at the 42 lattice points in

$$\{0, 1, 2, 3, 4, 5\} \times \{0, 1, 2, 3, 4, 5, 6\}$$

These are computed recursively by beginning with the $\delta(i, 0)$ and the $\delta(0, j)$:

$$\delta(1, 1) = \min[2, 2, \rho'(x_1, y_1)] = 0$$

$$\delta(1, 2) = \min[3, 1, 1 + \rho'(x_1, y_2)] = 1$$

$$\delta(2, 1) = \min[1, 3, 1 + \rho'(x_2, y_1)] = 1$$

$$\delta(2, 2) = \min[2, 2, \rho'(x_2, y_2)] = 1$$

$$\delta(1, 3) = \min[4, 2, 2 + \rho'(x_1, y_3)] = 2$$

$$\delta(3, 1) = \min[2, 4, 2 + \rho'(x_3, y_1)] = 2$$

$$\delta(2, 3) = \min[3, 2, 1 + \rho'(x_2, y_3)] = 1$$

$$\delta(3, 2) = \min[2, 3, 1 + \rho'(x_3, y_2)] = 1$$

$$\delta(4, 1) = \min[3, 5, 3 + \rho'(x_4, y_1)] = 3$$

$$\delta(1, 4) = \min[5, 3, 3 + \rho'(x_1, y_4)] = 3$$

$$\delta(3, 3) = \min[2, 2, 1 + \rho'(x_3, y_3)] = 2$$

$$\delta(4, 2) = \min[2, 4, 2 + \rho'(x_4, y_2)] = 2$$

$$\delta(2, 4) = \min[4, 2, 2 + \rho'(x_2, y_4)] = 2$$

$$\delta(5, 1) = \min[4, 6, 4 + \rho'(x_5, y_1)] = 4$$

$$\delta(1, 5) = \min[6, 4, 4 + \rho'(x_1, y_5)] = 4$$

$$\delta(5, 2) = \min[3, 5, 3 + \rho'(x_5, y_2)] = 3$$

$$\delta(4, 3) = \min[3, 3, 1 + \rho'(x_4, y_3)] = 1$$

$$\delta(3, 4) = \min[3, 3, 1 + \rho'(x_3, y_4)] = 2$$

$$\delta(2, 5) = \min[5, 3, 3 + \rho'(x_2, y_5)] = 3$$

$$\delta(1, 6) = \min[7, 5, 5 + \rho'(x_1, y_6)] = 5$$

$$\delta(5, 3) = \min[2, 4, 2 + \rho'(x_5, y_3)] = 2$$

$$\delta(4, 4) = \min[3, 2, 2 + \rho'(x_4, y_4)] = 2$$

$$\delta(3, 5) = \min[4, 3, 2 + \rho'(x_3, y_5)] = 2$$

$$\delta(2, 6) = \min[6, 4, 4 + \rho'(x_2, y_6)] = 4$$

$$\delta(5, 4) = \min[3, 3, 1 + \rho'(x_5, y_4)] = 2$$

$$\delta(4, 5) = \min[3, 3, 2 + \rho'(x_4, y_5)] = 3$$

$$\delta(3, 6) = \min[5, 3, 3 + \rho'(x_3, y_6)] = 3$$

$$\delta(5, 5) = \min[4, 3, 2 + \rho'(x_5, y_5)] = 2$$

$$\delta(4, 6) = \min[4, 4, 2 + \rho'(x_4, y_6)] = 3$$

$$\delta(5, 6) = \min[4, 3, 3 + \rho'(x_5, y_6)] = 3$$

Thus, $d(x, y) = 3$.

To apply the Levenshtein distance to the local feature-matching procedure of Section 8.6, let ρ be the segment distance function defined therein, and define the distance function ρ' required for the Levenshtein distance by

$$\rho'(x_i, y_j) = \begin{cases} 0, & \text{if } \rho(x_i, y_j) \le t \\ 1, & \text{if } \rho(x_i, y_j) > t \end{cases}$$

where it is assumed that x and y are images represented by the boundary-piece strings $x_1 \ldots x_n$ and $y_1 \ldots y_m$, respectively. The nonnegative number t, called the *threshold value*, is usually heuristically chosen. For perfect matching, the *no-noise* situation, $t = 0$ is utilized.

For the application at hand, the same algorithm should be used in finding the Levenshtein distance; however, it must be employed for all cyclic shifts of the entries in one of the strings. The reason for this is that the image is a closed curve, and the starting point for creating the boundary segments is not set a priori. After finding the distance between each cyclic permutation of a given image with another image, the minimum is taken.

Insofar as image recognition is concerned, a serious shortcoming in many local feature-matching methodologies, such as the Levenshtein procedure, is that a measure of similarity, not of congruence, is employed: pieces are shifted in attempting to find the best match. Global geometry is not taken into account, only local structure. The approach in the next section provides a partial remedy for this difficulty.

8.8 THE METHOD OF BRIDGING SEGMENTS

One approach for overcoming the lack of global geometric considerations in a local feature technique, such as the utilization of the Levenshtein distance to measure similarity, is the method of bridging segments. Here, geometric characteristics influence the recognition procedure.

Any boundary piece of the observed image that matches a boundary piece in one of the pattern images in the database is kept, and any that does not is discarded. In the other direction, any boundary piece of any pattern image that matches a boundary piece in the observed image is also kept; the others are discarded. Once this matching procedure has been accomplished, the remaining images, both the observed and those from the database, are usually comprised of disconnected boundary pieces. The essence of the method of bridging segments is to introduce straight line segments that connect, in an order-preserving fashion,

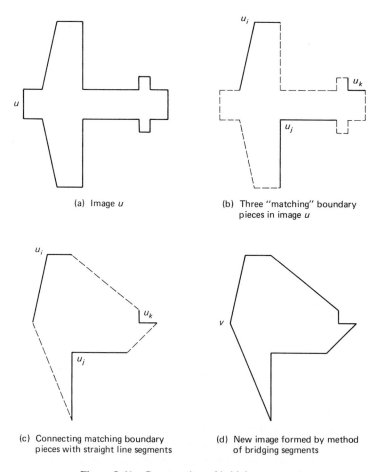

(a) Image u

(b) Three "matching" boundary pieces in image u

(c) Connecting matching boundary pieces with straight line segments

(d) New image formed by method of bridging segments

Figure 8.61   Construction of bridging segments

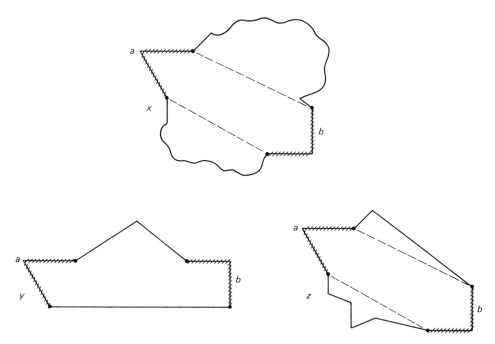

Figure 8.62   Matching by bridging segments

the remaining boundary pieces in each image, the net effect being to keep the structures intact (see Figure 8.61).

Once the new line segments have been introduced, each original image is once again a closed, boundary-type image, and the methods of Sections 8.6 and 8.7 can be applied.   Assuming the new closed-curve image is simple (the boundary does not cross itself), the feature methodology of Section 8.6 is directly applicable. Referring to Figure 8.61, all but the three boundary pieces u_i, u_j, and u_k have been removed in part (b), since it is being assumed that only these are involved in a match.   In part (c), the dashed lines illustrate the bridging segments, and in part (d), the resulting image is portrayed.   It is upon this image that the dynamic programming procedures discussed previously are applied.

Should the bridging process result in a closed curve that is not simple, a possible approach is to subdivide the bridged image into smaller ones that consist of simple closed curves.   Of course, not only is processing time increased, but the accuracy of the overall methodology is reduced.

Example 8.18

Consider image x of Figure 8.62, which is partially occluded by a cloud, and suppose that images y and z are archetypes in the database.   Boundary pieces a and b are identically matched in each of the three images, but local procedures do not result in a unique match.   However, the method of bridging segments does produce a match between the observed image x and the pattern image z.

8.9 FOURIER SERIES REPRESENTATION OF CHAIN-ENCODED IMAGES

The method of recognition by feature vector comparison is essentially a compression technique: images are replaced by a finite set of features, and it is on the features that we focus our attention. In the preceding sections we have assumed the existence of line-drawing-type images and have applied string-recognition procedures based on elementary geometric properties. In the current section, we will introduce a particular string-encoding technique and then apply a Fourier series compression methodology. (Those who are not familiar with the theory of Fourier series in one dimension should only skim this and the following section.) Two uses of the Fourier coefficients should be noted: (1) Using a finite number of the Fourier coefficients, a reasonable facsimile of the original image can be constructed, and (2) some predetermined collection of the Fourier coefficients can be employed as the components of a feature vector.

In the chain encoding of linear-boundary-type images, the alphabet $A = \{0, 1, \ldots, 7\}$ is employed. A *chain code* c is a string from A^*. Each letter (integer) corresponds to a directed line segment of length 1 or $\sqrt{2}$ in the x-y plane, the directions of the segments being multiples of $45°$. Figure 8.63 gives the numeration scheme for the chain code. For each letter a_i in A, the directed line segment v_i associated with a_i, as shown in the figure, can be written in phasor notation as

$$v_i = \left[1 + \frac{\sqrt{2} - 1}{2} (1 - (-1)^{a_i}) \right] \sphericalangle \left(\frac{\pi}{4} \right) a_i$$

If $c = a_1 a_2 \ldots a_m$ is a string of length m from A^*, then a line-type image can be associated with c by joining the segments v_i in a head-to-tail fashion while reading c from left to right. Specifically, if the string $a_i a_{i+1}$ appears within the

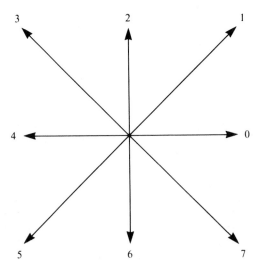

Figure 8.63 Chain-code line segments

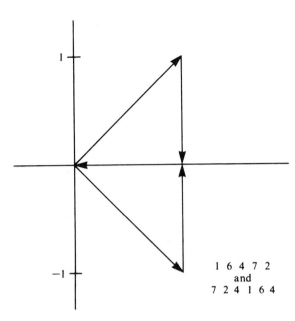

1 6 4 7 2
and
7 2 4 1 6 4

Figure 8.64   Non 1-1 nature of chain encoding

string c, then the head of v_i should touch the tail of v_{i+1}. The process is begun by positioning the tail of v_1 at the origin. Using this procedure, for every c in A^* there exists a unique piecewise linear line-type image v associated with c. Should c be the empty string, we let v be the null image. Note that the correspondence between strings in A^* and piecewise-linear line images is neither one-to-one nor onto (see Example 8.19).

Example 8.19

Consider the linear line image illustrated in Figure 8.64. This image is induced by the strings $c = 1\ 6\ 4\ 7\ 2$ and $d = 7\ 2\ 4\ 1\ 6\ 4$. Hence, the inducement of linear line images from A^* is not one-to-one. Moreover, if we were to choose a piecewise-linear line image that does not have a directed line segment with tail at the origin, then that image could not have been induced by a string from A^*. Hence, neither is the inducement onto.

In what follows, we shall assume that the piecewise-linear line image v has been induced by a fixed element c in A^*. Projections will be obtained by traversing the image $v_1 v_2 \ldots v_K$ from the tail of v_1 to the head of v_K using arc length t as a parameter. If $c = a_1 a_2 \ldots a_K$, then the total arc length is given by

$$T = \sum_{i=1}^{K} \left[1 + \frac{(\sqrt{2} - 1)}{2} (1 - (-1)^{a_i}) \right]$$

As an arc in the plane, $v = v(t) = (x(t), y(t))$, where $x(t)$ and $y(t)$ specify the x and y coordinates, respectively, of v, and where $0 \le t \le T$. $x(t)$ and $y(t)$

are called the x and y *projections*, respectively.   The time (arc length t being the parameter) required to traverse a particular link a_i is

$$\Delta t_i = 1 + \frac{(\sqrt{2} - 1)}{2} (1 - (-1)^{a_i})$$

where it should be noted that the apparently complicated expression yields either 1 or $\sqrt{2}$.   The time required to traverse the first p links in the chain is

$$t_p = \sum_{i=1}^{p} \Delta t_i$$

The changes in the x-y projections of the image induced by the chain as the link a_i is traversed (see Figure 8.65) are

$$\Delta x_i = \text{sgn}(6 - a_i) \, \text{sgn}(2 - a_i)$$

$$\Delta y_i = \text{sgn}(4 - a_i) \, \text{sgn}(a_i)$$

where sgn is the *sign function*, given by

$$\text{sgn}(z) = \begin{cases} 1, & \text{if } z > 0 \\ 0, & \text{if } z = 0 \\ -1, & \text{if } z < 0 \end{cases}$$

We now consider a direct procedure for obtaining the Fourier coefficients of a chain-encoded contour.   Since the starting point of the chain code corresponds to the origin, the projections on the x and y axes for the first p links of the chain are given by

$$x_p = \sum_{i=1}^{p} \Delta x_i$$

and

$$y_p = \sum_{i=1}^{p} \Delta y_i$$

The Fourier series expansion for the x projection, as a function of the parameter t, of the entire chain code consisting of K symbols is given by

$$x(t) = A_0 + \sum_{n=1}^{\infty} A_n \cos \frac{2n\pi t}{T} + B_n \sin \frac{2n\pi t}{T}$$

where A_0, A_n, and B_n are the nonnormalized Fourier coefficients

$$A_0 = \frac{1}{T} \int_0^T x(t) \, dt$$

$$A_n = \frac{2}{T} \int_0^T x(t) \cos \frac{2n\pi t}{T} \, dt$$

$$B_n = \frac{2}{T} \int_0^T x(t) \sin \frac{2n\pi t}{T} \, dt$$

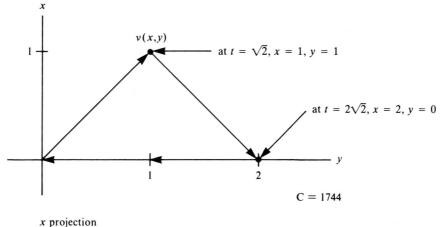

at $t = \sqrt{2}$, $x = 1$, $y = 1$

at $t = 2\sqrt{2}$, $x = 2$, $y = 0$

$C = 1744$

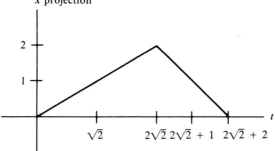

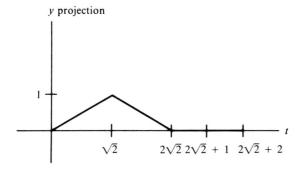

Figure 8.65   Projections of chain-encoded images

The Fourier coefficients A_n and B_n are easily found because the x projection $x(t)$ is piecewise linear and continuous for all time.   A simple calculation shows that

$$A_n = \frac{T}{2n^2\pi^2} \sum_{p=1}^{K} \frac{\Delta x_p}{\Delta t_p} \left[\cos \frac{2n\pi t_p}{T} - \cos \frac{2n\pi t_{p-1}}{T} \right]$$

$$B_n = \frac{T}{2n^2\pi^2} \sum_{p=1}^{K} \frac{\Delta x_p}{\Delta t_p} \left[\sin \frac{2n\pi t_p}{T} - \sin \frac{2n\pi t_{p-1}}{T} \right]$$

The Fourier series expansion for the y projection of the chain code of the complete contour is similarly found to be

$$y(t) = C_0 + \sum_{n=1}^{\infty} C_n \cos \frac{2n\pi t}{T} + D_n \sin \frac{2n\pi t}{T}$$

where

$$C_n = \frac{T}{2n^2\pi^2} \sum_{p=1}^{K} \frac{\Delta y_p}{\Delta t_p} \left[\cos \frac{2n\pi t_p}{T} - \cos \frac{2n\pi t_{p-1}}{T} \right]$$

$$D_n = \frac{T}{2n^2\pi^2} \sum_{p=1}^{K} \frac{\Delta y_p}{\Delta t_p} \left[\sin \frac{2n\pi t_p}{T} - \sin \frac{2n\pi t_{p-1}}{T} \right]$$

The DC components A_0 and C_0 in these Fourier series representations are given by

$$A_0 = \frac{1}{T} \sum_{p=1}^{K} \frac{\Delta x_p}{2\Delta t_p} (t_p^2 - t_{p-1}^2) + \xi_p(t_p - t_{p-1})$$

$$C_0 = \frac{1}{T} \sum_{p=1}^{K} \frac{\Delta y_p}{2\Delta t_p} (t_p^2 - t_{p-1}^2) + \delta_p(t_p - t_{p-1})$$

where

$$\xi_p = \sum_{j=1}^{p-1} \Delta x_j - \frac{\Delta x_p}{\Delta t_p} \sum_{j=1}^{p-1} \Delta t_j$$

$$\delta_p = \sum_{j=1}^{p-1} \Delta y_j - \frac{\Delta y_p}{\Delta t_p} \sum_{j=1}^{p-1} \Delta t_j$$

and $\xi_1 = \delta_1 = 0$.

Example 8.20

The chain code image for $V_1 = 0005676644422123$ is illustrated in Figure 8.66. Since the induced contour is closed, both the x and y projections begin and end at $t = 0$, and both $x(t)$ and $y(t)$ are uniform limits of their respective Fourier series.

Let $\tilde{X}_N(t)$, $N = 0, 1, 2, \ldots$, denote the function that is the Nth truncation of the Fourier series for x; that is, $\tilde{X}_N(t)$ is the Nth partial sum of the Fourier series for

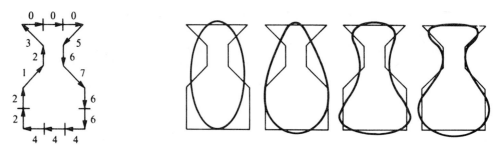

Figure 8.66   Chain code of image and first four harmonic approximations

x. We often say that $\tilde{X}_N(t)$ is the *N*th harmonic approximation, the number of harmonics being the number of Fourier coefficients, starting from 0, being employed in the truncation. In a similar manner, $\tilde{Y}_N(t)$ denotes the *N*th harmonic approximation to the *y* projection.

If we let $\tilde{v}_N(t) = (\tilde{X}_N(t), \tilde{Y}_N(t))$, then, as the parameter *t* runs from 0 to *T*, $\tilde{v}_N(t)$ traces out an approximation to the piecewise-linear line image $v(t)$ that has been induced from the chain code V_1. Since $\tilde{X}_N(t)$ and $\tilde{Y}_N(t)$ converge uniformly to $x(t)$ and $y(t)$, respectively, $\tilde{v}_N(t)$ converges uniformly to $v(t)$. Figure 8.66 gives the first four harmonic approximations, $\tilde{v}_1$, $\tilde{v}_2$, $\tilde{v}_3$, and $\tilde{v}_4$, superimposed on the original chain code image *v*.

For a given image, it is useful to be able to specify the number of harmonics required in order that a truncated Fourier approximation to a contour be in error no greater than some prespecified amount in the *x* or *y* dimension. Let

$$\tilde{X}_N = A_0 + \sum_{n=1}^{N} A_n \cos \frac{2n\pi t}{T} + B_n \sin \frac{2n\pi t}{T}$$

$$\tilde{Y}_N = C_0 + \sum_{n=1}^{N} C_n \cos \frac{2n\pi t}{T} + D_n \sin \frac{2n\pi t}{T}$$

be the Fourier series truncated after *N* harmonics for the $x(t)$ and $y(t)$ projections, respectively, and define the error ε as

$$\varepsilon = \max[\sup_t | x(t) - \tilde{X}_N(t) |, \sup_t | y(t) - \tilde{Y}_N(t) |]$$

It can be shown that, as long as $v(0) = v(T)$ (the induced image contour is closed),

$$\varepsilon \leq \frac{T}{2\pi^2 N} \max[V_0^T(x'(t)), V_0^T(y'(t))]$$

where the total variation of the derivative $x'(t)$ has been symbolized as $V_0^T(x'(t))$ and the total variation of the derivative $y'(t)$ as $V_0^T(y'(t))$. The derivatives for the link a_i, everywhere except at the end points, are

$$x_i' = \frac{\Delta x_i}{\Delta t_i}$$

$$y_i' = \frac{\Delta y_i}{\Delta t_i}$$

These can be tabulated according to the value a_i and are given in Table 8.7. The total variations of $x'(t)$ and $y'(t)$ are, respectively,

$$V_0^T(x'(t)) = \sum_{2}^{K} |x_i' - x_{i-1}'|$$

$$V_0^T(y'(t)) = \sum_{2}^{K} |y_i' - y_{i-1}'|$$

A graph of the actual error ε versus the number *N* of harmonics is shown in Figure

TABLE 8.7   x AND y DERIVATIVES OF LINK a_i

a_i	x'_i	y'_i
0	1.0	0.0
1	0.707	0.707
2	0.0	1.0
3	−0.707	0.707
4	−1.0	0.0
5	−0.707	−0.707
6	0.0	−1.0
7	0.707	−0.707

8.67 for the chain code V_1 of Example 8.20.   The predicted bounds on the error according to the maximum total variation estimate are shown superimposed on the graph.

Example 8.21

Consider the following four chain codes:

V_2 = 11172206667666444444422

V_3 = 54123430010100077110754545065413446

V_4 = 0031070454764457153450413314206000

V_5 = 2333446766544433267700012232545433221566770101444322110455667000321107733455671000776233445007776

As shown in Figures 8.68 through 8.71, for each of these codes there are image contours of increasing complexity (wiggliness).   Each figure displays the chain-code represen-

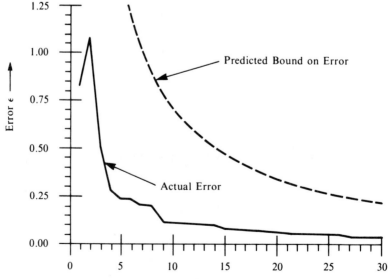

Figure 8.67   Predicted and actual error versus harmonic content

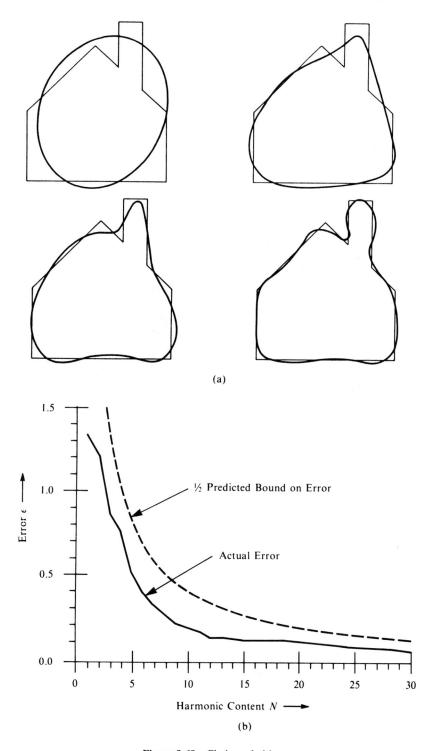

(a)

Error ϵ —→

½ Predicted Bound on Error

Actual Error

Harmonic Content N —→

(b)

Figure 8.68   Chain-coded house

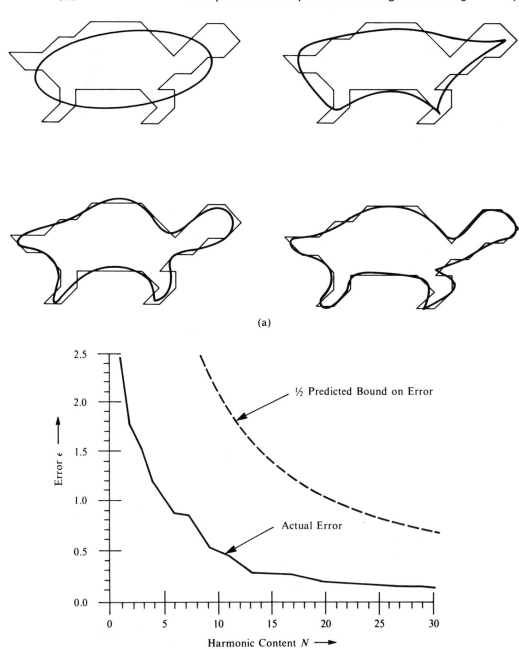

(a)

½ Predicted Bound on Error

Actual Error

Properties of the chain code $V_3 = 5412343001010007711$
075454506541344446

(b)

Figure 8.69   Chain-coded raccoon

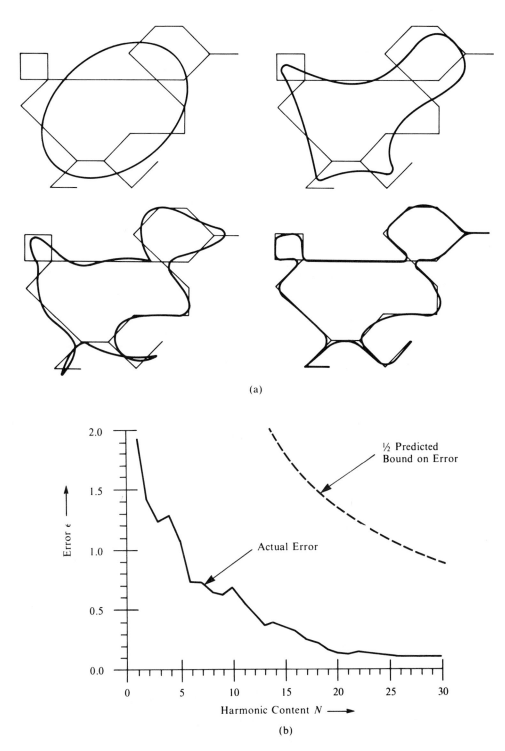

(a)

(b)

Figure 8.70 Chain-coded chicken

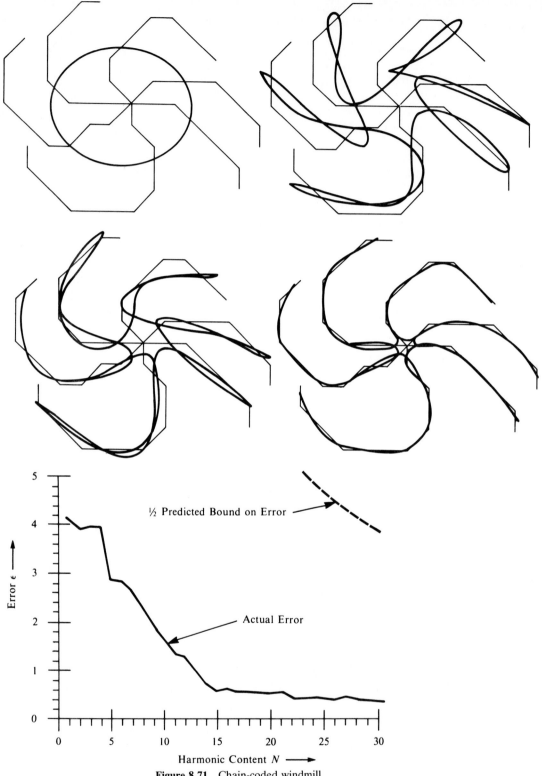

Figure 8.71 Chain-coded windmill

tation of the image contour together with superimposed Fourier approximations that incorporate increasingly higher harmonic content. The actual error and *one-half* the predicted bound on the error, in terms of the harmonic content N, are shown at the bottom of each figure. It is apparent from inspection of the figures that, as the contour becomes more complex, the predicted bound becomes more conservative. Consequently, to make a realistic comparison of the accuracy of harmonic reconstruction as it applies to different contours, both plots of ε should be normalized against $T = t_K$ (i.e., use $\varepsilon' = \varepsilon/T$). In any event, the predicted bound on ε offers the advantage of quick and easy computation as compared to the calculation of the actual error.

8.10 NORMALIZATION OF FOURIER SERIES REPRESENTATIONS

In the projection compression methodology of Section 8.9, normalization for feature recognition via the Fourier coefficients must be accomplished with respect to (1) the starting points for obtaining the Fourier expansion and (2) rotation, translation, and magnification. This can be done through the utilization of the *harmonic ellipsi*.

Using the results of Section 8.9, the truncated Fourier approximation to a closed piecewise linear line image can be written as

$$\tilde{X}_N(t) = A_0 + \sum_{n=1}^{N} X_n(t)$$

and

$$\tilde{Y}_N(t) = C_0 + \sum_{n=1}^{N} Y_n(t)$$

where, for $1 \leq n \leq N$,

$$X_n(t) = A_n \cos \frac{2\pi nt}{T} + B_n \sin \frac{2\pi nt}{T}$$

and

$$Y_n(t) = C_n \cos \frac{2\pi nt}{T} + D_n \sin \frac{2\pi nt}{T}$$

Let $v_n(t) = (X_n(t), Y_n(t))$ for any n. Then, as the parameter t runs from 0 to T, $v_n(t)$ describes a locus of points in the plane. This locus is elliptical. Indeed, suppose $A_nD_n - B_nC_n$ is nonzero. The elimination of the sine and cosine terms in the defining expressions for X_n and Y_n yields

$$\frac{(C_n^2 + D_n^2)X_n^2 + (A_n^2 + B_n^2)Y_n^2 - 2(A_nC_n + B_nD_n)X_nY_n}{A_nD_n - B_nC_n} = 1$$

which is an ellipse.   For the case where $A_n D_n - B_n C_n = 0$, we have an ellipse in a degenerate form—a straight line or a point.   Finally, it should be noted that the same elliptical loci will be obtained for the points $v_n = (X_n, Y_n)$ regardless of the starting point for taking projections of the contour.

We now proceed to the normalization problem outlined at the beginning of the section.   To begin with, a difference in the starting points is displayed in the projected space as a phase shift.   Hence, a starting point displaced λ units in the direction of rotation around the contour from the original starting point will have projections, for $n \geq 1$,

$$X_n(t^* + \lambda) = A_n \cos \frac{2\pi n}{T} (t^* + \lambda) + B_n \sin \frac{2\pi n}{T} (t^* + \lambda)$$

$$Y_n(t^* + \lambda) = C_n \cos \frac{2\pi n}{T} (t^* + \lambda) + D_n \sin \frac{2\pi n}{T} (t^* + \lambda)$$

where $t^* + \lambda = t$.   Expanding X_n and Y_n and collecting terms yields

$$X_n^*(t^*) = A_n^* \cos \frac{2\pi n t^*}{T} + B_n^* \sin \frac{2\pi n t^*}{T}$$

$$Y_n^*(t^*) = C_n^* \cos \frac{2\pi n t^*}{T} + D_n^* \sin \frac{2\pi n t^*}{T},$$

where

$$\begin{pmatrix} A_n^* & C_n^* \\ B_n^* & D_n^* \end{pmatrix} = \begin{pmatrix} \cos \dfrac{2\pi n \lambda}{T} & \sin \dfrac{2\pi n \lambda}{T} \\ -\sin \dfrac{2\pi n \lambda}{T} & \cos \dfrac{2\pi n \lambda}{T} \end{pmatrix} \begin{pmatrix} A_n & C_n \\ B_n & D_n \end{pmatrix}$$

To obtain a normalization with respect to rotation, note that a counterclockwise rotation of the X-Y coordinate axes through ψ degrees into the U-V axes is accomplished by

$$\begin{pmatrix} U \\ V \end{pmatrix} = \begin{pmatrix} \cos \psi & \sin \psi \\ -\sin \psi & \cos \psi \end{pmatrix} \begin{pmatrix} X \\ Y \end{pmatrix}$$

The effect of this rotation on the Fourier coefficients A_n^*, B_n^*, C_n^*, and D_n^* is readily apparent when the projections X_n^*, Y_n^* are expressed in matrix form:

$$\begin{pmatrix} X_n^* \\ Y_n^* \end{pmatrix} = \begin{pmatrix} A_n^* & B_n^* \\ C_n^* & D_n^* \end{pmatrix} \begin{pmatrix} \cos \dfrac{2\pi n t^*}{T} \\ \sin \dfrac{2\pi n t^*}{T} \end{pmatrix}$$

Then the projections μ_n, ν_n on the U-V axes are

$$\begin{pmatrix} \mu_n \\ \nu_n \end{pmatrix} = \begin{pmatrix} \cos\psi & \sin\psi \\ -\sin\psi & \cos\psi \end{pmatrix} \begin{pmatrix} X_n^* \\ Y_n^* \end{pmatrix} = \begin{pmatrix} \cos\psi & \sin\psi \\ -\sin\psi & \cos\psi \end{pmatrix} \begin{pmatrix} A_n^* & B_n^* \\ C_n^* & D_n^* \end{pmatrix} \begin{pmatrix} \cos\dfrac{2\pi nt^*}{T} \\ \sin\dfrac{2\pi nt^*}{T} \end{pmatrix}$$

A rotated set of Fourier coefficients A_n^{**}, B_n^{**}, C_n^{**}, and D_n^{**} may be defined by

$$\begin{pmatrix} A_n^{**} & B_n^{**} \\ C_n^{**} & D_n^{**} \end{pmatrix} = \begin{pmatrix} \cos\psi & \sin\psi \\ -\sin\psi & \cos\psi \end{pmatrix} \begin{pmatrix} A_n^* & B_n^* \\ C_n^* & D_n^* \end{pmatrix}$$

The combined effects of the rotation, together with a displacement of the starting point, on the coefficients A_n, B_n, C_n, and D_n of the original expression are readily described in matrix notation as follows:

$$\begin{pmatrix} A_n^{**} & B_n^{**} \\ C_n^{**} & D_n^{**} \end{pmatrix} = \begin{pmatrix} \cos\psi & \sin\psi \\ -\sin\psi & \cos\psi \end{pmatrix} \begin{pmatrix} A_n & B_n \\ C_n & D_n \end{pmatrix} \begin{pmatrix} \cos\dfrac{2\pi n\lambda}{T} & -\sin\dfrac{2\pi n\lambda}{T} \\ \sin\dfrac{2\pi n\lambda}{T} & \cos\dfrac{2\pi n\lambda}{T} \end{pmatrix}$$

The preceding matrix equation gives us a transformation

$$\begin{pmatrix} A_a \\ B_n \\ C_n \\ D_n \end{pmatrix} \rightarrow \begin{pmatrix} A_n^{**} \\ B_n^{**} \\ C_n^{**} \\ D_n^{**} \end{pmatrix}$$

call it Λ, which takes the original Fourier coefficients and outputs a collection of coefficients normalized with respect to both starting point and orientation. For a given contour v, these new coefficients can be compared to sets stored in the database in order to decide upon a classification for v.

To utilize the mapping Λ, some canonical methodology must be set for deciding on the starting point and the final spatial orientation of the Fourier approximations of the original image. In other words, for a given observed image v, we need to know the inputs ψ and λ in order to compute A_n^{**}, B_n^{**}, C_n^{**}, and D_n^{**}. These inputs are derived from the first harmonic ellipse. Intuitively, the transformation is made so that the starting point is at one of the semimajor axes and the ellipse v_1 is rotated according to the position of the chosen axis. Because of the two possible choices of the semimajor axis, two possible canonical classifications result. These are simply 180° rotations of each other.

Although we will not go through the geometric details, the values of ψ and λ, based on the first harmonic ellipse, are given by

$$\lambda_1 = \frac{T}{4\pi} \arctan\left(\frac{2(A_1 B_1 + C_1 D_1)}{A_1^2 + C_1^2 - B_1^2 - D_1^2}\right)$$

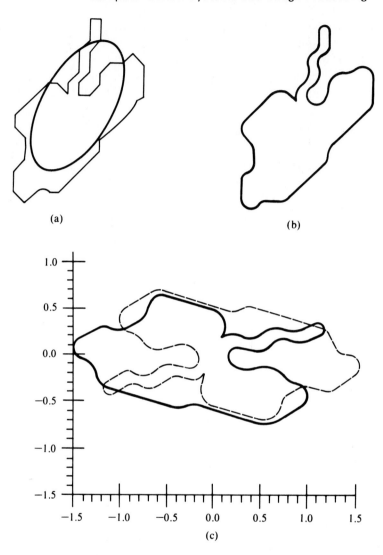

Figure 8.72   Tank image and normalization

and

$$\psi_1 = \arctan\left(\frac{C_1^*}{A_1^*}\right)$$

The normalization of the Fourier coefficients relative to starting point and orientation is achieved by using Λ, with the output coefficients based upon the first harmonic ellipse of the observed image.

If we desire a classification independent of size, this normalization can be accomplished by dividing each coefficient by the magnitude of the semimajor axis, which is given by

$$E^* = [(A_1^*)^2 + (C_1^*)^2]^{1/2}$$

Finally, classification independent of translation can be achieved by simply ignoring the terms A_0 and B_0.

Example 8.22

The elliptic classification procedure is shown for a tank on an incline in Figure 8.72. The image and the first harmonic ellipse are shown in part (a), and the 30th harmonic normalized approximation of the tank is given in part (b). Two possible classifications involving the 30th harmonic approximation, as generated by the normalized coefficients, are shown by solid and dashed lines in part (c).

EXERCISES FOR CHAPTER 8

8.1. Let

$$f = \begin{pmatrix} 0 & 1 & 1 & 0 & 0 & 1 & 0 \\ 0 & 4 & 5 & 1 & 0 & 0 & 0 \\ 1 & 7 & 6 & 1 & 2 & 9 & 0 \\ 2 & 6 & 5 & 3 & 2 & * & 1 \\ 2 & 7 & 8 & 1 & 2 & 0 & 0 \\ 2 & 6 & 5 & 7 & 6 & 3 & 1 \\ 2 & 7 & 8 & 5 & 7 & 1 & 2 \\ 3 & 2 & 2 & 1 & 3 & 0 & 1 \end{pmatrix}_{3,2}$$

Find
(a) THRESH$(f; 5)$
(b) TRUNC$(f; 6)$, where TRUNC is defined by

$$\text{TRUNC}(f; t) = \text{MULT}[f, \text{THRESH}(f; t)]$$

(c) SMOOTH$(f; M)$, where

$$M = \begin{pmatrix} 0 & 1/4 & 0 \\ 1/4 & \textcircled{0} & 1/4 \\ 0 & 1/4 & 0 \end{pmatrix}$$

(d) FILTER$(f; M)$, where M is the mask of Example 8.2.
(e) FILTER$(f; N)$, where N is the mask of Example 8.2.

8.2. Let

$$f = \begin{pmatrix}
0 & 1 & 1 & 0 & 1 & 0 & 0 & 0 & 0 & 1 & 1 & 2 \\
1 & 0 & 1 & 0 & 1 & 0 & 0 & 0 & 0 & 7 & 0 & 1 \\
1 & 2 & 0 & 1 & 6 & 6 & 6 & 7 & 1 & 1 & 0 & 0 \\
* & 2 & 1 & 1 & 6 & 7 & 7 & 6 & 1 & 2 & 1 & 1 \\
1 & 1 & 7 & 5 & 6 & 7 & 5 & 7 & 6 & 6 & 0 & 0 \\
1 & 1 & 6 & 6 & 7 & 6 & 5 & 7 & 6 & 6 & 0 & 0 \\
1 & 2 & 0 & 0 & 7 & 7 & 8 & 6 & 1 & 1 & 1 & 1 \\
1 & 1 & 0 & 2 & 5 & 7 & 6 & 6 & 0 & 0 & 0 & 0 \\
0 & 0 & 1 & 0 & 1 & 0 & 0 & 0 & 1 & 0 & 0 & 0 \\
0 & 0 & 1 & 2 & 0 & 0 & 1 & 1 & 1 & 1 & 0 & 0
\end{pmatrix}_{0,\,6}$$

Compute:

(a) VERTEDGE(f; 4)

(b) HOREDGE(f; 3)

(c) GRAD(f)

(d) GRADMAG1(f)

(e) GRADMAG2(f)

(f) GRADMAG0(f)

(g) PREWMAG1(f)

(h) PREWEDGE1(f; t)
  for $t = 12, 16, 20,$ and 24

(i) PREWMAG2(f)

(j) PREWEDGE2(f; 10)

8.3. In a manner appropriate to Figure 8.20, define the operators SOBELEDGE1, SOBELEDGE2, and SOBELEDGE0. Apply each of these operators to the image f of Exercise 8.2 with the threshold input $t = 12$.

8.4. Define the gradient operator NEWGRAD by

$$\text{NEWGRAD}(f) = [\text{FILTER}(f; Q1), \text{FILTER}(f; Q2)]$$

where the masks $Q1$ and $Q2$ are defined by

$$Q1 = \begin{pmatrix}
-1 & 0 & 1 \\
-1 & 0 & 1 \\
-1 & \textcircled{0} & 1 \\
-1 & 0 & 1 \\
-1 & 0 & 1
\end{pmatrix}$$

$$Q2 = \begin{pmatrix}
1 & 1 & 1 & 1 & 1 \\
0 & 0 & \textcircled{0} & 0 & 0 \\
-1 & -1 & -1 & -1 & -1
\end{pmatrix}$$

Using the norms MAXNORM, ONENORM, and TWONORM, define the operators NEWMAG0, NEWMAG1, and NEWMAG2 in a manner similar to PREWMAG0, PREWMAG1, and PREWMAG2. Then apply these three new gradient-type operators to the image f of Exercise 8.2.

8.5. Let

$$A = \{(0, 0), (0, 2), (2, 0), (2, 2)\}$$

$$B = \{(0, 0), (1, 0), (2, 0), (3, 0)\}$$

$$C = \{(0, 0), (1, 1), (2, 2)\}$$

Find each of the following sets (in set notation and pictorially):

(a) $(1, 1) + A$ **(j)** $[A + (-1, 2)] \oplus B$
(b) $A \oplus B$ **(k)** $A \oplus (B \cup C)$
(c) $(A \oplus B) \oplus C$ **(l)** $A \oplus (B \cap C)$
(d) $A \ominus B$ **(m)** $(A \oplus B) \cup (A \oplus C)$
(e) $B \ominus A$ **(n)** $(A \oplus B) \cap (A \oplus C)$
(f) $\mathscr{C}(A, B)$ **(o)** $A \ominus (B \cup C)$
(g) $A \oplus (2C)$ **(p)** $A \ominus (B \cap C)$
(h) $2[\tfrac{1}{2}A \oplus C]$ **(q)** $(A \oplus B) \cap (A \oplus C)$
(i) $(C \oplus A) \oplus B$ **(r)** $(A \ominus B) \ominus C$

Note that

$$tA = \{ta : a \in A\}$$

8.6. Let

$$A = \{(x, y): 0 \le x \le 2, 0 \le y \le 3\}$$

$$B = \{(x, y): x^2 + y^2 \le 1\}$$

$$C = \{(x, y): y = x \text{ and } 0 \le x \le 1\}$$

$$D = \{(x, y): 0 \le y \le |2x| \text{ and } -1 \le x \le 1\}$$

(See Figure 8.73.)   Give graphical representations of the following:

(a) $A \oplus B$ **(j)** $A \oplus \tfrac{1}{2}C$
(b) $A \oplus C$ **(k)** $O(A, B)$
(c) $B \oplus C$ **(l)** $O(A, C)$
(d) $A \ominus B$ **(m)** $O[B, \tfrac{1}{2}C]$
(e) $A \ominus C$ **(n)** $O[A, \tfrac{1}{2}B]$
(f) $A \ominus \tfrac{1}{2}B$ **(o)** $O[A, \tfrac{1}{4}B]$
(g) $A \ominus \tfrac{1}{4}C$ **(p)** $O(D, B)$
(h) $B \oplus \tfrac{1}{2}B$ **(q)** $C(D, B)$
(i) $A \oplus \tfrac{1}{2}B$ **(r)** $C(D, 2B)$

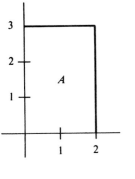
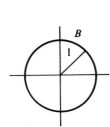
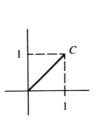
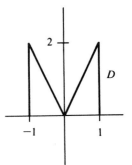

Figure 8.73   Images for Exercise 8.6

8.7. Let

$$S = \begin{pmatrix} 1 & 1 & 1 & 1 & 1 & * \\ 1 & 1 & 1 & * & * & * \\ 1 & 1 & 1 & 1 & * & * \\ * & * & 1 & 1 & 1 & 1 \\ * & \circledast & 1 & 1 & 1 & 1 \\ * & * & 1 & 1 & 1 & * \end{pmatrix}$$

$$T = \begin{pmatrix} \textcircled{1} & 1 & 1 & 1 & 1 & 1 & 1 \\ 1 & 1 & * & * & 1 & * & 1 \\ * & * & * & * & 1 & 1 & 1 \end{pmatrix}$$

$$E = \begin{pmatrix} 1 & 1 \\ \textcircled{1} & 1 \end{pmatrix}$$

Find

(a) $S \wedge T$

(b) $S \wedge T \wedge E$

(c) $S \vee T \vee E$

(d) TRAN$(E; 1, 2)$

(e) DILATE(S, E)

(f) DILATE(T, E)

(g) ERODE(S, E)

(h) ERODE(T, E)

(i) OPEN(S, E)

(j) OPEN(T, E)

(k) CLOSE(S, E)

(l) CLOSE(T, E)

8.8. Using the image S of Exercise 8.7, find

(a) $\psi_V(k)$

(b) $\psi_H(k)$

(c) $\Phi_V(k)$

(d) $\Phi_H(k)$

(e) Graph of $\Phi_V(k)$

(f) Graph of $\Phi_H(k)$

8.9. For the following figure U, find SKEL(U).

$$U = \begin{pmatrix} 1 & 1 & 1 & 1 & * & * & * & * \\ 1 & 1 & 1 & * & * & * & * & * \\ 1 & 1 & 1 & * & * & * & * & * \\ 1 & 1 & 1 & * & * & * & * & * \\ 1 & 1 & 1 & * & * & * & * & * \\ 1 & 1 & 1 & * & * & * & * & * \\ 1 & 1 & 1 & 1 & 1 & 1 & * & * \\ 1 & 1 & 1 & 1 & 1 & 1 & 1 & 1 \\ 1 & 1 & 1 & 1 & 1 & 1 & 1 & \textcircled{1} \end{pmatrix}$$

8.10. Find $\mathscr{F}(w_i)$, $i = 1, 2, \ldots, 6$, for the polygonal boundary image in Figure 8.74. Let v_1 be the indicated vertex in the figure. Find the inter-image distance tables for the image of Figure 8.74 and the images of Figures 8.59 and 8.60.

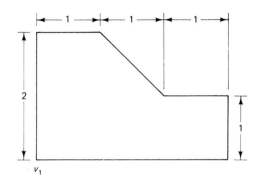

Figure 8.74 Image and boundary
pieces for Exercise 8.10

8.11. Consider the strings

$$x = a\,b\,a\,b\,a\,a$$

and

$$y = a\,b\,b\,a\,a$$

Using ρ' as given in Section 8.7, find the Levenshtein distance between x and y.

8.12. Let ρ be the boundary-piece distance defined in Section 8.6 and let ρ' be the corresponding distance function, based on the parameter t, given in Section 8.7. Using Table 8.3 and threshold parameter $t = 2$, find the Levenshtein distance between the local-feature strings resulting from the images in Figures 8.59 and 8.60. Repeat for $t = 1$.

8.13. Consider the chain code 000543, which largely corresponds to the upper part of the image shown in Figure 8.66. Find the projections of this image and the corresponding Fourier approximations using four and eight harmonics.

8.14. Find the first harmonic ellipse associated with the image of Exercise 8.13. Then find the angle between the major axis of the ellipse and the abscissa.

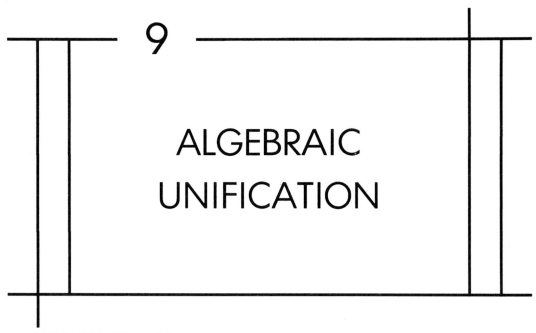

9

ALGEBRAIC UNIFICATION

9.1 MANY-SORTED ALGEBRAS

Throughout the text, a wide variety of algebraic structures have been introduced, from the propositional calculus, to bound matrices, to various classes of automata. It is the purpose of the present section to provide a unification of the underlying algebraic principles embodied in these diverse structures. The mechanism for the unification is the many-sorted algebra.

The outstanding characteristic of most of the structures heretofore discussed is their many-sortedness; that is, the entities within any given structure are of different mathematical *sorts*, or types. Rather than proceed directly to a general discussion of the many-sorted algebra concept, we will introduce it by means of an example from elementary calculus.

Consider the collection of all three-dimensional vectors, together with the operations of vector addition, scalar multiplication, and dot product. As a classical mathematical structure, the entirety forms what is known as an *inner-product space*. Let us examine the structure from the perspective of the sorts (types) vector and scalar. Specifically, there is a set of sorts

$$S = \{\text{vector, scalar}\}$$

Moreover, there are five binary operations of interest:

1. Vector addition: $(\mathbf{u}, \mathbf{v}) \rightarrow \mathbf{u} + \mathbf{v}$

$$(\text{vector, vector}) \rightarrow \text{vector}$$

2. Scalar multiplication: $(a, \mathbf{v}) \to a\mathbf{v}$

$$(\text{scalar, vector}) \to \text{vector}$$

3. Dot product: $(\mathbf{u}, \mathbf{v}) \to \mathbf{u} \cdot \mathbf{v}$

$$(\text{vector, vector}) \to \text{scalar}$$

4. Real addition: $(a, b) \to a + b$

$$(\text{scalar, scalar}) \to \text{scalar}$$

5. Real multiplication: $(a, b) \to ab$

$$(\text{scalar, scalar}) \to \text{scalar}$$

There are also unary operations:

6. Vector additive inverse: $\mathbf{v} \to -\mathbf{v}$
7. Real additive inverse: $a \to -a$
8. Real multiplicative inverse: $a \to a^{-1}, a \neq 0$

And there are zeroary operations (special elements within the sorts):

9. Vector zero: $\mathbf{0}$
10. Real zero: 0
11. Real unity: 1

Besides the aforementioned operations, there are also algebraic laws that apply, such as various commutative, associative, and distributive laws.

From an axiomatic perspective, the preceding operations, together with a list of relevant algebraic laws, characterize other particular mathematical structures besides the collection of three-dimensional vectors and the associated operations. Indeed, the terms *vector* and *scalar* are generic, having only a universal meaning relative to an abstract axiomatic description that includes the sorts, the operators that map elements of specified sorts into other sorts, and the equational constraints (laws). These characterize not a particular mathematical entity, but rather a class of entities, each of which has a collection whose elements are called "vectors" and another collection whose elements are called "scalars." These "vectors" might be mathematical functions defined on some specific domain, while the "scalars" might be complex numbers or the elements of some abstract field. From the perspective of AI, the matter of interest is the typification of the algebra of sorts. Natural intelligence operates in a many-sorted world, and, consequently, the algorithmic simulation of intelligent activity demands a precise delineation of the methodology by which sorts are operationally preserved and altered. The many-sorted algebra concept provides a rigorous mathematical framework for such a delineation. Moreover, the concept of a homomorphism (see Section 9.4) provides the mathematical tool necessary for a study of the structure-preserving qualities of mappings between different algebras.

Practically speaking, specifications employing the many-sorted algebra approach provide a modular technique for describing structure. At a global level, the structure is described in terms of the sorts of objects and the names of the operators between and among sorts. At a lower level, a precise specification, relative to the global structure, is made regarding the particular entities under consideration.

In a lattice structure, since only one type is utilized, the set of sorts can be given by

$$S = \{\text{elements}\}$$

In the cases of nondetermistic, fuzzy, and stochastic automata, three distinct sorts are employed: states, inputs, and values from a valuation space. Thus,

$$S = \{\text{states, inputs, values}\}$$

For a Petri net, four sorts are given; hence,

$$S = \{\text{places, transitions, values, markings}\}$$

The typification of both inter- and intrasort operations in a many-sorted algebra is done by means of the *signature sets*. The names of the operators with n inputs of types $s_1, s_2, \ldots, s_n$ and output of type s make up the signature set denoted by

$$\sum_{s_1 s_2 \ldots s_n, s}$$

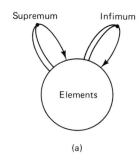

(a)

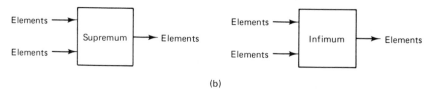

(b)

Figure 9.1 Polyadic graph and block diagram for lattice

Each element in the signature set is termed an *operation symbol*.   Although there is a signature set corresponding to each pair

$$(s_1 s_2 \ldots s_n, s) \in S^* \times S$$

in practice, only a finite number of these sets will be nonempty.

In a lattice, all signature sets, except one, are empty, the only nonempty one being

$$\sum_{\text{element element, element}} = \{\text{supremum, infimum}\}$$

This follows since, in a lattice, there are exactly two binary operators, the supremum and infimum.   In a fuzzy automaton, all signature sets are empty except

$$\sum_{\text{state input state, value}} = \{\text{transition function}\}$$

$$\sum_{\text{state, value}} = \{\text{final}\}$$

$$\sum_{\text{value value, value}} = \{\text{supremum, infinum}\}$$

$$\sum_{\varepsilon, \text{ state}} = \{\text{initial}\}$$

$$\sum_{\varepsilon, \text{ value}} = \{\text{one, zero}\}$$

The last two signature sets contain the names of the zeroary operations.   These operations are the names of the appropriate elements in the output sort.

A block diagram representation can be given to illustrate both the elements in the set of sorts and the names of all operations employed.   The name of an operation is placed inside a block, the sorts of the required inputs are written to the left, with arrows coming in, and the sort of the output is written on the right, with an arrow leaving the block and pointing to it.

A second graphical representation is the *polyadic graph*, which is a many-tailed, directed-type graph whose circular nodes contain the names of the sorts. There are also arrows, each of which is labeled with the operation it depicts.   Each arrow has tails emanating from the input sorts of the operation it specifies, the number of tails from each sort indicating the number of inputs of that sort required, and the total number of tails being the arity of the operation involved.   Further-more, the head of each arrow points to the appropriate output sort.   Figures 9.1 through 9.8 provide polyadic graphs of some of the important many-sorted algebras introduced in the text, with all but the last two also containing block-diagram descriptions.   Note that the graphs do not contain complete descriptions, since the equational constraints (laws) satisfied by the operators have not been listed.

The set of sorts and the signature sets provide a global view of structure, but

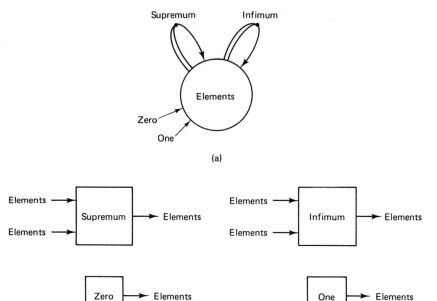

(a)

(b)

Figure 9.2 Polyadic graph and block diagram for bounded lattice

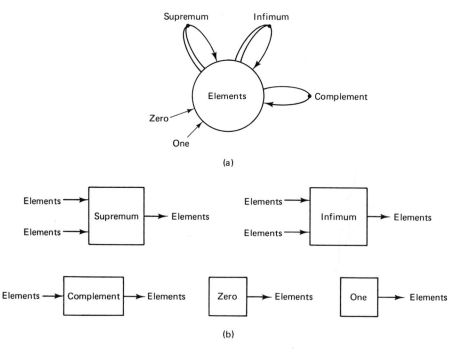

(a)

(b)

Figure 9.3 Polyadic graph and block diagram for Boolean algebra

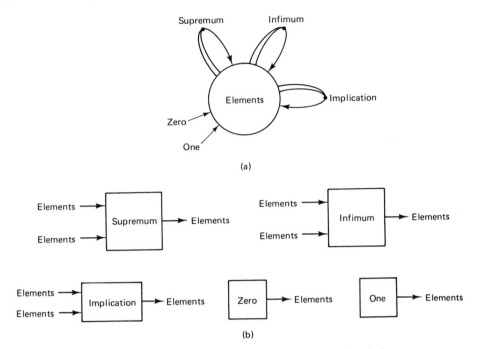

(a)

Elements ——→ ┌─────────┐
             │ Supremum│ ——→ Elements
Elements ——→ └─────────┘

Elements ——→ ┌─────────┐
             │ Infimum │ ——→ Elements
Elements ——→ └─────────┘

Elements ——→ ┌─────────────┐
             │ Implication │ ——→ Elements
Elements ——→ └─────────────┘

┌──────┐
│ Zero │ ——→ Elements
└──────┘

┌──────┐
│ One │ ——→ Elements
└──────┘

(b)

Figure 9.4   Polyadic graph and block diagram for Heyting algebra

do not address specifics.   Actual elements of the sorts specified are given in the *carrier sets*.   These provide a view of the structure at a lower, more individual level.   Specifically, associated with each sort s in S there is a carrier set A_s that contains the actual elements utilized.

Example 9.1

Example 2.7 discusses the directed graph illustrated in Figure 2.4.   Since there are only two sorts, points and arrows, to be denoted by p and a, respectively, there are

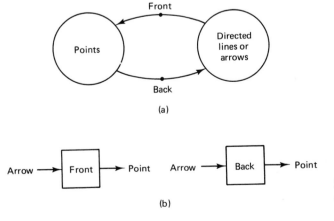

Figure 9.5   Polyadic graph and block diagram for directed graph

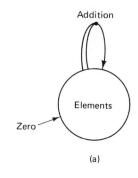

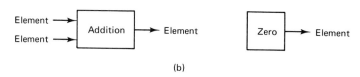

Figure 9.6 Polyadic graph and block diagram for monoid

two carrier sets:

$$A_p = \{1, 2, 3\}$$

and

$$A_a = \{x, y, z\}$$

Example 9.2

For an L automaton, the set of sorts contains three elements: states, inputs, and values. For the particular L automaton of Example 5.12, the corresponding carrier sets are given by

$$A_{\text{states}} = A_s = \{1, 2, 3\}$$

$$A_{\text{input}} = A_i = \{a, b\}$$

$$A_{\text{values}} = A_v = \{1, z, x, y, 0\}$$

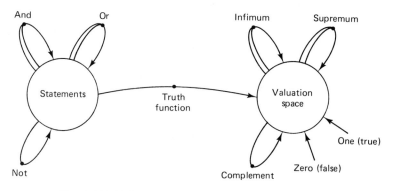

Figure 9.7 Polyadic graph for propositional calculus

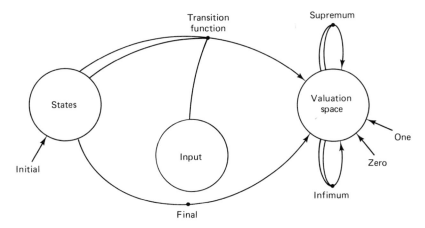

Figure 9.8   Polyadic graph for fuzzy automaton

Corresponding to each named operation, as specified by the signature sets, are the actual operations themselves.   Thus, to each

$$\sigma \in \sum_{s_1 s_2 \dots s_n, s}$$

there is an *n*-ary operator σ_A such that

$$\sigma_A \colon A_{s_1} \times A_{s_2} \times \cdots \times A_{s_n} \to A_s$$

Furthermore, for each zeroary operation named $\sigma \in \sum_{\varepsilon, s}$ there corresponds a special element σ_A in the carrier set A_s.

Example 9.3

The algebraic entity discussed in Example 9.1 is a directed graph.   Since FRONT and BACK are elements of the signature set

$$\sum_{a, p}$$

there correspond two functions f and b having the associated names FRONT and BACK, respectively, and for which

$$f \colon A_a \to A_p$$

and

$$b \colon A_a \to A_p$$

Moreover, in the example at hand,

$$f(x) = f(y) = f(z) = 1$$
$$b(x) = 1$$

and

$$b(y) = b(z) = 2$$

The process of precisely specifying the set of sorts, the names of the operations, the actual elements used (i.e., the carrier sets), and the actual operations themselves constitutes the many-sorted algebra methodology.

Mathematically, a many-sorted algebra is a seven-tuple

$$(S, \alpha, \Sigma, \beta, \Phi, \gamma, G)$$

where S is the set of sorts and Σ is the class of all signature sets. Recognizing that there exists a signature set (possibly empty) for any element in $S^* \times S$, we specify the mapping

$$\alpha: S^* \times S \to \sum$$

by

$$\alpha((s_1 s_2 \ldots s_n, s)) = \sum_{s_1 s_2 \ldots s_n, s}$$

Next, the set Φ is the class of all carrier sets; that is,

$$\beta: S \to \Phi$$

by

$$\beta(s) = A_s$$

Finally, G is the set consisting of all actual operators and γ maps the operational symbols (names) contained in the union of the signature sets into G:

$$\gamma: \bigcup_{S^* \times S} \left[\sum_{s_1 s_2 \ldots s_n, s} \right] \to G$$

such that for each $\sigma \in \sum_{\varepsilon, s}$, $\gamma(\sigma) \in A_s$, and for

$$\sigma \in \sum_{s_1 s_2 \ldots s_n, s}$$

$$\gamma(\sigma): A_{s_1} \times A_{s_2} \times \cdots \times A_{s_n} \to A_s$$

Example 9.4

Consider the L automaton of Example 7.2. There is the trinary function name

$$\text{TRANSITION} \in \sum_{s \ i \ s, \ v}$$

Thus,

$$\gamma(\text{TRANSITION}) = \delta$$

and

$$\delta: A_s \times A_i \times A_s \to A_v$$

where the actual function δ is specified in Example 5.12.   Furthermore,

$$\text{FINAL} \in \sum_{s,v}$$

$$\gamma(\text{FINAL}) = f$$

and

$$f: A_s \rightarrow A_v$$

Also,

$$\text{SUPREMUM} \in \sum_{v\ v,v}$$

$$\text{INFIMUM} \in \sum_{v\ v,v}$$

$$\gamma(\text{SUPREMUM}) = \vee$$

$$\vee: A_v \times A_v \rightarrow A_v$$

$$\gamma(\text{INFIMUM}) = \wedge$$

and

$$\wedge: A_v \times A_v \rightarrow A_v$$

Finally, special zeroary functions also exist, since

$$\text{INITIAL} \in \sum_{\varepsilon,s}$$

and

$$\text{ZERO, ONE} \in \sum_{\varepsilon,v}$$

Therefore, each carrier set of the proper sort has special elements:

$$\gamma(\text{INITIAL}) = 1 \in A_s$$

$$\gamma(\text{ZERO}) = 0 \in A_v$$

$$\gamma(\text{ONE}) = 1 \in A_v$$

9.2 UNIVERSAL IMAGE ALGEBRA

In this section we will discuss a particular many-sorted algebra called the *universal image algebra*.   The operators in this algebra are induced by the operands in the set of sorts and thus provide natural inter- and intrasort transformations.   They also provide a unified structure in which to express digital image-processing algorithms.   Because of the simplicity and powerful spanning capability of the operators, the algebra provides a frame within which to specify the ever-increasing collection of digital image-processing algorithms.   Furthermore, due to the gen-

erality of the definition of image that we adopt, the algebra has algorithm specification applications well outside the domain usually associated with image processing per se.

Four types of operands are employed in the universal image algebra. The
names of these types are specified in the set of sorts

$$S = \{\text{images, values, sets, parameters}\}$$

The universal image algebra is further characterized by the use of ten fundamental operators. Employing function composition, image-processing algorithms (and many others) can be expressed in terms of the ten operators. Thus,
these algorithms constitute terms within the algebra. The names of the fundamental operations appear in the following signature sets:

$$\sum_{\text{image image, image}} = \{\text{ADDITION, MULTIPLICATION,}\\ \text{MAXIMUM, DIVISION}\}$$

$$\sum_{\text{image, image}} = \{\text{ROTATION, REFLECTION}\}$$

$$\sum_{\text{image parameter, image}} = \{\text{TRANSLATION}\}$$

$$\sum_{\text{image, value}} = \{\text{GRAY}\}$$

$$\sum_{\text{image, set}} = \{\text{DOMAIN}\}$$

$$\sum_{\text{value set, image}} = \{\text{EXISTENTIAL}\}$$

The polyadic graph of Figure 9.9 summarizes the action of the operators on the
sorts.

In Section 4.8, we considered an image to be a bound matrix: it has a domain
that is a finite subset of $Z \times Z$ and codomain R, the set of real numbers. Such
images are usually called *digital images*. Other types of images are the *Euclidean*,
or *analog* images, whose domains are subsets of the Euclidean plane and whose
codomains are R, and the *fully digital* images, whose domains are finite subsets of
$Z \times Z$ and whose codomains are Z. In the current section, we wish to develop
the particular image algebra that applies to the class of digital images; however,
we will assume that such images possess domains in $Z \times Z$ that can be of infinite
cardinality. Although we do not wish to go into detail, the permissibility of infinite
domains is crucial to certain fundamental theoretical results in the area of image
processing. Let us simply note that, while a practical digital image will of necessity
possess a finite domain, there is certainly no upper limit on the number of elements
a digital image domain might contain; thus, in principle, it is necessary to allow
infinite domains. For instance, an image might have all of $Z \times Z$ for its domain.
Under this convention, the collection of bound matrices is a subcollection of the
collection of all digital images.

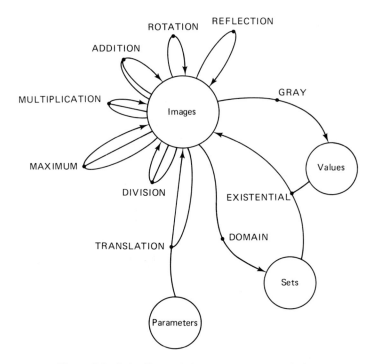

Figure 9.9 Polyadic graph for universal image algebra

The particular image algebra we will develop is only one among many that fit the frame of the universal image algebra: it is the specification of the carrier sets and the operators, together with the equational constraints, that characterize the particular algebra.   Throughout, one should keep in mind the bound matrix algebra of Section 4.9.

Given the set of sorts in the universal image algebra, we define the carrier sets for the *digital image algebra* (*DIA*) by

1. $\beta(\text{values}) = A_{\text{values}} = R.$
2. $\beta(\text{parameters}) = A_{\text{parameters}} = Z \times Z.$
3. $\beta(\text{sets}) = A_{\text{sets}} = 2^{Z \times Z}$, the set of subsets of $Z \times Z$.
4. $\beta(\text{images}) = A_{\text{images}} = X = \bigcup_{A \subset Z \times Z} R^A$, where R^A denotes the class of all functions from A into R.   Thus, an image is a function defined on some subset of the grid $Z \times Z$ with codomain R.

For each operation name contained in the signature sets of the universal image algebra, there exists an operator obtained by the γ function:

1. $\gamma(\text{EXISTENTIAL}) = E$, where

$$E: R \times 2^{Z \times Z} \rightarrow X$$

by $E(t, A) = t_A$, the constant image defined by

$$t_A(i, j) = \begin{cases} t, & \text{if } (i, j) \in A \\ \text{undefined}, & \text{otherwise} \end{cases}$$

The operation E allows the creation of any constant image (i.e., an image with a single gray value) defined on an arbitrary subset of $Z \times Z$.

2. $\gamma(\text{GRAY}) = G$, where $G: X \rightarrow R$, and for any $f \in R^A$,

$$G(f) = \begin{cases} f(0, 0), & \text{if } (0, 0) \in A \\ 0, & \text{if } f = \emptyset, \text{ the null image} \\ f(i, j), & \text{otherwise, where } \arctan(j/i) \text{ is minimized} \\ & \text{for minimum } i^2 + j^2 \end{cases}$$

If f is defined at the origin, $(0, 0)$, then $G(f)$ outputs the gray value there; if f is not defined at the origin, it picks out the gray value of the "closest" pixel to the origin that lies in the domain of f.

3. $\gamma(\text{DOMAIN}) = K$, where $K: X \rightarrow 2^{Z \times Z}$, and for any $f \in R^A$,

$$K(f) = A$$

This operator yields the domain for the specified image.

4. $\gamma(\text{ADDITION}) = \oplus$, where $\oplus: X \times X \rightarrow X$, and for $f \in R^A$ and $g \in R^B$,

$$(f \oplus g)(x, y) = \begin{cases} f(x, y), & (x, y) \in A - B \\ g(x, y), & (x, y) \in B - A \\ f(x, y) + g(x, y), & (x, y) \in A \cap B \\ \text{undefined}, & (x, y) \notin A \cup B \end{cases}$$

For each pixel in the intersection of the input domains, the output image has the arithmetic sum of the input gray values at that pixel. For a pixel that lies in one of the input domains but not in both, the decision has been made to leave its gray value unchanged. A similar decision has been made regarding the multiplication and maximum operators.

5. $\gamma(\text{MULTIPLICATION}) = \odot$, where $\odot: X \times X \rightarrow X$. If the domains of f and g are A and B, respectively, then

$$(f \odot g)(x, y) = \begin{cases} f(x, y), & (x, y) \in A - B \\ g(x, y), & (x, y) \in B - A \\ f(x, y)g(x, y), & (x, y) \in A \cap B \\ \text{undefined}, & (x, y) \notin A \cup B \end{cases}$$

6. $\gamma(\text{MAXIMUM}) = \bigcirc\!\!\!\vee$, where $\bigcirc\!\!\!\vee: X \times X \to X$. If the domains of f and g are A and B, respectively, then

$$(f \bigcirc\!\!\!\vee g)(x, y) = \begin{cases} f(x, y), & (x, y) \in A - B \\ g(x, y), & (x, y) \in B - A \\ f(x, y) \vee g(x, y), & (x, y) \in A \cap B \\ \text{undefined}, & (x, y) \notin A \cup B \end{cases}$$

7. $\gamma(\text{DIVISION}) = \bigcirc\!\!\!\div$, where $\bigcirc\!\!\!\div: X \times X \to X$. If f and g have domains A and B, respectively, then

$$(f \bigcirc\!\!\!\div g)(x, y) = \begin{cases} f(x, y)/g(x, y), & (x, y) \in A \cap B \\ & \text{and whenever } g(x, y) \neq 0 \\ \text{undefined}, & \text{elsewhere} \end{cases}$$

This operation always yields an image whose domain is a subset of the intersection of the input domains. It is useful in removing parts of an image that do not satisfy certain criteria.

8. $\gamma(\text{TRANSLATION}) = T$, where $T: X \times Z \times Z \to X$, and

$$[T(f, i, j)](x, y) = f(x - i, y - j)$$

The operator T moves an image over and up, while "leaving gray values unchanged." Accordingly, $T(f, i, j)$, or f_{ij}, is the original image "moved over i to the right and up j." This most important operation is used in almost all filtering procedures, including convolution, dilation, and erosion.

9. $\gamma(\text{ROTATION}) = N$, where $N: X \to X$, and

$$[(N(f)](x, y) = f(y, -x)$$

This operator rotates an image 90° in the counterclockwise direction about the origin while leaving the gray values otherwise unchanged. A double application of this operation produces a 180° rotation, which is essential for many filtering applications, such as convolution and erosion.

10. $\gamma(\text{REFLECTION}) = D$, where $D: X \to X$, and

$$[(D(f)](x, y) = f(-y, -x)$$

This diagonal flip operator flips the image in a manner similar to the matrix transpose. Together, N and D generate the "group of symmetries of the square." D plays an additional important role in the image algebra, in that it provides right–left orientation for digital images, a feature basic to the development of automatic spatial understanding.

The definition of the basic ten operators is complete. Together, they provide a simple and powerful collection from which to form, by function composition, digital image-processing algorithms.

Each of basic the operators in the DIA possesses a counterpart in the bound matrix algebra of Section 4.9. Some of the correspondences are direct: $\oplus$ and EXTADD, $\odot$ and EXTMULT, $\otimes$ and EXTMAX, $\ominus$ and DIV, T and TRAN, N and NINETY, D and FLIP, and K and DOMAIN, where in the latter case we simply interpret the output of DOMAIN, which in the bound matrix setting is a vector, as a set. The remaining two basic DIA operators can be expressed in terms of bound matrix operations as follows:

$$E(t, A) = \text{CREATE}(A, [t, t, \dots, t])$$

and

$$G(f) = \text{RANGE}(\text{SELECT}(f; 1, 1, i, j))$$

where $[t, t, \dots, t]$ is a constant vector of dimension $\text{card}(A)$ and (i, j) is either the origin, if the origin is in the domain of f, or the closest pixel to the origin that lies in the domain of f, if the origin is not in the domain of f.

In the other direction, all bound matrix operations can be expressed in terms of the basic ten operators of the DIA. Each bound matrix operation is either directly expressible as a basic DIA operator, or it is a macro-operator in the DIA (see Section 9.3). In sum, the bound matrix algebra can be viewed as a subalgebra of the digital image algebra.

Two dozen identities holding in the DIA will shortly be given. Essentially, they follow at once from the fact that several of the basic operations are range or domain induced. It is the inducement that results in both the simplicity and the power of the operations.

The general notion of range inducement is quite independent of the class X of images; however, we will only define it relative to binary operations on that class. To that end, a binary operator $Q: X \times X \to X$ is said to be *range induced* if there exists a binary operation $q: R \times R \to R$ such that for any images f and g in X, with respective domains A and B,

$$[Q(f, g)](i, j) = q[f(i, j), g(i, j)]$$

for any $(i, j) \in A \cap B$. In other words, on the intersection of the domains of f and g, Q is defined pointwise in terms of q. Two points should be noted in the definition of range inducement: First, as part of the definition, if $q[f(i, j), g(i, j)]$ is undefined, then so is $[Q(f, g)](i, j)$. Second, no stipulation is made regarding the definition of $Q(f, g)$ outside of $A \cap B$. It is a simple task to show that $\oplus$, $\odot$, and $\otimes$ are range induced. The last of the range-induced operations is $\ominus$; however, there is a slight variation in the definition due to the possibility of the gray value 0 in the divisor image.

As with the concept of range inducement, the concept of domain inducement is more general than the version we will employ. The operation

$$S: X \to X$$

is said to be *domain induced* by the lattice operation

$$s: Z \times Z \to Z \times Z$$

if, for any point $(i, j) \in Z \times Z$,

$$[S(f)](i, j) = f[s(i, j)]$$

Intuitively, assuming that the $Z \times Z$ to $Z \times Z$ mapping s is both one-to-one and onto, the gray values of $S(f)$ are exactly the same as f except that the entire image has been moved, the new location in the lattice depending on the isomorphism s.

Direct application of the definition shows that T, N, and D are domain induced.

The three remaining operations, E, G, and K, are structural in nature since they relate images, gray values, and sets of pixels. Taken together, the three structural mappings allow the formation and splitting of images by means of the diagram

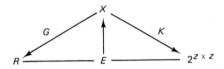

Once the appropriate operations within X are defined, the existential mapping E will provide isomorphic copies of R and $2^{Z \times Z}$ within X. The projections will permit recovery.

A principal reason for using inducement to define many of the operators in the DIA is that equational constraints are then induced from the properties of the domain and range. Indeed, the following are easily shown to hold:

1(a) $f \oplus g = g \oplus f$
  (b) $f \odot g = g \odot f$
  (c) $f \triangledown g = g \triangledown f$
2(a) $f \oplus (g \oplus h) = (f \oplus g) \oplus h$
  (b) $f \odot (g \odot h) = (f \odot g) \odot h$
  (c) $f \triangledown (g \triangledown h) = (f \triangledown g) \triangledown h$
3 $f \odot (f \ominus f) = f$ at (i, j) such that $f(i, j) \neq 0$
4 $f \triangledown f = f$
5 $D(D(f)) = D^2(f) = f$
6 $N^4(f) = f$
7(a) $N(f \oplus g) = N(f) \oplus N(g)$
  (b) $N(f \odot g) = N(f) \odot N(g)$
  (c) $N(f \triangledown g) = N(f) \triangledown N(g)$
  (d) $N(f \ominus g) = N(f) \ominus N(g)$
8(a) $D(f \oplus g) = D(f) \oplus D(g)$
  (b) $D(f \odot g) = D(f) \odot D(g)$

(c) $D(f \lor g) = D(f) \lor D(g)$

(d) $D(f \ominus g) = D(f) \ominus D(g)$

9(a) $T(f \oplus g, i, j) = T(f, i, j) \oplus T(g, i, j)$

(b) $T(f \odot g, i, j) = T(f, i, j) \odot T(g, i, j)$

(c) $T(f \lor g, i, j) = T(f, i, j) \lor T(g, i, j)$

(d) $T(f \ominus g, i, j) = T(f, i, j) \ominus T(g, i, j)$

Due to the inducements and structural nature of the operations in the DIA, numerous other identities hold. In particular, 7, 8, and 9 are special cases that result from the general principle that any domain-induced operation commutes with any range-induced operation.

9.3 MACRO-OPERATORS IN THE DIGITAL IMAGE ALGEBRA

Although the basic ten operators in the DIA can be directly employed to specify digital image-processing algorithms, they do so at a very low level. To provide a workable system of operations for practical algorithm expression, it is necessary to build a library of *macro-operators*, which, from an algebraic perspective, are simply *terms* in the algebra. From a programming point of view, these are stored procedures that can be called whenever the functions they specify are required in an algorithm.

Rigorously, all algorithms that are ultimately constructed from the basic ten operators are terms in the DIA and therefore might be called macro-operators; however, we will take the pragmatic view that the macro-operator library contains "standard" functions. Of course, since the carrier sets and operators of the DIA are mathematically quite general, and since the basic ten operators are either range induced, domain induced, or structural, the algebra itself can be employed in other areas besides image processing (for instance, signal processing), and hence the notion of which functions are standard is one that is certainly open to interpretation. Moreover, other important image algebras are obtained by only slight alterations in the carrier sets and the operators corresponding to the operation symbols, and, as a result, there is a close relationship between the corresponding macro-operator libraries.

In the sequel, a representative collection of DIA macro-operators will be presented, together with their expressions as terms within the algebra. Since the higher-level operations form tiers of increasing complexity, the latter ones presented will have basis representations that employ lower-level macro-operations, where, by a *basis representation* of an operator, we mean a description of the operator in terms of the basic ten operators (or macro-operators already represented) linked by function composition.

Some of the macro-operations in the following list will be recognized as slightly generalized versions of either operations on bound matrices (Section 4.9) or of certain image-processing transformations discussed in Chapter 8. All will surely be recognized by those who have taken courses in digital image processing.

Throughout the list, X will denote the class of all digital images, C the class of all constant images having single gray value 1, and Y the class of digital images having finite domains (i.e., the class of bound matrices). Note that both C and Y are subclasses of X, and that $C \cap Y$ is the class of constant $(1-*)$ bound matrices. Unless otherwise specified, it will be assumed that f and g have domains A and B, respectively.

1. Additive identity: For any set $A \subset Z \times Z$, there exists an additive identity in R^A; indeed, $f \oplus 0_A = f$. 0_A has a basis representation given by $0_A = E(0, A)$.

2. Multiplicative Identity: For any set $A \subset Z \times Z$, there exists a multiplicative identity on R^A. $f \odot 1_A = f$. 1_A has a basis representation given by $1_A = E(1, A)$.

3. Additive inverse: We define $\ominus: X \to X$ by $[\ominus f](i, j) = -f(i, j)$. $\ominus$ serves as an additive inverse in that $f \oplus [\ominus f] = 0_A$. A basis representation is given by $\ominus f = E[-1, K(f)] \odot f$. When the unary operator $\ominus$ is preceded by $\oplus$, it is customary to omit the $\oplus$.

4. Multiplicative inverse: We define $\oslash: X \to X$ by

$$[\oslash f](i, j) = \begin{cases} 1/f(i, j), & \text{if } (i, j) \in A \text{ and } f(i, j) \neq 0 \\ \text{undefined}, & \text{otherwise} \end{cases}$$

   If f is never 0 on A, then $f \odot [\oslash f] = 1_A$. In that sense, $\oslash$ serves as a multiplicative inverse. A basis representation is given by $\oslash f = E[1, K(f)] \oslash f$.

5. Minimum macro: $\wedge: X \times X \to X$ by

$$[f \wedge g](i, j) = \begin{cases} f(i, j) \wedge g(i, j), & \text{if } (i, j) \in A \cap B \\ f(i, j) & \text{if } (i, j) \in A - B \\ g(i, j) & \text{if } (i, j) \in B - A \end{cases}$$

   A basis representation is given by $f \wedge g = \ominus[(\ominus f) \vee (\ominus g)]$.

6. Scalar multiplication: $\triangle: R \times X \to X$ by $[t \triangle f](i, j) = t \cdot f(i, j)$. This operation is often denoted by $t \cdot f$. It has a basis representation $t \triangle f = E[t, K(f)] \odot f$.

7. Complementation: $\mathscr{C}: C \to C$ by

$$\mathscr{C}(1_A) = 1_{A^c}$$

   Basis representation:

$$1_{A^c} = (1_A \oplus E[-1, Z \times Z]) \ominus (1_A \oplus E[-1, Z \times Z])$$

8. Absolute value: $|\cdot|: X \to X$ by

$$|f|(i, j) = |f(i, j)|$$

   Basis representation: $|f| = (\ominus f) \vee f$.

9. 180° rotation: N^2: $X \to X$ by $[N^2(f)](i, j) = f(-i, -j)$. Basis representation: $N^2(f) = N(N(f))$. A 270° rotation macro N^3 is defined analogously. Horizontal and vertical flips can be constructed from N and D. For instance, a horizontal flip is given by $N[D(f)]$.

10. Threshold: A common variant of thresholding is given by $\mathscr{T}$: $X \times R \to X$, where

$$[\mathscr{T}(f, t)](i, j) = \begin{cases} 1, & \text{if } f(i, j) \geq t \\ 0, & \text{if } f(i, j) < t \end{cases}$$

To simplify notation, we write $\mathscr{T}_t (\cdot) = \mathscr{T}(\cdot, t)$. A basis representation is given for $\mathscr{T}_0$ by

$$\mathscr{T}_0(f) = [\ominus[(f \oslash 0_A) \oplus (f \oslash 0_A)]] \oplus 1_A$$

For arbitrary t, $\mathscr{T}_t(f) = \mathscr{T}_0(f \ominus E[t, K(f)])$. Other variants of thresholding can be constructed by using $\mathscr{T}_0$, including the operation of image truncation (image clipping).

11. Addition macro: The basic addition operation, $\oplus$, is defined on the symmetric difference of the input domains by leaving the input images unaltered thereon. An addition macro-operation can be defined so as to leave the output undefined on the symmetric difference of the input domains. We define $\mathscr{A}$: $X \times X \to X$ by

$$[\mathscr{A}(f, g)](i, j) = \begin{cases} f(i, j) + g(i, j), & \text{if } (i, j) \in A \cap B \\ \text{undefined}, & \text{otherwise} \end{cases}$$

Basis representation:

$$\mathscr{A}(f, g) = (f \oplus g) \ominus [(E[1, K(f)] \oplus E[0, K(g)]) \odot$$
$$(E[0, K(f)] \oplus E[1, K(g)])]$$

Multiplication, maximum, and minimum macros are analogously defined. In each case, however, the basis representation can be given utilizing the addition macro. For instance, for multiplication,

$$\mathscr{M}(f, g) = \mathscr{A}[f \odot g, \mathscr{A}(0_A, 0_B)]$$

12. Selection: A database-type macro $\mathscr{S}$: $X \times 2^{Z \times Z} \to X$ is defined by

$$[\mathscr{S}(f, B)](i, j) = \begin{cases} f(i, j), & \text{if } (i, j) \in A \cap B \\ \text{undefined}, & \text{otherwise} \end{cases}$$

Basis representation: $\mathscr{S}(f, B) = \mathscr{A}(f, 0_B)$.

13. Extension: Given a primary image f and a secondary image g, the extension of f by g is defined to be f on A and g on $B - A$. The extension operator $\mathscr{H}$: $X \times X \to X$ and has basis representation

$$\mathscr{H}(f, g) = [(0 \bigtriangleup \mathscr{S}(g, K(f))) \odot g] \oplus f$$

14. Restriction: We define $\mathcal{R}: X \times X \to X$ by

$$[\mathcal{R}(f, g)](i, j) = \begin{cases} f(i, j), & \text{if } (i, j) \in A \cap B \\ \text{undefined}, & \text{otherwise.} \end{cases}$$

Basis representation: $\mathcal{R}(f, g) = \mathcal{S}[f, K(g)]$.

15. Gray-level summation: $\sum: Y \to R$ by

$$\sum(f) = \sum_{(i,\ j) \in A} f(i, j)$$

Note that f in Y means that it has only a finite number of pixels in its domain. Basis representation:

$$\sum(f) = G\left[\bigoplus_{(i,j) \in A} \mathcal{S}[T(f, -i, -j), \{(0, 0)\}] \right]$$

where $\bigoplus_{(i,j) \in A}$ means summation with respect to $\oplus$. There also exist macros for the gray-level product, gray-level maximum, and gray-level minimum.

16. Dot product: Suppose f and g both have domain A. Then the dot product

$$\mathcal{D}_0(f, g) = \sum_{(i,j) \in A} f(i, j)g(i, j)$$

can be formed. If the images have different domains, then the dot product is undefined. Rigorously,

$$\mathcal{D}_0: \bigcup_{\substack{A \subset Z \times Z \\ A \text{ bounded}}} R^A \times R^A \to R$$

Basis representation: For $f, g \in R^A$,

$$\mathcal{D}_0(f, g) = \sum(f \odot g)$$

17. Filtering: One of the most common operations in digital image processing is that of filtering an image by a given mask. Since a mask is nothing but an image that is being employed for a specific purpose, no reference need be made to the term mask. We define $\mathcal{F}: Y \times Y \to Y$ by

$$[\mathcal{F}(f, g)](i, j) = \begin{cases} \displaystyle\sum_{(u,v) \in B} f(i + u, j + v)g(u, v), & \begin{array}{l} \text{if all terms in the} \\ \text{sum are defined and} \\ B \text{ is the domain of } g \end{array} \\[2em] \text{undefined}, & \begin{array}{l} \text{if there exists at least} \\ \text{one undefined term} \\ \text{in the sum} \end{array} \end{cases}$$

Basis representation:

$$\mathcal{F}(f, g) = \bigoplus_{(i,\ j) \in A} E[\mathcal{D}_0[\mathcal{R}(f, T(g, i, j)), T(g, i, j)], \{(i, j)\}]$$

where the convention is adopted that undefined summands are ignored.

18. Pixelwise norms for image vectors: Very often we must consider a vector of images $(f_1, f_2, \ldots, f_m)$. For simplicity, suppose each f_k has the same domain A. Then, for any $(i, j) \in A$, we can associate a real-valued vector

$$V_{i,j} = (f_1(i, j), f_2(i, j), \ldots, f_m(i, j))$$

Numerous norms can be applied to $V_{i,j}$, though, for the sake of explication, we restrict our attention to the supremum norm

$$\|V_{i,j}\|_\infty = \max_{k = 1,2,\ldots,m} |f_k(i, j)|$$

Correspondingly, the macro $N_\infty: X \times X \times \cdots \times X \to X$, m terms in the product, can be defined by

$$[N_\infty(f_1, f_2, \ldots, f_m)](i, j) = \|V_{i,j}\|_\infty$$

Basis representation:

$$N_\infty(f_1, f_2, \ldots, f_m) = \bigvee_{k=1}^{m} |f_k|$$

19. Gradient-type edge detector: Many edge-detection techniques involve filtering by two directional masks. Examples are the usual gradient, the Prewitt gradient, and the Sobel gradient. These operators each have three popular variants, the particular variant depending on the choice of norm. We restrict our attention to the supremum norm and define the edge operator

$$E_\infty: Y \times Y \times Y \times R \to Y$$

by

$$E_\infty(f, M, N, t) = \mathcal{T}_t[N_\infty(\mathcal{F}(f, M), \mathcal{F}(f, N))]$$

which is itself a basis representation. For instance, if

$$M = \begin{pmatrix} -1 & 0 & 1 \\ -2 & \textcircled{0} & 2 \\ -1 & 0 & 1 \end{pmatrix} \quad \text{and} \quad N = \begin{pmatrix} 1 & 2 & 1 \\ 0 & \textcircled{0} & 0 \\ -1 & -2 & -1 \end{pmatrix}$$

then E_∞ outputs a binary image depending on the threshold parameter t, and E_∞ is the Sobel edge detector (see Section 8.3).

20. Compass gradient operators: In a manner similar to the gradient-type operators, we can construct a compass gradient macro-operator. It can be used with any set of eight compass gradient masks such as the Kirsh or three-level masks. We leave out the thresholding operation and define $E_C: Y \times Y \times \cdots \times Y \to Y$, nine terms in the product, by

$$E_C(f, M_1, M_2, \ldots, M_8) = N_\infty[\mathcal{F}(f, M_1), \mathcal{F}(f, M_2), \ldots, \mathcal{F}(f, M_8)]$$

which is itself a basis representation.

21. Morphological operations: Four two-valued morphological macro-operators are defined, each taking $C \times C \to C$. They respectively yield the dilation, erosion, closing, and opening, and they are given in basis form by

$$\mathscr{D}(f, g) = \bigvee_{(i,j) \in K(f)} T(g, i, j)$$

$$\mathscr{E}(f, g) = \mathscr{C}[\mathscr{D}(\mathscr{C}(f), N^2(g))]$$

$$Cl(f, g) = \mathscr{E}[\mathscr{D}(f, N^2(g)), N^2(g)]$$

$$O(f, g) = \mathscr{D}[\mathscr{E}(f, g), g]$$

Many other important macro-operations could be provided, including convolution, the DFT (using a complexification of the image algebra), and the gray-level morphological operations; however, the preceding list should be sufficient to provide an indication of the representations within the DIA.

In the following examples we will employ the bound matrix subalgebra to illustrate some of the macro-operations in the DIA.

Example 9.5

Let

$$f = \begin{pmatrix} 2 & -1 \\ \underline{0} & * \end{pmatrix}$$

Then, as a set, the domain of f is given by

$$K(f) = \{(0, 0), (0, 1), (1, 1)\}$$

The additive and multiplicative identities on $K(f)$ are given by

$$0_{K(f)} = E[0, K(f)] = \begin{pmatrix} 0 & 0 \\ \underline{0} & * \end{pmatrix}$$

and

$$1_{K(f)} = E[1, K(f)] = \begin{pmatrix} 1 & 1 \\ \underline{1} & * \end{pmatrix}$$

respectively.

The additive inverse for f is given by

$$\ominus f = E[-1, K(f)] \odot f$$

$$= \begin{pmatrix} -1 & -1 \\ \underline{-1} & * \end{pmatrix} \odot \begin{pmatrix} 2 & -1 \\ \underline{0} & * \end{pmatrix}$$

$$= \begin{pmatrix} -2 & 1 \\ \underline{0} & * \end{pmatrix}$$

Since $f(0, 0) = 0$, f does not possess a multiplicative inverse; however, the image $①f$ is still defined:

$$①f = E[1, K(f)] ⊖ f$$

$$= \begin{pmatrix} 1 & 1 \\ ① & * \end{pmatrix} ⊖ \begin{pmatrix} 2 & -1 \\ ⓪ & * \end{pmatrix}$$

$$= \begin{pmatrix} 1/2 & -1 \\ ⊛ & * \end{pmatrix}$$

Example 9.6

Let f be the bound matrix of Example 9.5 and let

$$g = \begin{pmatrix} * & 4 \\ ⊖3 & 2 \end{pmatrix}$$

We will apply the basis representation of $⊘$ directly to f and g to compute $f ⊘ g$:

$$f ⊘ g = ⊖[(⊖f) ⊘ (⊖g)]$$

$$= ⊖\left[\begin{pmatrix} -2 & 1 \\ ⓪ & * \end{pmatrix} ⊘ \begin{pmatrix} * & -4 \\ ③ & -2 \end{pmatrix} \right]$$

$$= ⊖\begin{pmatrix} -2 & 1 \\ ③ & -2 \end{pmatrix}$$

$$= \begin{pmatrix} 2 & -1 \\ -3 & 2 \end{pmatrix}$$

Example 9.7

We will apply the basis representation of the threshold operator to threshold the bound matrix f of Example 9.5 at 0 and then at 1:

$$\mathcal{T}_0(f) = [⊖[(f ⊘ 0_{K(f)}) ⊖ (f ⊘ 0_{K(f)})]] ⊕ 1_{K(f)}$$

$$= \left[⊖\left[\begin{pmatrix} 0 & -1 \\ ⓪ & * \end{pmatrix} ⊖ \begin{pmatrix} 0 & -1 \\ ⓪ & * \end{pmatrix} \right] \right] ⊕ \begin{pmatrix} 1 & 1 \\ ① & * \end{pmatrix}$$

$$= \begin{pmatrix} * & -1 \\ ⊛ & * \end{pmatrix} ⊕ \begin{pmatrix} 1 & 1 \\ ① & * \end{pmatrix}$$

$$= \begin{pmatrix} 1 & 0 \\ ① & * \end{pmatrix}$$

and

$$\mathcal{T}_1(f) = \mathcal{T}_0(f \ominus E[1, K(f)])$$

$$= \mathcal{T}_0\left[\left(\begin{array}{cc} 2 & -1 \\ \boxed{0} & * \end{array}\right) \ominus \left(\begin{array}{cc} 1 & 1 \\ \boxed{1} & * \end{array}\right)\right]$$

$$= \mathcal{T}_0\left[\left(\begin{array}{cc} 1 & -2 \\ \boxed{-1} & * \end{array}\right)\right]$$

$$= \left(\begin{array}{cc} 1 & 0 \\ \boxed{0} & * \end{array}\right)$$

Example 9.8

Using the bound matrices f of Example 9.5 and g of Example 9.6, we find $\mathcal{A}(f, g)$ according to the basis representation:

$$E[1, K(f)] \oplus E[0, K(g)] = \left(\begin{array}{cc} 1 & 1 \\ \boxed{1} & * \end{array}\right) \oplus \left(\begin{array}{cc} * & 0 \\ \boxed{0} & 0 \end{array}\right) = \left(\begin{array}{cc} 1 & 1 \\ \boxed{1} & 0 \end{array}\right)$$

and

$$E[0, K(f)] \oplus E[1, K(g)] = \left(\begin{array}{cc} 0 & 0 \\ \boxed{0} & * \end{array}\right) \oplus \left(\begin{array}{cc} * & 1 \\ \boxed{1} & 1 \end{array}\right) = \left(\begin{array}{cc} 0 & 1 \\ \boxed{1} & 1 \end{array}\right)$$

Thus,

$$\mathcal{A}(f, g) = \left(\begin{array}{cc} 2 & 3 \\ \boxed{-3} & 2 \end{array}\right) \oslash \left[\left(\begin{array}{cc} 1 & 1 \\ \boxed{1} & 0 \end{array}\right) \odot \left(\begin{array}{cc} 0 & 1 \\ \boxed{1} & 1 \end{array}\right)\right]$$

$$= \left(\begin{array}{cc} 2 & 3 \\ \boxed{-3} & 2 \end{array}\right) \oslash \left(\begin{array}{cc} 0 & 1 \\ \boxed{1} & 0 \end{array}\right)$$

$$= \left(\begin{array}{cc} * & 3 \\ \boxed{-3} & * \end{array}\right)$$

The richness of the DIA can be seen from the number of important subalgebras it contains. For instance, within the DIA is an isomorphic copy of the Boolean algebra

$$\mathcal{B} = (2^{Z \times Z}, \cup, \cap, {}^c, \emptyset, Z \times Z)$$

of subsets of $Z \times Z$ under union, intersection, and complementation. Specifically,

$$E(1, \cdot): 2^{Z \times Z} \xrightarrow[\text{onto}]{1-1} C \subset X$$

Moreover, the set-theoretic operations of union, intersection, and complementation are preserved under the mapping (relative to the DIA operations of $\bigcirc\!\!\!\vee$, $\bigcirc\!\!\!\wedge$, and $\mathscr{C}$, where $\bigcirc\!\!\!\wedge$ denotes the minimum macro mentioned in 11). Indeed, letting

$$\Psi(A) = E(1, A)$$

we have

$$\Psi(A \cup B) = 1_{A \cup B} = 1_A \;\bigcirc\!\!\!\vee\; 1_B = \Psi(A) \;\bigcirc\!\!\!\vee\; \Psi(B)$$

$$\Psi(A \cap B) = 1_{A \cap B} = 1_A \;\bigcirc\!\!\!\wedge\; 1_B = \Psi(A) \;\bigcirc\!\!\!\wedge\; \Psi(B)$$

$$\Psi(A^c) = 1_{A^c} = \mathscr{C}(1_A) = \mathscr{C}(\Psi(A))$$

Among the other subalgebras of the DIA are real-valued matrix algebra, bound matrix algebra, and morphological algebra.

9.4 HOMOMORPHISMS BETWEEN MANY-SORTED ALGEBRAS

Homomorphisms are structure-preserving mappings between many-sorted algebras. They are useful for recognizing when certain structures appear within other structures. For instance, in the last section we determined that there is an exact copy of the set-theoretic Boolean algebra within the DIA. Instrumental in the recognition of the isomorphism was the Boolean algebra homomorphism $E[1, \cdot]$. In the present section we will present the concept of a homomorphism between two many-sorted algebras possessing the same sorts and operation symbols.

Consider the many-sorted algebras

$$A^1 = (S, \alpha, \Sigma, \beta^1, \Phi^1, \gamma^1, G^1)$$

and

$$A^2 = (S, \alpha, \Sigma, \beta^2, \Phi^2, \gamma^2, G^2)$$

A *many-sorted algebra homomorphism* (or simply, a homomorphism) from A^1 into A^2 is a family of functions

$$\mathscr{H} = \{h_s\}_{s \in S}$$

such that

$$h_s: A^1_s \to A^2_s$$

for any $s \in S$, and which preserves the operations, that is, (1) If $\sigma \in \sum\limits_{\varepsilon, s}$, $\sigma^1 = \gamma^1(\sigma)$, and $\sigma^2 = \gamma^2(\sigma)$, then

$$h_s(\sigma^1) = \sigma^2$$

and (2) If $\sigma \in \sum\limits_{s_1 s_2 \ldots s_n, s}$, $(a_1, a_2, \ldots, a_n) \in A^1_{s_1} \times A^1_{s_2} \times \cdots \times A^1_{s_n}$, $\gamma^1(\sigma) = \sigma^1$, and $\gamma^2(\sigma) = \sigma^2$, then

$$h_s(\sigma^1(a_1, a_2, \ldots, a_n)) = \sigma^2(h_{s_1}(a_1), h_{s_2}(a_2), \ldots, h_{s_n}(a_n))$$

Graphical representation of these two characterizing properties of homomorphisms is given in the commuting diagrams

1)

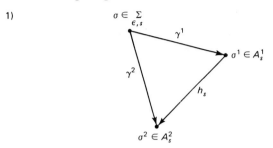

and

2)

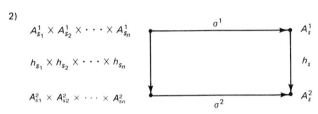

Note that it is implicit in the notion of a commuting diagram that the commutation must hold for every named operation in the many-sorted algebra being discussed.

A homomorphism $\mathcal{H} = \{h_s\}_{s \in S}$ from A^1 into A^2 is said to be an *isomorphism* if

$$h_s: A_s^1 \xrightarrow[\text{onto}]{1-1} A_s^2$$

for each $s \in S$. Thus, if two many-sorted algebras are isomorphic, then all corresponding carrier sets in the two algebras are identical except for the naming of the elements. Moreover, the corresponding n-ary operations in the two algebras are also identical up to the naming of the operators involved. Consequently, isomorphic algebras are usually identified.

Several examples will now be given to illustrate the steps involved in determining homomorphisms between two many-sorted algebras.

Example 9.9

Consider the lattices L^1 and L^2 illustrated in the Haase diagram of Figure 9.10. Define the mapping

$$h_e: A_e^1 \to A_e^2$$

by

$$h_e(0) = h_e(x) = l$$

$$h_e(1) = h_e(y) = u$$

$L^1 = (A_e^1, \vee^1, \wedge^1)$ $L^2 = (A_e^2, \vee^2, \wedge^2)$

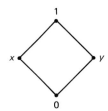

Figure 9.10   Two lattices

Since the following diagrams commute, $\mathscr{H} = \{h_e\}$ is a homomorphism from L^1 into L^2.

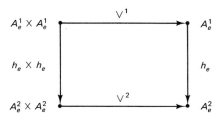

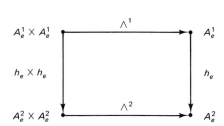

The first diagram commutes by observing that columns 6 and 7 of Table 9.1 are equal. Similarly, the equality of columns 9 and 10 shows that the second diagram commutes.

Example 9.10

The two lattices illustrated in Figure 9.10 are also Boolean algebras:

$$(A_e^1, \vee^1, \wedge^1, c^1, 0, 1)$$

and

$$(A_e^2, \vee^2, \wedge^2, c^2, l, u)$$

The lattice homomorphism described in Example 9.9 is also a Boolean algebra homomorphism since the three following diagrams also commute:

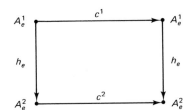

TABLE 9.1 HOMOMORPHISM VERIFICATION FOR EXAMPLE 9.9

① $r \in A_e^1$	② $s \in A_e^1$	③ $r \vee^1 s$	④ $h_e(r)$	⑤ $h_e(s)$	⑥ $h_e(r) \vee^2 h_e(s)$	⑦ $h_e(r \vee^1 s)$	⑧ $r \wedge^1 s$	⑨ $h_e(r) \wedge^2 h_e(s)$	⑩ $h_e(r \wedge^1 s)$
1	x	1	u	l	u	u	x	l	l
1	y	1	u	u	u	u	y	u	u
1	0	1	u	l	u	u	0	l	l
1	1	1	u	u	u	u	1	u	u
0	x	x	l	l	l	l	0	l	l
0	y	y	l	u	u	u	0	l	l
0	0	0	l	l	l	l	0	l	l
x	y	1	l	u	u	u	0	l	l
x	x	x	l	l	l	l	x	l	l
y	y	y	u	u	u	u	y	u	u

Commutativity of the first and second diagrams follows from

$$h_e(0) = l$$

and

$$h_e(1) = u$$

Finally, the table below shows that the third diagram commutes, since the last two columns are identical.

$r \in A_e^1$	r^{c1}	$h_e(r)$	$h_e(r^{c1})$	$(h_e(r))^{c2}$
x	y	l	u	u
y	x	u	l	l
0	1	l	u	u
1	0	u	l	l

Example 9.11

Two distinct directed graphs, G^1 and G^2, are illustrated in Figure 9.11. Define $\mathcal{H} = \{h_l, h_p)$ by

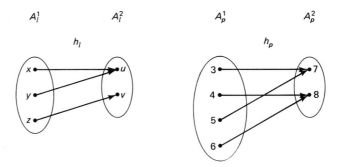

$G^1 = (A_l^1, A_p^1, f^1, b^1)$ $G^2 = (A_l^2, A_p^2, f^2, b^2)$

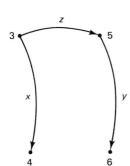
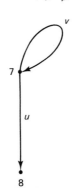

Figure 9.11 Two directed graphs

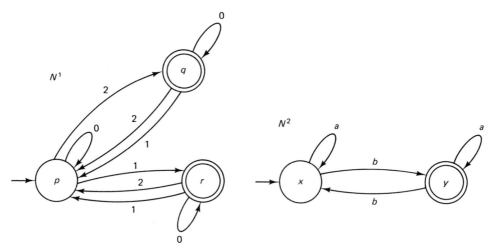

Figure 9.12   Two automata

To demonstrate that $\mathcal{H}$ is a directed graph homomorphism from G^1 into G^2, we need to show that the following two diagrams commute.

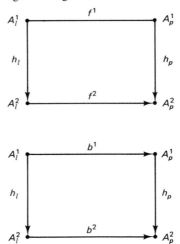

Justification follows from the table below, since columns 3 and 5 are identical, as are columns 7 and 8.

① $r \in A_l^1$	② $f^1(r)$	③ $h_p(f^1(r))$	④ $h_l(r)$	⑤ $f^2(h_l(r))$	⑥ $b^1(r)$	⑦ $h_p(b^1(r))$	⑧ $b^2(h_l(r))$
x	4	8	u	8	3	7	7
y	6	8	u	8	5	7	7
z	5	7	v	7	3	7	7

Example 9.12

Consider the automata N^1 and N^2 illustrated in Figure 9.12. A homomorphism is given by $\mathcal{H} = \{h_q, h_i, h_v\}$, where h_v is the the identity map, and h_q and h_i are defined as follows:

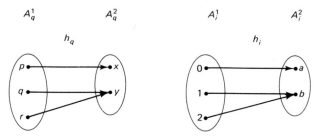

The three relevant commuting diagrams are

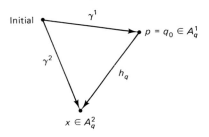

and

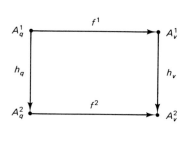

The first diagram commutes because

$$h_q(q_0) = x$$

The second diagram commutes because columns 3 and 5 are identical in the table.

① $u \in A_q^1$	② $f^1(u)$	③ $h_v(f^1(u))$	④ $h_q(u)$	⑤ $f^2(h_q(u))$
p	0	0	x	0
q	1	1	y	1
r	1	1	y	1

The third diagram commutes because columns 5 and 9 are identical in Table 9.2.

Example 9.13

Consider the two Petri nets P^1 and P^2 illustrated in Figure 9.13. A homomorphism from P^1 into P^2 is given by

$$\mathcal{H} = \{h_p, h_t, h_v, h_n\}$$

where h_v and h_n are the identity mappings

$$h_v: A_v^1 \rightarrow A_v^2$$

and

$$h_n: A_n^1 \rightarrow A_n^2$$

and h_p and h_t are defined as follows:

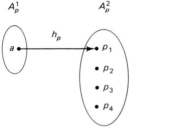
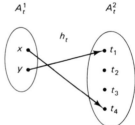

TABLE 9.2 HOMOMORPHISM VERIFICATION FOR EXAMPLE 9.12

① u	② v	③ w	④ $\delta^1(u, v, w)$	⑤ $h_v(\delta^1(u, v, w))$	⑥ $h_q(u)$	⑦ $h_i(v)$	⑧ $h_q(w)$	⑨ $\delta^2(h_q(u), h_i(v), h_q(w))$
p	0	p	1	1	x	a	x	1
p	1	r	1	1	x	b	y	1
p	2	q	1	1	x	b	y	1
q	0	q	1	1	y	a	y	1
q	1	p	1	1	y	b	x	1
q	2	p	1	1	y	b	x	1
r	0	r	1	1	y	a	y	1
r	1	p	1	1	y	b	x	1
r	2	p	1	1	y	b	x	1

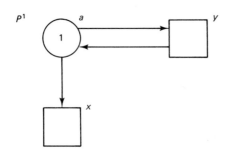

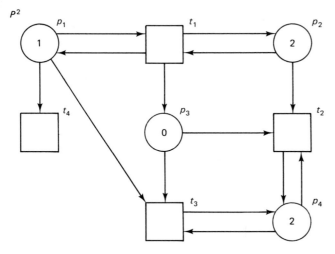

Figure 9.13   Two Petri nets

The following three diagrams commute:

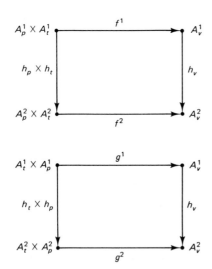

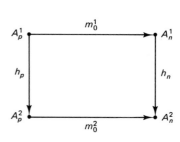

Verification that these diagrams commute follows by noticing that the last two columns in each of the three tables below are identical.

$u \in A_p^1$	$v \in A_t^1$	$h_p(u)$	$h_t(v)$	$f^1(u, v)$	$f^2(h_p(u), h_t(v))$	$h_r(f^1(u, v))$
a	x	p_1	t_4	1	1	1
a	y	p_1	t_1	1	1	1

$u \in A_p^1$	$v \in A_t^1$	$h_p(u)$	$h_t(v)$	$g^1(v, u)$	$g^2(h_t(v), h_p(u))$	$h_r(g^1(v, u))$
a	x	p_1	t_4	0	0	0
a	y	p_1	t_1	1	1	1

$u \in A_p^1$	$h_p(u)$	$m_0^1(u)$	$h_n(m_0^1(u))$	$m_0^2(h_p(u))$
a	p_1	1	1	1

9.5 CATEGORIES OF MANY-SORTED ALGEBRAS

For the sake of completeness, we close this chapter with a brief discussion concerning categories of many-sorted algebras.

A category C of many-sorted algebras consists of two entities: (1) a set, denoted by $|C|$, of many-sorted algebras having the same set of sorts and the same signature sets, and (2) a set consisting of all homomorphisms between the elements of $|C|$. The elements of $|C|$ are often called the *objects* of the category and the homomorphisms in C are often called *morphisms*. Thus, for any two, not necessarily distinct, objects A^1 and A^2 in $|C|$, there is in C a set, denoted by $\mathrm{MOR}(A^1, A^2)$, that consists of all homomorphisms from A^1 into A^2. Notice that

$$\mathrm{MOR}(A^1, A^2) = \mathrm{MOR}(A^i, A^j)$$

if and only if

$$A^1 = A^i \quad \text{and} \quad A^2 = A^j$$

since the objects in $|C|$ are distinct.

Morphisms may be composed under function composition (if the operation is well defined) and the resulting mapping will be a homomorphism. Specifically, if $\mathcal{H}_1 \in \mathrm{MOR}(A^1, A^2)$ and $\mathcal{H}_2 \in \mathrm{MOR}(A^2, A^3)$, then

$$\mathcal{H}_2 \circ \mathcal{H}_1 \in \mathrm{MOR}(A^1, A^3)$$

Since a many-sorted algebra homomorphism is itself a set of functions, one for each sort,

$$\mathcal{H}_2 = \{h_s^2\}_{s \in S}$$

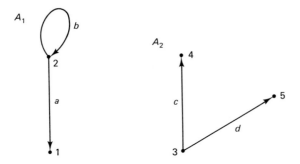

Figure 9.14 Two directed graphs

and

$$\mathcal{H}_1 = \{h_s^1\}_{s \in S}$$

Thus, $\mathcal{H}_2 \circ \mathcal{H}_1$ is a symbolic representation for the set of operators

$$\{h_s^2(h_s^1(\ ))\}_{s \in S}$$

Morphism composition satisfies the associative law: if

$$\mathcal{H}_1 \in \text{MOR}(A^1, A^2)$$

$$\mathcal{H}_2 \in \text{MOR}(A^2, A^3)$$

and

$$\mathcal{H}_3 \in \text{MOR}(A^3, A^4)$$

then

$$\mathcal{H}_3 \circ (\mathcal{H}_2 \circ \mathcal{H}_1) = (\mathcal{H}_3 \circ \mathcal{H}_2) \circ \mathcal{H}_1$$

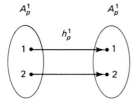
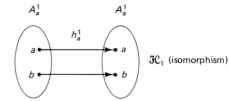

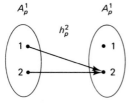
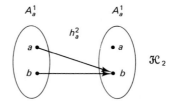

Figure 9.15 Homomorphisms from A^1 into A^1

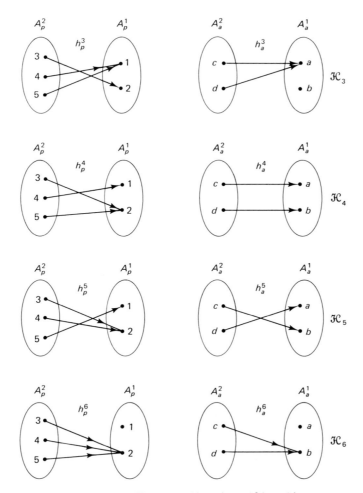

Figure 9.16   Homomorphisms from A^2 into A^1

Furthermore, there will always be an identity morphism I in each class $\mathrm{MOR}(A^1, A^1)$. For any $\mathcal{H} \in \mathrm{MOR}(A^1, A^1)$

$$I \circ \mathcal{H} = \mathcal{H} \circ I = \mathcal{H}$$

Example 9.14

   Consider the category consisting of the two objects A^1 and A^2, each a directed graph, having the carrier sets

$$A^1_a = \{a, b\}, \qquad A^1_p = \{1, 2\}$$

   and

$$A^2_a = \{c, d\}, \qquad A^2_p = \{3, 4, 5\}$$

respectively, and the respective front and back functions f^1 and b^1 and f^2 and b^2, where

$$f^1(a) = 1, \qquad f^1(b) = 2$$
$$b^1(a) = 2, \qquad b^1(b) = 2$$
$$f^2(c) = 4, \qquad f^2(d) = 5$$
$$b^2(c) = 3, \qquad b^2(d) = 3$$

Corresponding graphs are illustrated in Figure 9.14. The many-sorted algebra category comprised of these two objects also contains ten morphisms among the possible 192 mappings

$$\mathcal{H} = \{h_a, h_p\}$$

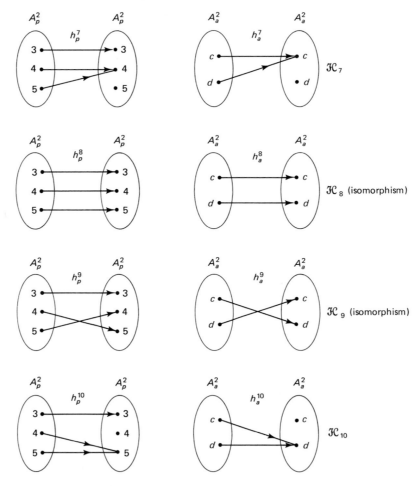

Figure 9.17   Homomorphisms from A^2 into A^2

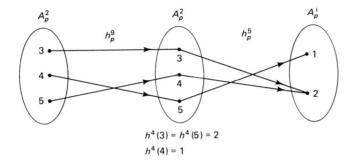

$$h^4(3) = h^4(5) = 2$$
$$h^4(4) = 1$$

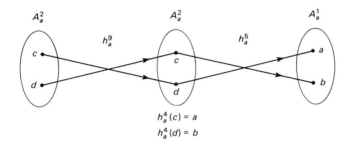

$$h_a^4(c) = a$$
$$h_a^4(d) = b$$

Figure 9.18   Closure of homomorphisms

Each morphism is a many-sorted algebra homomorphism, and there are two distinct homomorphisms from A^1 into A^1, one of which is an isomorphism (see Figure 9.15). There are no homomorphisms from A^1 into A^2; however, there are four homomorphisms from A^2 into A^1 (see Figure 9.16), and there are four homomorphisms from A^2 into itself (see Figure 9.17), two of which are also isomorphisms.   Specifically,

$$\text{MOR}(A^1, A^1) = \{\mathcal{H}_1, \mathcal{H}_2\}$$

$$\text{MOR}(A^1, A^2) = \phi$$

$$\text{MOR}(A^2, A^1) = \{\mathcal{H}_3, \mathcal{H}_4, \mathcal{H}_5, \mathcal{H}_6\}$$

and

$$\text{MOR}(A^2, A^2) = \{\mathcal{H}_7, \mathcal{H}_8, \mathcal{H}_9, \mathcal{H}_{10}\}$$

Figure 9.18 illustrates the closure of homomorphisms under function composition: $\mathcal{H}_5 \circ \mathcal{H}_9 = \mathcal{H}_4$.

EXERCISES FOR CHAPTER 9

9.1. Draw a polyadic graph illustrating the set of sorts and operation names in an inner product space.   Why is the structure somewhat different from most other structures discussed in the text?

9.2. Show that properties 1 through 9 of Section 9.2 hold in the DIA.

9.3. Property 3 of Section 9.2 states that

$$f \odot (f \ominus f) = f$$

Relate this property to the ordinary multiplication of matrices involving the pseudoinverse (see Section 7.4).

9.4. Let f^+ denote the operation

$$f^+(n, m) = \begin{cases} f(n, m), & \text{if } f(n, m) > 0 \\ 0, & \text{if } f(n, m) \leq 0 \end{cases}$$

Express f^+ in terms of the basic ten operations.

9.5. Refer to f^+ in Exercise 9.4. Is it true that $f^+ = |f| - f$?

9.6. Let

$$f = \begin{pmatrix} * & 1 & 4 \\ \textcircled{0} & -3 & 2 \end{pmatrix}$$

and

$$g = \begin{pmatrix} 1 & 2 \\ -3 & -2 \\ \textcircled{*} & 1 \end{pmatrix}$$

Using f and g, illustrate the basis representations in the macro-operation list of Section 9.3 for the following macro-operations:

(a) additive inverse
(b) multiplicative inverse
(c) minimum ($\oslash$)
(d) scalar multiplication ($t = 3$)
(e) absolute value
(f) horizontal flip
(g) threshold ($t = 2$)
(h) addition macro ($\mathscr{A}$)
(i) minimum, maximum, and multiplication macros (analogous to $\mathscr{A}$)
(j) selection ($B = \{(1, 0), (2, 1)\}$)
(k) extension
(l) restriction
(m) gray level summation

9.7. Using the image

$$f = \begin{pmatrix} 4 & 0 & 1 & 0 & 6 \\ 5 & 5 & 0 & 5 & 0 \\ 5 & 6 & 6 & 1 & 1 \\ 5 & 4 & 6 & 5 & 1 \\ 6 & 6 & 6 & 5 & 4 \end{pmatrix}_{4, -2}$$

and the mask

$$g = \begin{pmatrix} 0 & 1 \\ \textcircled{-1} & 0 \end{pmatrix}$$

utilize the basis representation of filter to find $\mathcal{F}(f, g)$.

9.8. For the structure given in Figure 9.10, find all lattice homomorphisms from L^1 into L^2. How many of these are isomorphisms?

9.9. Referring to Exercise 9.8, find all Boolean algebra homomorphisms from L^1 into L^2. How many of these are isomorphisms?

9.10. Referring to Figure 9.11, find all directed graph homomorphisms from G^2 into G^1. How many of these are isomorphisms?

9.11. Referring to Figure 9.12, find all automata homomorphisms from N^2 into N^1. Which of these are isomorphisms?

9.12. Consider the category whose objects are all directed graphs with two points from $A_p = \{1, 2\}$ and a single line from $A_a = \{a\}$. Find all morphisms involving these objects.

REFERENCES

ABBOTT, JAMES C., *Sets Lattices and Boolean Algebras*. Newton, MA: Allyn & Bacon, 1969.

AHO, A.V., J.E. HOPCROFT, AND J.D. ULLMAN, *Design and Analysis of Computer Algorithms*. Reading, MA: Addison-Wesley, 1974.

ALLEN, G.J., "Representation and Description of Curved Objects," *Report 173,* Stanford University Artificial Intelligence Laboratory, 1972.

ALLEN, JAMES, "Towards A General Theory of Action and Time," *Artificial Intelligence* 23 (2), 1984, pp. 123–154.

ANDERSON, JOHN R., "Acquisition of Proof Skills In Geometry," in *Machine Learning: An Artificial Intelligence Approach*, ed. Ryszard Michalski, Jamie G. Carbonell, and Tom M. Mitchell. Palo Alto, CA: Tioga, 1983, pp. 191–219.

ARBIB, MICHAEL A., AND ERNEST G. MANES, *Arrows, Structures and Functors: The Categorical Imperative*. Orlando, FL: Academic Press, 1975.

ASH, ROBERT B., *Basic Probability Theory*. NY: John Wiley & Sons, 1970.

BACH, EMMON, *Syntactic Theory*. NY: Holt, Rinehart & Winston, 1974.

BACHANT, J., AND J. MCDERMOTT, "R1 Revisited: Four Years In the Trenches," *The AI Magazine*, 5, no. 3 (Fall 1984).

BALLARD, DANA, AND CHRISTOPHER BROWN, *Computer Vision*. Englewood Cliffs, NJ: Prentice-Hall, 1982.

BARR, A., AND E.A. FEIGENBAUM, EDS., *The Handbook of Artificial Intelligence,* Vol. 1, William Kaufmann, 1981.

BARROW, H., AND J.M., TENENBAUM, "Recovering Intrinsic Scene Characteristics from Images," in *Computer Vision Systems,* ed. A. Hanson and E. Riseman, NY: Academic Press, 1978.

BARROW, H., AND J.M., TENENBAUM, "Interpreting Line Drawings as Three-dimensional Surfaces," *Proc. AAAI 1,* 1980, pp. 11–14.

BARROW, H., AND J.M., TENENBAUM, "Computational Vision," *Proceedings of the IEEE 69 (5),* 1981, pp. 572–595.

BARSTOW, D.R., N. AIELLO, R.O. DUDA, L.D. ERMAN, C. FORGY, D. GORLIN, R.D. GREINER, D.B. LENAT, P.E. LONDON, J. MCDERMOTT, H.P. NII, P. POLITAKIS, R. REBOH, S. ROSENSCHEIN, A.C. SCOTT, W. VAN MELLE, AND S.M. WEISS, "Languages and Tools for Knowledge Engineering," in F. Hayes-Roth, D.A. Waterman, and D.B. Lenat, eds. *Building Expert Systems,* Reading, MA: Addison-Wesley, 1983.

BECK, JACOB "Textural Segmentation," in *Organization and Representation in Perception,* ed. Jacob Beck, Hillsdale, NJ: Lawrence Erlbaum, 1982, pp. 285–317.

BEHZAD, M., G. CHARTRAND, AND L. LESNIAK-FOSTER, *Graphs and Digraphs*. Boston: Prindle, Weber, and Schmidt, 1979.

BELLMAN, RICHARD, *An Introduction to Artificial Intelligence: Can Computers Think?* San Francisco: Boyd & Fraser, 1978.

BLEDSOE, W.W., "Non-resolution theorem proving," *Artificial Intelligence*, 9 (1), 1977, pp. 1–35.

BOBROW, DANIEL G., AND TERRY WINOGRAD, "An overview of KRL, a Knowledge Representation Language," *Cognitive Science*, 1, 1977, pp. 3–46.

BODEN, MARGARET, *Artificial Intelligence and Natural Man.* NY: Basic Books, 1977.

BOYER, R.S., AND J.S. MOORE, *A Computational Logic.* Orlando, FL: Academic Press, 1979.

BRACHMAN, R.J., "On the Epistemological Status of Semantic Networks," in N.V. Findler, ed., *Associative Networks: Representation and Use of Knowledge by Computers.* Orlando, Fl: Academic Press, 1979.

BRACHMAN, R., S. AMAREL, C. ENGELMAN, R. ENGELMORE, E. FEIGENBAUM, AND D. WILKINS, "What are Expert Systems?" in F. Hayes-Roth D.A. Waterman, and D. Lenat, eds., *Building Expert Systems,* Reading, MA: Addison-Wesley, 1983.

BRITTING, KENNETH R., *Inertial Navigation Systems Analysis.* NY: Wiley-Interscience, 1971.

BROXMEYER, CHARLES, *Inertial navigation Systems.* NY: McGraw-Hill, 1964.

BRUCE, BERTRAM, "Case Systems for Natural Language," *Artificial Intelligence,* 6, 1975, pp. 327–360.

BRUNER, J.S., J.J. GOODNOW, AND G.A. AUSTIN, *A Study of Thining,* NY: John Wiley & Sons, 1956.

BUCHANAN, B., R. BECHTAL, J. BENNETT, W. CLANCEY, C. KULIKOWSKI, T. MITCHELL, AND D.A. WATERMAN, *Constructing an Expert System,* in Hayes-Roth, Waterman and Lenat, eds., *Building Expert Systems.* Reading, MA: Addison-Wesley, 1983.

CALLERO, M., D.A. WATERMAN, AND J. KIPPS, "TATR: A Prototype Expert System for Tactical Air Targeting," *Rand Report R-3096-ARPA,* Santa Monica, CA: The Rand Corporation, 1984.

CAMPBELL, A.N., V.F. HOLLISTER, R.O. DUDA, AND P.E. HART, "Recognition of a Hidden Mineral Deposit by an Artificial Intelligence Program," *Science* (217), September 3, 1982, pp. 927–929.

CARBONELL, JAIME, "Derivational Analogy and Its Role in Problem Solving," *Proc. AAAI 3,* 1983, pp. 64–69.

CHAKRAVARTY, INDRANIL, "A Generalized Line and Junction Labeling Scheme with Applications to Scene Analysis," *IEEE Transactions on Pattern Analysis and Machine Intelligence, PAMI-1, 2,* 1979.

CHANDRASEKARAN, B., "Expert systems: matching techniques to tasks." In W. Reitman, ed., *Artificial Intelligence Applications for Business,* Norwood, NJ: Ablex, 1984.

CHANG, C.L., AND R.C.T. LEE, *Symbolic Logic and Mechanical Theorem Proving,* Orlando, FL: Academic Press, 1973.

CHARNIAK, EUGENE, "ORGANIZATION AND INFERENCE IN A FRAMELIKE SYSTEM OF COMMON SENSE KNOWLEDGE," *Theoretical Issues in Natural Language Processions*, 1, 1975, pp. 42–52.

CHARNIAK, EUGENE, CHRISTOPHER K. RIESBECK, AND DREW V. MCDERMOTT, *Artificial Intelligence Programming,* Hillsdale, NJ: Lawrence Erlbaum, 1980.

CHARNIAK, EUGENE, "Passing Markers: A Theory of Contextural Influence in Language Comprehension," *Cognitive Science,* 7 (3), 1983.

CHARTRAND, G. *Graphs as Mathematical Models.* Boston: Prindle, Weber, and Schmidt, 1977.

CHILDS, D.L., "Feasibility of a Set—Theoretic Data Structure—a General Structure Based on a Reconstructed Definition of Relations," *IFIP Congress,* 1968.

CHOMSKY, NOAM, *Syntactic Structures.* The Hague: Mouton, 1957.

——, *Aspects of the Theory of Syntax.* Cambridge, MA: MIT Press, 1965.

CHURCH, ALONZOK, *Introduction to Mathematical Logic.* Princeton, NJ: Princeton Press, 1956.

CLANCEY, W.J., "Tutoring Rules for Guiding a Case Method Dialogue," *International Journal of Man-Machine Studies,* 11, 1979, pp. 25–49.

CLANCEY, W.J., "Methodology for Building an Intelligent Tutoring System," *Report STAN-CS-81-894,* Stanford CA: Department of Computer Science, Oct., 1981.

CLOCKSIN, W. AND C. MELLISH, *Programming in Prolog.* NY: Springer-Verlag, 1981.

COHEN, P.R. AND E.A. FEIGENBAUM, *The Handbook of Artificial Intelligence.* vol. 3, William Kaufmann, Inc. 1982.

CONOVER W.J., *Practical Nonparametric Statistics.* NY: John Wiley & Sons, Inc., 1971.

COOKE, S., C. HAFNER, T. McCARTY, M. MELDMAN, M. PETERSON, J. SPROWL, N. SRIDHARAN, AND D.A. WATERMAN, "The Applications of Artificial Intelligence to Law: a Survey of Six Current Projects." *AFIPS Conference Proceedings,* Vol. 50, 1981.

DAVIS, R., "Applications of Meta Level Knowledge to the Construction, Maintenance and Use of Large Knowledge Bases," *Report STAN-CS-552,* Stanford University: Stanford Artificial Intelligence Laboratory, July 1976.

DAVIS, R., "Expert Systems: Where are We? And Where Do We Go from Here?" *The AI Magazine,* pp. 3–22, Spring 1982.

DAVIS, RANDALL, BRUCE BUCHANAN, AND EDWARD SHORTLIFFE, "Production Rules as a Representation for Knowledge-Based Consultation Program," *Artificial Intelligence,* No. 8, pp. 15–45, 1977.

DAVIS, RANDALL AND DOUGLAS B. LENAT, *Knowledge-Based Systems in Artificial Intelligence.* NY: McGraw-Hillo, 1982.

DENNING, DOROTHY E.R., *Cryptography and Data Security.* Reading, MA: Addison-Wesley, 1982.

DOLD, A., AND B. ECKMANN, eds., *Lecture Notes in Mathematics.* Berlin, Springer-Verlag, 1972.

DOUGHERTY, E.R., AND C.R. GIARDINA, *Image Processing—Continuous to Discrete,* Vol. 1. Englewood Cliffs, NJ: Prentice-Hall, 1987.

DOUGHERTY, E.R., AND C.R. GIARDINA, *Matrix Structured Image Processing.* Englewood Cliffs, NJ: Prentice-Hall, 1987.

DOUGHERTY, E.R., AND C.R. GIARDINA, *Morphological Methods In Image and Signal Processing.* Englewood Cliffs, NJ: Prentice-Hall, 1987.

DOUGHERTY, E.R., AND C.R. GIARDINA, "A Structurally Induced Image Algebra." *Computers and Mathematics,* Stanford 1986.

DOUGHERTY, E.R., AND C.R. GIARDINA, "Morphological Algebra as a Subalgebra of Image Algebra," *SPSE International Conference,* Arlington, 1986.

DOUGHERTY, E.R., AND C.R. GIARDINA, "Image Algebra—Induced Operators and Induced Subalgebras," *SPIE Symposium on Optics in Medicine and Visual Image Processing,* Boston, 1987.

DOUGHERTY, E.R., AND P. SEHDEV, "A Matrix-Structured Image Processing Language For the VAX-11/780" *Electronic Imaging '87,* Boston, 1987.

DUBOIS, DIDIER AND HENRI PRADE, *Fuzzy Sets and Systems: Theory and Applications.* Orlando, FL: Academic Press, 1980.

DUDA, R., P.E. HART, N.J. NILSSON, R. REBOH, J. SLOCUM, AND G. SUTHERLAND, "Development of a Computer-based Consultant For Mineral Exploration," *SRI Report,* Menlo Park, CA: Stanford Research Institute, Oct. 1977.

DUDA, R., P.E. HART, N.J. NILSSON, P. BARRETT, J.G. GASCHNIG, K. KONOLIGE, R. REBOH, AND J. SLOCUM, "Development of the PROSPECTOR Consultation System For Mineral Exploration," *SRI Report,* Menlo Park, CA: Stanford Research Institute, Oct. 1978.

ENDERTON, H.B., *A Mathematical Introduction to Logic.* Orlando, FL: Academic Press, 1972.

FEIGENBAUM, E.A., "Expert Systems in the 1980's," in *Machine Intelligence, Infotech State of the Art Report*, series 9 no. 3, ed., A. Bond, Elmsford NY: Pergamon Infotech Limited, 1981.

FOSTER, C.C., *Content Addressable Parallel Processors.* NY: Van Nostrand Reinhold Co., 1976.

FRALEIGH, JOHN B., *A First Course in Abstract Algebra.* Reading, MA: Addison-Wesley, 1967.

GALLAIRE, H. AND JACK MINKER, *Logic and Databases.* NY: Plenum Press, 1978.

GASCHNIG, J., "PROSPECTOR: An expert system for mineral exploration," in *Machine Intelligence, Infotech State of the Art Report,* series 9, no. 3, Elmsford, NY: Pergamon Infotech Limited, 1981.

GASCHNIG, J. "Application of the PROSPECTOR system to geological exploration problems," in *Machine Intelligence 10,* J.E. Hayes, D. Michie, and Y.H. Pao, eds., Chichester, England: Horwood, 1982.

GAZDAR, GERALD, "On Syntactic Categories" *Transactions of the Royal Society, B-295,* pp. 267–283, 1981.

GOETCHARIAN, V., "From Binary to Grey Level Tone Image Processing by Using Fuzzy Logic Concepts," *Pattern Recognition,* Vol. 12, (1980), pp. 7–15.

GOGUEN, J.A., "Correctness and Equivalence of Data Types," *Proc. Conference on Algebraic Systems Theory*, Udine, Italy. Also in *Mathematical Systems Theory.* ed. G. Marchesihi and S.K. Mitter, NY: Springer-Verlag, 1976, pp. 352–358.

GOGUEN, J.A. "Abstract Error for Abstract Data Types," *UCLA Semantics and Theory of Computation Report* 6. Also in *Proc. IEIP Working Conference on Formal Description of Programming Concepts,* New Brunswick: St. Andrews, 1977, pp.21.1–21.32.

GOGUEN, J.A., J.W. THATCHER, E.G. WAGNER, AND J.B. WRIGHT, "A Junction Between Computer Science and Category Theory: I, Basic Definitions and Examples" Part I, *IBM Research Report RC 4526,* 1973.

GOGUEN, J.A., J.W. THATCHER, E.G. WAGNER, AND J.B. WRIGHT, "Initial Algebra Semantics and Continuous Algebras." *IBM Research Report RC 5701.* Also in *JACM,* 24, pp. 68–95, 1975.

GOGUEN, J.A., J.W. THATCHER, E.G. WAGNER, AND J.B. WRIGHT, "Abstract Data Types as Initial Algebras and Correctness of Data Representations," *Proc. Conference on Computer Graphics, Pattern Recognition and Data Structure,* 1975, pp. 89–93.

GOGUEN J.A., J.W. THATCHER, AND J.B. WRIGHT, "A Junction Between Computer Science and Category Theory: I, Basic Definitions and Examples," Part II *IBM Research Report RC 5908,* pp. 1976.

GROSSMAN, ISRAEL, AND WILHELM MAGNUS, *Groups and Their Graphs.* NY: Random House, 1964.

GUPTA, MADAN M., GEORGE N. SARIDIS, AND BRIAN R. GAINES, *Fuzzy Automata and Decision Processes.* NY: North-Holland Co., 1977.

HALL, E. *Computer Image Processing and Recognition.* Orlando, FL: Academic Press, 1979.

HALMOS, PAUL R., *Lectures on Boolean Algebras,* NY: Springer-Verlag, 1974.

HALMOS, PAUL R., *Naive Set Theory.* NY: Van Nostrand Reinhold Co., 1960.

HART, P.E., NILS J. NILSSON, AND B. RAPHAEL, "A Formal Basis for the Heuristic Determination of Minimum Cost Paths," *IEEE Transactions on Systems Science and Cybernetics, SSC-4 (2),* 1968, pp. 100–107.

HAYES, JOHN P., *Computer Architecture and Organization.* NY: McGraw-Hill, 1978.

HAYES, PATRICK "The Second Naive Physics Manifesto," in *Formal Theories of the Commonsense World,*" ed. J. Hobbs. Hillsdale, NJ: Ablex, 1984.

HAYES-ROTH, B., AND F. HAYES-ROTH "A Cognitive Model of Planning," *Cognitive Science*, 3 (4), 1979, pp. 275–310.

HAYES-ROTH, F., D.A. WATERMAN, AND D. LENAT, eds., *Building Expert Systems.* Reading, MA: Addison-Wesley, 1983.

HAYES-ROTH, F., D.A. WATERMAN, AND D. LENAT, "An Overview of Expert Systems," in Hayes-Roth, Waterman and Lenat, eds., *Building Expert Systems,* Reading, MA: Addison-Wesley, 1983.

HOEL, P.G. *Introduction to Mathematical Statistics.* New York: John Wiley and Sons, 1962.

HOPCROFT, J.E., AND J.D. ULLMAN, *Introduction to Automate Theory. Languages, and Computation.* Reading, MA: Addison-Wesley, 1979.

HORN, B.K.P., "Understanding Image Intensities," *Artificial Intelligence*, 8, 1977, pp. 201–231.

JOHNSON, P.E., "What Kind of Expert Should a System Be? *The Journal of Medicine and Philosophy,* vol. 8, pp. 77–97, 1983.

JOHNSON, P., "The Expert Mind: A New Challenge for the Information Scientist," in Th. M.A. Bemelmans, ed., *Beyond Productivity.* North Holland Publishing Co., The Netherlands, 1983.

KAHN, KENNETH AND G.A. GORRY, "Mechanizing Temporal Knowledge," *Artificial Intelligence,* 9, 1977 pp. 87–108.

KAPLAN, S.J., "The industrialization of artificial intelligence: from by-line to bottom line," *The AI Magazine,* vol. 5, no. 2, Summer 1984.

KAUFMANN, A., *Introduction to the Theory of Fuzzy Subsets* vol. 1. Orlando, FL: Academic Press, 1975.

KERNIGHAN, B.W. AND D.M. RITCHIE, *The C Programming Language.* Englewood Cliffs, NJ: Prentice-Hall, 1978.

KAYTON, MYRON AND WALTER R. FRIED, eds., *Avionics Navigation Systems.* NY: John Wiley & Sons, Inc., 1969.

KLIR, GEORGE J., *Architecture of Systems Problem Solving.* NY: Plenum Press, 1985.

KNUTH, E.E., *The Art of Computer Programming, Vol. I: Fundamental Algorithms.* (2nd ed.). Reading, MA: Addison-Wesley, 1973.

KNUTH D.E. AND R.N. MOORE, "An Analysis of Alpha-Beta Pruning," *Artifical Intelligence,* 6, 1975, pp. 293–326.

KOHAVI, ZVI, *Switching and Finite Automata Theory.* NY: McGraw-Hill, 1978.

KONOLIGE, K., "Bayesian Methods for Updating Probabilities," in R. Duda, P. Hart, K. Konolige, and R. Roboh, "A Computer-Based Consultant for Mineral Exploration," Menlo Park, CA: *Artificial Intelligence Center*, SRI International, 1979.

KOWALSKI, R., *Logic for Problem Solving.* NY: American Elsevier, 1979.

KOWALKSI, R. "Algorithm = Logic + Control," *ACM Communications,* vol. 22, no. 7, July 1979.

KRIPKE, SAUL, "Semantical Considerations on Modal Logic," *Acta Philosophica Fennica,* 16, 1963, pp. 83–94.

LARKIN, J., J. McDERMOTT, D.P. SIMON, AND H. SIMON, "Expert and Novice Performance in Solving Physics Problems," *Science,* vol. 208, June 1980.

LEBOWITZ, MICHAEL, "Generalization from Natural-Language Text," *Cognitive Science,* 7(1), 1983, pp. 1–40.

LENAT, D., R. DAVIS, J. DOYLE, M. GENESERETH, I. GOLDSTEIN, AND H. SCHROBE, "Reasoning about Reasoning," in F. Hayes-Roth, D.A. Waterman, and D. Lenat, eds., *Building Expert Systems.* Reading, MA: Addison-Wesley, 1983.

MACLANE, SAUNDERS, *Categories for the Working Mathematician.* NY: Springer-Verlag, 1971.

MARR, DAVID AND ELLEN HILDRETHK, "Theory of Edge Detection," *Proceedings of the Royal Society, B-207, 1980, pp. 187–217.*

MARR, DAVID, *Vision.* San Francisco: Freeman, 1982.

McCARTHY, JOHN AND PATRICK J. HAYES, "Some Philosophical Problems from the Standpoint of Artificial Intelligence," in *Machine Intelligence*, 4, ed. B. Meltzer and D. Michie, Edinburgh: Edinburgh University Press, 1969.

McDERMOTT, DREW V., AND JON DOYLE, "Non-Monotonic Logic I," *Artificial Intelligence,* 13(1,2), 1980, pp. 41–72.

McDERMOTT, DREW V., "Contexts and Data Dependencies: A Synthesis," *IEEE Transactions on Pattern Analysis and Machine Intelligence, PAMI-5,* 1983.

McDERMOTT, J., "R1's Formative Years," *AI Magazine,* vol. 2, no. 2, 1981.

McDERMOTT, J., "R1: A Rule-Based Configurer of computer Systems," *Artificial Intelligence,* vol. 19, 1982, pp. 39–88.

VAN-MELLE, W., E.H. SHORTLIFFE, AND B.G. BUCHANAN, "KMYCIN: a Domain-Independent System that Aids in Constructing Knowledge-Based Consultation Programs," in A. Bond, ed., *Machine Intelligence, Infotech State of the Art Report*, series 9, no. 3, NY: Pergamon Infotech Limited, 1981.

MENDELSON, ELLIOTT, *Introduction to Mathematical Logic.* NY: Van Nostrand Reinhold Co., Inc., 1964.

MINSKY, MARVIN, "A Framework for Representing Knowledge," in P. Winston, ed., *The Psychology of Computer Vision.* NY: McGraw-Hill, 1975.

MULSANT, B., AND D. SERVAN-SCHREIBER, "Knowledge Engineering: A Daily Activity on a Hospital Ward." *Computers and Biomedical Research*, vol. 17, pp. 71–91, 1984.

MYERS G.J., *Advances in Computer Architecture.* NY: John Wiley & Sons, 1978.

NATHANSON, FRED E., *Radar Design Principles.* NY: McGraw-Hill, 1969.

NELSON, W.R., "REACTOR: An Expert System for Diagnosis and Treatment of Nuclear Reactor Accidents," *AAAI Proceedings,* 1982.

NEWELL, A., J.C. SHAW, AND H.A. SIMON, "Empirical Explorations of the Logic Theory Machine," *Proceedings of the Western Joint Computer Conference*, 1957, pp. 218–239.

NEWELL, A., J.C. SHAW, AND H.A. SIMON, "Programming the Logic Theory Machine," *Proceedings of the Western Joint Computer Conference*, 1957, pp. 230–240.

NEWELL, A., AND H.A. SIMON, *Human Problem Solving.* Englewood Cliffs, NJ: Prentice-Hall, 1972.

NORMAN, D.A. AND D.E. RUMELHART, eds., *Explorations in Cognition.* San Francisco: Freeman, 1975.

O'CONNER, D., "Using Expert Systems to Manage Change and Complexity in Manufacturing" in W. Reitman, ed. *Artificial Intelligence Applications for Business.* Norwood, NJ: Ablex, 1984.

PARSEN, E., *Modern Probability Theory and Its Applications.* NY: John Wiley and Sons, 1960.

PEARL, JUDEA, "Reverend Bayes on Inference Engines: a Distributed Hierarchical Approach" *Proc. AAAI 2*, 1982, pp. 133–136.

PETERSON, W. WESLEY AND E.J. WELDON, JR. *Error-Correcting Codes* 2nd ed. Cambridge, MA: MIT Press, 1972.

PITMAN, GEORGE R. JR., ed., *Inertial Guidance.* NY: John Wiley & Sons, Inc., 1962.

PRATT, W., *Digital Image Processing.* New York: John Wiley and Sons, 1978.

RAPHAEL, BERTRAM, *The Thinking Computer: Mind Inside Matter.* NY: W.H. Freeman & Co., 1976.

REITER, J., "AL/X: An Expert System Using Plausible Inference," *Intelligent Terminals Ltd. Report,* Machine Intelligence Research Unit, University of Edinburgh, 1980.

REITER, RAY, "A logic for default reasoning," *Artificial Intelligence*, 13, 1980.

RICH, ELAINE, *Artificial Intelligence.* NY: McGraw-Hill, 1983.

ROSENFELD, A., AND A.C. KAK, *Digital Picture Processing.* vols. 1 & 2, 2nd ed. Orlando, FL: Academic Press, 1982.

ROSENFELD, AZRIEL, ROBERT HUMMEL, AND STEVEN ZUCKER, "Scene Labeling by Relaxation Operations," *IEEE Transactions on Systems, Man. and Cybernetics, SMC-6*, 1976, p. 420.

ROSS, S.M. *A First Course In Probability.* 2nd ed. New York: Macmillan, 1984.

SHAPIRO, S.C., *Techniques of Artificial Intelligence.* NY: Van Nostrand Reinhold, 1979.

SHORTLIFFE, E.H., AND B.G. BUCHANAN, "A Model of Inexact Reasoning in Medicine," *Mathematical Biosciences*, vol. 23, 1975.

SHORTLIFFE, E.H., *Computer-Based Medical Consultations: MYCIN.* New York: Elsevier, 1976.

SHORTLIFFE, E.H. AND L.M. FAGAN, "Expert Systems Research: Modeling the Medical Decision-Making Process," Palo Alto, CA: *Heuristic Programming Project Report HPP-82-3*, Departments of Medicine and Computer Science, Stanford University, March 1982.

SIKLOSSY, L., *Let's Talk Lisp.* Englewood Cliffs, NJ: Prentice-Hall, 1976.

SMITH, DAVID E., "Finding All of the Solutions to a Problem," *Proc. AAAI 3*, 1982, pp. 373–377.

SMITH, R.G., AND J.D. BAKER, "The DIPMETER Advisor System" *IJCAI Proceedings*, 1983, pp. 122–129.

STANDISH, THOMAS A., *Data Structure Techniques.* Reading, MA: Addison-Wesley, 1980.

STEFIK, M., J. AIKINS, R. BALZER, J. BENOIT, L. BIRNBAUM, F. HAYES-ROTH, AND E. SACERDOTI, "Basic Concepts for Building Expert Systems," in F. Hayes-Roth, D.A. Waterman, and D. Lenat, eds., *Building Expert Systems.* Reading, MA: Addison-Wesley, 1983.

STEFIK, M., D.G. BOBROW, S. MITTAL, AND L. CONWAY, "Knowledge Programming in LOOPS: Report on an Experimental Course," *The AI Magazine* Fall 1983, pp. 3–13.

STEFIK, M., J. AIKINS, R. BALZER, J. BENOIT, L. BIRNBAUM, F. ROTH-HAYES, AND E. SACERDOTI, "The Architecture of Expert Systems, in F. Hayes-Roth, D.A. Waterman, and D. Lenat, eds. *Building Expert Systems.* Reading, MA: Addison-Wesley, 1983.

TSUJI, S. AND SHORTLIFFE, E.H., "Graphical Access to the Knowledge Base of a Medical Consultation System," Palo Alto, CA: *Heuristic Programming Project Report HPP-83-6*, Departments of Medicine and Computer Science, Stanford University, February 1983.

TURING, ALAN M., "Computing machinery and intelligence," in *Computers and Thought*, ed. E. Feigenbaum, and J. Feldman. pp. 1–35. NY: McGraw-Hill, 1963.

WATERMAN, D.A., "Generalization Learning Techniques for Automating the Learning of Heuristics," *Artificial Intelligence*, vols. 1 and 2, 1970, pp. 121–170.

WATERMAN, D.A. AND A. NEWELL, "Protocol Analysis as a Task for Artificial Intelligence," *Artificial Intelligence*, vol. 2, 1971, pp. 285–318.

WATERMAN, D.A. AND F. HAYES-ROTH, eds., *Pattern-Directed Inference Systems*, Orlando, FL: Academic Press, 1978.

WATERMAN, D.A. AND F. HAYES-ROTH, "An Overview of Pattern-Directed Inference Systems," in D.A. Waterman and F. Hayes-Roth, eds., *Pattern-Directed Inference Systems.* Orlando, FL: Academic Press, 1978.

WATERMAN, D.A. AND B. JENKINS, "Heuristic Modeling Using Rule-Based Computer Systems," in R.H. Kupperman and D.M. Trent, eds., *Terrorism: Threat, Reality, Response.* Hoover Press, 1979.

WATERMAN, D.A. AND M. PETERSON, "Rule-Based Models of Legal Expertise," *Proceedings of the First Annual Conference on Artificial Intelligence*, 1980.

WATERMAN, D.A. AND M. PETERSON, "Models of Legal Decision-Making." *Rand Report R-2717-ICJ*, The Rand Corporation, 1981.

WATERMAN, D.A. AND F. HAYES-ROTH, "An Investigation of Tools for Building Expert Systems," In F. Hayes-Roth, D.A. Waterman, and D. Lenat, eds., *Building Expert Systems.* Reading, MA: Addison-Wesley, 1983.

WEISS, S.M. AND C.A. KULIKOWSKI, *A Pratical Guide to Designing Expert Systems.* Totowa, NJ: Rowman & Littlefield, 1984.

WHEELER, J. GERSHON *Radar Fundamentals.* Englewood Cliffs, NJ: Prentice-Hall, 1967.

WIDROW, BERNARD AND SAMUEL D. STEARNS, *Adaptive Signal Processing.* Englewood Cliffs, NJ: Prentice-Hall, 1985.

WINOGRAD, TERRU, *Understanding Natural Language.* Orlando, FL: Academic Press, 1972.

WINSTON, PATRICK H., *The Psychology of Computer Vision.* NY: McGraw-Hill, 1975.

WINSTON, PATRICK H. AND HORN, BERTHOLD, *LISP.* Reading, MA: Addison-Wesley, 1980.

WINSTON, PATRICK H., *Artificial Intelligence.* 2nd ed. Reading, MA: Addison-Wesley, 1984.

WONG, C.M., R.W. CRAWFORD, J.C. KUNZ, AND I.P. KEHLER, "Application of Artificial Intelligence to Triple Quadruple Mass Spectrometry," *Proceedings of the IEEE Nuclear Science Symposium, San Francisco, CA:* Oct., 1983.

YEH, RAYMOND T., ed., *Current Trends in Programming Methodology,* vol. 4, Englewood Cliffs, NJ: Prentice-Hall, 1978.

ZADEH, LOTFI A., KING-SUN FU, KOKICHI TANAKA, AND MASAMICHI SHIMURA, *Fuzzy Sets and Their Applications to Cognitive and Decision Processes.* Orlando, FL: Academic Press, 1975.

ZADEH, L.A., "Fuzzy Sets," *Information & Control,* 8, 1965, pp. 338–353.

ZADEH, L.A., "Fuzzy Sets and Systems," in J. Fox, ed., *System Theory,* Microwave Research Institute Symposia Series XV, Brooklyn NY: Polytechnic Press, 1965, pp. 29–37.

ZADEH, L.A., "Fuzzy Algorithms," *Information & Control,* 12, 1968, pp. 94–102.

ZADEH, L.A., "Probability Measures of Fuzzy Events," *J. Math. Anal. & Appln.,* 23, 1968, pp. 421–427.

ZADEH, L.A., "Biological Applications of the Theory of Fuzzy Sets and Systems," in L.D. Proctor, ed., *Biocybernetics of the Central Nervous System*, Boston, MA: Little, Brown, 1969, pp. 199–212.

ZADEH, L.A., "Towards a Theory of Fuzzy Systems," in R.E. Kalman and R.N. DeClaris, eds. *Aspects of Networks and Systems Theory.* NY: Rinehart and Winston, 1971.

ZADEH, L.A., "Quantitative Fuzzy Semantics," *Information Science*, 3, 1971, pp. 159–176.

ZADEH, L.A., "Similarity Relations and Fuzzy Orderings," *Information Science,* 1971, pp. 177–200.

ZADEH, L.A., "A Fuzzy Set Interpretation of Linguistic Hedges," *J. Cybernetics,* 2, 1972, pp. 4–34.

ZADEH, L.A., "Linguistic Cybernetics," in J. Rose, ed., *Advance in Cybernetics and Systems,* 3. London: Gordon & Breach, 1975, pp. 1607–1615.

ZADEH, L.A., "Fuzzy Logic and Approximate Reasoning," *Synthese,* 30, 1975, pp. 407–428.

ZADEH, L.A., "Calculus of Fuzzy Restrictions," in L.A. Zadeh, K.S. Fu, K. Tanaka, and M. Shimura, eds., *Fuzzy Sets and Their Applications to Cognitive and Decision Processes.* Orlando, FL: Academic Press, 1975, pp. 1–39.

INDEX